BOSS KETTERING

On the cover of Time *in* 1933.

BOSS KETTERING

STUART W. LESLIE

COLUMBIA UNIVERSITY PRESS
New York   1983

This book received the Columbia University prize in American Economic History in honor of Allan Nevins.

Clothbound editions of Columbia University Press books are Smyth-sewn and printed on permanent and durable acid-free paper.

Library of Congress Cataloging in Publication Data

Leslie, Stuart W.
  Boss Kettering.

  Includes bibliographical references and index.
    1. Kettering, Charles Franklin, 1876–1958.
  2. Inventors—United States—Biography. I. Title.
  T40.K4L47 1983 620'.0092'4 [B]   82-17906
  ISBN 0-231-05600-1

Columbia University Press
New York   Guildford, Surrey

For Lynwood, Tab, and Susan

CONTENTS

Illustrations begin p. 103 and p. 245

PREFACE

Charles F. Kettering thought studying history was a waste of time. You never get anywhere looking in your rearview mirror, he liked to say. He preferred to concentrate on the future because, he said, "we will have to spend the rest of our lives there." In many ways he embodied the best aspirations of his own generation. As much as any one man, he helped shape that future in which we live out our lives.

Today some remember him as the inventor of the electric self-starter for automobiles. Others associate his name with the cancer research center in New York. But in his own time he was acknowledged as America's greatest living inventor and engineer. He won every major professional honor, including a special award established in his name by the joint engineering societies. Leading universities bestowed on him honorary doctorates of engineering, science, and even law. He served government committees on topics ranging from patent reform to technological mobilization. And in the twilight of his career he enjoyed the singular distinction, for an engineer, of being elected president of the American Association for the Advancement of Science.

Nor was such acclaim undeserved. Kettering contributed to a surprising array of technical and scientific fields: accounting machines and inventory control systems; nontoxic refrigerants; high-speed diesel engines; magnetism and solar energy research; and to a host of in-novations—leaded gasoline, high-compression engines, four-wheel brakes—that converted the automobile from plaything to big business and a fixture of American aspiration. His pronouncements on the need for fuel-efficient engines and fuel conservation, uttered more than fifty years ago, still sound contemporary. And twenty years after his death, we are just beginning to understand the full social and environmental implications of some of his work, like leaded gasoline and freon.

Dedicated to hard work as he was, Kettering was no colorless technician. He spoke eloquently, with an ear for the memorable metaphor and a rare gift for making science understandable to the layman. His quotable aphorisms and commonsense wisdom made him the most talked about and admired engineer since Thomas Edison. In his field, Kettering's stature as a public figure was unrivaled. His public celebrity was confirmed in that peculiarly American way with his appearance on the cover of *Time*.

Kettering's personal achievements and immensely creative energies seem even more remarkable when seen as part of a career spent mostly with General Motors, an enterprise synonymous with the faceless modern corporation. He made corporate bureaucracy work for him. Within the largest private organization of his time he fashioned a managerial role that proved technological entrepreneurship could flourish, and one man could still make a difference.

ACKNOWLEDGMENTS

Lynwood Bryant gave me the idea of a Kettering biography, and took time off from an otherwise peaceful retirement to read several drafts. John Beer and Glenn Porter also offered many valuable suggestions. Eugene Ferguson carefully read the manuscript several times, helped me through more than one discouragement along the way, and set a wonderful example of unselfish scholarship.

Without my friends at General Motors, this biography could never have been attempted. Mr. E. N. Bowen, Engineer for Administrative Services at the GM Research Laboratories, went out on a limb to open Kettering's files for the first time, and corrected many mistakes in the early drafts. Mr. C. N. Frank of the Records Retention Unit guided me through virtual mountains of material and pointed out many things I might otherwise have overlooked. Mr. Ernest Horne and the staffs of the GM Research Library and Kettering Archives were most generous with their time and resources.

Mr. Eugene Kneiss of the Patent Division of NCR Corporation gave me access to his collection of Kettering papers, and shared his own recollections of Kettering's later years.

At the Kettering Foundation in Dayton, Mr. Robert Daley and Mrs. Patricia Piety led me to several new and important sources, and arranged a delightful tour of Kettering's home, Ridgeleigh Terrace.

To the staffs of the Dayton Public Library, the Eleutherian Mills Historical Library (especially Richmond Williams, who opened so many doors at GM), the Kettering Moraine Museum, the Wright Patterson Air Force Museum Archives, the Mohican Historical Society of Loudonville, Ohio, and the Dwight D. Eisenhower Library, I owe a debt for prompt answers to my many questions.

Earlier versions of chapters 6 and 9 appeared as "Charles F. Kettering and the Copper-cooled Engine," *Technology and Culture* (October 1979), 20(4):752–76, and "Thomas Midgley and the Politics of Industrial Research," *Business History Review* (Winter 1980) 54(4):480–503; I am grateful to the publishers of those journals for permission to use the material here. I am also grateful to *Time* for permission to reprint as a frontispiece the Kettering cover that appeared on January 9, 1933 (copyright 1933 Time Inc.; all rights reserved). The rest of the illustrations appear courtesy of the General Motors Institute Alumni Foundation's Collection of Industrial History, Flint, Michigan.

And finally, a debt of gratitude to two of Kettering's long-time coworkers, John Campbell and Thomas Boyd. Both of them read through the entire manuscript, saving me from many mistakes. Occasionally, we have differed on interpretation, but I have much profited from their generous criticism. To Thomas Boyd goes a special thanks for doing so much to collect and save Kettering material, and for being so generous in sharing his special knowledge of this remarkable man with others.

BOSS KETTERING

1 / THE EARLY YEARS

Long after he had become America's most famous, and wealthiest, living engineer, Kettering returned to his boyhood home for a community birthday celebration. Turning on the charm for an audience of old friends and family, he recalled his early days on the farm. "Now, I didn't know at that time that I was an underprivileged person because I had to drive the cows through the frosty grass and stand in a nice warm spot where a cow had lain to warm my feet," he remembered. "I thought that was wonderful. I walked three miles to the high school and I thought that was wonderful too. I thought of all that as an opportunity, and I thought the only thing involved in opportunity was whether I knew how to think with my head and how to do with my hands."[1] And yet however nostalgically he invoked his rural past, about all that was left was the nasal twang of his down-home delivery. With a generation of Americans, Kettering had grown up in the country but moved to the city, and what he had done there forever changed the small-town world he left behind.

Kettering was born on August 29, 1876 on a family farm three miles north of Loudonville, a town of a few hundred in the rolling hills of central Ohio, forty miles northeast of the state capital at Columbus. He was the fourth child and third son of Jacob and Martha

Hunter Kettering, third-generation emigrants from Alsace-Lorraine and Scotland.[2]

Nothing in the family's background would have predicted fame and fortune for the youngest son. Jacob was said to be a tall, "hard-bitten" farmer and occasional barn carpenter with something of an interest in politics. Martha was a quiet woman, with a stern face, rough features, and an interest in music. Though each parent left an imprint on Charlie, as he was called, neither filled him with tales of their past. Years later when a genealogist asked about a commission for a family tree, Kettering confessed to a friend, "I told the guy we didn't care for a genealogist. All we knew about the Ketterings and Hunters was they had to work hard for a living."[3] Neither of Kettering's older brothers, David and Adam, distinguished himself in any way. One became a farmer, the other a handyman and later a car dealer when his famous brother secured him a franchise. Kettering's sisters, Emma and Daisy, led equally ordinary lives as schoolteachers and housewives in Loudonville. Only Charles, for whatever quirk of genes and personality, broke away from his past.

Every American inventor is expected to show an early inclination for experiment and a precocious ingenuity, and Kettering apparently was no exception. Stories of the boy's mechanical abilities were handed down in the family, acquiring dignity as they became legend. Usually the tales had the clever young man fixing his mother's sewing machine or taking apart some familiar gadget to see how it worked. One apocryphal story had him inventing a reading stand for a plow, "a patent reading device" the caption of a popular cartoon later read, "which enabled him to study engineering and plow at the same time."[4] Most of this can be safely dismissed as harmless stories that surround the boyhood of any famous man. But one family tale rings true, and in an unusual way pointed toward Kettering's research style. His brother Adam recalled, with an older brother's expected lack of sympathy and no appreciation for the roots of genius, "He sure experimented digging potatoes. He was always coming back out of the potato patch, looking for some other kind of fork, shovel, spade— anything there was a chance he might get 'em out of the ground easier. Till he had half the tools on the farm out there. And the potatoes not dug."[5] With a few twists, that could have been the lament of any of Kettering's corporate superiors over the years.

Young Kettering did display an uncommon interest in scholarly pursuits. He read voraciously, particularly on scientific subjects, though a sensitive eye condition that caused headaches and dimmed vision often curtailed these activities. His most vivid childhood memories were not the chores on the farm or playing with friends but the lessons of John Rowe and Neil McLaughlin, two teachers at the Big Run School, a one-room schoolhouse straight out of McGuffey's Reader and a mile's walk from the Kettering homestead.[6]

Perhaps too Kettering's lack of success in social matters encouraged his more academic ventures. Jacob was a strict father who discouraged parties and other afterschool affairs.[7] Rapid growth made Charlie look gangly, and his nearsightedness gave him an awkward, stumbling gait. With hand-me-down clothes, disheveled hair, and his curious habit of stooping forward to compensate for his poor eyesight, he offered an easy target for adolescent taunts. He became withdrawn and seldom participated in games, parties, or dating. Only his sister Emma became his close friend and counselor.

But in the classroom, Kettering shone. He won himself a tuition-free education at the Loudonville High School by passing a competitive examination. He did well in all his classes, though he particularly excelled at physics and mathematics. The rigor and clarity of his geometric proofs won high praise from his teachers. Experimental science fascinated him. C. E. Budd, a young physics instructor, was Kettering's favorite. He let his best student undertake several independent investigations, and together they assembled a surprisingly complete physics laboratory.[8] With this enthusiastic teacher, Kettering learned to explore the orderly, precise world of science.

Surprisingly, this shy student was also a respected orator. Perhaps to compensate for his quiet private voice, he developed a stirring public one. With clear and quick thinking, and his intuitive grasp of the essence of any argument, he became a feared debater. He once represented Loudonville in an oratorical contest in the nearby college town of Wooster. That speech, entitled "The Four Square Man," employed a caustic wit to lampoon what Kettering, with some personal conviction, considered a useless contemporary preoccupation with fashion. "By the study of human nature, it is found that every person who is capable of intelligent exercising of the mind has an ideal toward which he is working," he said. "A large number of people see their ideal in fashion. . . . The sum of their thoughts is: Bang and dress and friz, and friz and dress and bang. . . . And what becomes of such people? Did you ever hear of any of them rising to eminence? It would not be so hard for them to die if they could only arrange their funeral dress. Thus their lives end."[9] The young speaker never did develop any interest in dressing fashionably or well. Indeed he may have been the worst-dressed multimillionaire in America.

Much of Kettering's early education came not from books but from his sharply inquisitive awareness of his surroundings. Simple technology was as familiar a scene in the rural landscape as the corn and the pastures, and through frequent encounters with local mechanics, Kettering learned to appreciate the workings and power of technology. His lessons began at home. From Jacob each of the Kettering sons acquired a knowledge of rudimentary mechanics. His skill as a carpenter taught them craftsmanship. Watching his father lay the framework for barns and houses with only a steel square and chalk, Charlie observed the skill and art of workmanship that only experience could teach.[10]

Kettering and the other young men of the town often gathered at the local grist mill, where the patient miller shared lessons in elementary engineering as he ground flour from the Kettering grain. Later, they congregated at the new Corliss steam engine in a competing mill, just as a later generation would meet at the local garage. The mill and the engine became the focal point of Kettering's limited social life. The practical engineers who tended the engine, flattered by youthful adulation, spent many hours explaining the design and operation of the machine to their eager students.[11] Out of these informal lessons grew Kettering's profound respect for the intimate knowledge to be gained by close observation and direct experience. "There is a great difference between knowing a thing and understanding it," he later said. "You can know a lot and not really understand anything. But from those practical men there in that mill . . . I learned how to understand things."[12]

Kettering's early education was thus a combination of academic basics from books and the classroom and practical mechanics learned while peering over the shoulders of sympathetic "instructors." By the time he graduated from high school in 1895, Kettering felt equally comfortable reading a physics text or bruising a knuckle on a stubborn machine part.

Yet despite considerable ambition and talent, the graduate had nowhere to go. A general depression in the mid 1890s closed many doors, and he was still unwilling to travel far from home. Only teaching offered a realistic escape from farming. His sister Emma was already teaching at Bunker Hill, a country school three miles east of town, and since his boyhood idols were teachers, it was a natural choice. When Emma transferred to another school, a position opened up for her recently graduated brother, who on the strength of his outstanding secondary school record got the job at a salary of $250 a year.[13] To save money, he commuted to school on horseback and lived at home.

The first days were not easy for the young teacher. Scarcely older than many of his charges, he worried about discipline. "I was sixteen then, and Charlie Kettering was only three years older," one of the students recalled. "We had the name of being pretty tough up there, and the first day of school Charlie showed up with a big stick and tried to look fierce through his glasses."[14] Later, staying with the student's family on stormy days, the equally tough teacher eventually admitted that the show of force was only a bluff.

An entertaining and innovative instructor, Kettering soon won the respect of his class. He delighted in classroom demonstrations and applied a commonsense approach to his students' problems. Spelling homework often came from popular magazines. Science lessons focused on agricultural subjects of direct interest to many older pupils. In the evenings, he conducted special courses on electricity and magnetism for the advanced students.[15]

The new teacher augmented classroom studies with field trips to local technological landmarks. One excursion took them to the new Loudonville electric light plant. Another introduced the country scholars to an X-ray machine displayed in a railroad-car traveling exhibit promoting California products. The latter provoked angry protest from several fundamentalist parents and preachers appalled at the thought of "stripping" the decency of clothing with a machine.[16]

His attention to the individual needs of his students and his ability to apply novel solutions to achieve practical results were his strengths as a teacher. "One of the very peculiar things I had happen [as a teacher] was this very bright kid came to school and the only thing she would do was to read upside down; she had to hold the book upside down," Kettering remembered. "Well it was quite simple. She learned to read from her grandmother and the kid sat on a little stool in front of her grandmother and her grandmother had the book right-side up and she learned to read over the top."[17] Having unraveled the mystery, Kettering constructed a book stand, and by gradually varying the angle of the stand, he taught the little girl to read properly.

Kettering's gift for teaching left a lasting imprint on many of his students. Because of his many responsibilities, Kettering was unable to attend a Bunker Hill homecoming thirty-eight years later, but Emma reported back to her brother, "One of your school girls, Emma Coble, said I should tell you that she has her reader in which you had them write the date and 'I wonder where we will be forty years from now.' "[18]

After a year of teaching, the young instructor enrolled in a summer session for teachers at Wooster College, the same campus where he had given his speech on fashion four years before. Strangely, Kettering ignored the college's many offerings in the physical sciences and even passed over a special Science Training Class designed specifically to acquaint rural teachers with a laboratory approach to physics.[19] Instead, he registered for one course in Greek. The story goes that he did so because his parents wanted him to enter the ministry. How the almost-atheist Kettering would have made out as a minister is an intriguing question, but more likely he viewed Greek as a good preparation for further work in science.

Kettering took his course seriously, and spent very little time on sports or other summer amusements. What time remained in his busy days he put to use in the library poring over technical and scientific periodicals. A flare-up of his childhood eye ailment, the result of overwork, cut short his stay and forced him to resign his teaching assignment in the fall.[20] Dark glasses, cold compresses, and imposed rest brought some improvement, and in the winter of 1897 he accepted a new appointment at the upper-division school in Mifflin, ten miles north of home.

Kettering brought his innovative teaching to Mifflin and remained for a year and a half as a popular and respected instructor. Emma joined him during the second year and took charge of the younger students. Brother and sister continued to live at home. As if to foreshadow his later conversion to engineering, Kettering traded his horse for a bicycle and became a familiar figure on the country roads.[21]

As before, he seemed drawn to the company of men interested in mechanics and science. He became close friends with Hiram Sweet, an ingenious local carriage maker fond of building self-computing cash registers and primitive orreries. Such practical inventiveness reinforced Kettering's appreciation for self-taught knowledge.

Kettering continued his informal scientific education in company with John Robinson, the town druggist, and George Gruenwald, a fellow teacher. Together the men explored photography and chemistry and conducted simple electrical experiments. They even rigged a telephone set between the Robinson home and store. Emma recalled that during the year in Mifflin her brother "spent most of his evenings at John Robinson's store, 'experimenting.' "[22]

With their contemporaries, these would-be scientists learned the fundamentals from periodicals like *Scientific American* and home study kits ordered through a flourishing mail order market. From such sources, Kettering not only absorbed a sound scientific background but learned something of patents, the dynamic growth of electrical technology, and the notion of the inventor/engineer as a prime mover of social progress. Moreover, he glimpsed in such literature a world far more exciting than country teaching. In the summer of 1898, his eyes recovered, the schoolteacher applied for admission to the engineering college of Ohio State University and was accepted.

Few students were as well prepared. Kettering brought along to college a solid academic background and a broad exposure to contemporary technical and scientific literature. From his teaching he had learned to distill the key facts of a concept and to present complex ideas in understandable form. From his independent investigations in chemistry and electricity he had acquired the thrill of discovery not found in bookish pursuits. And, from having witnessed firsthand the liberating power of technology in rural America—the improved reapers, plows, and planters that had done so much to change farming while he was growing up—he readily accepted prevailing notions of technology as a force for spiritual as well as material progress.

Setting him apart in some ways from other student engineers of his time, Kettering's interest in the theoretical side of things, and perhaps his humanistic leanings, helped temper in him the age's enthusiasm for engineering as a means of dominating a hostile, unforgiving natural environment. While other engineers of his generation often talked about subduing nature, he chose to describe his relationship with a metaphor of cooperation. "When we talk about science triumphing over nature we sometimes want to picture ourselves as the gala knight of old with his sword held high and with his foot on the dragon's head," he later told a younger generation of engineers. "I don't like that picture at all, because . . . I would sooner picture this thing as a humble worker who is thankful that he has had an opportunity to work with these things, who is thankful that he has had an opportunity . . . to do something for his fellow man." [23]

As the freshman aspiring engineer settled into Mrs. Leonard Young's Boarding House near the campus in Columbus in September 1898, paid his $2.25 for his first week's room and board, and began to explore his new surroundings, he had no idea of the vast differences between his untutored notions of engineering and the rigorous academic discipline the field was rapidly becoming.

Some aspects of Columbus were familiar. The mills, power plants, machine shops, and factories were just larger and more sophisticated examples of the kind of engineering he had known back home. Kettering resourcefully parlayed his experience into an opportunity to finance his college education and a chance to expand his knowledge of practical technology. He talked the university's maintenance supervisor into a position at the power plant. [24]

Whatever his background, it would have been difficult for any intelligent, ambitious engineering student to resist the attraction of electrical engineering, the most dynamic specialty in the college. A glance at the college catalogue reveals that the electrical engineering laboratory was the newest and best equipped on campus, and that top students often received two or three offers after graduation. The pioneering work of electrical explorers like Thomas Edison had mapped out an exciting new terrain that could be penetrated only by academically trained minds equipped to handle complex problems. And the rapid growth of electrical engineering as a business enterprise heightened the drama and intensified the social importance of a field only decades old wrestling with new questions of ethics, ideology, and organization. By choosing electrical engineering, Kettering placed himself in one of the most vibrant and tension-filled fields of the day. Moreover, a new laboratory built with $10,000 in state funds and the best equipment Ohio manufacturers could donate put Ohio State's department of electrical engineering on an equal footing with the nation's best.[25]

The hard work invested in an outstanding secondary school record paid off for Kettering at registration. On the strength of his previous academic work, he entered college with twelve credits, or better than half a term's work.[26]

The first-year curriculum for Kettering and every other student in the engineering college consisted of chemistry, mathematics, rhetoric, drawing, and foreign language courses. The longstanding relationship between engineering and the military made military science, with a four-hour-a-week drill that Kettering detested, another required course.

Older than his fellow freshmen, and bookish by nature, Kettering devoted himself to his studies and excelled. He earned merit grades, the highest possible mark, in every subject except drawing, where his weak eyes held him to a solid pass. So enthusiastic was he about the laboratory section of chemistry that he went into debt for extra laboratory supplies.[27]

As in high school, Kettering was too serious to be popular. Among his few social acquaintances was Frank O. Clements, a solemn but ambitious graduate student who served as Kettering's laboratory instructor and who years later would join his former student as technical director of the General Motors Research Corporation. Harry F. Smith, a fellow boarder and a comrade on the parade field, also enjoyed with Kettering the limited social activities of diligent students and would one day be a partner in several business ventures.[28]

In the spring, though, the fine print in the textbooks began to fade, and the mysterious eye problems returned. Kettering's roommates prepared oversized drawings of important illustrations and read some of the assignments aloud. Though his grades held up, his weakened eyes did not, and in the late spring Kettering returned home for medical attention. He made another try in the fall, but a convulsive seizure that Mrs. Young mistook for a stroke dashed any hopes of completing the term. "If my eyes won't let me finish my schooling, I hope the train runs off the track and kills me," the dejected young scholar reportedly told his landlady as he left.[29]

It did not, and Kettering arrived in Loudonville to find an unexpected opportunity awaiting him. Visiting with some old friends in Mifflin, he signed on with his brother Adam's telephone line gang.[30] Though his first assignment for the Star Telephone Company was as a hole digger and wire stringer, his education and experience moved him up rapidly. His slender, six-foot frame hardened under physical strain, and Kettering even gained something of a reputation for feats of endurance and strength. Surprisingly, the once-shy scholar thrived among the rough-and-tumble workers, cultivating the saltiness of language for which he was later famous and winning his share of roadside brawls. Explaining later his rapid rise to foreman, he joked that it was because he could lick anyone on the job.[31] If a little college education and a lot of home study and practical experience were important ingredients in the making of a foreman, physical courage and strength did not hurt.

Working on a telephone line crew at the turn of the century was still a valuable supplement to traditional engineering education. Urban telephone systems were relatively sophisticated, but rural systems were still developing as local conditions and ingenuity allowed. Opportunities for native talent had never been better.[32]

The new foreman brought a measure of professionalism to his post. He studied periodical literature and ordered technical publications through the mail. Unaware that most of the challenges he faced had already been solved by engineers at Western Electric, he attacked the inconveniences of the existing technology with an independent, imaginative, and empirical spirit that he would use again and again. He isolated and solved the problem of selective ringing, so that each customer would have an individual signal. With almost no technical assistance, he wound his own coils, located trouble spots, and even installed the first common-battery system in central Ohio over Thanksgiving, thus doing away with the magneto at each customer's telephone.[33]

Kettering met many interesting people during his tenure with the telephone company, most notably Olive Williams, his future wife. Her brother Ralph worked on the line gang with Kettering and as a practical joke, introduced the two during a test call. The dark-haired daughter of a Star stockholder and pianist of the Ashland Methodist Church and the rising engineer from the farm soon became more than casual friends. By the next summer, Kettering was a frequent guest at Olive's piano recitals in the Williams' parlor.[34]

Though the position with the telephone company offered good pay and a first-rate practical education, what Kettering really wanted to do was complete his college training. His eyes and finances strengthened by almost two years of rugged work, and his technical horizons further broadened by reading and experience, Kettering returned to Ohio State in the fall of 1901, a mature man of twenty-five.

The change from foreman to student after a two-year absence was difficult. Kettering managed to pass each of his first-term courses—analytics and differential calculus, mechanics and heat, quantitative chemistry, and expository writing—but without a merit grade. At least he escaped cadet service. Olive taught him the clarinet and he joined the marching band, which conveniently met at the same time as the cadets.

As Kettering became reaccustomed to the academic world, the grades improved. He continued to do well in fundamental science courses and enrolled in advanced chemistry and physics. Less gifted students remembered admiring his ability to digest the new Steinmetz classics and distill the essential points of these difficult volumes. Impressed by Kettering's grasp of physics, the department asked him to teach an undergraduate laboratory section. His students recalled their instructor's gift for demonstrations and unorthodox metaphors like "a thermometer is a molecular speedometer," or "the second law of thermodynamics says you can't push something faster than it's already going." He rarely focused on the standard curriculum, and while this made for entertaining classes, many of Kettering's students subsequently failed their departmental examinations.[35]

Kettering took his practical knowledge outside the classroom and landed several consulting positions. An original technique he devised for locating malfunctioning telephone lines made Kettering something of a legend in the engineering college, and earned the young instructor a $125 consulting fee for a single night's work. Embellished as the story was handed down from one admiring class of electrical engineers to another, the tale had the hearty student suffering from malaria and braving the worst rain and hail in decades to pinpoint the trouble spot.[36] Nonetheless, Kettering's feats did win the respect of his professors and peers. During the summer months, he kept up with things by returning to the Star Telephone Company, which also left him ample time for courting Olive Williams.

Under the pressure of heavy course loads and outside work, Kettering's social life on campus, always rather restrained, suffered even more. Only Carl P. Leibold and Herbert L. Bostater, two fellow engineering students and boarders, became close friends. Leibold, tall and svelte with close-cropped dark hair and an engaging smile, moved easily through the university's social currents, joined a prestigious fraternity, and later won election as class president. He could not, however, carry his less socially inclined friend along with him. When Leibold nominated Kettering for membership in his fraternity, the brothers rejected the country scholar with no money, no social connections, and very little charm.[37] The financial consequences of their blunder were only realized years later when the wealthiest and most influential graduate of the university would have nothing to do with fraternities of any sort.

Bostater, pudgy, plain, and sharing Kettering's rural background, became his closest companion. Together they haunted the Columbus Theater on Saturday nights, enjoying symphonies and the opera. A touring company called the Bostonians was their favorite, Bostater recalled. Kettering particularly liked one light opera, "Bohemian Girl." On other occasions they studied together, Bostater reading textbooks aloud to his nearsighted friend as Kettering closed his eyes and lay back, puffing on his pipe. [38]

The three friends came together to write their senior thesis, with Kettering supplying the inspiration. Drawing on his telephone experience and his Steinmetz studies in alternating current, he decided to evaluate the relative merits of available alternating-current telephone apparatus, and convinced his friends to assist him. Like all young men they believed that with closer attention to proper "principles" they could drastically alter things.

As things turned out they did not, but they did devise more sensitive measuring instruments to evaluate the performance of different telephone circuits. Their work also suggested that for the best transmission the coefficient of self-induction should be low, the resistance of the primary circuit low, and the magnetism held to a minimum. [39] If the project did not revolutionize telephony as its authors expected, it was a good example of Kettering's emerging technical style. Instead of striking out into completely unexplored areas, he focused his attention on a commercial bottleneck where improvements seemed possible.

In later years, Kettering frequently repeated the theme that engineering depended on commercial success. "We've always said that we are great believers in the fourth dimension," he remarked. "Most engineering problems consist of length, of breadth, and of thickness, and our fourth dimension is cost. We feel that instead of calling cost the fourth dimension, it should be the first dimension, because we have got to design against cost continually if we are going to get a product which will meet the requirements in the field." [40] That theme too grew directly out of Kettering's education at Ohio State.

The connections between business and engineering were not always obvious to underclassmen. Seniors were encouraged to see the relationship in a new light. Francis Caldwell, chairman of the electrical engineering department and himself an example of the relationship he wished his students to accept (he had worked at Thomson-Houston Electric Company for several years before joining the faculty), was Kettering's favorite instructor. He filled his classes as much with information on patents and contracts as with mechanics and formulas. Kettering became further acquainted with the commercial aspects of his profession through the American Institute of Electrical Engineers (AIEE), an organization he was invited to join during his senior year. Despite occasional rumblings for reform of ethics and accountability, the dominant ideology of this group was that the business of engineering was business. From such sources—professors whose careers straddled the communities of engineering and business, discussions of the student chapter of the AIEE, the commercial orientation of his classes—Kettering assimilated the assumptions and expectations of his profession.[41]

Kettering's first position made good use of his commercial bent. When an executive with the National Cash Register Company (NCR) of Dayton, Ohio wrote asking about a practical-minded student for the firm's invention department, the university recommended Kettering. And after a visit to the company in April 1904, he returned with a signed contract as "electrical inventor" at a rather remarkable salary of $50 a week. He was to begin July 1.[42]

The job at NCR appealed to Kettering. A man who would later think nothing of traveling to Europe on business each year, he had yet to venture beyond Columbus, and NCR was comfortably close to home. More important, he saw in the job an ideal opportunity to test both his experience and his professional training. If a generation older, he would probably have tried his hand at independent invention or worked his way up the corporate ladder without the benefit of a university degree. If a generation younger, he would likely have aspired to the surrogate academic environment of a corporate research laboratory or perhaps stayed in academia. But Kettering's training, while well grounded in the fundamental sciences, had also made him persistently practical. So the NCR position turned out to be an excellent starting point for a career of commercially focused corporate research.

On June 22, 1904 Kettering, now twenty-seven, received his diploma as a mechanical engineer in electrical engineering with a class of fifty. His academic record earned him membership in Sigma Xi scientific honorary society, and his oratorical talents won him a speaking role in the ceremony. He and Bostater, the "committee" in charge of program invitations, nearly sabotaged the commencement by ordering the invitations COD and then finding themselves short of cash when they arrived.[43] Disaster was averted, however; invitations were sent, and the program proceeded smoothly as his proud parents and Olive Williams, now Kettering's fiancée, looked on.

The years at Ohio State filled in the outline of the education begun at Loudonville. Courses in quantitative chemistry, the physics of magnetism, heat, and sound, and advanced mathematics gave Kettering a solid base of scientific knowledge. For this aspect of his education he was later grateful:

If I were writing the engineering course, I would write only three things— four years of physics, four years of chemistry, and three years of mathematics, and then you might fill in with anything else you want, including a little history and economics. The "how" and "why" of fundamentals should be inculcated to form the foundation for the approach to any problem.[44]

Yet Kettering recognized that theoretical knowledge had to be blended with experience to create a good engineer, just as he had blended consulting and work for the phone company with his college studies. In a letter of advice to his son written twenty-five years later, he listed the crucial ingredients of the engineer:

The first essential of being a good engineer was that you knew a lot about mechanisms just from your observations of them. The second was, that you could form a picture of some new form of mechanism in your mind, and the third, that you ought to have enough mathematics and physics to be able to calculate whether this new mechanism would work satisfactorily or not.[45]

Reflecting on the circumstances of his life on his eightieth birthday, and the happy combination of practical and scientific skills, Kettering held aloft a pliers, screwdriver, and monkey-wrench. "I'm always a screwdriver and pliers type," he mused, "but then someone threw a monkey-wrench in there."[46]

2 / THE CASH

In later years, after Kettering had left his mark on American business and engineering, he received what must surely rank as a unique honor for a man in his profession. The National Federation of Sales Executives conferred on him a custom-made award for "outstanding accomplishments as salesman and scientist," recognizing his ability not only to discover new things but to sell his inventions to business and the public. In his acceptance speech Kettering remarked that "to get out of a rut sometimes should deserve a greater patent than getting a new idea."[1] In these words he hinted at the principles he felt had carried him to the top of the engineering profession: systematic and incremental improvement, close attention to the market, and persistent promotion of the product. These, he felt, could count for more than originality alone. He could certainly look back to the experiences of his first five years as an electrical inventor for the National Cash Register Company (or as it was fondly known to its employees, the Cash) for proof that this was so.

Kettering arrived in Dayton at the end of June 1904 and found himself a modest apartment at 513 West First Street, a few blocks from the sprawling NCR complex. On the morning of July 1 he reported to Charles Lundgren in Inventions Department No. 4 to start his career with NCR. After signing the usual waiver agreeing "to transfer, assign, and deliver to said company my entire rights, title and interest in and to all inventions relating to cash registers and like machines," he took his place as the company's first electrical inventor and officially joined what one of his colleagues who would later rise to the presidency of the company called the "NCR circus."[2]

Indeed, "circus" aptly described a corporation better known for sales gimmicks and managerial eccentricity than for innovative products. John H. Patterson, the president, had built NCR from scratch, putting it on the corporate map with new marketing schemes and programs in industrial welfare. Among his ideas were direct mail advertisements, the "canned" sales pitch, protected territories with statistically calculated quotas, formal classes in the art of selling, and the annual sales convention. Within two decades these strategies had transformed the cash register from a local curiosity (it had been invented by two Dayton brothers, the Rittys) into a common tool of retailers everywhere.[3]

Unhappily, there was another side to John Patterson. He fired his best managers capriciously, or when they threatened to become too powerful. He subjected his subordinates to all manner of bizarre fads: drinking only bottled water, riding horseback at dawn, eating peculiar diets. And more detrimental to the company, he paid virtually no attention to product development. So despite a near monopoly and some of the best sales talent in the country, NCR had barely weathered the financial panic of 1903–4. Only Thomas J. Watson, who would later found the rival IBM, kept the firm afloat with a profitable secondhand reselling operation, a good indication that NCR had saturated its primary market and had nothing new to offer.[4] Even the so-called inventions departments were still the province of self-taught mechanics, who carried out specific assignments adequately but lacked the imagination to exploit the cash register in new ways.

When Kettering joined the company it boasted only one professionally trained engineer, Edward A. Deeds, an ambitious, moon-faced, thirty-year-old vice-president known for his financial skills rather than technical expertise. Yet alone among NCR executives, Deeds recognized the need to upgrade the product line to match innovative marketing. After a few unsuccessful tries at doing it himself, Deeds looked around for someone more expert, and thanks to his connections with Ohio State, found Charles Kettering.

Kettering's arrival signaled an important shift in corporate direction. The sales force was already chafing under the restraints of a limited offering, and salesmen were being urged to stall customers until the new inventor's talents could be put to use.[5]

Because he was such a special catch, Kettering immediately had an unusual degree of autonomy. Kettering's boss, A. J. Lauver, head of the Future Demands and Improvements Committee, told the paymaster something of the remarkable freedom the new employee would be allowed:

Mr. Kettering, as you will see by the put on slip, will be known as an electrical expert. His headquarters will be in Inventions No. 4 to which department his expenses should be charged, but he will be independent of Mr. Lundgren so far as working out his own ideas, and he and Mr. Lundgren will work together, neither having special authority over the other.[6]

Kettering had independence, but he also had the backing of first-rate draftsmen, machinists, and technicians who could translate his schemes into hardware, and who could free him for imaginative ventures. Kettering could occasionally become prickly with supervisors, and in his few personal encounters with Patterson he was told more than once not to report for work the next day. But to those under him he communicated an infectious enthusiasm that could rally men in the directions he chose.

Kettering first attacked an inconvenience that had troubled NCR customers for years. As cash registers had grown more complex and offered more features, the keys became harder to push until weary cashiers begged for relief. To lighten the burden Kettering applied a well-known electrical principle in a novel way. He backed a flexible keyboard with a powerful electromagnet so that when the operator touched a key the solenoid completed the entry automatically. Flushed with the pride of his first professional invention, he presented it to the Future Demands Committee. Shockingly, they rejected it, not because it didn't work but because it seemed too bulky and expensive to sell. They sent him back to the drawing board, sadder but wiser.

Autonomy had a price, and if he wanted to be successful he would have to invent things that meshed better with NCR marketing objectives. Because he learned from this minor setback, Kettering's next invention would get a better reception.[7]

Patterson's NCR has often been called America's first "sales university," and while it was nothing so grand as that phrase implied, marketing did receive a formal emphasis rare in business at that time. All employees in managerial positions were required to enroll in a salesmanship class called the Owls Course. In the weekly roundtable discussions Kettering learned to appreciate the economic dimensions of invention and NCR expectations for his work. He also met Richard H. Grant, the new sales manager in charge of cash register sales to department stores. During one of these informal sessions, Grant told the inventor about a particular obstacle blocking the sale of the registers, and planted the seed for Kettering's next invention. Department stores resisted registers, Grant explained, because they preferred to handle all sales, cash and credit, from a central location. However, unlike cash sales, credit required prior approval from the credit manager. Of course, a clerk could always call the credit department on the telephone, but then a messenger (or pneumatic tube) still had to carry the charge slip to the manager for written authorization. A credit system that could monitor credit without delaying the customer or inviting collusion between clerk and buyer could open a vast new market for NCR registers, said Grant.[8]

Drawing on Grant's knowledge of department store needs and his own experience with telephones and solenoids, Kettering combined two rather simple ideas into an important innovation. By fitting together a standard telephone and a solenoid-actuated stamping device, he developed the first automatic credit approval system, the forerunner of today's bank cards. To transact a credit sale, the cashier lifted the telephone receiver at his station, which lit a small lamp in the credit office and alerted the manager. Then the credit office checked the record of the customer in question and, if credit was approved, tripped the stamping solenoid. The cashier then simply rang up the sale normally.[9]

This project also taught the inventor something about patents as well as marketing. John B. Hayward, a partner in a New York law firm and an expert in the field of business machines (he later joined Watson in founding IBM) handled the patent for Kettering and NCR. From Hayward, Kettering learned the importance of protecting fundamental ideas, not particular applications, and the art of supplementing existing patents. As Kettering refined his ideas, adding, for instance, a circuit to lock the sending register until the credit office cleared the transaction, he secured a patent on each improvement.[10]

No sooner had Kettering won approval for his new O. K. Credit System from the Future Demands Committee than he was dispatched on a promotional tour with Grant to sell the invention.[11] An NCR maxim that Kettering took to heart was that any invention, no matter how good, must be sold. To sell this one, he and Grant visited a number of large eastern department stores and finally convinced John Wanamaker to try it in his Philadelphia store.

By year's end, only six months after joining NCR, the new inventor had earned himself a promotion to the head of the inventions department with nine employees and a budget well into five figures. With well-deserved pride he noted in his year-end report, "Whenever shown this electrical credit system has met with immediate and enthusiastic approval. Many large department stores in which demonstrations of this system have been made, have given orders for both the No. 400 registers and the credit system."[12] Clearly the new innovation was on its way toward meeting its profit objective and justifying the company's faith in its designer.

As would happen often in his career, Kettering's innovation was carried further by others. The inventions department machinists had been building all the early units themselves under Kettering's direct supervision, severely overtaxing its slender resources. Deeds recognized that Kettering was being wasted on what should have been a routine assembly operation and, noting that the credit system no longer needed refinement, ordered the "device assembled by the factory instead of the Inventions Department."[13]

At the end of the yearly report, Kettering inserted a short paragraph that would become the slogan for the coming year. "The demand for electrical operation of labor-saving devices is becoming greater every day," he wrote, "and we are working overtime to bring out electrical cash registers to supply the quick service required in the stores of our large cities."[14] What NCR needed was an electrically powered register, a deceptively simple project that had so far defeated all inventors who had tackled it, including Deeds himself.[15] Fortunately for the new department head, he took on a chief assistant who became a natural complement for his own talents. William A. Chryst, tall, slender, and bespectacled, a man who might easily have passed for Kettering's brother, was a self-taught but ingenious engineer who had worked his way up from messenger to machinist to technician until his talents caught Kettering's eye.[16] A gifted nonverbal thinker, Chryst could transform the schemes Kettering outlined verbally or in rough form into workable sketches and blueprints. And of equal importance, Chryst could then translate these two-dimensional drawings into three-dimensional hardware. Their talents meshed perfectly. Their collaborative efforts produced a workable electric cash register in a few short months, but the partnership continued on for many years.

When Chryst and Kettering began discussing their ideas for the electric cash register design in the early months of 1905, they faced two major obstacles. First, they needed a motor light enough and small enough to fit comfortably into a standard housing but with enough power to drive the unit. Second, they needed a sufficiently sensitive clutch mechanism to engage and disengage the counting wheels at precisely the correct instant.

For higher torque, Kettering simply rewound the motor. Unlike his untutored predecessors, he knew that a light-weight motor capable only of intense, short spurts would be adequate for the intermittent operations involved. Later he switched from a direct to an alternating current design which was more flexible and safer, because the current could be stepped down by a transformer. Eventually this became the basis for a "universal motor" able to accommodate a wide range of cycles and voltages and therefore well suited for NCR's expanding international market.

The clutch proved more difficult than the motor. Initially, Kettering and Chryst devised a magnetic clutch, but it could not operate on alternating current. Then they came up with a successful variant of the "overrunning" clutch, a mechanical version of spring-mounted rollers in a series of sleeves. Kettering, by now wise in the way of patents, protected both ideas.[17]

In April Kettering unveiled the prototype of the register to the Future Demands Committee, which was impressed enough to ask him to demonstrate it to a meeting of district sales managers. The salesmen marveled at the device, even though its inventor explained that it was only a primitive model for which he had in mind a number of improvements.[18]

Like the credit approval system, the electric register was almost an immediate success, and an NCR staple by the end of the year. Trying to explain why he and Chryst had succeeded when established electrical companies that NCR had approached to build such a motor had failed, Kettering scribbled in his notebook not one outstanding insight, but a collection of integrated refinements: the universal AC motor, a condenser to eliminate sparking at the contact points, better windings. Nothing startling, but little things that added up to success. Summing up, the inventor wrote, "We have never placed a machine upon the market which has caused less trouble or opened up a greater field for increased business."[19]

Kettering's co-workers in those years recalled how he bubbled over with ideas, and with energy. He got to work by six-thirty in the morning and often worked late into the evening. He barely had time to outline one idea to his assistants before he was ready with another. In the midst of perfecting the electrical register, for instance, he worked out a distant indicator, a device to display sales graphically at some point removed from the register. A saloon could use it, for example, to display the sale both in the bar room and in the pool room to show customers that their fees had been properly recorded.

As with so many of Kettering's inventions, the idea for the distant indicator came directly from the market, in this case from a tavern owner in Alabama. The suggestion had been toyed with in NCR's other inventions departments for several years, but no one had done much with it. Their models were either bulky mechanical monsters, or confusing electrical ones which simply illuminated painted glass plates scattered by denomination, dollars in one part of the box, cents in another.

When Kettering took over the project he substituted a monogram display for the awkward box. A selective relay translated information from the register onto a single set of lights, illuminating them so they "spelled out" the amount of the purchase, much as a modern scoreboard flashes names and numbers. When finally marketed the units cost fifty dollars and performed as promised, but except in foreign markets they did not sell very well. Nonetheless, they were the forerunners of the stadium scoreboards of today.[20]

Kettering's next major project marked a turning point in his career. Previously, he had attacked a single problem at a time, with little attention to how his ideas fit together. Now he began not only to notice how his inventions fit the existing market, but how they could come together in a system of innovation. Thus, Kettering emerged as a professional inventor.

About the time he completed the electric register, Kettering began to realize that the cash register and the credit approval system were simply parts of a potentially bigger system. Separately, they could speed up individual transactions and keep accurate records at each station, but the sum of the store's daily take could still be totaled only by collecting and counting the individual register returns. What Kettering saw was that a system which could collect and tabulate data from the entire store would be far more valuable to the retailer.

First, Kettering worked out a technique for electrically connecting two sending machines and a receiving totaler, so a simple pull of a lever could relay information about the amount and type of sale to the auditor's office.[21] As the system evolved, Kettering added other features until the sending unit could convey the total of all business, total cash business, total taken by each regular cashier, total taken by relief cashier, and other kinds of information.[22] By giving the merchant an up-to-the-minute record of all store transactions, this innovation anticipated much later computerized inventory control systems and set the stage for a revolution in retail accounting. Only the inherent limitations of electromechanical processing stalled further advances until the advent of electronic circuits. Yet the potential implications of the idea did not escape the young inventor. "A complete balance of the store could be obtained in about twenty minutes after active business had ceased," he wrote, "and this would require but the services of not more than two or three people."[23] Modern improvements such as computer scanning may be viewed as merely refinements of Kettering's conceptual breakthrough.

On August 1, 1905, Kettering and Olive Williams were finally married. A rising young inventor of twenty-nine earning a substantial salary of $303.46 a month, Kettering at last felt able to shoulder the responsibilities of marriage.[24] Following a modest ceremony in the front parlor of the bride's home in Ashland, the groom's new brother-in-law, Ralph Williams, drove them to the train station in Mansfield, where, while waiting for the train, the couple enjoyed their first ride in an automobile.[25] For the first few days of the honeymoon, they stayed at the Cadillac Hotel in Detroit, then traveled to Niagara Falls and returned to Ashland at the end of the week.

As Olive packed her things and prepared to move into their new house in Dayton, the bridegroom wrote to his best friend Chryst, complaining that while he "had a fine trip, gained five pounds," he "didn't find married life such a wonderful change." Nor, presumably, did Olive, for to judge from the letter to Chryst, her husband must have spent most of the honeymoon hatching new schemes for an alternating motor drive for the #79 register, watching Western Union stock tickers, and trying to sell a multiple drawer register to a Detroit department store. "I am now firmly convinced that the #79 electric is a comer and we must make sure that everything is the best we can make it," he wrote. "I have got some ideas up my sleeve about the AC stuff. I think we can get a motor that will be just as good as a DC."[26]

Additional duties at the office followed the new responsibilities at home. The inventor's success pushed him into a broader, though sometimes unwelcome, managerial role within the inventions departments, accompanied by the expected number of administrative headaches.

On the most fundamental level, he had to disburse a weekly payroll of $400 among his eighteen assistants, apportion the limited time and funds of the department among competing interests, and fight for money and space in a bureaucracy increasingly dominated by the idiosyncratic temperament of President Patterson.[27] Pleasing this tyrant could be difficult, as many senior officers found to their chagrin. On matters of broad policy, at least in the technical realm, Kettering and Patterson agreed, but on issues of petty discipline (an obsession with the president) they often clashed. The habitual tardiness of semiautonomous inventors and mechanics, a matter of little concern to Kettering, bothered Patterson enormously. Consequently, Kettering's department consistently earned a mediocre "B" performance rating.[28]

Nor was the inventor able to measure up to some of the president's other unorthodox standards. Convinced that good horsemen made good managers, Patterson insisted that each NCR manager from department head up learn to ride properly. Each morning, the men donned white trousers and white turtlenecks and religiously executed Patterson's regimen of calisthenics and horsemanship. On one occasion, the hapless inventor fell from his mount directly in front of the reviewing stand, earning the president's severe displeasure and nearly losing his job.[29]

More significant administrative responsibilities arose from the inventions themselves. New products demanded machinists able to build them and skilled service men to repair them. To keep a close watch on the evolution from prototype to marketable product, Kettering set up a small manufacturing station within the inventions department where he could personally oversee the slow process of working the bugs out of each device before it was turned over to the regular production departments.[30] In an intuitive way, he recognized the conflicts of interest that divided research and production engineers. This breach would become obvious again and again in later projects, never failing to cause him trouble. He also put aside one hour an afternoon for a class in advanced products. By teaching repairmen the intricacies of the new electric registers and credit systems, he helped build confidence in the field and assured his innovations a warmer reception in the market. No corporate inventor had done this before, but it did have its advantages.

Another of his duties paid handsome dividends in later years. Because NCR did not manufacture its own electrical subassemblies, Kettering became an informal purchasing agent and ambassador to the electrical industry.[31] His buying trips to firms like the Kellogg Supply Company and the Robbins and Meyers Company kept him in touch with recent industry trends, and built a valuable network of business and technical acquaintances that would serve him well when he went into business for himself.

Sometimes, of course, the roles of inventor and manager came into conflict. In the flush of enthusiasm over a new idea, the inventor often promised what the manager could not deliver, leading to disappointed customers and angry sales representatives. "In the future, under no circumstances, should a promise be made by any of our inventors or anyone else to which we cannot live up," came the stern warning from the executive office after one such incident. "If it is thought that a certain machine or improvement can be gotten ready for market in sixty days, the time should be doubled when announcement is made, in order to allow for mishaps and delays."[32]

Other times, the rush to introduce an innovation into the market resulted in shoddy prototypes and technical oversights. Some of the new #79 registers clogged with dust because the inventions department forgot to design a simple dust plug.[33] R. H. Grant reported that one of Wanamaker's O. K. Credit Systems was "so poorly assembled that, in the endeavor to find several short circuits, the mere touching of the wires with a screw driver, caused them to break."[34] Yet, criticism from the field helped the inventor refine his ideas. Customers' suggestions inspired several improvements, including a warning bell to indicate the end of the paper roll.[35]

At the beginning of April 1906, a corporate realignment placed Kettering, and with him William Chryst, at the head of Inventions Department No. 3 with a salary increase to $346.67 a month.[36] The new department head quickly gained his usual measure of loyalty and respect from his men. To work out the design of a small store register, the Class 400, one-half of the staff volunteered to spend the normal two-week summer shutdown period completing the project. "Over one half of our men prefer to work," Kettering told the Future Demands Committee, "and I believe it more advisable to work at this time than to have a number of countermanded orders. I will personally superintend the work." The committee gladly consented to this unprecedented request.[37]

Besides bringing an uncommon enthusiasm and esprit de corps to the department, Kettering also initiated several farsighted reforms. Dismayed by the amount of time wasted completing drawings and specifications for the patent department, he requested a full-time draftsman to develop ideas from the "paper patent standpoint." That would, in his opinion, "leave a greater part of my time to work upon the engineering and . . . inventions."[38]

A meeting of the Future Demands Committee on July 25, 1906, assigned the new department head his first major project, something that would occupy much of his inventive activity for the next two years. Recognizing that hotels and restaurants, like department stores, suffered from outdated accounting and inventory control methods, the committee asked Kettering for an innovation that would do for the restaurant owner what electric cash registers, automatic credit approval systems, and auditing registers were already doing for the retail market.[39]

Before discussing any specific designs, Kettering set off on a fact-finding tour of eastern hotels and restaurants.[40] Only after careful study of the particular needs of the industry would he be prepared to begin actual design. For the next three weeks, he lived in unaccustomed luxury in such surroundings as the Hoffman House in New York and the Bellvue-Stratford in Philadelphia, consorting with waiters and cashiers. With the help of a little cash, he managed to loosen some tight lips, and learned all about erasures, double checks, and the other common frauds of the business. On August 27, he returned to Dayton, and he and Chryst began work on a series of preliminary sketches that would take them four months.[41]

The design they proposed incorporated the lessons of Kettering's field research. The rush of lunch and dinner trade, with long quiet spells in between, demanded a machine capable of rapid operation but with lower power draw. To fulfill both these requirements, Kettering developed a motor that could operate either continuously or intermittently, with a simple button for changeover between modes.[42] Since this register was only as fast as the person using it, Kettering ran the release bar across the entire right-hand side of the machine and arranged the keyboard so that the cashier could strike the keys and release bar at the same time.[43]

Accurate business statistics and tight security were perhaps even more important than convenience and speed, and the inventor gave these considerable thought. To guard against fraud, he incorporated a series of special locks with keys for each cashier and a lockout device which prevented printing unless the check was properly positioned under the printer. To preserve a tamper-proof record of each transaction, he included a mechanism that printed a duplicate stub and dropped it into a locked box for later review by the manager.

Because a restaurant needed sales totals for a variety of items, Kettering included counting wheels for "Food," "Wine," and "Cigars," with a separate color printer for each category. Thus at any time during the day, the manager could retrieve subtotals by kind of sale or individual waiter, and if he liked, compare them to either the main counting wheels' total or the duplicate stubs.[44]

Kettering also developed several other options that could make the machine even more convenient. With the addition of another entry key, for instance, the manager could subtotal sales of a luncheon special or keep track of a temporary waiter. Another option printed a duplicate stub that could be used as payment at the bar.[45]

Throughout the design phase of the project, the inventor kept in close contact with restaurant owners and employees, soliciting their suggestions and refining his ideas in light of their recommendations. Even when he felt sure that "this machine would cover all the conditions met with in the field" he advised the company to "have a meeting of our best restaurant people and submit a plan of this machine, and obtain from them just what a restaurant checking machine would embody."[46] Ongoing communication with restaurant representatives ensured that the new register would receive a favorable reception in the field. Following Patterson's sales precepts, Kettering himself introduced the machine at the Hotel Men's annual convention in Saratoga Springs, New York in July 1908.[47]

Another innovation which seemed minor at the time finally allowed restaurant owners to subtract as well as add on the machine. According to his own account, Kettering first conceived of a true subtracting machine while discussing designs for an automobile differential with Chryst. By connecting a pair of numbered wheels through a differential of spur and bevel gears so that the sum presented by the pair was always nine, and by employing an intermediate mating gear to rotate one wheel backwards while the other rotated forwards, Kettering got his checking machine to register additions as subtraction on the totalizer with but the touch of a "subtraction" button.[48] His idea was both simple for the cashier and simple mechanically, because the drive unit moved in one direction only. And while the idea was put only to minor use in the hotel checking system, it laid the foundation for important advances in later accounting and banking machines.

By the end of 1906, after only two and a half years as an inventor, Kettering's ideas were beginning to have significant effects on NCR sales strategy. The annual company convention in December devoted an entire session to the selling points of the electric cash register. After the meeting a district manager told Kettering, "I am becoming more convinced than ever that the field for these registers is greater than we have any conception of, and it is a matter of educating the selling force, supplying them with knowledge and arguments to use in demonstrating them."[49]

Kettering knew full well why his innovations had been so successful. "The convenience of the electrical attachment is one of its strongest points," he noted. "A man will use the electric machine for the same reason that he will use the automatic gas lighter and any other conveniences, because it reduces the actual work, saves time, and makes the apparatus readily accessible."[50] Justly proud, he pointed out that over a thousand units had been sold since June 1906, without any complaints about durability or performance.

Important as they were, Kettering's specific innovative contributions to NCR were overshadowed by the more general changes in outlook and direction he initiated, particularly his insistence that haphazard trial-and-error invention give way to more formally organized industrial research. Responding to constant pressure from Kettering, the Inventions Department started to look more like a laboratory and less like a machine shop, as orders for oscillographs replaced the usual requisitions for lathes and grinders.[51] Following a meeting with an independent inventor and promoter who was trying to interest NCR in an adding machine, Kettering filed a report revealing his growing skepticism of traditional invention. "He is one of the old school of inventors," he wrote. "While he is a practical man, I do not believe that he could take hold of a new machine and develop it from a manufacturing and commercial standpoint." Not only did such men often base their inventions on shaky technical foundations, he remarked, but they too often neglected the demands of the market in their designs, confusing ingenuity and practicality. "Like a great many other inventions that have been worked up from the mechanical rather than commercial side, things which are talking points on Mr. Schneider's type of construction would be eliminated when the machine would be designed for commercial use," he said.[52]

Commercial orientation did not mean fundamental studies were being neglected, and under Kettering's leadership Inventions Department No. 3 reflected the foresight and educated curiosity of the professional engineer. Instead of the project-by-project approach that had characterized previous departments, Kettering divided projects into Electrical and Mechanical subgroups, and then further into sections, e.g., special work on motors, motor drives, distant adding and printing, electrical transmission of accounts.[53]

Among the most forward-looking of the sections was the one devoted to special motor studies. Having discovered that "in designing the motor for the general cash register work we were forced to do a great deal of work without having the proper information and data at hand," Kettering began, on his own authority, a series of basic investigations of the electric motor.[54] For one phase of the study he had his engineers compare the efficiency and durability of commutation brushes and windings on different AC motors. And after Kettering saw a display of graphite brushes at a street railway convention, the department looked into graphite as a better bearing lubricant.

Nonetheless, Kettering did not overlook the importance of hands-on experience. One assistant, a recent engineering school graduate, returned from an assignment on the angular deflection of a certain cash register shaft with a complexly argued and mathematically intricate answer that Kettering immediately recognized as wrong. Rather than rework the problem on paper, Kettering took the engineer into the shop, fastened one end of the shaft in a vise and the other to a dial indicator for measuring angular deflection. In a few minutes, the assistant had a lifetime lesson in commonsense engineering.

Kettering's encouragement of basic research represented a significant departure in corporate strategy for NCR, and a new philosophy of industrial research. In one of his many proposals he revealed something of his broader plan for research. "It has always been my desire since I have been with the National Cash Register Co. to make the work in my department more comprehensive than what the individual orders specify," he wrote. "The mechanical experiments should be the working out of the general solutions rather than the specific case."[55] Kettering included a paragraph appealing for executive support and funding for the basic research. However, knowing the capricious and arbitrary management as he did, he reconsidered this request, and finally slashed it from the final copy.[56]

Ironically, the department's best-remembered innovation under Kettering's leadership required the least amount of advanced engineering. In an attempt to meet the stiff competition in the low-priced market, Kettering and his engineers began to design a spring-powered cash register in December 1907. This project had top corporate priority, and lest Kettering and his staff forget, the Future Demands Committee pointedly reminded them that "everything possible should be done to get this completed within the next three months."[57]

Indeed, all that winter, Inventions Department No. 3 dropped everything else to concentrate on the drawer-operated register. On February 15, Chryst entered in his personal diary, "Talked with CFK about rushing work on the D.O. machine faster. About all designing done. Details only to get out."[58] Three days later a conscripted force of machinists joined Kettering's team to translate the blueprints into hardware. Less than one month later a prototype emerged from the machine shop, and in the middle of March a tired department head formally presented it to an NCR convention.[59]

Outwardly the little register closely resembled its bulkier predecessors, down to the floral detailing on the brass Tiffany cabinet. The muscle, however, came from neither crank nor motor. Instead, a push of the drawer forced a spring into a recoiled position, and this spring then powered the register.

Early models suffered a variety of ills, especially jostled counting wheels from hard slams of the drawer. Continuous refinement corrected the difficulties, and by the end of April Chryst noted, "#1000 assembled. Working very satisfactorily. Still able to jar down transfers on extraordinarily hard drawer slam. No longer able to open drawer without registering."[60]

With persistent overtime the department completed an improved version and presented it to President Patterson, in a command performance, before his European sailing in May. On the fifth, Kettering personally accompanied the prototype to New York and demonstrated it to Patterson. "Looks fine in new cabinet with marble and slab and indicators," one of the engineers commented before wishing both Kettering and the #1000 a fond farewell from Dayton.[61]

So anxious was NCR for a new weapon in the low-priced sales war that the instruction books were printed even before Patterson's return from England and the units were readied for market. Kettering, showing a remarkable appreciation for customer frustrations, suggested "that in addition to sending out this book, we have two labels printed—one for tape printer instructions, to be pasted on the inside of the printer drawer, one giving directions for resetting the counter, to be pasted inside the lid over the counters."[62]

In July, the #1000 hit the market and the first complaints hit the Inventions Department. Thomas Watson, now assistant sales manager, lodged the first protest. Keys on early models sold in the Boston territory stuck "unless the drawer was closed with considerable force, or forced home."[63] Other units jammed when the heavy springs shoved the drawers past their limits. At one time, Lauver even asked Kettering to replace the spring drive with a standard crank, a suggestion that tied up twenty-three engineers, draftsmen, and machinists before it was abandoned. [64]

Kettering eventually worked the bugs out of the #1000 and developed a reliable line of office registers that ran the gamut from two-bank, nontotaling models to sophisticated versions with multiple counters. [65] The drawer-operated register proved a long-lived and lucrative innovation. To critics who questioned the durability of the motive power, the inventor always replied, "Have you got a watch? It runs well and keeps good time, doesn't it?" [66]

Between such pressing projects, Kettering still found time to squeeze in work of his own, exploring areas seemingly unrelated to the cash register, but with potential commercial value. Beginning in June 1908, he and Chryst worked out a scheme for synchronizing a motion picture projector and a phonograph. [67] The dream of "talkies" had captivated many inventors, including Thomas Edison, who, though he could claim invention of both moving pictures and the phonograph, had not been able to put them together. Edison had noted in August 1909, "There are more than 40 patents combining phonographs with motion picture film. None are successful. There is a wide gap between an idea and its reduction to practice." [68]

Kettering and Chryst opted for a synchronizing motor connecting a phonographic disc and a silent movie, similar in concept to Edison's "kinetophone." Their idea was some twenty years ahead of its time, but it pursued the same false lead as Edison, who abandoned his device in 1913 after spending considerable funds developing and promoting it. [69] Perhaps fortunately, a series of distractions at the end of the summer prevented Kettering from exploring the limits of the "Motion Picture Machine."

The years at NCR were personally, as well as professionally, maturing. A wife, and on April 20, 1908 a son, Eugene Williams, brought stability to the often harried and overworked inventor. Olive organized the household finances, put up with his unusual moods and hours, and reminded her husband of a life beyond invention in the arts and in music. Besides playing the piano in their home, and performing in local churches, she occasionally dragged her spouse to the symphony and opera. Although the inventor's attention frequently wandered during these performances, his boredom occasionally paid unexpected dividends in the form of technical sketches on the program notes.

He found congenial companions among the men in the Inventions Department. He particularly enjoyed weekend camping excursions to southern Ohio with Chryst, geological expeditions with B. M. Shipley, and skeet shooting with W. Schutte.[70] Kettering and Schutte once displayed their marksmanship at the annual company talent show when, after a few minor stunts, the more myopic of the "deadeyes" aimed with such startling accuracy that his bullet split on a knife edge and extinguished two candles. Only later did he confess the fraud: a cleverly designed bellows, and not the bullet fragments, had actually put out the flames.[71]

Still, invention dominated Kettering's life. Beginning in the fall of 1908, he launched a project that would cap his career at NCR and open a new chapter in the history of integrated accounting and statistical systems.

From his earliest work on the sending and receiving register, Kettering had envisioned a truly integrated inventory control system that could tabulate data from a number of individual registers. While such a system remained on the drawing board, its inventor impatiently reminded his superiors that "this is a line of work which is capable of being developed to a state which will produce results surprising to those who are not familiar with its capabilities."[72] Thanks to an innovative New York banker, Charles E. Sprague, Kettering finally got a chance to prove his point, though in a slightly different context.

Sprague, linguist, philosopher, and professor of accounting as well as president of the Union Dime Bank, wanted to mechanize bank accounting. Gifted mechanically as well as intellectually, Sprague himself invented several machines to do the job, but these proved costly and unreliable. He once mentioned his frustration to Thomas Watson, who relayed the problem to Kettering.

Nobody had ever built a machine like the one Sprague wanted, and the NCR patent department frankly doubted anyone could. But the sales department, noting that Sprague was "very enthusiastic on the subject of machines in banks," and that he intended to build a huge new bank and equip it with automated accounting machines, decided selling the machines to the Union Dime "would be a splendid way to initiate this type of machine before the public."[73]

The problem was, Kettering had no workable design for such an instrument. While he pondered options, Deeds stalled Sprague by offering to rebuild and service Sprague's faulty units until the new ones were ready. At best it was a risky bargain. Nonetheless, as Deeds pointed out, this "would keep them [the Dime management] in the proper frame of mind toward us, and would also give us an opening in trying out some of our new machines when we could get some models built."[74]

In August 1909, Kettering submitted a general proposal for the system, drawing heavily upon the hotel and restaurant checking machine and the auditor's register. According to the plan, each unit would include six rows of keys and eleven counting wheels, allowing totals up to a billion dollars and permitting the bank to retrieve data from past months. Every bank customer would receive a special passbook. When he came into the bank, he would simply give the book to the cashier, who would then insert it into the accounting machine and enter the transaction. The machine would register the deposit or withdrawal, automatically send a record to the central accounting unit, and simultaneously print the total and "Paid" or "Rec'd" in the customer's passbook. Thus the depositor would have an accurate printed record of each transaction and the bank management would have access to individual and composite data on all accounts at all times.[75]

On September 1, Kettering received a formal order for seven prototypes of the accounting machine, with delivery set for the following February.[76] A month later the Dime management reviewed the blueprints and enthusiastically endorsed the program. After talking with Sprague, Watson reported, "They had inquiries from three banks in other cities asking for information in regard to these registers. I believe it will be the means of opening up considerable business with the banks."[77]

Eight months and dozens of excuses later Inventions Department No. 3 finally delivered the accounting machines. As one NCR vice president crowed, "These machines have more functions really than any machines we have ever constructed and if you could see the machines themselves, even in their partly completed condition, you would realize the immense amount of work there is in them." To finish the order the Inventions Department worked overtime until management decided that "we have reached a stage where the night work was not doing any particular good as the men were worn out."[78]

Kettering, however, did not stay around to see his machines completed. On September 18, 1909 he resigned from NCR, neither the victim of one of Patterson's notorious purges nor a defector to a rival firm. Rather, he gave in to the allure of technological challenge and entrepreneurship.

On August 10, 1908 Chryst had noted in his diary, "CFK full of auto ignition project," a project that had gradually captured his interest during the year.[79] As Kettering himself often said, he did not want a man to have a job, he wanted the job to have the man. His talents and hard work had taken NCR from the simplest of registers to electromechanical accounting and inventory control systems, and clearly pointed the way to the future. Later developments would be left to others. He turned to a newer field of invention, automotive technology, where he would spend the rest of his long career.

Five years at the Cash stamped Kettering with an engineering style that became his trademark. In his commercial orientation and his ability to anticipate the market, he reflected the influence of master salesman John Patterson. Recalling the most significant lessons of his tenure at NCR, Kettering observed, "I didn't hang around much with other inventors or the executive fellows. I lived with the sales gang. They had some real notion of what people wanted."[80] That was a shrewd insight for a young engineer seeking to make his way in the world of commerce.

These years also laid the philosophical and technical foundations for his career in industrial research. In pursuing both fundamental principles and commercial products, Kettering set a corporate precedent and accumulated a reservoir of data and ideas that would shortly launch him into national prominence as he put them to use in his work on the automobile.

Twenty years later, when NCR named Kettering to its board of directors and officially reunited the corporation and its greatest inventor, the current chief engineer suggested that Kettering was still the company's head of engineering. What made this only a slight exaggeration was that Kettering had indeed opened so many avenues of innovation that other NCR engineers were still refining and exploiting them a generation after his resignation. More than that, Kettering left NCR with a new outlook on research. "Essentially, research is nothing but a state of mind—a friendly, welcoming attitude toward change," he said. That attitude, as much as any innovation, transformed the business machine from a defensive measure against weak-willed cashiers into a powerful tool of management planning.

3 / THE DELCO YEARS

Like many engineers of his generation, Kettering claimed to have little use for the "experts." "If I want to stop a research program," he once said, "I can always do it by getting a few experts to sit in on the subject, because they know right away that it was a fool thing to try in the first place."[1] Yet what seems like a paradox, a university-trained engineer finding fault with academic training, was actually a strength. For if, as one observer of American history has commented, the nation found in the automobile a perfect technological expression of its personality, of its quest to level space, time, and class, then the automobile found in Kettering an inventor whose technological style perfectly matched the needs of its early years.[2] On the basis of a thorough knowledge of what was scientifically and technologically possible, Kettering was always willing to try what others said was unworkable. Neither backyard mechanic, eager to try anything, however fanciful, nor smug academic, apt to dismiss an idea solely on the basis of misguided theory, Kettering had an eclectic, inventive research style that gave him a powerful advantage in the field he chose to conquer.

Kettering did not move into the automotive field by chance. Rather, circumstances of personal acquaintance, professional interest, and the state of automotive electrical technology all drew him into a new technical field at a most fortuitous moment. The personal connection came through Deeds, who was at the time building a kit car behind his home on Central Avenue and needed help with the electrical system. The professional interest grew out of discussions with P. M. Lincoln, a consulting engineer for NCR who often argued with Kettering about one of the inventor's idiosyncratic theories of magnetism (a debate which drove Kettering to build an ignition coil to prove his point). The final prodding came from Earl Howard, a former NCR salesman who had taken a position with the Cadillac Motor Car Company, and who frequently asked Kettering's advice on automotive ignition systems over business lunches with his old associates.[3]

Kettering's contacts with all three suggested that an astute electrical engineer might find the automotive field quite lucrative. The ignition system was, perhaps, the weakest link in the internal combustion engine system. A proper ignition for such a variable, high-speed engine had frustrated inventors for decades.[4] Continental engineers, led by Robert Bosch, had eventually worked out an acceptable magneto around the turn of the century. Americans still preferred dry cell battery ignitions, which were cheaper though less reliable. However, battery ignition had its own shortcomings. To provide a spark of adequate intensity from a relatively small bank of batteries, the dry cells were connected to an induction coil in such a way that the primary circuit was repeatedly interrupted by a master vibrator that created a shower of sparks, which then depleted the nonrechargeable batteries after a few hundred miles of driving.

At Deed's urging, Kettering turned his talents to this problem in the early summer of 1908. Apparently, Kettering had no qualms about borrowing men and machines from his employer for some moonlighting ventures. He started by appropriating a new oscillograph to study the electrical characteristics of ignitions, and recruiting several technicians in his inventions section to machine odds and ends for his experiments.[5]

On July 23 Kettering prepared a preliminary sketch of the design that would later become the basis for his ignition patent. Deeds and Lincoln witnessed and signed it.[6] Essentially, Kettering's idea was an adaptation of the magnetic relay he had previously developed for the cash register, a kind of holding coil that would release the ignition contact only at the proper moment in the cycle and send one intense spark instead of the usual shower. This, he surmised, would prolong the life of the dry cells significantly.

Kettering's early tests on Deeds' car were encouraging, and by August he was looking around for a company willing to manufacture and market his invention. Here his contacts with electrical suppliers for NCR paid off. He discussed the proposal with the Kellogg Company, suppliers for the O.K. Credit System, and received strong encouragement. About the same time he tested a prototype of the ignition in Deeds' Packard and found, according to an associate, that its performance exceeded all expectations.[7]

By the end of the summer Kettering had recruited two of his NCR engineers to assist with the project on a regular basis, his assistant Chryst and another promising electrical technician, William P. Anderson. An air of mystery surrounded the secret enterprise as the three men met evenings and Sundays in the barn behind Deeds' house. Kettering sometimes even arrived at the meetings with a beaver cap pulled over his face, and entered the barn only after glancing in all directions to see whether he had been followed. Gambling on the venture and short of cash, Kettering borrowed $1,500 from his wife's savings account to invest in a lathe and milling machine for the workshop.[8]

Increasingly, Kettering found himself torn between prior commitments at NCR, particularly the accounting machine, and his new invention. Letters written to personal friends betrayed his growing detachment from NCR affairs and his desire for more inventive freedom. On April 13, 1909 he wrote Chryst, then in Oregon recovering from a bout with asthma, under the letterhead, "Charles F. Kettering, Consulting Engineer." Realizing that Chryst would be surprised at the new title, he would only say, "I am taking the liberty of using some paper which I got recently. Please do not throw eggs." His description of the research at NCR was almost an afterthought: "We are getting some of the new machines hammered into a pretty fair shape and will try to get the things in such shape that when you take hold of them they will take tangible form."[9] To friends who knew him well, such uncharacteristic lack of enthusiasm could only mean an intense interest in something new.

Entries in Chryst's diary for the spring of 1909 showed quite clearly the extent of Kettering's new interest. Often, the journal reads simply, "Working on CF's ignition stuff till 10:30." Occasionally, a note of success: "CF and EA [Deeds] finished putting new ignition system on EA's Packard. Fine results."[10]

While Kettering and the moonlighting engineers struggled to refine the ignition system, Deeds began promoting the invention among local automobile makers. Deeds especially hoped his connection with Howard at Cadillac might pay off. Toward this end, the partners purchased a new Cadillac roadster as a test vehicle. As it turned out, Deeds' instincts about Cadillac were right. In the late spring of 1909, Henry Leland, the stern old man of the automobile industry whose quests for precision and technical innovation were legendary, made an overture to Kettering and Deeds. Leland sent his best engineer, F. E. Sweet, to Dayton to examine the ignition. The night before he was to arrive, Chryst's diary notes that everyone in the barn worked until 2:00 the next morning readying the system.[11]

The ignition worked flawlessly the next day, and Sweet returned to Detroit impressed with the idea. Other company engineers were less enthusiastic when independent tests at Cadillac were inconclusive. But Kettering continued to push the idea, pointing out, for instance, that his battery ignition had a larger spark advance, which gave the slow steady idle that luxury car owners appreciated.[12] He also made frequent visits to Detroit to clarify technical details for company engineers. Then almost unexpectedly, on July 7, Leland telegraphed Kettering and asked to see him immediately. Two weeks after the meeting, Kettering received an order for 8,000 ignition units.[13]

The order caught the partners by surprise, for they did not even have a formal charter, much less manufacturing facilities. After frantic negotiations, Deeds arranged a loan of $150,000 to capitalize the venture, evenly splitting the liability between himself and Kettering, and formally incorporated the company on July 22, 1909. Eventually, the partners issued 100,000 shares of common stock (at $100 per share) and 50,000 shares of preferred (at a $100 per share) to raise more capital.[14]

Collaboration with Deeds at this point was particularly opportune. Although Kettering had a good eye for the market, he had no plan for organizing the business to reach it. Deeds did. With expertise in finance, incorporation, law, and accounting, he handily complemented his partner's technical skills. Deeds gave the engineer a solid business education. In later years Kettering liked to portray himself as an innocent among the corporate wolves, but Deeds' instruction, if it did not make him into another Jay Gould, certainly taught him to hold his own in the world of business.

Because they had no intention of forming a manufacturing enterprise, Deeds wanted to call the firm the Dayton Laboratories and Engineering Company, emphasizing the research aspect. Taking a cue from "Nabisco," Chryst suggested instead the Dayton Engineering Laboratories Company, which shortened to the agreeable acronym "Delco," an idea the partners liked and adopted.[15] Kettering and Deeds solved the initial manufacturing problem by subcontracting the order to the Kellogg Company, which would ship the completed ignitions directly to Cadillac.

Deeds handled the business transaction and, with the assistance of NCR attorney John Hayward, steered the ignition through conflicting patent claims and licensing. Kettering applied for his own patent on ignition improvements on September 15, 1909,[16] three days before he formally resigned from NCR.

Meanwhile, Kettering and Chryst, collaborating as they had done in the Inventions Department, continued to work on the ignition. Wherever Chryst happened to be, Kettering kept him informed of the developments at Delco. Their correspondence displayed the innovative thinking they had shared in their work at NCR, and a new spirit of adventure that had been missing in their last days together at Inventions Department No. 3. "I am satisfied if you came back here and loafed around the Delco joint a while the cash register business would look so tame to you that you would never care to go into it again," Kettering assured Chryst.[17]

Significant technical refinement was accomplished in a few short months. Kettering told his friend:

We have been doing some rather remarkable things in way of speeds of battery systems—getting about 10,000 sparks per minute with fairly good timing. We have some magneto stunts worked out now which are fine, and I am sure that by another year we will have something out which will have everything skinned that has been hatched yet. We could get this out for 1911 by extraordinary effort but I am afraid we would only get what the boy got who could not wait for the apples to get ripe. He got green apples and the belly ache, and we might get out something not fully developed and which would cause us trouble.[18]

A few technical flaws did appear. Some engines fitted with the new ignitions suddenly died after cold-weather starts, a mysterious phenomenon until Kettering noticed that this only occurred when the negative terminal of the coil was connected to the spark plug. Other holding coils would not release their armatures and froze the relays. According to Kettering, he discovered the solution to this puzzle during an all-night train ride to Detroit. Fingering one of the defective units in the darkness of the Pullman car, he realized that the end of the core was rounded, thus concentrating the magnetism and holding the armature more tightly against the pole piece than intended.[19] A few personal visits to the Kellogg manufacturing plant in Chicago and their closer attention to machining eliminated the defect.

Kettering thought selling the system would be easy. He reported to Chryst that "the Cadillac Company is so thoroughly enthused over Delco that they are making a demonstration of it a part of their exhibit at all the auto shows" for the spring of 1910.[20] Using his NCR skills, Kettering wrote several advertisements himself. The new ignition, he asserted, would increase battery life, eliminate timing troubles, and give easier starts.

Some promotional pieces bent the truth a little for the sake of the sales pitch. Claims of 10,000 miles without adjustment and a change of dry cells only every 2,000 miles were accurate. But "unsolicited" testimonials from satisfied customers, including one E. A. Deeds of Dayton, who wrote, "I have run my Packard Thirty 3280 miles on one set of six dry cells. Have driven 6800 miles on Delco without a single adjustment of contact points or a spark plug removal," raised some suspicions among those familiar with the little company.[21]

One early promotional campaign turned out to be a complete failure. A Dayton automobile maker entered three of its cars in one of the first races at the new Indianapolis Speedway, two equipped with Delco, the other with a magneto. Delco representatives stood by with banners and other advertisements waiting for the victory that never came. To their disappointment and embarrassment, the wax holding the ignition coils melted during the race and disabled both battery-ignition automobiles.[22]

Even without an endorsement from the Speedway, early customers seemed satisfied with the ignition. By the spring of 1910, several motor car companies, including Stoddard-Dayton, Republic, Speedwell, and Cadillac had equipped some models with Delco ignition. To celebrate what seemed to be a promising start, the partners rented office space for the firm in the United Brethren Publishing Company in downtown Dayton, and hired a secretary.[23]

Among inventor/entrepreneurs in the field of electric automotive technology, Kettering distinguished himself by his ability to survive and prosper in the stiffly competitive marketplace. No longer backed by the research and sales resources of a large corporation, he found that his experience with Patterson served him well in the new enterprise. Focusing on a commercially viable product with his specialized electrical engineering skills, Kettering made an impressive debut in his new field.

Yet he was already looking to the future, as his notebook entries for that spring show. On March 6, 1910, while on a train ride from Syracuse to Dayton, he told patent attorney John Hayward about an invention for magnetizing steel.[24] He was thinking of a process for tempering and magnetizing simultaneously, by immersing a steel bar in a cooling bath of oil and water, and at the same time magnetizing it with a special coil mounted in the bath. Nothing came of the invention, but Kettering continued to think about useful inventions and possible patents.

It was about the time when he was considering ways of magnetizing steel that he also started tinkering with an electric self-starter for automobiles. That idea, it turned out, had a truly promising future.

Henry Leland often told his friends, including Kettering, a story that illustrated why self-starting was so crucial a challenge to the automotive industry. One afternoon on the Belle Isle Bridge in Detroit, Leland said, an acquaintance of his chanced upon a woman stalled in traffic and offered to crank her engine. Unfortunately, the woman forgot to retard the spark, and the kickback broke the man's jaw; gangrene complications later killed the unlucky Samaritan. Whether the tale was true or not, Leland's point was clear. Starting a car could be difficult and even hazardous. A tremendous opportunity existed for the inventor who could perfect an efficient self-starter.[25]

Inventors had certainly tried. Some had worked with springs. Others had combined acetylene gas with automobile lighting systems, or compressed air with tire pumps. Several had even experimented with electrical versions which converted the flywheel into a giant motor.[26] Cadillac engineers were working on such a system about 1910, and Kettering learned something about it from them. The idea of electrical self-starting was continually circulating among automotive engineers looking for a break.

"If I have any success, it's due to luck, but I notice the harder I work, the luckier I get," Kettering once observed.[27] As usual, he worked hard on this project, often from early in the morning to late at night. However, it was not so much the hard work as his previous experience at NCR which produced his "luck" this time. The cash register work had taught him the importance of systems of innovation. From the first, Kettering envisioned not just an electrical starter but an integrated system of starting, lighting, and ignition. The relationship between the individual components, how they fit together, turned out to be the key to the problem.

The Delco team that translated Kettering's inspiration into workable hardware this time was a far cry from the legions of specialists he would later command at General Motors. It hardly mattered to him. He often noted, "A research problem is not solved by apparatus; it is solved in a man's head."[28] Seven NCR expatriates gathered in the Deeds' barn in the fall of 1910: Robert S. DeMaree and Zerbe Bradford in drafting, and William Anderson, R. R. Todd, John Reece, H. C. Phillips, and W. H. Mooney in the machine shop.[29] A few others, like Chryst, lent a hand in the evenings and on weekends. Kettering himself spent so many hours in the barn (at 319 Central

Avenue) that the Dayton City Directory inadvertently listed it as his official address. Known collectively as the "Barn Gang," these men were an independent lot and a creative fraternity. Their leader, affectionately called the "Boss," often observed that the only rank in the group was when one man was ranker than the next. Long into the nights they pushed themselves with only an old phonograph for diversion and Mrs. Kettering's coffee and sandwiches to keep them going.

Along with the Cadillac engineers and almost everyone else working on electric self-starting, Kettering began with a flywheel unit. Like everyone else, he ran into the same obstacles—lack of torque, poor voltage regulation, excess size and weight. What distinguished his effort from the others was his ability to recognize the crucial lessons of his early failures, along with his conviction that the challenge could be met only by considering the entire system. Kettering had already decided in the first few weeks that the key was to make the starting motor also serve as a generator for ignition and lighting.[30] While many false leads and dead ends lay between this brilliant insight and its final execution, he moved far ahead of his competitors.

One major goal was a motor powerful enough to turn an automobile engine but small and light enough to fit into the car. A flywheel starter, like the one Kettering originally built, had to be fixed in a 1:1 ratio with the crankshaft, which meant that it needed an impossibly powerful battery to move it. Where other inventors simply gave up, concluding that the battery would have to be as large as the engine itself, Kettering looked at the problem from a new perspective. "After thoroughly investigating the subject, we decided to abandon the flywheel type generator," he wrote, "and to make some other form which could be attached to the motor the same as is customary with a magneto."[31] He tested a variety of generators until he found one that could produce 7 pounds of torque at 30 amperes and 12 volts. That was too little to crank the engine by itself, but since the unit was mounted separately, it could be mechanically amplified. So Kettering and his mechanics worked out a gearing mechanism that allowed the generator to run on a 1:1 ratio with the engine while driving, but which could be geared up for more torque during starting. Thus the generator could run slowly enough for proper battery charging most of the time and still give sufficient torque at only 25 amperes during starting.[32] The arrangement was something like the motor Kettering had developed for the cash register at NCR, in which a relatively small motor gave a large amount of current for a short spurt.

Another important link in the system was the voltage regulator. Regulating the output of the generator over the variable speed range of an internal combustion engine demanded a special design to prevent the generator from overloading the storage battery. Kettering experimented with a number of alternatives, from a reaction winding arranged so that as the current increased the output of the generator weakened, to a relay and ballast device that kept the charge flowing from the generator to the battery at less than 7.5 volts, to a carbon-block rheostat that gradually reduced current in proportion to load.[33] The last was eventually adopted when the other options proved too costly, complex, or insensitive.

Finding a generator to provide an adequate charge for the storage battery across such a range of variable speeds was another pressing problem. After testing several commercial generators and playing with different coils and windings, Kettering found that "by proper proportioning of the fields, the air gap, and the number of bars on the commutator, such a generator could be made to pick up at a speed of about 300 revolutions per minute, and to stand abnormal speed of 3,000 to 4,000 revolutions per minute without perceptible sparking. At speeds within the range of automobile driving, the commutation was perfect."[34]

Bringing the headlamps into line with the rest of the system was the final obstacle. To weather the shock of unpaved roads, headlamps came with rugged tungsten filaments that could only be run off 6-volt current. Kettering's motor-generator needed at least 12 volts for starting. To provide both adequate starting power and proper current for lighting, Kettering came up with a series-multiple battery arrangement. For starting, the four 6-volt batteries could be linked in series, for a total output of 24 volts. Then for lighting, the system would be switched into a parallel setup supplying 6 volts only.[35]

These developments came together with surprising speed, and in November Kettering wrote John Hayward, who was now his patent attorney, a detailed proposal for a complete starting, lighting and ignition system:

Our scheme, therefore, at the present time consists of a generator which is arranged to be driven at engine speed, a gearing mechanism by which the generator can be cut loose from the engine at driving speed, and coupled to the engine through a system of gearing most effective for starting. Combined with this is a series multiple controller, which throws the batteries from multiple to series. We have a storage battery made up of the required number of cells, a series multiple controller, and the ampere hour regulator and low voltage cut-out. The battery, ampere hour regulator, series multiple cut-out, and low voltage cut-out are preferably mounted in one compartment. Inasmuch as a continuous supply of current is at hand, this system permits the elimination of the magneto or other forms of generator for ignition. [36]

Consulting a patent attorney was a wise move, for while the self-starting system was progressing rapidly in a technical sense, the patent situation was far from resolved. Even Kettering admitted to Hayward that "there are many things old in this apparatus, and which are well known to the art," though he went on to explain that he believed that "the combination of all these pieces of apparatus represents an improvement and a production of results not hitherto obtained." He pointed to the automatically controlled ammeter and rheostat as examples of novelty.

Inventor and lawyer got together at the end of the month. Hayward brought a list of possible infringements, and at his suggestion, Kettering bought licenses on several related patents as insurance. Such caution was well warranted, and in later years Delco sued a number of infringers and won on the strength of these patents.

"If you can tell what a patent is by reading the language of the patent attorneys, you're better than I am," Kettering liked to joke. Notwithstanding the stilted language and the tedious process, the patents proved indispensable in the successful launching of Delco.

Cadillac watched the developments with keen interest. In December, the company sent Kettering an engine to use for testing a self-starter. On the seventeenth, Kettering, Chryst, Anderson, and several assistants attached the starting unit, and after several failures caused by a faulty armature, the engine sputtered into life.[37]

Word of this success got back to Cadillac a few days later, and on January 6, 1911, Earl Howard sent Delco a new Cadillac automobile for further experiments. For the next few weeks, the Barn Gang struggled to reduce the size of the starting-generating system so that it would fit in the car.

The men finished the reduced-size system on January 14, and after 100 trials it was still working well. On February 8 they installed the complete unit in the Cadillac, and Kettering tried the lighting system for the first time.[38] One week later, Chryst noted in his diary that shortly after supper, he and Kettering had taken a ride in the starter-equipped Cadillac. A couple of "bugs," particularly a "battery [that] would not turn [the] engine after charging," still bothered them. However, the next evening, Chryst wrote, "At 4:30 went with Clements to Delco and saw car being finished. Rode with CFK out up Oakwood hill to Peach Orchard drive testing self-starter."[39] Delco then sent the Cadillac, with the new starter, to Henry Leland for his evaluation.

Thomas Watson, who was still with NCR, was the first person outside of the Delco group to enjoy a ride in the self-starting automobile. The evening of the trial, Kettering spied his old associate at the train station in Dayton, and offered him a lift home. The men got into the car, Kettering depressed the clutch and pushed the starter button, and off they went. Watson was astonished. He later remembered thinking that the absentminded inventor must have forgotten to crank the car. In the course of the trip, Kettering did explain the new system to his duly impressed friend.[40]

Occasionally the strains of time and technical frustration disrupted the harmony of the Barn Gang. Kettering and Chryst, according to one of the members, fought "hammer and tongs," though they usually patched up their differences quickly. Outsiders got a cool reception. When one of Hayward's lawyers arrived at the barn for the first time, he was confronted by Anderson, who informed him that no eastern stuffed shirt was about to look through the company papers without his permission.[41]

Progress never continued without setbacks. In the rush of testing and design reevaluation, Kettering broke his ankle when his test car slid off an icy road near Dayton on April 12. To compound the misfortune, he was told the next day that the only other self-starting automobile had been destroyed in a fire in Henry Leland's garage. The Cadillac engineers were unable to reconstruct it, and Kettering had to hobble to Detroit for consultations.[42]

Still, Leland seemed pleased with the starter. On June 13, 1911, Cadillac decided upon a full commitment to the self-starter. That day, a Cadillac engineer wrote a memorandum to Leland outlining the steps needed to adapt the automobile for the starting system.[43]

In the course of the development of the starter, Cadillac limited its comments to general evaluation of the finished product. As the self-starter became a real possibility for Cadillac, it was obvious that the two groups of engineers would have to work together more closely. Kettering became a frequent visitor to Detroit. While he ignored most of the Cadillac engineers' suggestions, he listened carefully to a few, particularly those concerning how the starting, lighting, and ignition system had to fit together with other components on the car.[44]

In November, Leland ordered 12,000 starting, lighting, and ignition systems from Delco. The quantity came as something of a surprise to the small consulting firm, and forced Kettering out of his accustomed role of inventor into the broader role of manufacturer and entrepreneur. Initially, the Delco partners tried to arrange a network of outside suppliers as they had done for the ignitions— armatures from Robbins and Meyers, ammeters from the Sangamo Instrument Company, storage batteries from the Electric Storage Battery Company, and ignitions from Kellogg. The potential suppliers were somewhat suspicious of massive orders from a relatively unknown enterprise. O. Lee Harrison, the Cleveland representative of the Electric Storage Battery Company, visited the barn just to meet the person who wanted so many batteries. After an informative tour with Kettering, and with Leland's recommendation, Harrison accepted the order.[45]

Smaller companies, with more to lose on one order, refused, and that meant a hasty change of plans. The only way Delco could fill the Cadillac order was if they started machining their own small parts and assembling the final systems. The partners hurriedly rented one floor of the Beaver Power Building for these operations. Kettering and Deeds also sold preferred stock (50,000 shares at $100 per share) and mortgaged life insurance and a vacant lot to enable them to purchase supplies and hire the staff they needed.[46] Among these new recruits was O. Lee Harrison, who became the first sales manager.

Kettering was justifiably proud of his technical achievement and took special pleasure in the fact that Delco had done something "experts" had said could not be done. He loved to tell the story about his 1912 speech to the Detroit section of the American Institute of Electrical Engineers. The details varied with each retelling, but he usually said that several members came up to him after the meeting and accused him of profaning every known law of electrical engineering. The punch line never changed. Kettering explained to these unimaginative plodders that he had not broken any laws, he had simply made his self-starter 90 percent automobile and 10 percent electrical.[47] In other words, commercial practicality, not theoretical efficiency, was the key to success.

Kettering liked to play on this idea of outwitting the experts. In a promotional piece that he wrote for the *Saturday Evening Post,* he said, "Not one man in a thousand imagined a year ago that the day was at hand when motor car engines would be started and cranked by electricity—many engineers declared that it could not be done— automobile manufacturers shook their heads, looked wise—and doubted."[48]

While Kettering was busy outwitting his fellow engineers, he let his management responsibilities slide. He much preferred the technical puzzles, and when business associates called, they usually found him in overalls hunched over some apparatus or other in a corner of the plant. It was rare to find him sitting behind the elegant double desk he shared with Deeds. Things only got worse when Chryst left NCR to work full time for Delco in the fall of 1911. Kettering and Chryst worked up several ingenious inventions together, including a mercury voltage regulator of particular note, but Delco still needed a firmer hand on the reins. Deeds continued as a full time vice-president at NCR, and had little time for the new enterprise. Left to his own devices, Kettering delayed decisions and neglected vital correspondence.[49]

He did, however, investigate any number of new ideas. On a visit to Thomas Edison's laboratory in New Jersey, he toured the famous facilities and spent the morning with the great inventor discussing a new alkaline storage battery. Ultimately, Kettering had technical reservations about Edison's battery and nothing contractual came out of the meeting. His evaluation, it turned out, was correct. Henry Ford later invested $1.2 million in the battery without result.[50]

For Leland, Kettering became an informal technical adviser and engineering consultant. When Cadillac switched to a V-8 engine, Kettering test-drove the early prototypes and then helped the engineers evaluate them. One problem seemed to be faulty ignition, which was of course made by Delco. The Cadillac testers had noticed that after a few miles the motor started missing. Yet when the distributor contacts were changed, the car started and ran well, at least for another dozen miles. Kettering looked over the engine and discovered the trouble was an air leak into the intake manifold caused by overheating. Never one to miss a good practical joke, Kettering joined the Cadillac men on a test run. When the engine began missing, he pulled over to the side of the road and solemnly tightened the rim nuts. To everyone else's amazement, the now cool engine started perfectly. After a couple more times, the other engineers caught on, though Kettering could not resist teasing that tightening rim nuts seemed so much easier than changing contacts that Cadillac should include this advice in its instruction book.

A company like Delco that depended on the close coordination of scattered suppliers could not survive without careful management, and Kettering's neglect was costly. The firm had grown steadily, and by the fall of 1912 counted Cadillac, Oakland, Oldsmobile, Jackson, Auburn, and other car companies among its customers. With 1,200 employees, they had moved to a four-story building on East First Street.[51] But the company scarcely turned a profit until Deeds came over from NCR full time and rationalized the company's accounting and purchasing.

By early 1913, Delco occupied the basement and two floors of the rented factory building on East First Street, employed 1,500 workers, and had sold a total of 35,000 starting, lighting, and ignition systems.[52]

The Dayton Flood nearly destroyed the promising young company. On March 25, 1913, after several weeks of heavy rains and spring thaws, the dams and levees holding the four rivers flowing through Dayton to the Ohio gave way. At dawn a torrent of water twelve feet high crashed down on the unprepared city, choking the downtown with mud, and leaving the city without gas, water, or electricity.[53]

In the confusion, witnesses could only guess the extent of the damage. One early news dispatch claimed that "Dayton is tonight nothing less than a seething river three miles wide, a mile and a half on each side of Main Street, its principal thoroughfare. It is estimated that 2,000 to 5,000 people have perished."[54] Actually, the damage was much less, and when the waters receded two days later, about 350 people were found dead and $120 million in property destroyed.

However, the Delco factory was in the middle of the hardest hit area. The first work shift arrived about 8 o'clock on the 25th, and found the basement, with the heat-treating furnaces and punch presses, already flooded and the water rising fast. They carried some of the lighter equipment and supplies to the first floor, but within an hour, the machine shop, shipping department, and assembly areas on the first floor were also under water. The men retreated to the second floor to await rescue, which only came three days later.[55]

George Smith (later Kettering's financial adviser), president of the Dayton Chamber of Commerce and head of the rescue operations on the east side of the Miami River, was confronted with fire, looting, and civil chaos. He sent a telegram to Ohio governor James Cox asking for food, medical supplies, and the state militia.

Years later, at a reunion of flood survivors, Smith asked if anyone knew how that telegram was delivered. From the back of the room, Kettering spoke up:

Well, maybe I can help you out George. I guess I was the guy. I took one of the copies of the telegram when you called for volunteers. I had a buck-board automobile out at the curb, with no top, no dash, no fenders, and no body excepting a slat bottom and a seat for two. Bill Chryst of the

Delco factory was with me. It was raining and sleeting but we had on our rubber coats, hats, and boots. We had an idea that if we went far enough north, we would find a bridge across the river. We rode for hours, it seemed. I have no idea how long. We came to a railroad bridge and drove across it. At the other end we got water in the carburetor and the car stopped on the submerged track. I climbed out and lifted the hood and wiped the water out of the carburetor with my handkerchief and got the car going. Then we started northward again. We drove some distance and finally saw a light ahead. It appeared to be in a tower. When we reached it we found it to be a railroad train dispatcher's tower, and he had a telegraph key open, and a limited line of communication available. . . . It was still raining and sleeting. We reached home about daylight. That was how it happened.[56]

Kettering could not get to the Delco factory until after the flood receded. Then he personally directed the salvage operations. He slept on a wooden platform with the rest of the crew, cooked on an electric grill, and took his turn on the shovels. To pump the water out of the basement, he rented an Ahrens-Fox fire engine from Cincinnati, and talked his way past the militia, who wanted to take it for relief operations.[57]

The hard work of carrying and shoveling seemed to restore Kettering's health. Before the flood, the strain of meeting orders and the endless travel had affected his nerves. Sometimes he could not eat for days. One of the engineers recalled that during the salvage, Kettering once ate half a dozen eggs and drank three cups of black coffee. He then announced that he had not felt so good since his days on the telephone line gang. He reminded the men that he had been the boss of that gang because he could lick anyone on it. "Do any of you fellows want to fight me now?" he asked.[58] On April 12, less than three weeks after the flood, Delco was back in limited production.

By the end of 1913, the factory had expanded to all four floors of the building, and had completed 45,000 units. Production was three times what it had been the year before. Output grew steadily to 600 units a day. In 1915, the company built a new seven-story factory across the street from the original plant, doubling the floor space to 500,000 square feet. That year Delco employed 2,000 workers.[59]

At the same time, Delco also started taking a more active role in worker affairs. It purchased a tract of land south of town and set up prefabricated company housing. Originally, these houses were intended as emergency shelter for flood victims, but the village eventually became a summer recreational area for employees, called Delco Dell.

Kettering and Deeds personally underwrote Triangle Park, another employee recreational area. They bought 143 acres along the Miami River in the north section of the city and constructed swimming areas, baseball fields, boathouses, picnic tables, a dance pavilion, and other facilities. It cost each of them $80,965.[60]

Kettering enjoyed the park as much as his workers. One Fourth of July an alert Delco photographer caught him in an uncharacteristic pose with a baseball and bat. On the tennis court, he was known for his awkward stroke, and deadly lob.

Delco Dell and the Triangle Park also pointed to a new interest in corporate paternalism that Kettering picked up from Patterson and NCR. Like many self-made men, Kettering had a hard time accepting the changes in relationships brought about by growth. He preferred the intimacy and equality of the Barn Gang days, and had little sympathy for, or understanding of, organized labor. During a brief strike, he coauthored an ultimatum to the workers which promised them "fair treatment, as high wages as we can afford, as good working conditions as we can provide and at all times a kindly interest in your well being and progress," and threatened to fire anyone who did not return on the company's terms.[61] Yet, Kettering kept enough of his good humor to wear a sign during the strike which said, in response to demands for an eight-hour day, "I want eight hours sleep!"

Deeds' managerial skills put Delco back in the black. At the end of 1915 the company reported profits of $1.5 million, and had about one-quarter of the automotive starting, lighting, and ignition market.[62] It had good accounts with Hudson and Packard, small orders from local automobile firms, and at least hopes of business from Ford. Most of its market, however, was with General Motors. Its survival as an independent company depended upon conditions within the automobile industry, and the trend was toward consolidation.

In 1915, the automobile industry was chiefly the story of Henry

Ford and William Crapo Durant. That year, Ford sold his millionth Model T and took control over a market he would dominate for more than a decade. At the same time, Durant reorganized one of his many automotive investments, the Chevrolet Motor Car Company, into a holding company, and through a complex series of financial maneuvers used it to regain control of another of his creations, General Motors.

Durant had founded General Motors in 1908 and built it into Henry Ford's only real competitor. His career with the company had been a series of spectacular rises followed by equally spectacular falls. He was a superb promoter and a terrible administrator. He had a sharp eye for the future of the automobile industry and looked forward to a time when it would be dominated by integrated enterprises with full model lines. Yet he acquired companies with only passing attention to their real worth or future, and burdened his company with crushing debts. He built an automotive empire, watched it fall into the hands of the receivers, and fought his way back into the presidency. "Irrepressible," one observer called him.[63]

One of Durant's good ideas was to bring together a group of independent accessories manufacturers and combine them with General Motors. In the fall of 1915, he started negotiations with five independent accessory manufacturers—Hyatt Roller Bearing Company, Remy Electric Company, New Departure Ball Bearing Company, Perlman Rim Corporation, and Delco.[64] The companies were scattered throughout the country, and even worse, contained two sets of direct competitors, Delco and Remy in the electrical field, and Hyatt and New Departure in the bearings market.

Nevertheless, Durant had an easy time convincing the firms to join his proposed United Motors Company. For one thing, he tended to be overly generous in his financial offers, even if most of it was in stock. More important, the prospective members faced a common dilemma. All depended on either Ford or General Motors for most of their business. As Alfred Sloan, then the forty-year-old president of Hyatt Roller Bearings, explained to Kettering and Deeds during the negotiations, if one or both of the automotive giants chose to make their own accessories, the independents might go under, so it seemed prudent to align themselves with one or the other.[65] The merger had special appeal for Kettering, who had little interest in managing Delco anyway, and thought the merger would free him from some administrative tasks and make available a ready source of seed money for new inventions.

On May 11, 1916, Kettering and Deeds cast their lot with Durant and United Motors. They sold out for $2.5 million in cash and 15,000 shares each of United Motors stock, with a bankers' price of $50 a share.[66] They retained their positions as president and vice-president.

For Kettering, the merger represented two important changes. It brought him together for the first time with Alfred Sloan, the man with whom he would later build General Motors into the largest manufacturing enterprise in the world. And, it gave him the financial resources to begin exploring the technical ideas that would do so much to effect that change.

However, Kettering's new wealth placed upon him the burden of managing it properly, a task for which he knew he was poorly equipped. He needed a full-time financial adviser, and at the end of May, he hired George Smith, a successful Dayton businessman who had been president and treasurer of the Kinnard Company. Smith resigned his former positions on June 1 and opened an office for Kettering in a downtown Dayton bank.[67]

Smith accompanied Deeds to New York later in the month as Kettering's official representative at the signing of the papers for the Delco sale. Only an hour after the sale, he sold several thousand shares of Kettering's new stock, then selling at a high 85½, and opened several bank accounts for him.[68] The sale touched off a brief controversy with Durant, who thought he had an agreement with Kettering and Deeds not to sell any stock until after a "decent" interval. Durant immediately telephoned Deeds, and demanded to know what had happened to the understanding. Deeds made some excuses for Kettering, who he said, was no financier. To their relief, Durant dropped the subject.[69] Kettering, however, was no innocent in these matters, and despite what Deeds said, was probably well aware of what had happened.

Smith proved a wise and able financial counselor, and under his management Kettering's investments grew into one of the largest fortunes in America.[70] The portfolio was comprised mainly of blue chip investments like U. S. Steel, General Motors, Pennsylvania Railroad, National City Bank of New York, and others, and included real estate holdings worth several millions.

Kettering was primarily interested in the fund as a source of capital for technical ventures and investments. These investments, as a whole, did poorly. He lost $15,000 in a local aircraft design firm, another $22,000 in a dirigible company, and $286,000 in a gasoline engine venture. He invested, and lost, $85,000 in the Dayton Steel Racket Company, a farsighted enterprise trying to develop a steel tennis racket decades ahead of its time. Kettering's generosity with friends and distant relatives also proved costly. He lost $4,000 on a loan to his personal physician, $8,000 on a debt to Henry Leland's son, and $2,000 more on a loan to his niece.[71] In all, he wrote off about $7 million on speculative investments and bad debts. And yet, thanks to Smith's careful management of the rest, he was one of the twenty wealthiest men in the country when he died.

Not all of Kettering's technical investments turned out badly, especially when he invested in himself. Some of them even helped him repay a long-standing debt to his rural heritage.

A bit of folklore from Kettering's youth ran, "Better stay on the farm a while longer / Though profits come in rather slow / Remember you've nothing to risk boys / Don't be in a hurry to go."[72] Most of the ambitious farm boys left the homestead anyway, not only because the profits were bad but because the conveniences were few. Some of them, like Henry Ford and Charles Kettering, remembered what it had been like, and recognized that there was a huge rural market for the right kinds of inventions.

By 1913, many of the conveniences of the city had found their way to the farm, but electricity, perhaps the greatest technological marvel of the age, was conspicuously absent. Isolated homesteads did not provide concentrated loads, and the early utility companies could not economically extend their service to farm areas. A number of inventors had tried their hands at developing a portable power source for the farm. None of their solutions—small air and steam engines—did the job efficiently or conveniently.

Kettering had a better idea, a portable electric generating and lighting system. What he had in mind was a small gasoline engine which would drive a generator and charge a bank of storage batteries. The batteries would then power small electric appliances and lights. Kettering got the idea from Delco customers who wrote him about using their automobile generators for this purpose.

In the fall of 1913, Kettering gathered a small staff to pursue the idea. Initially, he tried to design and build his own internal combustion engine. After tinkering with it for a time, he showed it to some Cadillac engineers, who suggested he go back to electrical engineering and subcontract for the engine. Kettering took their advice, and hired one of them, Ernest Dickey, to help with the project.[73]

Kettering and Dickey put together a prototype of the system with a six-horsepower Fairbanks-Morse gasoline engine, a Delco generator, and a 32-volt bank of automobile storage batteries. Kettering installed the unit on his parent's Loudonville farm, and wired the house and barn himself.[74]

With so many other projects commanding their attention, it was not until 1916 that Kettering and Deeds incorporated the Domestic Engineering Company to develop, manufacture, and market the home lighting plants. Deeds was president, Kettering vice-president and technical consultant. The company was capitalized at $800,000.[75] They anticipated a big market for the product.

Kettering took charge of the technical development. He and Dickey put together a new air-cooled engine to eliminate winter freeze-ups, an automatic starter switch to cut in when the charge in the batteries dropped below a certain point, and specially designed (and patented) valves cooled internally with a mercury-tin amalgam. Occasionally, he lost patience with the staff, and himself, when progress slowed. "It seems to me that there has been enough time for us to clean up some of these troubles, and if we can not clean up the troubles, let's quit making the apparatus until we do get them cleaned up," he told one of the engineers.[76] Generally, things went more smoothly than this, and such reprimands were unnecessary.

Kettering took a strong stand on customer relations, out of concern for the safety of both the consumers and the company's competitive position. When told of a harrowing episode in which a customer nearly lost his life in an encounter with an exposed flywheel, he ordered the staff to immediately add a protective screen, reminding them that "if anybody should be seriously injured through a happening of this kind . . . [the competition] would . . . immediately jump upon it and give their business a considerable boost." He also secured the Underwriter's Laboratory seal for the plants, a distinction he put to good use in advertising.[77]

Hiring Richard Grant, the sales manager with whom Kettering had worked on the O.K. Credit System, to head the company's sales campaign turned out to be another stroke of genius. Grant dubbed the units the "Delco-Light" and sold them as a way of upgrading rural life and keeping the younger generation down on the farm.[78] The units sold so well that within a year Domestic Engineering began construction of a new factory, the largest single-story steel and concrete building in the world. By 1918 it was selling 60,000 Delco-Lights a year and employing 2,370 workers.[79]

The Delco-Light plants sold briskly until the mid-1920s, when the spread of rural electrification began to erode the market. In developing countries, the market lasted much longer. In the 1930s, Kettering led an expedition of his friends on a tour of the Mayan ruins at Chichen Itza, and was surprised to find one of the plants still working away in a hacienda in the Yucatan jungle.[80]

Another Kettering project in the small engine field turned out less profitably. In December 1915, he invested heavily in the Smith Gas Engineering Company, a small research firm founded by his college roommate Harry Smith. Kettering bought nearly half the original stock. For a time the firm did well, but it did not survive the recession of 1920, and when the company folded, Kettering wrote off $300,000 in bad debts. A similar investment in the Dayton Fan and Motor Company did even worse. Kettering poured over a million dollars into the company before it too went bankrupt.[81]

Kettering's involvement with the motorcycle industry was somewhat more successful. He supposed that building factories and bringing industry to the rural areas was the only way the small town and farm could enjoy the economic advantages the rest of the country took for granted. In 1915, he was given a unique opportunity to test his theories in a most appropriate setting, Loudonville, Ohio.

The focus of the experiment was Hugo Young, a sometime artist and motorcycle dealer who had an idea for a flexible sidecar suspension, the forerunner of the independent suspension. Young had secured patents for his idea and had built up a respectable business in one of the little towns near Loudonville.[82] Kettering heard about Young's company and was anxious to invest in it. The firm was technically interesting, the market for motorcycle sidecars was booming, and the investment would give him a chance to build a manufacturing industry in Loudonville.

In the fall of 1915, Kettering met with Young and offered to put $180,000 into the company if Young would move it to Loudonville.[83] Young jumped at the chance, and in return for the capital, gave Kettering a controlling block of stock and the presidency of the new enterprise, the Flxible Side-Car Company. Young, who would actually run the company, was executive vice-president and general manager.

Flxible turned out to be quite profitable, and as Kettering had predicted, it became the major Loudonville industry. During the First World War it did a good business in sidecars for the military. And in the 1920s, when low-priced automobiles put the squeeze on the motorcycle industry, the company lived up to its name and moved into the production of funeral cars, ambulances, and intercity buses.[84]

Flxible's success in the bus market later put Kettering into a curious conflict of interest. Long after the other major bus competitors— White, Mack, Beck, Aerocoach, Brill, and Fitzjohn—had left the field to General Motors, Flxible remained a prosperous thorn in the side of the automobile giant. Kettering, as vice-president and primary instigator of the General Motors bus development, and as president and consultant to Flxible, found himself backing both David and Goliath.

As a prominent local citizen, Kettering took an active role in community affairs. When Arthur Morgan, head of the Miami Conservancy District, a flood-control project, and later chief of the Army Corps of Engineers, called a meeting of Dayton businessmen and engineers in April 1917, Kettering attended. Over lunch, Morgan told his nine friends that with their financial support, he hoped to embark upon an experiment in progressive education. At each man's place was a pamphlet entitled "The Specifications of a Teacher," in which Morgan outlined his proposed experiment in individual, vocational instruction. After lunch, Morgan asked the group to serve as the board of directors for the school, and to pledge their sons for the entering class. Kettering, Orville Wright, Deeds, George Smith, and the others enthusiastically endorsed the idea, and the Moraine Park School was born.[85]

The board hired a progressive educator from Pueblo, Colorado named Frank D. Slutz as headmaster, and initially appointed two other instructors. After a futile search for suitable quarters, Kettering offered his old greenhouse on Southern Boulevard, quipping that he would rather raise kids than cucumbers anyway. With a few alterations, the "School in a Glass House" opened in the fall with an enrollment of 66, including Eugene Kettering, Charles Deeds, Ernest Morgan, Theodore and Martha Chryst, and Frederick Hooven.[86]

From the beginning, Moraine Park stressed an innovative curriculum. The school had no formal classes below the fifth grade. Instead, the younger children progressed at an individual pace. Discipline was minimal. The children drilled each other in spelling and arithmetic, chose their own books, and read aloud to each other without supervision. A peer assembly heard recitation. Should a young scholar become bored or restless, he could leave the classroom without permission and vent his frustrations at a carpentry bench provided for the purpose.[87]

Kettering eventually put $220,000 into the school, and worked on various projects with some of the teachers.[88] He and Slutz put together a program of cooperative education which included an extensive work-study program. Before graduation, each student had to run a small business of some sort, demonstrating his ability to use his classroom knowledge in a practical way. Over the years, the budding entrepreneurs organized a ping-pong parlor, a holly wreath company, a dance agency, a book bindery, and a grocery store. Some of the enterprises actually turned a profit that helped cover the operating expenses of the school. Kettering also insisted that students work around the school, and even the sons of millionaires could frequently be seen lending a hand with custodial duties.

Moraine Park caught the public's attention at a time of educational reform in America. Groups of businessmen in other cities were founding private schools based on similar educational philosophies. Commentators from national magazines like *Collier's* and *Atlantic Monthly* reviewed Moraine Park and talked with Kettering and some of the other organizers. The school's progressive methods, particularly the lack of emphasis on drill and discipline, drew protest from traditional educators, but others thought Moraine Park was a breath of fresh air in the stale educational environment.

Kettering and Deeds supported the experiment for a decade largely with contributions from their own pockets. Then, when it appeared that many wealthy "supporters" were not willing to share the financial burden, and that the ideas had been taken up by others, they discontinued the venture.

The school produced many fine graduates destined for success in a wide range of fields. Sadly, though, it ultimately failed the one student Kettering was most interested in, his son Eugene. Principal Slutz naturally was concerned about Eugene's work, and he tried hard to encourage and guide him. At the end of the school year of 1922, when Eugene was thirteen, Slutz wrote Kettering a detailed report of Eugene's scholastic progress. Eugene had missed some classes with a broken ankle, and he had "been rather careless" in some of his courses, so he would have to finish the term in the summer, Slutz explained. Slutz thought that "in a few days Gene can complete his English entirely," but he cautioned that Eugene's "trouble in mathematics is more serious because he does not take the necessary drill."[89]

Slutz suggested that Eugene accompany him to a Minnesota camp for some remedial work during the summer. "The independent out door life in camp will be good for the lad. He always responds well when he is put upon his own resources and I think he fails to respond as well when he has persons around him to do many things for him," Slutz told Kettering. "Gene is headed towards a fine success if we can keep him from failing to meet situations with his own hands. I think he is tempted to depend on others too much. If we work together we can see him over this hill."[90]

Kettering had tried to make things easier for his son, perhaps too easy, and he acknowledged that Slutz's plan might help Eugene. In August, he packed Eugene off to Camp Wanaki. Eugene loved the swimming, fishing, and hiking. His letters home revealed little academic improvement, however, leading Kettering to scold him, "You had a couple of bad 'spells' when you wrote this one. You know, it is awfully bad taste to scratch a word on a card or letter and it would only take a half minute more to find out how to spell it before you write it."[91] Later letters showed some progress, and the old school master noted approvingly, "This last letter is very much better than any other you have written but it still shows a little raggedness that I would like for you to improve on."[92] When Eugene announced that he would return from camp on the six o'clock train on August 36, his father teased, "It must be a great camp up there because you have different kinds of months than we have here. . . . I have looked through all of our calendars here and can find none that has more than thirty-one days in August."[93]

The following summer, Eugene again joined Slutz in Minnesota. His teacher commented on Eugene's love of camping, but wrote to Kettering also about an unappealing spoiled streak:

I want to help Gene to see that he must not expect special favors in camp but that he must abide gladly by what we think is best for his health and training. He feels that when we make a decision not to his liking, that someone has it in for him, which of course is not true. I want him to get that democratic good will and fair sportsmanship for which the men who know you admire you so much.[94]

Despite Slutz's best efforts, Eugene did not become much of a scholar, causing his father occasionally to question the value of the Moraine Park experiment. "Of all the boys who come up to the house with Gene, I have never yet heard any of them discuss a single thing about school, with the exception of athletics," he told the principal. "Nor have I been able to find out from a single one of them where their interests lay in the question of studies. I have repeatedly asked why they did not bring work home and they said they did not have to—that they did it all in school."[95]

Eugene's sloppy study habits and his problems with basic mathematics and English distressed Kettering. He wrote Slutz:

I do not want you to think that I have in any wise lost faith in our experiment, because I have not, but I feel that we are neglecting the fundamentals which you will never be able to get the boys to learn after they get past a certain age. An example of this is Gene's inability to spell or write well. I find that the other boys are not better off than he is and after he is beyond fifteen years of age you will never be able to teach him these things.[96]

Kettering's prediction proved accurate. Although Eugene did inherit some mechanical talents, and would later use them in a successful engineering career, he never developed his father's love of knowledge. The effects of Eugene's pampered and inadequate secondary schooling would plague him throughout his life.

In the early days of Delco, Kettering had turned down an opportunity to invest in some Oregon land with Chryst. He told his friend, "I know I could never persuade Mrs. Kettering to leave the borders of a city. Personally I can think of no more elegant place to live than the country."[97] In 1913, with Delco's business booming, Kettering finally convinced Olive to move out of the city. In the fall, he began building a mansion crowning a high moraine five miles south of Dayton. Completed in early 1914, the half-timbered Tudor of gray wood and fieldstone, called Ridgeleigh Terrace for its open porch, overlooked the Miami Valley. With its dark teak paneling in the entry hall, gold-leafed doorknobs, solid marble tubs and sinks, and sumptuous Persian carpets, Kettering's home attested to his financial success and Olive's good taste.[98] Only in the music room, where he occasionally wrestled with some work problems, did he modify Olive's decor. There, he ordered the carpet torn up and linoleum put down because, he said, "nobody would spit on that nice carpet and when I'm working I like to spit."[99]

Kettering also added some technical touches that reminded visitors that Ridgeleigh Terrace was the home of an outstanding engineer as well as a prosperous businessman. He purchased a rare player organ for Olive, which they placed at the top of the grand stairway. Partly to protect the delicate instrument, but mostly to satisfy his technical curiosity, Kettering designed and installed a central air-conditioning system, perhaps the first in a noncommercial building. And on Sunday afternoons, Olive often gave organ recitals for friends and the servants.

Despite the long hours, Kettering found time to be a family man. He took Eugene on long nature walks in the moraines, pointing out the fragile beauties of nature. Kettering loved animals, especially cats, and he always had two or three around the house. So that they could come and go as they pleased, he built a trap door and ramp out the basement. And whenever one climbed on his lap, even in the middle of wrestling with a tricky technical problem, Kettering simply quit working until the cat finished its nap.

Olive became a leading social and philanthropic figure in Dayton. She entertained lavishly and contributed huge sums to civic and artistic causes. Among the many recipients of her charity were the Dayton Art Institute ($8,059), the Good Samaritan Hospital ($17,500), the University of Dayton ($2,059), the Dayton Symphony and Philharmonic ($1,325), the American Red Cross ($32,140), and the YMCA ($90,141).[100] Her parties were memorable affairs, though not always because of their elegance. Kettering loved to play practical jokes on the guests. One time, he cleared off all the china and silverware set out for a formal luncheon, and left instead a single saucer of milk at each place, as if the meal were for a family of cats, instead of Dayton's richest ladies.[101]

Kettering also played an active role in Dayton's professional community. In February of 1914, he and Deeds called together prominent local engineers to see if they could channel the professional interests of various engineering groups into some concrete, influential expression.[102] Frank Clements, Kettering's laboratory instructor at Ohio State and at that time a local chemist, presented the meeting with the results of a survey commissioned by Kettering of similar clubs throughout the country. Kettering and Deeds then announced their intention to donate to the new society a remodeled Victorian mansion in downtown Dayton. Their generous offer put an end to any wavering, and two months later the fifteen men met again to sign the group's official charter of incorporation. The charter members included Kettering, Deeds, Arthur Morgan, Clements, J. H. Hunt (once professor of electrical engineering at Ohio State, then with Delco), Orville Wright, and Bill Chryst.

With an active membership campaign, the Dayton Engineers' Club grew rapidly from its original handful of members to 136 at the end of the first year. The club offered an ambitious series of guest lectures that year. Henry Leland and Leo Baekeland, chemist and inventor of the first commercially successful plastic, were among the speakers, and both appeared at the personal invitation of Kettering. Kettering followed the formal presentations with his inimitable impromptu remarks that, according to the participants, "gave an anticipation and zest to each meeting."[103]

The club was so popular that it soon outgrew its original quarters. On July 31, 1916, Kettering and Deeds announced a gift of $300,000 for a new clubhouse. Completed a year later, the imposing brick edifice on Monument and Jefferson housed sumptuously furnished meeting and dining rooms, lounges, a pool hall, and a technical library.[104]

Kettering was particularly interested in the library and helped it acquire an impressive collection of engineering texts and periodicals. Believing that one of the strongest foundations of an engineering career was intimate knowledge of the technical literature, he encouraged the younger members to browse freely, despite his occasional outbursts about disregarding experts. In the early years the club published a proceedings, which included contributions from C. E. K. Mees (research director of Kodak), William Gorgas (U.S. Army surgeon-general), and Louis Agassiz Fuestis (the naturalist).

Kettering served three terms as president of the Engineers' Club over the years, and did perhaps more than any other member to make it a success. Its luncheon sessions usually included an enthusiastic summary of his current work which members recalled even years later.[105] In 1923, the members voted him honorary president for life. The club could not, by itself, either make Dayton into a leading technical center or prevent its eventual decline. It did strengthen the local engineering community, keep Dayton's engineers in close touch with national trends, and inspire a number of young men to enter the profession.

At the opening of the new clubhouse on February 2, 1918, attended by Elmer Sperry, Jesse G. Vincent, and Leo Baekeland among others, the members recognized the founders' contributions with a bronze plaque:

Thus do we, the members of the Engineers' Club of Dayton, Ohio, inscribe on this memorial our appreciation of the energy, thoughtfulness, and generosity of our esteemed leaders, Col. Edward Andrew Deeds and Charles Franklin Kettering, which prompted them to erect and equip this splendid building and present it to us with its beautiful grounds. We accept it as an expression of their deep interest in scientific research and their abiding devotion to the cause of truth. Already their efforts have resulted in bringing into frequent and intimate touch with one another men of ability, progressiveness and achievement as well as those eager to learn and advance by such associations.[106]

The Delco years were ones of achievement for Kettering the inventor. In less than a decade he had perfected battery ignition and the self-starter, thus assuring that the gasoline automobile would become the dominant form of personal transportation in America. The claims of automotive journalists of the time that the self-starter did more for the emancipation of women than Susan B. Anthony may have been exaggerated, but the rapid spread of the starter did open a new market for the car.

These years also saw Kettering move into a new role as an entrepreneur. No longer backed by the managerial and marketing talent of NCR, he had to select his own problems, anticipate the trends of a largely unknown market, and learn something about promotion and patents, raising capital, and managing a large enterprise. Some lessons he learned well. In areas where he showed less interest or ability, such as finance and management, he learned to rely on experts more skilled in these matters.

Most important, this period marked Kettering's final maturing as a professional. He joined the Society of Automotive Engineers (SAE) in 1912, and by 1916 was a leading member. He published several papers, made frequent comments at the regular meetings, and gave more than one memorable speech.

Perhaps Kettering's best remembered talk during those early years was entitled "Science and the Future Automobile" and was given to the 1916 summer meeting of the SAE on board a Great Lakes steamer. Kettering delighted and educated his audience with thrilling visual effects and commentary on the changing American automobile. He frequently turned to his props, including a thermos jar of liquid air. He explained to his listeners, "I always like to use liquid air in these talks, because it helps to counteract by its extreme coldness the effect of the hot air which is disseminated along the line."[107]

Yet along with the humor came some shrewd insights into the changes taking place in the automotive industry, changes in which Kettering would shortly play an important role. He left his listeners with an impassioned plea for organized research:

The only reason I have come here is not to tell you anything wonderful, anything new, but simply to get us looking ahead, because down the road for years to come this automobile industry is going to advance. It is going to advance just in proportion as we can cooperatively have our formative engineers design new features and influence our research engineers to produce for us new materials. We must advance through scientific research in the future.[108]

4 / WORLD WAR I

One Sunday evening in the spring of 1916, Kettering invited several local engineers and businessmen to Ridgeleigh Terrace for a discussion of aviation and its likely role in the impending European war. Grover Loening, a recognized aeronautical engineer and one of the participants, recalled that during the meeting, "Kettering, in his high-pitched, Ohio-accented voice, joined in above . . . [Olive's] organ strains, 'You know, if the U. S. does get into this war, we want to help to do it right. We are building a factory for Domestic Lighting [Engineering] Company down here in Moraine, near this house. In a jiffy we could turn this into a plane plant if it was needed.' "[1]

In a sentence, Kettering unwittingly revealed both his foolish over-confidence that techniques borrowed from making automobiles could give a quick shot in the arm to aviation, and an important change in direction in his own career. Kettering was now forty years old, an accomplished inventor with nearly one hundred patents, a successful entrepreneur at the head of two corporations, and a millionaire. But he had not ventured very far from his narrow field of specialization. All his innovations had been applications of electrical technology to specific problems of business machines or internal combustion engines. The rush to supply and perfect the tools of war would broaden Kettering's technical and business interests to include aircraft design and manufacture, high-performance aviation fuels, and guided missiles, projects that would set the stage for many of his later commercial innovations and bring him into close contact with the evolving military-industrial complex.

Better than most military experts, Kettering appreciated the potential military implications of aircraft. Before the war, he publicly predicted that America had too few aircraft and would never have enough unless it found a way to transplant automotive production technology into the infant industry.

To this end he joined with five Dayton businessmen, including his chief business adviser Edward Deeds and famous aviator Orville Wright, in forming a syndicate for aircraft manufacturing in 1916. The Dayton Wright Airplane Company was capitalized at $500,000, with Deeds as president and Kettering as vice-president and technical consultant.[2]

About the same time the United States and Germany broke diplomatic relations. Secretary of War Newton Baker, belatedly recognizing the country's woeful military aviation preparations, hastily assembled an Aircraft Production Board. As automotive executives were thought to know the secrets of mass production, Baker appointed Howard Coffin, president of the Hudson Motor Car Company, to the head of the board. Coffin, in turn, filled his committees with other automobile men, including Edward Deeds, who joined the board just after the formal declaration of war on April 6, 1917. To avoid charges of conflict of interest, Deeds resigned his office as Dayton Wright president, placed his stock in a nonvoting trust, and accepted a commission as colonel in the army.[3]

The Aircraft Production Board lacked everything except confidence. Coffin announced that the United States would have 3,500 airplanes in the war before the end of the year.[4] Kettering's new partner, Orville Wright, told the press that several times that number was more likely.[5] Such rosy predictions rested heavily on a $640 million congressional appropriation for military aircraft and the assumption of the automotive engineers on the board that American manufacturers could simply select a foreign design and, with a few modifications, mass-produce it with assembly line technology. A technical delegation, after a European tour and conferences with French and English aviation experts, chose the British De Haviland, a sturdy observation and bombing craft, as the design best suited to American methods.[6]

Dayton Wright won the coveted De Haviland contract over several established aviation firms, a testimony to the strength of its Washington connection and the influence of the automotive lobby. The contract called for 400 training aircraft, the so-called J-1, to be completed by the end of December, and an unspecified number of De Havilands for the following spring. The guaranteed profit was to be $620 an airplane.[7]

Kettering's official position at Dayton Wright, apart from being a partner, was head of engineering, a post that paid $35,000 a year. He had little interest or expertise in financial matters, which he considered the responsibility of the other partners. As Kettering later testified, "I never paid any attention to the financial side of it. I simply operated the business. I had a financial secretary."[8]

Engineering an unfamiliar product would be challenge enough. The Delco-Light plant was requisitioned for the venture, and was expanded. But time and space were so limited that Dayton Wright moved into the building bay by bay, one step behind the wet cement. As the walls set behind him, the factory manager wrote on his office blackboard, in perfect echo of Kettering's unshakable optimism, "Impossibilities are the half-hearted attempts of quitters."[9] Kettering, meanwhile, kept his office in Gray Manor, an old residence in downtown Dayton where the other officers also worked.

For a novice in aviation, the technical and logistical problems were nearly insurmountable. First the wrong blueprints arrived, and when the right ones came, they were in unfamiliar British terms. Kettering complained, "It was all in English, and we . . . had to translate all that stuff into American terms so our men could know what it all meant."[10] Expected government shipments came so sporadically that one of the partners, when told only tires and toilet paper had arrived on time, reportedly snapped, "there's no landing gear for the tires and you guys are supposed to be too busy for the other."[11]

Lengthy approval procedures and bureaucratic red tape were also new and unpleasant experiences for Kettering. His daily ten o'clock calls to Washington frequently ended in violent shouting matches. After one particularly tedious series of water resistance tests for fuselage glue, Kettering exploded at one of the army engineers, "Hell, Major, we're trying to make aeroplanes, not soup!"[12]

Typically, Kettering had no patience for the managerial frustrations that were bound to arise out of such an operation and often neglected his management duties altogether to work on technical projects. But even on these, he made little headway against the bureaucratic current. His design for an electric air-speed indicator only found its way onto the De Haviland after heavy lobbying from his Washington friends.[13] His nonexploding gasoline tank was killed in committee, which was unfortunate, as the idea was farsighted. It employed a rubber casing that plugged the hole left by the bullet. Kettering sharpened his marksmanship skills testing the tanks; he simply could not convince the army to buy them. To make the whole experience even worse, his airplane crashed on the return flight from the conference with the army engineer about the tank. Roland Hutchison, then a young engineer on Kettering's staff, recalled that the plane "stubbed its toe, turned over, and the Boss bit the instrument panel, losing some teeth."[14]

Military aircraft, unlike automobiles, needed constant redesign in light of combat experience, and the process continually troubled the Dayton Wright staff. The placement of guns and other combat accessories unexpectedly upset the De Haviland's delicate balance.[15] Grover Loening later commented, "It was much easier than at first supposed to mount guns and other items if done by competent, versatile, aircraft people. But when the auto people (unfamiliar with exacting aircraft 'tricks') started on their own to mount this equipment on foreign copies, they made a sorry mess."[16]

Kettering himself became a victim of this inexperienced and hasty engineering effort. Once, while he was a passenger on a test flight, a rough running engine jolted its fuel line, sprayed gasoline over the fuselage, and caught fire. A quick-thinking technician doused the craft and its crew with soda until a wet and surly Charles Kettering screamed at him to stop.[17]

Technical foul-ups, red tape, and poor planning took their toll. Dayton Wright did not complete the last of its trainers until March 1918, three months behind schedule. And the De Haviland contract fell even farther behind. Political leaders, dismayed by the performance and misled by the overly optimistic predictions of the year before, started to ask some pointed questions of the aircraft industry, and about Dayton Wright's informal ties to Deeds and the Aircraft Production Board.

An army investigating team arrived in Dayton in May 1918 to look into charges of corruption and inefficiency. Its meetings with the Dayton Wright businessmen were not cordial. George Mixter, the commission leader, set the tone for the investigation by bursting unannounced into a meeting of the company directors and trumpeting, "I am Major George Mixter. The product of this plant has so far consisted principally of Goddams and Sonsabitches. I am here to discover the names of your directors and to obtain a list of the active ones." Kettering, never one to be intimidated by authority, was sitting at the far end of the table. According to an eyewitness, he recrossed his legs, took another bite out of his cigar, and glared back at Mixter. "My name is Charles Franklin Kettering," he replied. "I am one of the directors of this corporation and am, incidentally, its consulting engineer. I was born up in the Ohio hills near Loudonville and am consequently an American citizen. I have all the respect in the world for the flag of the United States, and the uniform of the Army, but it's the so and so inside that uniform I may be out to get. Now, what can I do for you, sir?" [18]

Over the summer, a Senate committee led by Attorney General Charles Evans Hughes, already famous for his probe of corruption in the utility industry, came to Dayton to complete the investigation. Hughes personally grilled Kettering and the other directors for a solid week, and poked through the business records of Dayton Wright. What particularly troubled Hughes was the informal business arrangements of Dayton Wright and its sister companies, which Hughes felt must be concealing something illegal. [19] The tangled web of notes and mortgages and directors seemed to hint at a conspiracy that Hughes could not prove. In the end, Hughes settled for censuring

Dayton Wright for inefficiency and recommending Deeds be court-martialed for conflict of interest. A military board later dropped all charges against Deeds. Hughes never found a conspiracy because there was none, only unrealistic expectations on the part of both the public and the Dayton Wright board.

No De Havilands did roll off of Dayton Wright's "assembly line" because airplanes simply could not be manufactured that way. With specifications changing frequently, the best they could do was produce one batch of similar planes, and then make adjustments for the next batch. On July 31, 1918 the firm completed its thousandth De Haviland and the directors called a company holiday.[20] Eventually the firm built 3,000 of them. And though most of the planes reached Europe too late to see action, Dayton Wright could still take some pride in its performance. It had manufactured most of the De Havilands made in America, and produced an aircraft that won high praise in the army's final technical report on American aircraft.[21]

Kettering also played a minor role in the development of the most important American aviation innovation of the war, the Liberty engine. Like the De Haviland, the Liberty engine grew out of the Aircraft Production Board's conviction that American automobile "know-how" could make up for lack of aviation experience. This time the expectation was closer to the mark, for aircraft engines were still enough like car engines so that the same production technology could be used for both.[22]

The engine itself was designed by Elbert Hall and Jesse Vincent, two automotive engineers with almost no background in aviation. Again, Secretary Baker predicted instant success, and expected that the Liberty design would "solve the problem of building high-class, powerful, and yet comparatively delicate aviation engines by American machine methods—the same standardized methods which revolutionized the automobile industry in this country."[23]

Delco won the ensuing competition for the ignition contract, for several reasons. First, Kettering, who was vice-president of engineering and who had become the nominal president (at a salary of $50,000) upon Deeds' resignation had obvious personal connections. Second, Delco belonged to United Motors, which had an active lobby in Washington. Since the first days of the war, when rumors that civilian production would be curtailed circulated through the industry, United Motors had kept a watchdog in the capital, as Sloan told Kettering, to "work with the different departments of government . . . and to keep our Companies advised of the demands of Government . . . with a view to making up the reduction in the automobile industry by taking on Government business and bringing our different units in touch with Government business." [24] Third, Vincent had designed the Liberty with a battery ignition in mind because he liked the light weight, reliability, safety, and easier starting. He stuck with his design in the face of, as he put it, "every kind of pressure" from "certain people having magnetos to sell." [25]

Kettering's ignition design, for which J. H. Hunt deserves much of the credit, was quite similar to standard automotive ignitions. Among its novel features was a special generator drive shaft that also ran the oil and water pumps, and synchronized sparkplugs, two to a cylinder. It also had a light-weight battery that did not leak during loops and rolls, and a safety system to prevent the propeller from reversing during starting. [26]

The official army trials in July 1917 supported Kettering's design. Hunt, who went along as Delco representative, wrote from Langley Field in Virginia that "very much to everyone's surprise, [the army testers] had obtained 1000 feet less climb in ten minutes with the . . . magneto than they had obtained with Delco." [27] And Vincent added that he "was very pleased with the ignition because I found it lighter than magnetos, probably more reliable, and best of all . . . it made for easier starting." [28] Competing magneto manufacturers accused the Aircraft Production Board of playing favorites. But in any event, Delco got the order for 20,000 ignitions at $112 apiece. Eventually the army switched to an improved magneto, but the Delco ignition had ably fulfilled combat requirements early in the war and under a great deal of pressure.

Kettering first met Henry Ford as part of the Liberty engine venture. The army wanted a faster production method for the steel engine cylinders, and sent Kettering to negotiate with Ford. The two businessmen met in Ford's office and discussed the engine, Ford's ill-fated peace ship, and other things. Later, Kettering invited Ford to Dayton, where they looked at some early experiments with wireless. When discussion flagged and Ford plainly grew weary of the technical talk, Kettering enlivened the conversation by swapping a few homely stories.[29]

One other Kettering company made a significant contribution to the war effort, Dayton Metal Products. This firm had been incorporated by Kettering and his five partners from Dayton Wright in 1915 and capitalized at $200,000. It was intended as a manufacturer of specialty pumps and refrigerating accessories but turned to war materiel and fuses instead. Kettering was again an engineering consultant and vice-president, at a salary of $25,000.[30]

Kettering gradually assumed an active part in the enterprise. For some time he had been studying the relationship between fuels and engines, first in response to complaints that his Delco ignition worsened knock in car engines, and later when some Delco-Light units started getting the same complaints. He had even set up a small laboratory on the second floor of the Domestic Engineering Company to study the problem, headed by Frank Clements, his Ohio State acquaintance who had also worked for NCR. Thomas Midgley, another NCR recruit, was chief chemist.

The equipment was crude and the staff shorthanded, but thanks to Kettering's farsighted appreciation of the issue, and his correct assumption that engine performance was closely related to fuel type, the laboratory had better data on the relationship between fuel and engine than anyone else in America at the time. Consequently, when the Army Air Service needed information on the erratic performance of aviation combat fuels, it turned to Kettering.

Subsequently, Kettering transferred his little laboratory to an old Victorian mansion on Ludlow Street downtown, and renamed it the Research Division of the Dayton Metal Products Company, because the parent company had priority for the restricted chemicals the researchers needed. It had a staff of less than a dozen men and the most primitive of facilities; the test engines were in the kitchen, the chemical "laboratory" in the butler's pantry.[31]

The laboratory's first government contract was for a project to evaluate combat gasolines from various parts of the world and find out why some were so much better than others. To do this, the researchers compared the samples in a single-cylinder, variable compression engine. The results were wildly inconsistent. Not only did performance vary by the geographical provenance; it was affected by compression ratio, carburetor setting, and fuel-air mixture. Even more puzzling to Kettering, Midgley, and the others was that for any given variable, one gasoline was usually best, most others nearly as good, and one or two others slightly but distinctly inferior; yet there seemed little discernible reason for this. "No way was found of predicting the power performance from any one, or from any group of properties," they admitted.[32]

Still, the data supported Kettering's original contention that knock and performance were more a function of fuel than engine. And it showed conclusively that California gasolines offered more power than others, a conclusion of some immediate interest to the Air Service.

A closer look at California gasolines revealed that they contained a high percentage of naphthenes. This observation led the chemists to wonder about the role of specific hydrocarbon groups in fuel performance. They subsequently experimented with ethers, paraffins, aromatics, and olefins.[33] None of these groups performed as well as the naphthenes, but the data from these investigations suggested that fuel structure had something to do with behavior. For instance, cyclic compounds did better than chain compounds. When this discovery was combined with a report from the army that indicated that German combat aircraft were using a cyclic cyclohexane fuel (a report that was, ironically, mistranslated), Kettering redirected the research toward artificially produced, cyclic fuels.[34]

One promising possibility was to synthesize cyclohexane from benzene. Theoretically this could be done with a simple catalytic reaction. However, the professional chemists that Kettering consulted on the problem were not hopeful; Leo Baekeland, in fact, was so skeptical, that he offered Kettering a wooden medal for the first pint of cyclohexane produced from the laboratory.[35]

For a time, Baekeland's pessimism seemed justified. Kettering and the chemists stayed up the entire night of October 22, 1917 trying to make a nickel oxide catalyst work, to no avail. Then Kettering, who always ran down the value of professional expertise but when desperate was just as eager to take advantage of it, sent one of the researchers to the Ohio State University library to study benzene catalysts. The results of this literature search gave the team some clues to better catalytic reactions, purer raw materials, closer attention to impurities, and a new technique for bringing together the benzene and the catalyst. With these improvements the chemists began to get a better yield, and on November 7 they tried an engine test which gave encouraging results. [36]

The freezing point of cyclohexane was something of a problem. It froze at 40°F, far too high a temperature for aviation use. However, the researchers soon discovered a convenient mixture of cyclohexane and benzol with a freezing point of −40°F that they called "Hecter." [37]

The fuel worked near miracles with the Liberty test engines. One withstood nearly twice the compression of engines powered with the best California gasolines. Another, with new piston rings, better-timed exhaust valves, and improved exhaust stacks, pulled sixteen more horsepower than a production Liberty. [38]

Unfortunately, "Hecter" only offered important military advantages if it could be made available in quantity. And by March 1918, the Dayton Metal Products laboratory could still produce only a liter or two at a time.

That summer, Kettering hired two chemical engineers from Ohio State to help with the problems of cyclohexane production, Thomas A. Boyd, a recent graduate, and Carroll A. Hochwalt, a precocious sophomore. The two young men brought badly needed expertise into the project, and with a careful study of catalysts and reaction temperatures they steadily increased cyclohexane output to twenty-eight gallons a day by the end of November 1917. [39] They might have done even better had it not been for inferior and infrequent shipments of raw materials because of the war. F. O. Clements complained to Baekeland, "The boys have had considerable difficulty producing cyclohexane since you left due to the fact that they received a shipment of very poorly refined benzol, carrying very large quantities of carbon disulphate and thiophenes." [40]

Although the laboratory had stockpiled sufficient cyclohexane to start flight testing by the fall of 1917, Kettering delayed the trials for weeks on one pretense or another. Publicly, he said that the ground tests were inconclusive. To close associates, he told the truth. He had suffered so many recent embarrassments in front of military committees that he did not want to risk another failure. Nor did he "want to run the risk of adverse reports on this fuel due to some inherent fault of the motor itself." [41]

His fears were groundless. "There was a very perceptible increase of power, both on the ground and at all altitudes reached in our tests (maximum 22,000 ft.) and the pickup was greatly improved," test pilot Howard Rinehart told Kettering after the first trial. "It was found to be exceptionally free from vibration. The motor with this fuel gave one the impression of flying behind a steam engine or an electric motor . . . this by reason of its smoothness, even exhaust, quick response to the throttle and absence of the usual sharp report of a gas motor exhaust. . . . In short, it could almost be said that by the use of 'Hecter' a new sensation in flying had been created." [42]

Even with the addition of the chemical engineers, the Dayton Metal Products Company was unable to manufacture enough synthetic fuel to power one combat plane. However, the idea of specially tailored synthetic fuels would find many later applications in both the civilian and the military market. And the knowledge gained in the project was put to good use in later investigations.

Leo Baekeland, at least, received formal recognition for his important contributions. At a special postwar meeting of the Dayton Engineers' Club, Kettering and Midgley presented him with the first pint of cyclohexane prepared at the laboratory, along with plans for an appropriate medal, a benzene ring surrounded by cats, to suggest "catalysis." [43]

In December 1917, in the midst of the fuel investigation, the De Haviland contract, and the Liberty engine ignition venture, Kettering accepted another government assignment, a guided aerial torpedo. This project would be more forward-looking and more technically interesting than any of the other wartime projects, would occupy more of Kettering's time, and yet, in the end, would be the least successful.

The idea of a self-guided flying bomb was not new. Elmer Sperry, an inventor already famous for his contributions to gyroscopic navigation and stabilization, had been at work on one for over a year under the sponsorship of the navy. Drawing on his earlier work with gyroscopic compasses and automatic feedback control, Sperry had developed a successful control system for a full-sized naval airplane, but he had not yet come up with a practical torpedo.[44]

Kettering first observed the Sperry guidance system in early December 1917 as part of an army committee watching trials of the device at Amityville, Long Island. Most of the members were not very impressed, and the committee returned a negative verdict. Kettering, however, contributed such an enthusiastic minority report that General George O. Squier, the officer in charge of the committee, was persuaded to continue the investigation.[45] As Kettering explained in his report, and later to a secret meeting of designers, draftsmen, and engineers from Dayton Wright and the Dayton Metal Products Company, the only serious drawbacks of Sperry's system were its cost and complexity. "It's got to be simple," Kettering said. "We haven't got time to make it complicated."[46] In his opinion, if an aerial torpedo was to be of immediate benefit, it would have to be cheap and expendable.

Kettering faced a two-sided challenge as the engineering head of the army torpedo project. He had to develop a body and power plant for the weapon, and he had to devise a suitable guidance system.

For the former task, he could rely on an impressive array of aeronautical engineering talent from Dayton Wright, notably Orville Wright and two of his assistants, Roland V. Hutchinson and Louis Luneke. Together, this design team worked up a prototype that met Kettering's cost requirements. What emerged from their drawing boards was a biplane with a fifteen-foot wingspan, steel tubing for structural support, and pasteboard on the control surfaces to save weight. For the wing covering, the designers chose a muslin and brown paper covering, with a protective coating of hide glue, water, glycerine, and creosote.[47] For some reason, Kettering, who knew very little about aviation design, felt compelled to offer his advice on ailerons. He and Wright argued at some length on this point, but in the end Kettering bowed to Wright's view that dihedral in the wings would be the cheapest and most efficient form of lateral control.

C. H. Wills, the former chief designer at Ford, and Ralph de

Palma, a race car builder and driver, had charge of the torpedo's engine. Here too Kettering felt qualified to give advice. Initially, he insisted on an air-cooled, two-stroke, opposed cylinder design, a configuration he thought would save weight. Though they did build such an engine, even the best efforts of Wills and de Palma could not get it to run very well. They later convinced Kettering that a more conventional four-cylinder, inline design would be better. Their final model pulled a strong forty horsepower and cost only $40.[48]

Subsequent efforts to improve performance and save weight had mixed results. A model with aluminum pistons gave forty-two horsepower on a test stand, and then exploded spectacularly in front of the terrified spectators.[49] Wills did improve cooling by repositioning the carburetor to feed the front and rear cylinders individually.[50]

Kettering, Midgley, and the Dayton Metal Products staff developed the guidance system. Kettering was actively involved in the technical details of this project, and his suggestion that they use the vacuum from the engine crankcase to operate the controls was ingenious. To control altitude, the engineers used an aneroid barometer. When the torpedo strayed from the correct height, the aneroid barometer would open a valve and adjust the elevator. The distance control, a small airscrew on the wing that drove a mileage counter, was another of Kettering's personal contributions. At a preselected range the counter would hit zero, cut off the ignition, and send the nose-heavy craft toward the target. For directional control, the designers borrowed Sperry's gyroscope.[51] Kettering resisted the idea for a long time, but in the end he could not come up with a workable alternative. Sperry generously gave Kettering detailed drawings of the system, and even visited Dayton several times to help out with the installation.

In September 1918, Kettering brought together the various parts of the project and Dayton Wright assembled for flight testing a somewhat larger version than the original prototype. Howard Rinehart, who had flight-tested Hecter, piloted the craft, called the Messenger. The test participants were advised to describe the craft as an alternative to motorcycle deliveries to the front in case any explanations were needed.[52] With a pilot, the torpedo performed flawlessly.

The last remaining problem was to develop a launching track for the torpedo. With slotted gas pipes and discarded carriages from hand-powered railway cars, the men fashioned a cheap and portable unit.

On September 13, 1918, the trials of the real torpedo began. At five o'clock in the evening de Palma whirled the engine into life, and at Kettering's signal, sent the biplane down the test track. Four times the men stopped the carriage just before launch. On the fifth run, the brake failed and the torpedo went into an awkward somersault.[53] That ended the first day of trials, but after a hurried repair during the night, the plane seemed ready for another test.

For this trial, Kettering invited Colonel Bion J. Arnold, the military commander of the project. Instead of stopping the carriage, the men let the torpedo fly. It flew respectably for about a hundred yards at a height of a few feet.

A full-scale flight on October 2 was more erratic. After a perfect launch, the machine reached the preset altitude, stalled, recovered with a loop followed by a half turn (an Immelmann), and dove directly at the observers, scattering them across the field. It recovered again, stalled, and crashed in the middle of another Immelmann.[54] Despite the momentary panic, military observer Colonel F. E. Harris wired a superior, "Maiden flight of ship successfully accomplished at six thirty this afternoon. Congratulations."[55] That sporadic flight and crash earned the aerial torpedo the nickname, "The Bug," and the next full flight confirmed the torpedo's new name. C. H. Wills recounted the event for Elmer Sperry:

You probably heard of the flight that they made at Dayton last Friday. I think it was terribly funny. A great many were skeptical and thought the engine would not fly, but they have given up that thought now . . . the ship went up about 500 feet and she nosed right straight up into the air and then dropped back, and went up again to about 1000 feet and tipped over backwards. The instrument board came loose and broke the hose connecting the controls. When all the controls were disconnected the ship side-slipped and started up in circles about a mile in diameter. The machine had been set to drop at 1000 feet. Mr. Kettering watched it until it was up about 12,000 feet and out of sight and with disgust said, 'Let the thing stay up there' and went home to bed. There were a couple of hundred people there and they got into automobiles and started to chase it and they began to get messages from various towns. One town in the valley telephoned that there was an aeroplane loose there and it was doing all kinds of didos. They finally located it twenty one miles away and there were about a dozen farmers out with lanterns looking for the aviator. There wasn't a thing hurt on the engine, not even a spark plug broken, but the gasoline tank was dry. It would have been going yet probably had it not been for the lack of gasoline. It had traveled approximately 90 miles for it was in flight just one hour. One farmer asked Mr. Kettering who drove it and he told him he did and the farmer wanted to know where he put his legs. I never saw anything that had so many tales and stories about it as that flight. Everybody had a different story about the capers it cut up. Some of the aces in France could have learned a few new tricks.[56]

While everyone was sufficiently impressed with the bug's range and durability, there was some doubt about its accuracy. Colonel Arnold told one of his superiors, it was "at present lacking in sufficient accuracy of control," a vast understatement.[57] Nonetheless, on October 22, another torpedo climbed to the preset altitude, leveled off, and dove on a target 500 yards away, missing by less than fifty feet to the right.

A flight that short hardly proved the torpedo was ready for combat situations, but it was enough to prod the army into purchasing one hundred prototypes from Dayton Wright. In November, Arnold received a telegram from the company, "Thirty carriages complete, thirty five by November twentieth, twenty motors on hand now complete. Kettering anxious for instructions."[58]

Those instructions significantly altered the aerial torpedo's destiny. On November 11, 1918 the Armistice ended the war. Arnold wanted Kettering to meet with the Secretary of War and prepare a brief for President Woodrow Wilson's forthcoming Versailles Peace Conference. On December 3 Kettering met in Washington with Arnold, Squier, Wright, and the Navy's Chief of Ordnance. The outcome of the meeting was the decision to combine the army and navy torpedo programs.[59]

This turn of events did not entirely please Kettering, who feared, with some justification, that the navy personnel would not appreciate the background, and therefore the fairly limited performance, of his aerial torpedo. He did not want the navy observers to forget that his device was much simpler and cheaper than its Sperry counterpart.

"There is one point that I want to raise," he told an associate, "and that is in sending these machines to the Navy, we do not want to be put in the position of having them try them out and condemning them, and then being obliged to prove their practicality."[60] In other words, he feared that the navy would compare absolute and not relative performance, regardless of the implications for combat use.

Kettering was also concerned about patents. He had become involved in a patent dispute with Sperry over certain technical details of their respective designs. Moreover, he found he would soon have to worry about foreign patent rights as well. The army was planning to ship half a dozen Dayton Wright torpedoes to Great Britain, when an alert Dayton Metal Products patent attorney discovered that British law held patents invalid on any invention imported without patent application. Since Kettering had not yet filed on the aerial torpedo, he refused to ship any of the machines until after the final papers could be filed at the end of August 1919.[61] The government suppressed these applications anyway, in the interests of national security. However, a military patent attorney noted at the time, "This will work practically no hardship on the inventor as the invention is of practically no commercial value and the Government would evidently be the only party interested in the purchase of same."[62]

In September 1919, the military began a series of flight tests of the Kettering torpedo at Carlstrom Field, Florida, as part of an evaluation of the two competing designs. Kettering did not attend personally, but instead sent Midgley and one other assistant.[63]

From Dayton Wright's viewpoint the trials were disastrous. Officials from the army, navy, and the British Air Corps watched a humiliating display of technical failures. The initial test on the twenty-sixth ended when the elevator controls lifted the bug off the carriage too quickly, crushing it on the runway. A week later a defective rudder setting caused a similar runway crash. On October 13 and 15, the torpedo did somewhat better. But when the second flight had gone about a mile, "it was observed to go into a steep dive and then suddenly fell to pieces," the flight log reported.[64]

After more than a month of frustration, the embarrassed Dayton Wright representatives dismantled the distance control and sent the torpedo off over the ocean. To everyone's surprise, the bug climbed to the preset height of 700 feet and held course for thirteen minutes and twenty miles. Finally, the engine gave out and the torpedo dove sharply.[65] In a mild understatement, the commanding officer concluded that the device was still "not sufficiently reliable to be trustworthy for carrying high explosives over friendly troops."[66]

On November 25, the commanding officer decided to continue the self-guided Sperry Curtiss J. N. H. and to scrap the Kettering design. Kettering, with pride intact, bowed out just as the decision became obvious. A week after the announcement he notified the army that he was "thru with the Bug job, especially since the General Motors work really required that none of the high engineering talent be spent in anything but work having to do with the allied interests of the G.M.C. [General Motors Corporation]."[67]

Sperry's success and Kettering's failure in developing the torpedo may have been due to the fundamental differences in their backgrounds, inventive styles, and divergent careers. They both began as electrical engineers, but there the similarity ended. Sperry's path had taken him into the specialized fields of gyroscopic stabilization and navigation. Because the navy was the only market for these sophisticated instruments, Sperry had been drawn into the evolving military-industrial complex. From a technical perspective too, Sperry's work had given him an excellent preparation for designing a guided torpedo, for much of it involved automatic feedback and control.

Kettering, on the other hand, came to the aerial torpedo from automotive engineering, a field in which cost efficiency counted far more than technical sophistication. Further, the automobile had been a creation of private enterprise at its freest. The industry had had little government support; only after the war did state authorities initiate a gasoline tax and the federal government begin a national highway program. Consequently, Kettering had not cultivated intimate connections with military engineers. When he did work with the government, he chose to work on a contract basis, rather than as part of a joint military-civilian team.

Sperry's torpedo was much like his other innovations, expensive, complex, and carefully tailored to military requirements. The Kettering bug, though promising and economical, sacrificed too much accuracy and performance for cheapness. It was a good idea, ruined by the home-built technology and the part-time, cost-conscious approach. Sperry's better government contacts simply dealt the final blow to a technically incomplete project.

Kettering, with limited funding from the army, did continue developing his version of the aerial torpedo after the war. Sperry's venture was likewise carried on by his son Lawrence under navy sponsorship. Budget cuts killed both projects in the later 1920s. Ironically, it was Kettering's torpedo that the American government revived in the next war. The German V-1 and V-2 were the true successors of the original Sperry torpedo.

If the bug rarely left the ground, its inventor often did, sometimes in record-breaking cross-country jaunts. Howard Rinehart piloted Kettering on several record flights and taught him to fly the plane.

Before leaving for the Washington meeting on the torpedo on December 2, 1918, Kettering and Rinehart announced that they would seek the nonstop flight record. Donning polar clothes, they left Dayton at eleven o'clock in the morning and arrived, cold but happy, four hours and ten minutes later at New York's Mineola Field. After a brief stopover for dinner and the theater, they continued on to Washington. Kettering greeted a crowd of reporters at the terminal. "The trip from Dayton was perfect," he said. "The big engine ran true throughout. At no time did Mr. Reinhart, who was driving, experience any difficulty in keeping the plane at an even pace. At no time did he race and at no time did he poke along. The plane responded beautifully to every demand."[68]

Six months later the two aviators set another cross-country record with a nonstop flight from a tractor convention in Wichita, Kansas to Dayton. Only foul weather prevented them from extending the trip to Long Island.[69]

Kettering became an enthusiastic pilot until Olive's protests finally grounded him. He also became a vocal supporter of the aircraft industry. Publicly he predicted a bright future for American aviation. Privately he told John J. Raskob, then treasurer of Du Pont and General Motors, that "the airplane has not been developed far enough to be any good from the standpoint of commercial work."[70] He was optimistic that the situation would soon change, and he knew just the group to do it. Kettering also told Raskob:

There has been a tendency on the part of a great many aeronautical engineers to make the public believe that the airplane is a highly technical, difficult-to-understand-piece of apparatus, and that the rules and regulations of ordinary engineering do not apply here. I believe that we have here in America, engineers who are far more capable of handling the situation in this country than any foreign people could do. I think we have an organization here in Dayton which, if properly coupled up, is capable of doing the best work possible along this line. I have always felt that the General Motors Corporation should take an active part in Aviation, and I hope that I shall have an opportunity of discussing this matter with you when the proper time comes.[71]

Throughout the 1920s, Kettering supported aviation in every way he could. He urged his alma mater to offer engineering courses in the field, saying the university "would be making a great mistake if they did not do something at this time along the line of aeronautics."[72] Not heeding his own warnings about commercial prospects, he also invested heavily in several aviation enterprises. One firm concentrated on metal-clad dirigibles and tried to interest the United States Postal Service in them. Kettering later wrote off the entire project as a loss.[73]

More successful financially were his interests in National Air Transport and United Aircraft and Transportation (later merged to form United Air Lines). Deeds and other insiders from the Dayton Wright days put together these companies in the mid-1920s to tap the new market in federal airmail. Deeds tipped off his friend Kettering, who subsequently shared in some spectacular paper profits and became a director of both firms.[74] In the 1930s he also shared the embarrassment of a Senate investigation into collusion and price-fixing in airmail rates. Still, whatever the side effects, such contacts kept Kettering in touch with aviation, knowledge that led to such profitable General Motors aviation investments as Allison Engineering.

Kettering's wartime experiences illustrated both the strengths and shortcomings of his automotive background. The least successful venture, the Dayton Wright De Haviland, was a failure Kettering could share with the entire automobile industry. Aircraft frames, especially those for combat airplanes, could not be built with mass-production technology borrowed from the automotive assembly line. In the industry's defense, bureaucratic mismanagement and unrealistic public expectations also contributed to the failure. Since the automobile makers actually produced most of the American aircraft built during the war, "failure" is probably too harsh a judgment anyway.

If the De Haviland project exposed a weakness of the assembly line, the Liberty engine showed its advantages. Kettering's personal contribution, the battery ignition, while hardly a radically innovative piece of technology, was much like the rest of the engine, solid, reliable, and thoroughly conventional.

The aerial torpedo was in some ways a remarkable bit of engineering that anticipated technical developments decades in the future. But its disappointing performance revealed a characteristic pitfall of Kettering's inventive style. Because he could not break away from cost-conscious automotive engineering, Kettering made the wrong choice between technical and cost efficiency.

In the fuel investigation, Kettering was at his best. His insight that engine performance was closely related to the chemical nature of fuel foreshadowed later triumphs with leaded gasoline and high-compression engines. The work on synthetic fuels marked a milestone in the evolution of the gasoline engine.

The war also set an important precedent for Kettering's relationship with the military. Like many engineers in the automotive industry, he did not become part of government-sponsored military technology. Although he would contribute technological innovations to the military throughout his long career, the successful ones grew out of his civilian work.

Kettering's many engineering successes, before the war in automobile electrical systems and during the war in fuels and engines, earned him a respected place in his profession. In January 1918, his peers elected him president of the Society of Automotive Engineers.[75] At the age of forty-one he, perhaps better than anyone else, personified the youth, boldness, and potential of the automobile industry.

5 / JOINING GENERAL MOTORS

By the end of the war Kettering was a partner in some half-dozen business enterprises. Playing even a limited role in their administration, management, and external coordination would have been work enough for several full-time executives. Consequently, while many of his technical ideas showed promise, he lacked sufficient time to work them through. He would have preferred a different arrangement, allowing him the freedom to work as long and as hard as he liked on each problem that interested him. When Kettering set up the fuel laboratory at Dayton Metal Products, he suggested to the administrative director "that what we should do was to set up an organization as a means of studying from various angles and without any immediate industrial implications, the application of fuel to an engine. 'Let's treat it,' I said, 'as our intellectual golf game, because I am sure that we will have to do a great deal of work before this will crystallize into useable form.' "[1]

Eventually, the sheer size and diversity of the Kettering companies easily defeated his half-hearted attempts at unified management and coordinated research. While Delco was relatively small, and Kettering's engineering investigations were limited to automotive electrical systems, informal management sufficed. The market was personal and familiar. As the enterprise grew and Kettering branched out into new technical areas, the weaknesses of loose administration started to show. Even if Kettering had been able to keep on top of the technical side of things, it would have been impossible for him to know the potential market for each invention, or assemble the right amount of capital to enter it at the most opportune moment. Before Kettering's inventions could become commercially valuable innovations, they needed financial resources and skilled management that were beyond his grasp.

A corporate merger of the Dayton companies and General Motors in 1918–19 brought Kettering together with a team of executives that could solve these organizational dilemmas. Pierre S. du Pont and Alfred Sloan, respectively president and executive vice-president of the revamped General Motors, came from technical backgrounds and recognized the importance of industrial research. They gave Kettering his first chance to pursue research free of business distractions. More important, they took the first steps to integrate his work with the overall operation of the corporation. The arrangement suited them both, held Kettering until retirement, and made automotive history.

Since May 1916, Delco (but not the other Dayton companies) had been part of United Motors, a loosely connected group of automobile accessories firms. Its president and principal architect was Alfred Sloan, one of the best organizational minds in the history of American business. Its founder and promoter, with equal influence over its destiny, was William Durant, among the worst organizational minds in American business. Durant's control over Sloan delayed Kettering's progress, at least in an institutional sense, for several years. And yet it was the organizational plan developed at United Motors that anticipated the institutional structure at General Motors, a structure that would, in turn, play an important role in Kettering's later work.

Almost from the beginning, Sloan perceived the weaknesses inherent in United Motors' sprawling structure and sought to correct them. Durant's lack of interest and the distractions of the war thwarted him. Sloan also wanted to take advantage of the technical ingenuity scattered throughout the corporation. What he had in mind was a central engineering laboratory which could solve production problems and serve as a source of innovation for the member companies. It was no secret that he thought Kettering should lead it. Again, Sloan's suggestions were ignored. Durant had little time for technical matters. As one close observer said of him, "His greatest weakness in the technological area was his disregard of it—his assurance that he could always play his hunches and his unawareness of the desirability of a systematic program for technological experimentation and development."[2]

Sloan did not let Durant's disinterest deter him completely. In July 1917, he wrote Kettering a detailed outline of his scheme for institutionalized research. "You will sooner or later be arriving at the time when you will want to organize the Engineering Division," he said. "We might as well consider the organization of it now and have it on record, and then when you get around to it we will know exactly how to proceed."[3] However, war work soon caught up with both executives and the plans were never formalized.

The war did not prevent Sloan from implementing other essential reforms. He introduced new accounting procedures and rationalized United Motors' organizational structure to eliminate needless competition among the members.

An important corporate realignment in 1918 made United Motors part of General Motors and smoothed the way for Sloan's reforms, including the engineering laboratory. Durant was the founder of General Motors, as well as United Motors, but his career with the former had been much less successful. Once he had even been voted out of office, only to fight his way back in. His main problem was that he was more interested in acquiring companies than in managing them, and consequently overextended himself financially. The war, with its rumors of civilian production being curtailed, sent the stock prices of automotive companies plummeting. Durant, who was using his General Motors stock as collateral for speculative investments, found himself in serious trouble.[4]

Pierre du Pont, chairman of the board of the Du Pont Company and, at least in name, the chairman of General Motors as well, came to Durant's rescue. General Motors offered an ideal investment opportunity for the Du Pont Company wartime profits, and a potentially vast market for Du Pont chemical products. So chairman du Pont agreed to invest $25 million in the automotive company, purchasing stock on the open market to drive up the price of Durant's shares.[5]

Du Pont tied this offer to two specific conditions. First, he insisted that Durant implement the Du Pont Company's cautious financial and accounting controls to provide sounder management. Second, he demanded that Durant bring together his scattered investments (General Motors, United Motors, and others) under a single corporate entity.[6] Durant accepted the terms. On December 31, 1918, General Motors officially acquired United Motors for $45 million in stock, making Kettering a formal, if peripheral, member of the General Motors family.

The corporate reorganization left Durant as president, and despite his promises to Pierre du Pont, it did little to change his casual way of doing business. As before, Durant spent most of his time speculating in the stock market, and almost no time on institutional reform. Sloan recalled, with some bitterness, how he spent hours waiting outside the president's office until Durant had finished talking with his brokers or old friends:

We scarcely felt like doing anything else until he rang the bell, so tempers soured. I was constantly amazed by his daring way of making decisions. My business experience had convinced me facts are precious things, to be eagerly sought and treated with respect. But Mr. Durant would proceed on a course of action guided solely, as far as I could tell, by some intuitive flash of brilliance. He never felt obliged to make an engineering hunt for facts.[7]

Even though Kettering was less involved with administrative affairs than Sloan, he too suffered from Durant's capricious management. For instance, because Durant did not clearly define spheres of marketing influence among the many General Motors divisions, Delco found itself competing in the electric starting, lighting, and ignition field against Remy. Remy's general manager, O. F. Conklin, complained to Kettering:

We have gone along for a couple of years with a sort of general understanding that we would not interfere with each others customers . . . [but] I think we should and must arrive at a more definite policy than we now have. It would be small satisfaction for me, as Manager of this Division, to take a piece of business and return to the Corporation a $5.00 profit which I know Delco might have had and returned a $6.00 profit. On the other hand, of course, we must do everything possible to keep our factory full and to encourage our Sales force. WHAT'S THE ANSWER???[8]

The ill effects of Durant's mismanagement extended to other areas of Kettering's business too. The United Motors Service Company, a feeble attempt by Durant to achieve corporate coordination by combining separate service units into one company, illustrated the basic trouble. Like so many of Durant's schemes, the idea was good, but the execution was faulty. Because the company was so poorly managed, service was much worse than before. Kettering complained to Sloan, "I have gone through this thing pretty thoroughly and you are going to run absolutely amuck with this organization unless you get a different type of management. There is no use to muff words about this situation but it is the rottenest organization we have ever tried to do business with. If this is the modern way of doing business I am ready to drop out and quit."[9]

If Durant was not much good at management himself, he did have a knack for spotting men with this talent. His best choice was Alfred Sloan, who rose rapidly from the head of the Hyatt division, to the president of United Motors, to a vice-president and a member of the board of directors of General Motors. From his new post, Sloan could clearly see the debilitating effects of mismanagement. In June 1919 he came up with an organizational plan to bring some order to the corporation. He circulated a sketch of his idea to key General Motors executives, including Kettering, for comment. In part he pointed out what most of the men already knew. General Motors had been run to that time as a series of independent companies, not as an integrated enterprise. In his words, "there has been no co-operation between the different units in any way, shape, or manner."[10] Sloan went beyond that diagnosis to a remarkable recommendation. He proposed a series of centralized staff departments, not to take over the functions of the operating divisions but to coordinate their work and eliminate some of the awkwardness of their relationships to each other. Without such a reform, Sloan said, General Motors could never be more than a collection of competing enterprises.[11]

Sloan's proposal set out, in somewhat abbreviated fashion, a managerial philosophy that would shape the institutional future of General Motors. Sloan believed that in a corporation the size of General Motors, the operating divisions must not be too strictly supervised in their day-to-day operations, and yet their work had to be kept in the best interests of the corporation as a whole. To achieve these sometimes contradictory goals, Sloan wanted to implement an organizational structure of semiautonomous line units held together at the top by a series of central staffs.

From Kettering's point of view, the most important result of Sloan's organizational adjustments was the creation of a central research staff. Before 1920 General Motors, along with most of its competitors, had done little in the way of research except for modest efforts at quality control, including a staff of about twenty chemists and metallurgists which ran a testing laboratory in Detroit. Sloan had recognized the disadvantages of such a situation as early as the United Motors days, when he had written to Kettering with his suggestions for organized research. Finally, in the fall of 1919, he began drawing together the plans for a research laboratory headed by Kettering.

Sloan envisioned a technical staff in Detroit with a broad range of engineering responsibilities. Specifically, Sloan had in mind: "intensive study of the problems ahead of the Automotive industry . . . examination and report upon engineering and research problems of a broad character, which are beyond the limitations of the equipment and personnel of the individual operations. Examination and reports upon inventions and ideas submitted to the Corporation for consideration. Development of new devices that may be required by an operating unit. Consultation on, or complete development of, any engineering or research problem." [12]

Because Kettering was still connected with several Dayton firms, Sloan divided his scheme into two parts. In Dayton, he wanted Kettering "to continue to direct the engineering, research and other experimental developments in connection with the Dayton Metal Products and Dayton Wright." And in Detroit, Sloan urged him to "at once assume entire control of the Central Laboratory and Technical School, creating the necessary departments, appointing your staff, and selecting such equipment and apparatus as in your discretion seems desirable and necessary, devoting as much of your time to the Detroit projects as may be required."[13]

Kettering, Sloan, and several other corporate executives met to discuss the proposal a couple of times in the summer of 1919. Kettering liked what he heard. "I could see his eyes glitter with desire," Walter Chrysler, then in charge of the Buick division and later head of Chrysler Corporation, said of Kettering at the meetings.[14] But he tied his acceptance to several special provisions. "I told Mr. Sloan that I would take it on three conditions," Kettering recalled, "that I would have no responsibility and no authority, and that I would never be held accountable for the money I spent."[15] He believed the laboratory would need that freedom to thrive. Further, Kettering insisted that the laboratory be set up in Dayton.

While the negotiations dragged on, General Motors embarked upon an expansion program that helped tie Kettering more closely to the corporation. On September 25, 1919, General Motors acquired the Dayton Metal Products Company for 25,338 shares of GM debenture stock ($2,107,000 par) and 21,457 shares of GM common stock ($2,145,700). At the same time, the corporation purchased the Dayton Wright Airplane Company, with assets of $1,200,000, for 10,960 shares of GM debenture stock. Four months later, on January 20, 1920, General Motors reincorporated the company as the Dayton Airplane Company. In December 1919, the Domestic Engineering Company was acquired for 35,451 shares of GM common stock in exchange for 33,070 shares of its stock, valued at $9 million.[16]

Meanwhile Kettering took on another assignment for General Motors, a tour of the European automobile industry. As part of a postwar expansion move, General Motors was interested in acquiring Citroen as a toehold in the continental market. Kettering joined Sloan, Walter Chrysler, and other GM executives on a trip to France for a close look at the French company's facilities. Kettering and Chrysler, as the mission's technical consultants, thought that the plant might be too old for American production standards. The legal experts ran into governmental opposition to selling a potential military resource, and the administrative specialists worried that General Motors could not spare qualified managers to run the plant. The delegation dropped the negotiations and sailed home.[17] For Kettering, the trip was the beginning of important technical contacts with European automotive engineers, and a first look at Paris, a city to which he and Olive would return many times.

By the time Kettering returned to Dayton, General Motors was ready to grant his request. He told a friend, "Since I last saw you the whole plan on the Detroit Laboratory has been dropped. We have come to the conclusion that we will simply enlarge the Laboratory here in Dayton."[18]

On January 13, 1920, General Motors named Kettering a vice-president. Six months later, on June 12, he officially became general manager of a new division, the General Motors Research Corporation. And on December 30, 1920, he was appointed to the board of directors.[19]

The Research Corporation's first home was the old Dayton Wright factory south of Dayton, and its staff the chemists and engineers from the Dayton Metal Products Research Laboratory. While the laboratory had the look of the airplane factory the building had recently been, Kettering gave the cavernous interior the feel of a more traditional lab by dividing the space (1,000 feet by 270 feet) into forty-four individual labs 20 feet by 30 feet, each complete with compressed air, vacuum, and a variety of electrical outlets. Except for the pattern shop, foundry, and heat-treating plant, which required special heavy equipment, the lab spaces were designed to be flexible so that when one project was finished, the space could be rearranged to accommodate another.[20] No expense was spared in furnishing the laboratories, or in supplying backup technicians. Some labs were so well equipped, in fact, that they impressed academic scientists on summer stints with the Research Corporation. One Antioch College physicist, who worked as a consultant on several projects in those early years, remarked to a fellow academic, "The slip-shod methods used by physicists in Universities to secure high vacuum seem absurd to me now after I've seen how easily it can be done in a factory where you have a few skilled mechanics."[21] For the time and industry, the staff had a high proportion of college graduates. Thomas Midgley, Carroll Hochwalt, and Thomas Boyd had earned bachelor's degrees;

J. H. Hunt and F. O. Clements had taught college before joining the laboratory. Kettering himself, of course, had an outstanding academic background. Compared to competitors like Ford, whose engineering departments were dominated by self-taught mechanics, the Research Corporation was quite progressive. Moreover, thanks to Kettering's academic contacts (such as Baekeland and various professors at Ohio State), the Research Corporation had ready access to the best professional expertise of the day.

University training and contacts did not mean narrowly focused investigations. Kettering watched closely for overspecialization and sometimes assigned men to projects remote from their field of expertise. He looked for a grasp of fundamentals and a freedom from orthodoxy. Nor was he reluctant, when the occasion demanded, to put a mechanical engineer on a chemical problem or ask a physicist to do a bit of chemistry. However, when he did put someone on an unfamiliar project, for instance when he placed Midgley, a mechanical engineer by training, in charge of fuel studies, he backed him with more specialized talent, in this case Boyd and Hochwalt, who had degrees in chemical engineering.

To give some order to the engineering studies under him, Kettering divided the work into five sections, each with a head, an assistant, and a staff of about a dozen men. At first, these categories were largely arbitrary, reflecting Kettering's outlook in 1920 more than any natural subdivisions of automotive engineering. Combustion Fundamentals covered studies of fuel chemistry, antiknock additives, and work on compression. Engine Fundamentals had charge of piston design and cooling, vibration studies, and lubricants. Engine Materials worked on finishes, metallurgy, and bearings. Carburetion and Distribution covered studies of fuel mixture ratios, filtration, and fuel pumps. And the Car and Dynamometer Test section had responsibility for road tests, brakes, transmissions, and tires.[22]

As the investigations progressed, Kettering focused his sections into eleven narrower divisions. Most of these fell into traditional groupings like mechanical and electrical engineering, or chemistry. However, Kettering also introduced some organizational innovations. He set up a division for chemical and metallurgical control, which investigated current manufacturing problems in these fields, and another division for chemical and metallurgical research, to look into the future of manufacturing processes. Moreover, he established divisions of experimental production and semiworks engineering to explore the challenges of converting research designs into commercial processes. All these organizational schemes revealed Kettering's near obsession with commercial orientation, a focus that would remain a distinguishing feature of his lab. A reporter from an automotive trade journal who visited the laboratory during that first year noted: "A strict point of practicality is made in all of the laboratory work that is undertaken. All of the development and research points to some commercial end, which, although it may be in the remote future, is, nevertheless, some day going to find its way onto the market as a practical product."[23]

Kettering had little patience for day-to-day administration. For this work he hired F. O. Clements, who had held a similar post at the Dayton Metal Products Research Laboratory. Clements, a studious, meticulous man with thick white hair and round glasses, would hold this kind of post under Kettering for the next two decades, handling correspondence, interviewing and hiring, conducting literature searches, and generally relieving his boss of administrative details. This taking care of details earned Clements an undeserved reputation as a nagger. "I guess he watched whether people got there on time," grumbled one of the chemists.[24] In spite of the insults and gossip, Clements was invaluable.

Kettering also hired a business director to handle accounting, budgeting, and other administrative matters not part of Clements' job. Department heads, after consulting with Kettering and Clements, submitted a special form to the business director explaining the nature of the project they had in mind, how long they thought it would take, how much it would cost, and how it would fit in with related laboratory interests. However, to prevent excessive red tape from stifling initiative, Kettering made sure that each section head had a small discretionary fund for exploring new ideas outside the formal budget.[25]

Kettering's idea of management was the exact opposite of Clements' careful attention to procedure and details. For the Boss, management was an informal, personal affair. He arrived at the Moraine City laboratory, just a short drive from Ridgeleigh Terrace, about nine o'clock in the morning. For the first hour or so he read the mail, dictating replies to the most urgent and interesting letters, and turned the rest over to Clements and his secretary. If he had a meeting with someone, he took care of it then. If he did not want to see someone, he told his secretary to tell them he was dead. Then he went off to the laboratories for his favorite part of the day.[26]

Unlike many research directors, Kettering was not an armchair engineer. He did read technical literature, though he preferred condensed reports prepared by his assistants, but he liked to pick up most of his information firsthand, either through chats with the researchers or from the instruments themselves. Startled section heads and young assistants often looked up to see Kettering unexpectedly blocking the doorway. The Boss usually asked a few pointed questions about the research and sat down at the bench to look at the data, tinker with an engine, or record an observation or two. Many of his questions seemed superficially easy, sometimes outrageously so. For instance, he sometimes asked the chemists what a catalyst was, and queried mechanical engineers about what kind of piston an internal combustion engine would like.[27] Yet in reexamining the apparently obvious, the researchers often stumbled on new insights and ideas.

Kettering's unusual questions sometimes frustrated the younger men, especially those just out of college. He liked to tell a story about two university-trained engineers he asked to study the fundamentals of friction. "We put them to work on a little machine that rubbed two pieces of metal together. That's all they were doing, rubbing one piece of metal against the other and they thought we were crazy," he recalled. The engineers complained to their section head, saying their talents were being wasted. When word got back to Kettering, as it almost always did, he told the young men, "Look here, you think the old man is crazy, but he's been wrong 99.9 percent of the time and doesn't mind being proved wrong again. You go ahead and prove it and quit talking to the other engineers or the boss will fire you one of these days." [28] Indeed, the Boss had a reputation for firing uncooperative assistants, but in this case the engineers stuck with the study, and the final outcome was a lubricant able to withstand 6,000 pounds of pressure.

One of Kettering's favorite maxims was, "Anything more than two feet away from the job you are working on is too far." [29] What he meant was that a good research administrator should be intimately acquainted with the work going on under him. Kettering did this, but at a price. At any one time he had one or two pet projects to which he devoted himself; the rest he virtually ignored until another idea caught his fancy. Consequently, his whims played a major role in determining which research at the Research Corporation would have priority.

The section heads could do little to change this fact. Formally, they had an opportunity to express their opinions every Saturday afternoon at a section heads meeting in Kettering's office. But as J. H. Hunt recalled, they had little input. "Well, he was the meeting! Because he did most of the talking and partly because we didn't find out exactly what was on his mind until the meeting had lasted as long as most of us wanted to stay there." [30]

If the internal organization of the Research Corporation was a bit haphazard, integration with the other General Motors divisions did not exist at all. Kettering dealt with the general managers of the other divisions as casually as he did with his section heads, but with more serious consequences.

Kettering met Albert Champion on the European tour of 1919. At that time, Champion was the head of a division that manufactured spark plugs, but he was eager to expand into other fields. During 1920, he heard that Kettering had invented a new speedometer at the Research Corporation and asked his permission to develop it in the Champion division. Kettering gladly consented, and never bothered to say anything about the arrangement to the top management of General Motors.

What Kettering, with his rather narrow view of corporate affairs, did not realize was that this seemingly simple arrangement with

Champion disrupted corporate operations in ways he did not understand. "The facts in the case are that Champion went into the development [of the speedometer] not after making a study of the situation but simply because the Stewart Company [a major instrument maker] started to make spark plugs," Sloan explained to the politically naive engineer when he discovered the agreement.[31] "Now, of course, we are not going to get anywhere by investing our capital on the basis of prejudice or to get square with somebody else, but only on the basis of a logical profit." To avoid similar misunderstandings in the future, Sloan strongly suggested that "it might be well in talking with the different Divisions, to impress upon them the fact that it is not within the province of the Research Corporation to determine who will make the devices when they are actually developed."[32]

Another problem with the poorly coordinated management under the Durant regime was that it wasted Kettering's talents on innovations for faltering divisions with no future. A classic case was his involvement with tractors and agricultural machinery.

The tractor market seemed like a natural outlet for automobile investments in the early 1900s. With steam models gradually giving way to gasoline tractors by the First World War, it seemed only a matter of time before the assembly-line techniques and gasoline engine experience of the automobile makers took over the industry.[33] Indeed, in 1916, Ford brought out the Fordson light-weight tractor, and Durant bought up the Samson Tractor Company.

Kettering knew of both developments almost from the beginning, through his membership in United Motors. He saw the tractor as a potential market for electrical accessories, and believed "that it was only a matter of time, and perhaps a very limited time, when tractors would be equipped with starting and lighting apparatus."[34] On the advice of his business associates, he visited several tractor fairs, a kind of rural carnival where tractors were sold in those pre-dealer days. One of these was the famous Freemont, Nebraska show of August 1916, which Sloan told him "will give you an opportunity to see under practical demonstration, every American tractor that is worthwhile and incidentally, a whole lot that are not worth-while."[35]

As a twenty-one-year-old schoolteacher in Mifflin, Ohio, 1897.

Supervising Inventions Department No. 3 at the National Cash Register Co. in 1905.

At the wheel of a 1913 Buick test car with Bill Chryst.

The first batch of Delco electric self-starting units ready for shipment to Cadillac in August 1911.

First lot of Delco Generators built.

An early promotional stunt for the Delco self-starting systems.

Cleaning up the Delco factory after the 1913 Dayton flood.

Ridgeleigh Terrace, Kettering's Dayton home.

Top secret "bugs" (self-propelled torpedoes) on the test track during the First World War.

The architects of General Motors. From left to right: E. A. Deeds; J. L. Pratt; G. Rentschler; E. G. Biechler; C. S. Mott; A. Sloan; and C. F. Kettering.

Kettering's air-cooled tractor with rein control.

"Road testing" the copper-cooled car on the back roads of Ohio in 1921.

THE FOUR
COMING THROUGH ON THE ROAD TO
IRONTON O
SUNDAY AUG 21, 1921

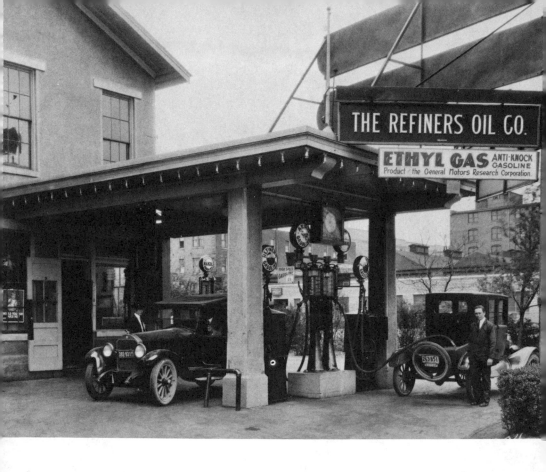

The debut of Ethyl gasoline at a Dayton filling station in 1923.

Kettering learned a lot about tractor technology from these meetings, and came up with a few ideas which he shared with the Samson engineers in early 1917. He had in mind a light-weight tractor with tracks instead of wheels. But the war kept him busy with other projects, and Samson spent only $6,500 working on Kettering's ideas in 1917.[36]

The war completely changed the character of the tractor market. A shortage of labor on the farm made it difficult to meet the wartime demand for foodstuffs. With a machine that offered some assistance, Fordson made significant gains in the rural market and emerged from the war as the dominant force in the industry.

Meanwhile, Samson lagged far behind. Durant and Sloan urged Kettering to focus on the technical aspects of the tractor in hopes of catching up with Ford. Sloan pointed out, "The tractor business is big business now and is going to be a tremendous business in the future. We have hopes that we will be able to work out something in our regular line that will meet this situation."[37]

As a result of Durant's special interest in the tractor market, Kettering devoted much of his first year as the head of research for General Motors to tractor innovations. He did rather well at it too. His experiments with air-cooled engines and kerosene fuel produced an intriguing prototype with a four-cylinder air-cooled engine, rear wheel drive, a clearance of 27", a weight of under 1,600 pounds, and rein control. The last was a nostalgic concession to traditional plowing, for a pull on the reins changed direction, worked the clutch, and shifted gears, so that the machine was controlled just like a horse. However, it was really too small for more than gardening, and the air-cooled engine tended to collect dust and overheat.[38]

While Kettering was busy reinventing the horsedrawn plow, the Samson division was headed for bankruptcy. Its production and marketing methods were obsolete, and it was pitted against the financial resources, experience, and name of Henry Ford. Even with General Motors money, it was an uneven contest. J. A. Craig, Samson's general manager, told Kettering, "I think the only way we are going to beat Ford's terrific competition is to step the Model M up in size about three more horsepower on the draw bar, which will put us entirely out of his class or any possibility of rating near him; then develop a tractor of the cultivation type and sell it stripped as a tractor at Ford's price or less and then charge a good, round sum for the cultivator attachment, on which we would expect to make our profit." [39]

For the long run, Samson's management expected Kettering to come up with some innovation that would save the division. Craig even told him at one point, "It looks as though we have made a turn in the road for our business, we feel the Samson Division will be on the way to redeem its reputation. We know you never lost faith in us and I want you to know how much I appreciate personally the support you have given me all along. . . . You surely have been a friend in need and we hope some day to be able to repay you." [40]

Perhaps, in time, Kettering could have introduced important tractor innovations and made Samson profitable. But in 1920, General Motors had already poured $30 million into the venture and, beset by other financial problems, could not afford to wait. Three months after the encouraging note from Craig, Kettering received more realistic news from Sloan:

Both the Executive Committee and Finance Committee have viewed the loss at Samson up to now, as necessary liquidating losses of a past situation, but this picture can not continue indefinitely. I think that the real constructive thing to do is to close the whole outfit down, disband the organization, continue with the Engineering Department either in Janesville or move such parts of it as are worth anything to Dayton. [41]

From Sloan's point of view, the Samson affair had been a disaster. It had drained precious corporate investment funds at an alarming rate, and clearly illustrated the dangers of Durant's uncontrolled acquisitive tendencies.

Kettering saw the affair through very different eyes. He told Sloan, "If we never got anything out of the tractor development but our reaction on the carbureting problem, it would be worth all that it has cost." [42] Perhaps that was an exaggeration, but the data on ignition, air cleaning, carburetion, and cooling would find later automotive applications.

More important, Kettering recognized that poor coordination of corporate activities could have serious implications for research. "The general tendency, looking at any research problem, is to make it too ingrown," he told Sloan. "By that I mean referring to research as the solving of manufacturing difficulties only and not to the bigger problems of the future. That is why it is so difficult for a Laboratory to work in conjunction with a manufacturing organization as its entire time is taken up in shooting troubles."[43] That observation was worth more than any amount of technical data.

If Durant's lack of management occasionally sidetracked the Research Corporation, its effects on the rest of General Motors were just short of catastrophic. Durant had not put proper financial controls into place, and consequently the corporation did not really command the actions of the individual divisions. Throughout the boom period of early 1920, when most everyone expected the postwar demand for automobiles to continue uninterrupted, the divisions expanded output. As the market began to soften in the summer and prices started to slide, the divisions piled up larger and larger inventories at "bargain" prices, despite repeated warnings from some corporate officers. In the fall, they found themselves dangerously overextended as the bottom fell out of the automobile market. By December, General Motors would have to write off $90 million in losses.[44]

Durant found himself in even more trouble than the corporation. He had again been using his General Motors stock as collateral for speculative loans and investments. As the price of the stock fell, he faced personal bankruptcy.

Durant's predicament sent reverberations through the financial community, for it was generally feared that if Durant went bankrupt, the blow to public confidence would be so critical that General Motors would follow him to the receivers. That possibility particularly disturbed Pierre du Pont, the man responsible for the huge Du Pont Company investment in the automobile company. At the end of November 1920, du Pont arranged a financial bailout of Durant in return for his General Motors stock and his resignation as president. On December 1, du Pont became the corporation's new president, and appointed Alfred Sloan as his executive vice-president.[45]

With du Pont's election, General Motors was on its way to becoming a modern corporation in such traditional areas as finance and administration. The change in leadership also signaled a new attitude toward research. No longer would the Research Corporation be the stepchild of General Motors.

On December 7, 1920, just a week after taking office, du Pont, Sloan, and a select group of corporate executives visited Dayton for a firsthand look at Kettering's work.[46] Kettering took his distinguished guests through the laboratories and pointed out some of the research highlights, including the fuel studies, the light-weight tractor project, and an air-cooled automobile engine he said was the "most important thing, not only in General Motors' work but in the whole automotive industry."[47]

After du Pont and the others left, Kettering sent the new president a long letter thanking him for the visit and answering in detail some of his questions about the Research Corporation and its work. He also included a few comments on the lack of attention to research in the past. "We have just received some money, with which we will be enabled to pay our August bills, but we are still in very bad shape so far as our 'bills payable' are concerned."[48]

Following du Pont's lead, other executives showed new interest in the Research Corporation. Harry Bassett, general manager of the Buick division, spent a day with Kettering touring the laboratories in February 1921. Like most of Kettering's visitors, Bassett left an enthusiastic supporter of industrial research. Bassett wrote to his host, "I cannot tell you how much impressed I was by the wondrous things I saw you doing at the research laboratories and I want you to know that I feel that the work of your organization is absolutely the only real foundation that the General Motors Company should have in future designs or models."[49]

The main institutional challenge facing Sloan and du Pont was to get the research division into the corporation as a whole. Durant had failed in this because he had not been able to coordinate the Research Corporation to meet the practical needs of the operating divisions. Sloan shrewdly recognized that to be most effective the Research Corporation should look toward the future, but at the same time it could not forget about practical results. That would satisfy the corporation's need for innovation and at the same time defuse arguments about wasting money on impractical research, which he knew would arise in some quarters. He offered Kettering a bit of corporate political wisdom:

Although [the Research Corporation] is not a productive unit and a unit that is supposed to make a profit, nevertheless the more tangible result we get from it the stronger its position will be. . . . It may be inferred at some future time . . . that we are spending too much money down there and being in a position to show what benefits had accrued to the Corporation, would strengthen our position materially.[50]

In May 1921, Kettering called a special meeting of the top divisional engineers as a first step in bringing together the Research Corporation and the operating units. Everyone seemed to have a different idea about what should be done, and after the meeting Kettering had to report that "on account of the wide variation of General Motors products it is very difficult to write out any formal method of doing this work."[51] Nevertheless, he thought the conferences had been useful. "We are going ahead in a very practical way and I feel that the engineers of the different divisions will present to the research laboratories for some discussion and approval such new devices as they contemplate," he told GM vice-president Charles Mott.[52]

Security was another immediate concern of the Research Corporation. Kettering's laboratory was unique in the industry. It attracted considerable attention from the competition, and Kettering's off-the-cuff remarks about automobiles capable of sixty miles a gallon and revolutionary air-cooled engines were obviously intriguing to the rest of the industry. Closer contact with the divisions brought a host of new visitors to the Research Corporation, a few of them industrial spies. More than one divisional engineer showed up at the laboratories, looked at confidential research, and disappeared from divisional payrolls. "I'll bet that there are more men on the outside who know how to build an air cooled motor than there are on the inside who know how to do it," Kettering once said to Mott.[53]

While Kettering's openness occasionally posed a security risk, it also kept General Motors' reputation for technological leadership before the public. Kettering was becoming a popular speaker for professional and business groups, and his usual topic was the importance of industrial research. When the meetings were held in Dayton, he often followed the formal talk with an informal tour of the Research Corporation.

General Motors' executives were divided on the question of the tours. Oldsmobile's general manager, A.B.C. Hardy, applauded. He thought that the only real benefit of the Research Corporation was public relations, and like so many up-through-the-ranks, practical engineers, he doubted that the research would have much of an impact on the automobile. He did not underestimate the public relations value of the venture, however. Said Hardy, "There certainly is an enormous quality, trade and sales value in the General Motors Research Corporation to be capitalized and that is the only way we can get real money out of it as it certainly has nothing for direct sale or profit." [54]

Sloan, on the other hand, took a dim view of showing off the research facility. When told that Kettering had taken a local Chamber of Commerce tour through the fuel section and had given them a demonstration of an antiknock additive, Sloan issued an uncharacteristically harsh reprimand:

Now, frankly, I question the propriety of this, and while I know that it could probably be staged so that no damage might be done, at the same time I see no reason why we should take any risk whatsoever and in dealing with a large organization as you have there it is almost impossible to prevent things being exposed, whether you like it or not. I am absolutely against taking Tom, Dick, and Harry through our research laboratories and I do not think it is fair to our stockholders to take any chances in that direction. [55]

Kettering defended the practice. "I find that if you allow nobody in your Laboratory, or have the thing bone-tight, then you are always going to have people on the outside hiring employees into your place." [56] And, at the same time, the value of public relations would be lost.

Ultimately, Kettering resorted to a bit of deception, a laboratory just for "tourists." He took his visitors past an impressive array of white-coated technicians and complex instruments, all engaged in trivial research. They gave a suitable backdrop for his lectures on industrial research without the usual risks. Hardly anyone knew the difference, and the few who did—such as Henry Ford, who was interested in learning more about the air-cooled engine—got no closer to the real laboratories. Kettering slyly observed once to Sloan that if you refused all visitors, "they will go to all sorts of extremes to get in, but if you have some well defined way by which people can walk through a place which they are told is your Research Laboratory, the difficulty is avoided."[57]

At a time in the automobile's history when "development consisted of working on next year's model and research was thinking of what to do for the year after that,"[58] the Research Corporation marked a clear departure from traditional practice. If the proposed coordination with the divisions was still imperfect, it was a precedent with tremendous implications for the future.

Kettering thought the Research Corporation was so unique he even took out an unusual insurance policy, naming "automotive research" as the beneficiary. On his death, $1.6 million would go to a trust fund exclusively targeted for automotive research. The policy was among the largest ever issued in Dayton and required the underwriting of six companies.[59] Years later, when General Motors was still the only automotive company seriously interested in research, Kettering teased Sloan, "It is quite interesting to see somebody is paying attention to our General Motors Research Plant, as Ford has almost copied our dimensions."[60]

Joining General Motors signified the end of Kettering's career as an independent inventor and entrepreneur. Henceforth the business side of his engineering work would be handled by experts in that field. His managerial activities would be restricted to the administration of research.

The new financial and technical resources at Kettering's disposal were ample compensation for the autonomy he surrendered. Practically overnight, he was able to expand his research to encompass the entire field of automotive engineering, not just those parts of it related to electrical technology. Of course, broad scope demanded its own compromises. Kettering now had to spend much of his time identifying important research areas and less time exploring them himself. Still, his unmatched ability to become intimately involved with a few favorite projects and still keep reasonable track of the rest let him contribute personally to scores of studies, and still fulfill his other responsibilities.

Very rarely can it be said that a single man or even a group of men altered the destiny of an entire industry, especially one as large and influential as the automobile industry. Certainly Henry Ford's perception that a mass-produced, inexpensive automobile could find a mass market could be cited as the insight that made the automobile big business. However, Ford must share his place with Sloan and Kettering, the "dream team" of creative businessman and imaginative engineer. With the institutional and technical innovations begun in 1920 by the formation of the Research Corporation, they would completely reshape the American automobile and the business environment that gave it birth.

6 / THE COPPER-COOLED ENGINE

"Industries are like some watches," Kettering frequently observed; "they have to be shaken hard every so often to keep them going." For his technical debut in General Motors, Kettering proposed to shake up the corporation with a radical innovation, an air-cooled engine that he hoped would be a powerful sales weapon aimed at General Motors' major competitor, the Model T.

The new air-cooled engine promised numerous advantages over its water-cooled competitors: it weighed less per horsepower, did not freeze in winter, dispensed with the radiator and other bulky cooling accessories, and achieved better fuel economy. Prospective owners would no longer need to garage their vehicles to ensure easy cold-weather starts. All in all, the new engine seemed, both to Kettering and to top executives in the corporation, an ideal antidote for General Motors' slumping sales position. But the bright promise of 1919 turned into a corporate nightmare, as Kettering's innovation shook apart the corporation in ways he could never have foreseen. By 1923 a dejected Charles Kettering would be considering resignation.

After four costly years of development, the failure of the project came rather unexpectedly and taught both Kettering and his new employers some valuable lessons about corporate research. The maturing of consumer tastes beyond inexpensive, strictly utilitarian automobiles and the more important reason of various technical difficulties helped account for the lack of success. Some technical problems encountered in this project were symptomatic of deeper problems relating to the role of, and the tensions between, competing engineering groups within General Motors. All during the project, poor coordination and lack of effective dialogue between design and production engineers resulted in crippling disputes and delays. Each group felt that only it was capable of developing the new engine successfully. Production engineers remained blind to the problems of perfecting a relatively new and radical technology, while design men failed to appreciate the difficulties involved in moving from a carefully tuned prototype to a trouble-free assembly-line automobile ready for mass production.

While internal dissension alone would effectively have sabotaged the project, the combination of this factor with declining profit possibilities was lethal. For as Alfred Sloan once remarked, "the principal object of the corporation was not only to make cars, but to make money."

A relatively brief exposure to the internal combustion engine had taught Kettering the rudiments of engine cooling. A major problem of an automobile's internal combustion engine was that it produced excess heat that had to be drawn off in some fashion. On small versions, the cooling effect of the surrounding air was sufficient. In larger engines, the heat flow from cylinder gases into piston heads, valve heads, and cylinder walls was slightly less per unit of exposed area than in small engines, but the inside temperatures of larger engines were higher because of longer heat flow paths to the cooler outside parts of the engine. Larger and more powerful engines, therefore, required a more sophisticated cooling system. Two methods were generally employed on automobiles. The first was relatively simple. Metal fins were cast onto the cylinders. Heat was conducted from the cylinders and cooled the engine. On larger models the surrounding air could not absorb, quickly enough, all the heat that was generated, and soon the attendant problems of overheating appeared—"burned" valves, sticking pistons, loss of power.

If an engineer wanted to increase the power and efficiency of an automobile engine, he had to employ a more effective cooling system. One answer was to use a cooling medium with both higher specific heat than air and the ability to "wet" the surface for better heat transfer. Many substances might do, but water was the cheapest and most readily available. Water thus conducted the heat away from the cylinders and was then circulated through a radiator where air provided the final cooling. Although water cooling effectively prevented overheating and allowed the construction of more powerful engines, it required a more expensive and complex design.

Finding a way to cool an engine by air as efficiently as by water would result in a major breakthrough in automotive design, many thought. An air-cooled engine would eliminate the radiator, hoses, and ducts needed to circulate the water through the engine, and greatly simplify the design. Further, it would have the additional advantages of not freezing in cold weather and offering greater power for a given weight.

Many automotive engineers realized the potential of air cooling even before the war. Numerous European makers used this system on their smaller cars. John W. Wilkinson developed the Franklin air-cooled engine in the United States in 1901. And while this particular model was not completely successful, subsequent efforts produced a marketable automobile.[1]

Aircraft engine builders during the war also developed several air-cooled designs. The power-to-weight ratio of airplane engines was obviously crucial, so air cooling looked promising. British engine designers built several sophisticated versions. The high velocity made air cooling more suitable for airplanes than automobiles, however.

Kettering learned about air cooling during the war. In 1919, he gave the research staff at General Motors a 1915 publication on the use of copper in the air cooling of engines—a principle pioneered by the brilliant, eccentric English inventor, Frederick W. Lanchester.[2] As copper was thought to conduct heat nine times more readily than iron, the chances for success looked good. Kettering hoped that copper's superior thermal properties would allow an engine design with greater compression ratios than other air-cooled engines, and thus better economy and more power for a given displacement. His concurrent campaign to reach the same goal with chemical fuel additives did not look very promising at the time, and he was inclined to favor the "copper-cooled" engine.

Copper was too soft a metal for cylinder construction, so some method was needed to join the iron cylinder to copper fins. The different thermal properties of the two metals made the problem more difficult than it appeared at first.

Roland V. Hutchinson took charge of the project at the laboratory. First, he attempted to cast the copper fins directly onto the iron cylinders without success. Thomas Midgley next hit upon the idea of machining the cast-iron cylinder on the outside, then attaching the fins with molten zinc.[3] This effort too failed. Next came the idea of brazing on the fins with a blowtorch. The difference in the coefficients of expansion of the copper fins and the iron prevented bonding with heat alone.

Midgley and an assistant solved the vexing problem of mass-producing the fins in January 1920. They produced a wooden model of an eccentric finning machine on the twenty-third, and Midgley told Kettering that the team was now "in [a] position to complete [the] motor design very rapidly with [a] high degree of intelligence."[4] Their model worked well, and by the end of February they had drawn up specifications for "a machine to fold copper into the shape of a fin of any height automatically and any number of fins to the set and cut them off. . . ."[5] They thought that the machine could eventually produce sixty fins a minute, though they held early runs to only thirty.

Attaching the fins to the cylinders remained a problem. Kettering devised a method of piercing a series of holes in the fins and then feeding the brazing wire through the holes. The idea worked quite well, though developing an automatic furnace to do the job took the laboratory nearly a year.[6]

Midgley's team first designed a horizontal furnace, but various difficulties involving discomfort and danger to the operator forced them to scrap this design. By January 1921, they perfected the idea. The operator placed the cylinder to be brazed into the furnace in a vertical position. He then rolled the furnace into a horizontal position and pushed it over the burner at the rear of the machine, where it engaged a rotating and timing device to complete the brazing. Remembering Kettering's insistence on simplicity, they noted that "the operator can be an unskilled workman. All he needs to learn is how to put the cylinder in the furnace and how to take it out."[7]

The gas-fired furnaces and their later electrical replacements cost forty to fifty thousand dollars each, but they reduced the tedious job of manufacturing the fins and cylinders to a cost-efficient operation. The furnace took in the fins, pressed them against the thin brass bonding metal, heated the metals to create a proper union, and gave back a complete copper-cooled cylinder for about two dollars.[8]

In final form the cylinders resembled a daisy, the center being the cylinder, the outlines of the petals represented by the elliptical copper fins with airspaces between them.

Kettering decided to test the new cylinders in a Chevrolet chassis. He constructed three four-cylinder engines. To provide additional cooling, he positioned fans on either side of the block. While test reports on these cars have not survived, he apparently considered them only marginally successful. Work on the project continued, but so far, no major breakthrough had been made in engine cooling.

Before Kettering could develop any kind of marketable product, the organizational realignments at General Motors placed the copper-cooled engine in a new environment. During the Du Pont acquisition, Kettering appeared before the Finance Committee to explain his work on the engine.[9] Pierre du Pont and John Raskob expressed great interest in the project. John T. Smith, who conducted the legal negotiations for General Motors, even believed that the copper-cooled engine played a vital role in making Kettering the head of research for the company. "It was not so much that they wanted CFK to head research for GM in the abstract," he recalled, "as they were 'sold' on him through that one concrete development, the copper-cooled car."[10]

Sloan's and du Pont's unfolding corporate policy conveniently created a niche for the project. Sloan planned a corporate product line that would range from the high-volume but low-priced Chevrolet to the low-volume, high-priced Cadillac, a car for every purse and taste.

While the models themselves would not overlap, divisions would share many common parts and technologies.[11] Kettering's air-cooled engine seemed ideally suited for the new marketing strategy, particularly for the lower end of the product line. Promising good performance and little maintenance at relatively low price, the copper-cooled engine would be the basis for a new series of Chevrolets.

The Executive Committee gave the final go-ahead for the project in January 1921, when it resolved that Kettering develop a four-cylinder air-cooled engine and that the engine first be targeted for a low-priced car in the Chevrolet division.[12] There was also considerable support for an improved version of the same engine for more expensive cars. At the same time, the top executives of the corporation agreed that Kettering should develop a six-cylinder engine for the Oakland division, scheduled for production a year and a half later.[13] Fred Warner, Oakland's general manager, and Kettering began a series of technical conferences to discuss the proposed innovation.[14] No one expected any difficulties, and as Sloan observed, "any differences that may exist I feel sure will, of course, be ironed out in conferences."[15]

Since the air-cooled Chevrolet was to be pitted against the Model T, low weight and low price were essential. Kettering appointed a special committee to draw up a list of standards for the new engine. Fred W. Davis, one of the engineers later responsible for testing the engine, recalled the strict guidelines imposed on the project. The committee limited the size of the engine to 135 cubic inches with a weight of less than 375 pounds. Further, it required at least 14 horsepower at 1,000 rpm. In addition, the cost could not exceed $75. More conferences pared pounds from the proposed frame, axles, and steering gears, for the whole car was to weigh no more than 1,450 pounds.[16]

Development progressed smoothly throughout the first half of 1921. The project weighed quite heavily on Kettering's shoulders, though, and his unremitting efforts on its behalf began to worry his superiors. Kettering's mother died during the winter after an extended illness. The combination of these strains showed plainly, and Sloan suggested a short European vacation to ease the burdens. Kettering refused. "I regret exceedingly that you and Mrs. Kettering are not going with us on this trip," Sloan replied. "As I explained to you, one of the reasons why I thought of the trip was because it would give you a change from the strenuous work that you are carrying on and would be a protection to the Corporation." [17]

By the summer of 1921, Kettering and his engineers felt sufficiently confident to begin road-testing the vehicles. General Motors still lacked a testing facility, and new products were either taken to the Indianapolis Speedway for trials or put through their paces on public roads. Kettering preferred the latter and assembled a fleet of copper-cooled cars, standard Chevrolets, competitors' cars, and a parts truck for an assault on the back roads of Ohio and Kentucky.

The expedition set off in late July for what the participants would later recall as one of the most grueling tours of their lives. Most of the driving was over very bad roads which "showed up the deficiencies in the industry's cars as well as the copper-cooled." [18] Kettering relished the harsh conditions. The expedition camped, cooked out, and generally roughed it. Many of the members enjoyed this a lot less than Kettering. O. T. Kreusser, who accompanied the group and who later headed the General Motors Proving Ground that would one day replace actual road tests, remembered, "The cars took it a lot better than the drivers, because after you came off one of those road test trips to Southern Ohio and Kentucky, it would take at least three baths to get all the dust out of the inside and outside of you. . . ." [19]

None of the cars survived this severe test without damage. Axles and drive shafts broke, teeth pulled out of pinion gears. After several weeks of testing, however, Kettering was at least satisfied with the performance of the new engine.

The division managers who were to receive the engine were fully cooperating with Kettering. George Hannum of Oakland and Karl Zimmerschied of Chevrolet agreed completely with the final production schedule. [20] Somewhat wary of the Research Corporation's control of the project, they stated, for the record, that they had no wish to interfere with Kettering's proposed design. As Zimmerschied noted, "the responsibility for design being Mr. Kettering's, the manufacturing Divisions are in no position to do more than make suggestions on this subject, and in this respect the normal relations are reversed, the line organization becoming an advisory body."[21] But the hard feelings showed as he remarked further that "while the advice of practical men may be of negligible value on those questions of design which affect the functioning of a part, it cannot be so considered with relation to factors affecting ease and cost of production."[22] The unusual organizational alignment of the project had already opened the door to future tension between competing groups of engineers.

The Executive Committee was ready to make an important commitment to the Chevrolet copper-cooled experiment. Sure that the corporation was on the verge of an important innovation, Pierre du Pont reassured Zimmerschied in September of 1921, "we have no doubt that you will fight out the problems, and the whole organization of General Motors is available to you for assistance."[23] He also confessed to Kettering, "Now that we are at the point of planning the production of the new cars, I am beginning to feel like a small boy when the long expected circus posters begin to appear on fences, and to wonder how each part of the circus is to appear and what act I will like the best."[24]

The laboratory completed design specifications in the fall of 1921, and the copper-cooled engine received its final form. A continuous strip of thin sheet copper surrounded each cylinder, with the bases of the crimps contacting one another. Thirteen fins per linear inch appeared the most satisfactory arrangement. The optimum ratio of fin length to the distance between the fins was established at 70:1. With a lesser gap the air turbulence was suppressed, which reduced air velocity at the fin surface, lowered the heat transfer from the fins to the air, and caused the fin temperature to rise.[25] To provide additional cooling the engineers employed a front-mounted fan, driven by a special V-belt at faster than engine speed, to push air through the copper fins and out through louvres in the hood.[26]

Other improvements on the car included a new oiling system for the engine consisting of a groove in the flywheel that picked up the oil and delivered it through a series of tubes to the rest of the engine (an interesting idea but perhaps an unnecessarily complex addition to an already complex engine).[27] For the car itself, the designers chose a tubular frame with one-quarter elliptical springs.

The design looked so good that the Executive Committee instructed the Oldsmobile division to help Kettering develop a six-cylinder version to plug a gap in the model line in the $1,900 to $2,100 range.[28]

Since Oakland sales were sagging badly, the executives decided to introduce the engine on an Oakland before Chevrolet got the innovation. Hannum received the new copper-cooled, six-cylinder automobile for final testing before full production in November 1921. Plans to end the production of water-cooled Oaklands within six weeks and replace them with the new design were pending. Assuming that the initial trials were successful, Chevrolet would follow suit and introduce a four-cylinder version in the early months of 1922. General Motors thus prepared to launch the most ambitious technical innovation of its short history.

A completely unexpected blow befell the copper-cooling program when Hannum failed the Oakland test car on November 8, 1921. He told du Pont that at least six months would be needed to make the necessary changes. To soften the blow to Kettering, the Executive Committee wrote him with encouragement and a vote of confidence. "In the development and introduction of anything as radically different from standard practice as the air-cooled car is from a regular water cooled job, it is quite natural that there should be a lot of 'wiseacres' and 'know-it-alls' standing around knocking your development," they said.[29] They also expressed confidence that Kettering would eliminate any problems and bring the car onto the market by 1923.

Du Pont wrote Kettering privately, explaining that his personal optimism was undimmed. "This whole affair seems to have developed into a tremendous 'tempest in a tea-pot,'" he explained. "For the life of me I cannot see how the situation has changed from a month or so ago, when everybody was satisfied and enthusiastic."[30]

No one doubted the final result. On the last day of November, the Executive Committee confidently predicted the expected profits from the new cars: $50 for the four-cylinder, at a manufactured cost of

$320 and a selling price of $475; and $60 per six-cylinder model at a manufactured cost of $525 and a selling price of $750.[31]

The complaints from Oakland were rather vague—overheating, loss of power, and other imprecise malfunctions. Interoffice memorandums were filled with evidence of the controversy as the engineers tried to apportion the blame. Interestingly, Louis Ruthenberg, who later became a liaison between the laboratory and the divisions, sided with Hannum. He believed that the Oakland test only confirmed the troubles already discovered at Dayton. The research engineers, he argued, were fooling themselves. When they read their own reports they naturally concluded that the troubles could be corrected with slight adjustments. Hannum, on the other hand, merely reported the defects of the engine without comment.[32]

Kettering disagreed completely, but resolved to reexamine the engine and correct any remaining troubles. He feared a certain resistance to his innovation, however. "If we can ever get the right receptive attitude into the minds of the General Motors people, so that they will really find out what the air-cooled motor means to the future of our industry," he confided to du Pont, "we will not spend time and money laying out garden variety motors of the ordinary type."[33]

On December 21, 1921, Kettering called a special conference with his top engineers to consider any necessary modifications. The conference lasted two days and covered the most minute details, from engine to drivetrain to chassis. Were the oil pan bolts spaced too far to prevent leakage? Was the gas tank properly supported? Might redesigning the fan help reduce cost? Was the Ford technique of manufacturing connecting rods better? Should alloy bolts be used to hold the flywheel onto the crankshaft?[34] After a lengthy discussion of these and many other questions, the meeting adjourned to begin the slow process of implementing the reforms.

The principal thrust of the modification program was in the direction of the frame, axle, transmission, and other aspects of the automobile divorced from the engine. The Oakland test disclosed as many problems with these details as with the engine, and Kettering intended to eliminate all objections.[35]

Chevrolet received the new chassis in March, and after a thorough test offered a few minor suggestions but was satisfied in general with the changes.[36] In the middle of the month the laboratory turned over detailed blueprints of the chassis but hesitated in releasing similar information on the motor.[37]

Everyone seemed pleased with the project's renewed progress. William S. Knudsen, vice-president in charge of operations at Chevrolet, outlined a tentative production schedule calling for over a thousand cars a month by the next January. In March, he replaced Zimmerschied as division president. The pressures of the project and personal difficulties had pushed Zimmerschied to a nervous breakdown.

A few ominous signs appeared at the laboratory too. Kettering became convinced that Chevrolet was sending saboteurs into the Research Corporation. He complained to O. E. Hunt at Chevrolet about a new divisional inspector: "I do not feel that we should be burdened in this proposition any further with these 'conscientious objectors.' You know, no battle was ever won with an army of 'conscientious objectors.' The thing that we should like to do is to get some real, damn fine, enthusiastic American Volunteers to come and help this situation along a little bit."[38] The conflict was beginning to make everyone somewhat paranoid.

Kettering gave the results of a new 20,000-mile trial to du Pont in late May 1922. They were impressive. The tappets had been adjusted twice, but no other maintenance had been necessary. Kettering claimed:

The valves and all the bearings were in perfect condition. There was no carbon deposit in the motor and the oil mileage had been in the neighborhood of a thousand to twelve hundred miles per gallon. In all of our road tests here, we have never seen anything like this; yet I am not surprised, because this simply proves out the fundamental principle.[39]

Under the influence of this optimistic report du Pont wrote to his friend Harry McGowan, an executive with the Nobel Company of Great Britain: "All goes well in the copper-cooled car development, we still expect to start manufacture in September and hope that developments will warrant production of 500 per day in March."[40]

Kettering pressed for immediate production of the new car. Some divisional engineers were reluctant. Their test reports over the summer indicated that much more development work was needed. R. K. Jack, chief engineer at Oldsmobile, conducted some independent evaluations in July. He told Kettering that the six-cylinder car was noisy, leaked oil at the front end, and sometimes knocked badly at speeds exceeding 30 mph. Minor things like windshield fasteners broke. The car started poorly and pumped oil. Worst of all, from Jack's point of view, the seat cushions were uncomfortable, "very hard after sitting for any length of time—like sitting on a board." [41]

Kettering dismissed the report as showing merely the kinds of troubles likely to be encountered with any "first job." "I do not think that we need to worry so far as getting these things ironed out in a short time," he told Jack. [42]

Yet the specter of organized divisional resistance began to grow in his mind. Many executives and engineers simply failed to appreciate his idea, he believed, and were "looking upon this work as being just a slight advance over the present thing instead of being a tremendous asset." [43] To assuage the divisions' objections, and to stifle recurring rumors that he was using his high corporate connections to circumvent normal engineering channels and shove a bad idea off on the divisional engineers, Kettering invited several divisional engineers to Dayton to offer their design suggestions. "The only way for us to get this situation straightened out was for the organization who was to build the car to come down to the laboratories and help analyze it so that we could work together in solving these particular problems," he noted. [44] But the growing rift between laboratory and divisions could only be solved by true cooperation, and Kettering actually expected their acquiescence.

Other aspects of the program were progressing more hopefully. James McEvoy, head of the GM Patent Department, issued a comprehensive fifty-page document on all possible patent infringements which indicated that only the design of the pistons and the clutch posed any potential problems, and getting around the infringement did not look too difficult. [45]

Meanwhile, sales of water-cooled automobiles, and especially

Chevrolets, increased rapidly during 1922.[46] Division executives openly questioned the wisdom of adopting a new engine at such a time. But staff executives, under great pressure from Kettering and du Pont, stuck by the original policy. In September, Kettering placed a copper-cooled four-cylinder in a Chevrolet chassis and sent it to O. E. Hunt for evaluation. Besides being the chief engineer for Chevrolet at the time, Hunt also had responsibility for developing a chassis for the copper-cooled automobile.

Hunt's tests continued to disclose low power. Much alarmed, Kettering dispatched Hutchinson and his assistant Walter Geise to the Chevrolet plant in Flint, Michigan to investigate. They first discovered that the dynamometers (instruments used to measure engine horsepower on a test stand) that General Motors had distributed to each division to systematize testing procedures were still resting in their shipping crates.[47] After unpacking them, they found that the power trouble had nothing to do with the engine. The wrong axle had been assembled in the car. The incident marked the beginning of a long, sometimes almost comical series of blunders and misunderstandings that were to plague the project. The divisional engineers were obviously not going out of their way to assist with a project in which they felt they played only a minor role.

While dealers sold standard Chevrolets in near record numbers, Kettering prodded the copper-cooled engine along. On October 24, 1922, Knudsen drew up another plan for introducing the new automobile. One of two options would be followed. One plan would begin manufacture of copper-cooled cars the next July at a rate of 1,000 per day, increasing to 2,000 per day by October 1. The production of water-cooled cars would end in June. Option two envisioned a more gradual introduction. Beginning the next July, 700 new cars would be produced each day, while the manufacture of water-cooled automobiles would continue at the rate of 1,000 a day.[48] Since water-cooled Chevrolets were selling well, the second option seemed wiser and was adopted. The new copper-cooled engine would appear as an option, not a complete replacement, for the standard Chevrolet until the design was perfected.

As additional insurance, the members of the Executive Committee requested that development continue on the water-cooled engine. Since the laboratory was preoccupied with the copper-cooled project, they assigned the task of improving the old design to the divisions. The Dayton design group, under Kettering, and the divisional design teams scattered about the corporation, now had vested interests in different designs, a situation that could only lead to further tensions between them.

Superficially, the situation resembled normal competitive engineering. Each team would develop a design, and the best would become standard. Yet in two very important respects this case was different. First, the decision to market the copper-cooled car had already been made; it was no longer supposed to be in the development stage. To begin work on a competitive engine at such a time showed a lack of faith in Kettering's team. Second, the very divisional engineers engaged in developing the water-cooled design were also responsible for testing Kettering's product, certainly not a situation guaranteed to produce an objective evaluation.

The organizational strife began to wear on Kettering. On seeing a redesign of his copper-cooled car clutch by R. K. Jack, he lodged a rather vicious protest with one of the corporation's vice-presidents. "How long, I wonder, is General Motors going to run a 'back door' organization?" he asked. "I am sending you this letter to say, frankly, that if some Executive arrangement is not made in the General Motors, whereby certain definite lines of handling things are worked out so that the Laboratory, at least, knows what is going on and why it is going on, I believe it is time to discontinue the research division."[49] To the Patent Department he drafted a letter taunting, "If the Patent Department can design better . . . then let's turn the Research Department over to the Patent Department."[50] He thought better of the last statement, though, and did not send the letter. While he still asserted that the copper-cooled engine was the most innovative project ever undertaken by the corporation, he worried that the endless and disorganized changes had created a "design which is neither 'fish' nor 'fowl.' "[51]

The conflict reached a head in November 1922. On the eighth, the Executive Committee, including Sloan, Kettering, and du Pont, met to consider the future of the copper-cooled project. Kettering confided to du Pont before the meeting that he believed that the divisions were out to "scuttle" the innovation.[52] At the meeting, Sloan urged cautious consideration before adopting an untried innovation during a peak sales period, while du Pont countered by reminding the participants that adoption was not the issue. That had already been decided. Only the when and how remained.[53] Kettering limited his comments to technical details. The pro-copper-cooled forces prevailed, and the committee voted to continue the project. The unveiling would occur at the New York Automobile Show in January, less than two months later.

Two days after the meeting the first orders for copper-cooled cars arrived in Detroit.[54] Irénée du Pont, Pierre's brother, requested six of the new coupes, a purchase he would come to regret during the next year.

The Chevrolet Copper-Cooled Superior proved the surprise hit of the New York show. Information on the new car leaked to the trade press in late December 1922. Reviewers expressed greatest surprise at the successful brazing of copper to iron. As late as April 1922, the *SAE Journal* had noted that "copper has been used extensively for air-cooled cylinders and was employed on some of the earliest air-cooled cars. The high conductivity is of considerable advantage, but there are many practical objections to its use. Principal of these was the difficulty of attaching sheet copper fins to the cylinder head."[55] Kettering earned high praise for overcoming this obstacle.

Journalists also stressed the low price of the automobile—only $200 more than the standard Chevrolet Superior. For the first time, the American public was offered a reasonably priced air-cooled car.[56] If the higher price seemed contradictory, since the point of the engine was to cut initial as well as operating costs, it merely reflected the novelty of an engine that offered advantages not available from competitors. The copper-cooled automobile made as great an impression on the public at the show as it had on the journalists. Success seemed assured.

Kettering was also gaining a measure of celebrity from the publicity. Just before the New York show the Harvard Medical Society invited him to address its members. His speech hinted at an inner conflict that was at the root of the corporate dilemma. "The day of the cross-roads inventor is over," he said, implying that integrated research teams would soon replace the lone wolf.[57] Yet he gave no clue about how troublesome fitting the individual genius into the organization could sometimes be.

Chevrolet's subsequent efforts to introduce the copper-cooled automobile to the public would encounter problems of technical malfunction, intracorporate communications breakdowns, and changing market conditions. In all, only 759 copper-cooled Chevrolets were manufactured. Some 239 were scrapped by production men. The other 520 were delivered to the sales organization. Of these, 100 were sold to retail customers while the rest were either driven by factory representatives or remained in inventory.[58] A couple eventually found their way into museums.

After initial sales, Kettering and the divisions were swamped with complaints about noise, clutch problems, wear on cylinders, carburetor malfunctions, axle breakdowns, and fanbelt trouble. The failure of the car had three primary causes. First, because the standards committee had demanded light weight, numerous components were redesigned. As Kreusser remarked, "When you tried to make automobile frames, drive shafts, rear axles, and steering gears you got into so many unconventional methods in order to get weight and price out that the car wasn't too successful."[59] Kettering remained perplexed by the laboratory's inability to produce a car as light as the Model T for the same price. In fact, Ford seemed able to fabricate the same car for about two-thirds the cost.[60]

The second cause of failure was less obvious, but probably more crucial. It involved a lack of communication between Kettering's men and the production engineers at Flint and Pontiac. Without adequate coordination of the two groups, minor difficulties grew into major conflicts, and small rivalries escalated into crippling disputes and delays. Even careless assembly may be traced to this tension.

The third cause was even less clear on the surface of things, but perhaps most important of all. Product development in this case was only of value to General Motors if it promised reasonable return within a relatively short period. The copper-cooled car was designed specifically to compete with the Model T, at least from the point of view of top management. (Kettering had pretensions of reforming an entire technology.) Chevrolet was holding its own against the Ford without the new engine or lightweight design. American consumers showed less enthusiasm for the copper-cooled car on the showroom floor than they had at automotive shows. Tastes were changing. Buyers no longer seemed to want a light-weight and inexpensive automobile, but looked instead to the style and comfort that water-cooled Chevrolets provided quite adequately.

Many of the technical difficulties related to engineering, but not necessarily to the air cooling of the engine. Several customers and divisional testers complained that oil worked its way through the cylinder walls and disabled the vehicle. Detractors of the copper-cooled engine proposed the theory that brazing of the copper fins sometimes changed the structure of the cast iron, making it porous enough to permit the passage of oil.[61] Little evidence was produced in support of this theory except the fouled cylinders themselves. Other explanations seemed far more plausible. Most likely the oil was pumping past the piston rings and entering the combustion chamber where it fouled the plugs and formed carbon deposits.

Sloppy assembly was behind the oil pumping. One Chevrolet owner reported that his new touring car, on inspection, was found to have scored cylinders, badly fitted rings, and cylinders out of true. "Mr. Taylor of the Wilmington Auto Company informed me it is pumping oil," the owner told an insurance agent for the corporation, "and added that the last three carloads of Chevrolets received by them have been giving similar trouble, a very serious defect for the reputation of a car."[62] Kettering never reported any pumping in his tests, nor did anyone else associated with the trials mention it. The problem appears to have been related to quality control and not to design. Production engineers, and not Kettering's staff, had responsibility for this aspect of the project.

The fanbelt also caused considerable anguish among owners. Du Pont wrote to Knudsen in March 1923, "It has been reported to me that copper-cooled car No. IC—1187, one of the four shipped to my brother, developed trouble with the fan belt at less than 100 miles."[63] Another customer reported a similar defect in his car.[64] To Kettering, these complaints were baffling, especially since none of the testers mentioned such a problem. The explanation was really quite simple, however. The belt had failed because it was placed on the car in the reverse direction. "The replaced belt has been correctly installed on the car," the customer explained, "and so far . . . has not broken."[65]

Other small defects surfaced. The clutch plagued several owners. Irénée du Pont's car went in for service once again in April 1923. (His driving time in this car was rather limited!) Replacement of the clutch collar ended the trouble.[66] Clutch problems were quite common, but the design came out of the Chevrolet division and not the Research Corporation. Another problem involved rapid wear of the copper-cooled engine's cylinders. An investigation revealed loosely adherent core sand in the intake manifold.[67]

One design problem eluded solution—the excess engine noise that was a common problem with air-cooled engines. Joseph Butz, a research engineer responsible for road-testing the car, discovered that the problem lay in the camshaft. He removed the offending part, gave it slightly different contours and a high polish, returned it to the engine, and was astonished to find it ran almost silently.[68] Kettering asked Butz to duplicate the design, but after several trials he could not. Later Butz took the part to another machinist for reproduction, but somewhere along the line someone misplaced the original. Since the project ended a short time later, further efforts in this direction ceased.

Nor did chassis improvements proceed smoothly. Hunt of Chevrolet had charge of this development, but by the summer of 1923 he had made only limited progress. Even du Pont began to wonder about the delays. He expressed his frustration to Sloan, saying, "I am inclined to believe that part of the trouble lies in the lack of support of the copper-cooled car from the top";[69] the top of the divisions, that is.

Many of the complaints about the new car centered on details only marginally related to either the design of the engine or the design of the rest of the car. Irénée du Pont's case seemed almost typical. "Trivial items were not in order, indicating careless work; for instance, fasteners on carpets were placed at wrong point, steering wheel out of adjustment, and similar items not having anything to do with the design of the car or the copper-cooling."[70] Lack of attention to assembly details was responsible.

The laboratory aggravated detail problems by continually introducing new, untried designs, always with an eye toward further cost reductions. The fan, for example, was completely and unnecessarily redesigned for a very slight cost savings.[71] Each change only added to the confusion.

Kettering believed that organized resistance within the divisions was the major problem, and he was partially correct. But most evidence suggests a poorly coordinated engineering effort rather than a grand conspiracy. Take, for instance, the troubles surrounding the rear axle and the carburetor. A three-month feud simmered over the proper design of the rear axle. After Kettering sent the copper-cooled car to Chevrolet, he discovered that "immediately the axle which we developed and proven on road test was thrown away," and replaced with an axle developed and promoted by the divisional engineers.[72] The carburetor caused a similar misunderstanding. Division engineers objected to a lack of power as the engine warmed up. "We told you," Kettering wrote to Sloan, "that their real trouble was in the carburetor system and valve setting. Trips to the Indianapolis Speedway have proven these points which have been supported on the dynamometers."[73] At least one design engineer disagreed with Kettering's assessment, evidence of schisms even within the laboratory. Fred Davis thought that a design flaw in the ducting system was responsible for poor power on starting.

Design and production engineers seemed increasingly unwilling to cooperate in solving these problems and quick to put blame on each other. As Knudsen put it, "Unhappily, the engine troubles when reported divulged a wide range of differences in opinion between the creators and the producers, both as to their cause and their remedies."[74]

Kettering felt trapped by this "organized resistance," and openly expressed his belief that "because of the way in which the Research Corporation is regarded by some of the General Motors Divisions, we can never expect to carry out the constructive programs which we have planned."[75]

Divisional engineers were equally disappointed. One wrote to du Pont complaining that his report on the project was very negative because Chevrolet found it nearly impossible to "produce the car within the limits set by Dayton, and rightly or wrongly demonstrated by their sample car."[76] Divisional letters had a more subdued tone than Kettering's, for no one at Chevrolet wished a confrontation with the powerful chief of research. Still, the divisional engineers felt betrayed by their counterparts in research. As Knudsen explained, "We ourselves were at sea as to the existence of troubles which had previously been lauded [by Kettering] as non-existent, which put the burden of proof on us."[77]

Some divisional engineers even began to wonder if Kettering had fallen prey to an overinflated ego and was trying to push through a pet project, regardless of the interests of the corporation. Perhaps they had a valid point. Louis Ruthenberg, whose headaches as liaison between the Research Corporation and the divisions finally forced his resignation, claimed, "Kettering was too emotionally involved in the controversy to appreciate my position."[78]

These problems peaked during the spring of 1923. At the end of May, the Executive Committee ordered a final test for the six-cylinder copper-cooled automobile. E. A. DeWaters from Buick and Hunt from Chevrolet supervised the trials and submitted another negative report to the committee.[79]

Sloan's ascension to the presidency in the spring cut off much of the top managerial support for the project. Sloan's cold calculations left little room for the kind of enthusiasm du Pont brought to the program. After considering the test results and the general position of the corporation, Sloan decided to terminate the copper-cooled engine by the end of the summer.

Kettering was visibly annoyed by the decision. He still believed quite strongly in the commercial possibilities of the engine. "If we cannot get some practical way of commercializing this product, in our organization," he suggested to Sloan, "I should like very much to discuss with you the possibility of taking this outside of the corporation."[80] Sloan would not hear of such a thing, and reminded Kettering that he was an important partner in the total enterprise.[81] Further, du Pont, Raskob and he had stood by Kettering in the past, and Sloan implied that Kettering now owed them continued loyalty despite any personal disappointment he might feel.

Kettering would not be appeased. On the last day of June, he offered his resignation. Deeply hurt, he told Sloan, "I regret very much that this situation has developed. I have been extremely unhappy and know that I have made you and Mr. du Pont equally unhappy. . . . I know that work here at the Laboratory has been almost 100% failure but not because of the fundamental principles involved. Enough may come out of the Laboratory to have paid for their existence but no one will care to continue in Research activities as the situation now stands. My only regret in severing my connection with the Corporation would be the wonderful association I have had with yourself, Mr. du Pont, Mr. Mott and others."[82] He did leave open the possibility that if conditions changed, he might stay.

Sloan, recognizing a temperamental engineer when he saw one, tried to reassure Kettering. He reminded him that the decision was not to scrap the entire project, only the production end of it. Orders supposedly given to shut down the brazing furnaces and other special laboratory developments were just rumors. Only the timing of the project had been bad, Sloan said, and Kettering would certainly bring it to fruition sometime in the future.[83]

On July 6, 1923, Sloan, Kettering, and two other corporation executives met to discuss the future of the project. They devoted much of their meeting to the morale problems. Everyone agreed that forcing the divisions to take part in a project that they did not firmly believe in had been a grave mistake. The discussion ended with a resolution to place the copper-cooled engine under Kettering's control at Dayton and remove the project from the divisions until a later date.[84]

Antagonisms lingered at the laboratory and in the divisions, and began to interfere with unrelated projects. A new production model promised to the laboratory did not arrive on schedule, and Kettering dictated an angry letter to Sloan. "We do not know what Olds are bringing out. We will never be allowed to know. Since this thing with the Copper-Cooled car has come up the Laboratory has been practically isolated from Corporation activities," he said. "This I resent, as I also resent the criticism upon the work of the Laboratories."[85]

The real intent of Sloan's decision for postponement also troubled him. A few days later he wrote Sloan another letter. "If we build 25 or 30 cars in Dayton, and they prove satisfactory, what do we do then?" he asked. "Are you going to allow us to build up an operation the size of Oakland, or Olds, or Buick if we can prove our case? My position in the matter is just this; that before I will undertake any further work for the General Motors Corporation, you will have to outline a perfectly definite policy and we will have to have some assurance that you are willing to help carry it through."[86]

Kettering's idea of "assurances" included firing the offending divisional engineers and managers. Naturally, Sloan refused. He pointed out that it was not within his power, or even within the power of the Executive Committee, to make the kind of changes that were really necessary. "The Executive Committee can remove anybody in the organization; it can make any changes in personnel it wants to; it can adopt any policies that in its judgement are desirable for the benefit of the Corporation, but there are certain things it cannot do," Sloan argued, "and that is, it cannot order a co-operative spirit to be developed in the organization—it has got to be done in an entirely different way."[87] Wholesale sacking of valuable division talent to appease Kettering or anyone else was certainly not the way.

Pierre du Pont regretted Sloan's decision nearly as much as Kettering did. He agreed to abide by it, but worried about the negative influence such a decision might have on prospective customers. "We should stand by our product even though we have offered an exchange for another car when our customers have expressed their preference for copper-cooled," he counseled. "I advise strongly that those still owning copper-cooled cars be written a letter stating that the Chevrolet Division will continue to service these cars and assume any other responsibility usual with their product."[88]

Nonetheless, the decision stood. All copper-cooled cars already sold were recalled. By the end of the summer of 1923, copper cooling ceased to be an active concern of the corporation.

Kettering never lost his enthusiasm for the engine, nor his bitterness about the handling of the situation. As late as November, he was still complaining to Sloan about the laboratory's relationship with the divisions. "Your manufacturing divisions at Detroit have made the most derogatory remarks regarding this research work and are permitted to go unchecked," he whined. "It makes no difference to me as to who designs our motors, but it certainly makes a difference to me as a stockholder, and to all other stockholders, as to whether we capitalize on the information which the Corporation has relative to a very advanced knowledge of motor design."[89] In a rare attack on Sloan he added, "[You] have been very free in your criticisms of the Laboratory methods, but I have never heard you offer any criticisms on the people who have thrown into discard every advanced principle known in the design of motors today" and substituted in their place "motors designed in the most superficial way we can possibly think of."[90]

Time slowly healed the wounds. Northway division and the laboratory cooperated in producing several more copper-cooled engines. Kettering set up a number of cars for experimental purposes, testing such innovative ideas as crankshaft vibration dampers and crankcase ventilators.[91] He promoted the engine to various interests, including the Yellow Cab Company of Chicago. And as late as March 1924, he was preparing chassis with copper-cooled power plants.[92]

The copper-cooled automobile lingered in the laboratory until 1925, but Kettering increasingly turned his attention to the study of fuel problems and to a host of incremental improvements on the automobile. The fruits of these investigations finally gave General Motors a product to defeat the Model T in the marketplace, the "secret weapon" the copper-cooled car had never become.

Naturally, the project was not a total loss. As with any technical failure, lessons were learned and ideas for future projects salvaged. Many of Kettering's later triumphs owed something to the copper-cooled engine. Durex, an oilless bearing, first appeared on the overhead camshaft on the engine.[93] New cylinder metals came out of the project. These efforts later contributed to the use of titanium and various alloys in cylinders. The metallurgical experience gained in manufacturing the brazed-copper fins helped in the development of permanent molds for brakedrums. A system for torsionally balancing highly stressed rotating parts like crankshafts also grew out of this project.[94]

More important, perhaps, Kettering and the corporation learned valuable lessons about coordinating research and production teams. In response to the tensions created by the controversy, Sloan suggested formation of a General Technical Committee to initiate contact between the operating divisions and research at the laboratories. In a letter circulated to a number of top executives in September 1923, Sloan proposed:

1. That co-operation shall be established between the Car Divisions and the Engineering Departments within the Corporation, including the engineering and research activities of the General Motors Research Corporation and that cooperation shall take the form of a Committee to be established to be termed the General Technical Committee.

2. The Committee will consist as to principle, of the Chief Engineers of each Car Division and certain additional members.[95]

The chief divisional engineers, Kettering and his top staff members, and selected general officers of the corporation met, under Sloan's leadership, as the General Technical Committee on September 14, 1923. At first the committee served largely as an engineering seminar. Topics of current interest were discussed; brakes, steering mechanisms, lubrication, metallurgical advances. Longer-range plans included a proving ground (a welcome improvement after the back roads of Ohio) and fuel research.[96] This administrative experiment was quite successful and proved its worth in subsequent engineering campaigns.

The failure of the copper-cooled engine taught hard lessons as well. Kettering learned that the development process could be unexpectedly difficult. When he first conceived of the air-cooled engine in 1919, he never imagined that incremental improvements would require so much time, or be so painful. It seemed, in his mind, only a short step from the initial inspiration to a successful engine. He thought that the fundamental principles were so sound that the process from laboratory to market would follow more or less automatically. Obviously, good fundamental engineering was not enough; the obstacles of development defeated him. With the typical myopia of a design engineer, he grossly underestimated the difficulty of converting a prototype into a reliable, mass-produced article ready for sale to the public.

The controversy also illustrated the conflicting demands placed on Kettering in his dual role as businessman/investor and engineer. Despite his enthusiasm for any particular project, sooner or later he faced the bottom line of economic calculation. The conflict between the laboratory and the divisions created a situation in which the technical success, and thus the profitability of the copper-cooled car, was endangered. Consequently, the project had to be dropped, however great his personal enthusiasm. He never fully acknowledged this conflict, however. Kettering thought and continued to think that good engineering would always be good business. He never admitted that the copper-cooled automobile was anything less than a technical success, and years after everyone else had forgotten about the project, he still maintained that the idea should be resurrected. Only preoccupation with more successful ventures spared him further embarrassment. The basic problem remained corporate politics, not engineering, and even a good innovation could not overcome the opposition.

In retrospect, the project also suggests a characteristic of professional engineering behavior that is easily overlooked, one that Kettering would never have admitted. For the copper-cooled car, pride, jealousy, and simple petulance played as large a role in determining the destiny of the project as thermal efficiency or rated horsepower.

Although the motives of all the project's participants can never be fully known, it does seem that objective evaluations of hard data did not completely determine the outcome. Ironically, personal motives and subjective evaluations could often be concealed behind technical jargon and well-ordered equations. The same problem would hinder Kettering in later projects too, though never to the same extent. Perhaps these tensions are an inherent problem of corporate research.

General Electric faced similar difficulties with its scientific staff and its engineering departments.[97] Group organization and dynamics, while difficult to assess, may be the key. Perhaps engineers develop group loyalties stronger even than corporate ties. Certainly Kettering's staff showed a loyalty and esprit de corps more appropriate to a military command.

General Motors, and Kettering too, eventually benefited from a better understanding of how to manage research and development. The paralyzing conflict between design and production engineers gradually gave way to cooperation. The Technical Committee helped coordinate future engineering projects and opened better and more formal channels of communication between technical staffs.

General Motors was not the first corporation to institutionalize research, but it was one of the first to realize the necessity of integrating research with production and marketing. By doing this, the Technical Committee improved the management of technological innovation throughout the corporation. That, in turn, increased the prospects of success for Kettering's future innovations as they took the treacherous path from laboratory to market. So while the copper-cooled car was a failure, it was the sort of failure Kettering could build on. "You must learn how to fail intelligently," he said, "for failing is one of the greatest arts in the world."[98]

7 / STUDYING THE KNOCKS

For his presidential address to the Society of Automotive Engineers in 1918, Kettering chose a topic of current and compelling interest, the fuel shortage. The internal combustion engine, already a keystone of the American economy and in Kettering's view "the most wonderful thing that has ever been given to mankind," was threatened by a petroleum crisis. Wartime fuel needs and an apparently insatiable demand for automobiles had combined to put a severe strain on world oil reserves. As Kettering reminded his audience, the future growth of the automobile industry depended upon a speedy solution to this crisis.[1]

In the years immediately following the war, the remedies independently pursued by oil companies and automotive designers tended to work at cross-purposes. Automotive engineers wanted to increase compression ratios, the cheapest and easiest way to improve the power, efficiency, and economy of an internal combustion engine. Oil companies, however, could only meet short-term demand by refining more gasoline from each barrel of oil. In practice, this meant including a greater percentage of less volatile distillates in the final product. These poorer grades of gasoline did not burn as easily and aggravated knock, a perplexing malfunction of gasoline engines violent enough to crack pistons, usually accompanied by overheating and loss of power. Since an engine's tendency to knock rose rapidly with increasing compression ratios, engineers' plans to curb the fuel shortage by boosting compression were unfortunately restricted.[2]

Studies of the fuel situation which Kettering finished in early 1920, just after taking office as head of General Motors research, concluded that "this year will see the maximum production of petroleum that this country will ever know."[3] Since this pessimistic estimate was corroborated even by such usually unruffled sources as *Scientific American*, the studies convinced Kettering that fuels and engines demanded top corporate priority.[4]

Kettering brought to this important investigation several years of experience in studying the relationship of fuels and engines, and the conviction, based on this experience, that knock was somehow related to the fuel and not to the motor. This deceptively simple idea was still very rare among Kettering's colleagues but would ultimately allow him to piece together the puzzle. "He took us to the mountain and showed us the kingdom," one of Kettering's more poetic associates later declared.[5]

Convinced that the problem was chemical, Kettering somewhat surprisingly turned not to an experienced chemist but to his twenty-seven-year-old mechanical engineer, Thomas Midgley. When he received the assignment, Midgley protested that he knew practically nothing about petroleum chemistry and very little about internal combustion engines. Perhaps it would be wiser to enlist the services of an acknowledged expert, he argued. Any chemist, Kettering firmly explained to his young colleague, would "come in with a pack on his back; we're going to make a very steep climb here and it may be that that very pack is going to keep us from getting up. Let's you and I go up and survey the road without any packs on our back and then we'll get some chemists."[6] Thus did Kettering warn of the pitfalls of preconception.

Still, he was not sure exactly what they should be looking for. He assumed that enough trials of different fuels would reveal the common denominator of knock. So he set up a single-cylinder engine, equipped it with variable compression, and had his assistants begin testing different fuels. To visitors who wondered why he did not experiment with a full-sized engine, Kettering joked that he was not smart enough for that, and if he could only understand what happened in a one-cylinder engine, he would be doing well.[7]

To better understand what was going on inside that one cylinder in the fleeting one- or two-thousandths of a second of combustion, Kettering bought a Dobbie-McInnes indicator, an instrument for measuring pressure in a cylinder at changing volume. Comparisons of pressure-volume cards for normal and knocking engines showed that knock was a very specific problem. It was different from preignition, a premature ignition of the fuel before the spark that contemporary engineers often confused with knock. Rather, knock occurred only after the piston reached top dead center. Further trials pinned down knock to a narrow area of combustion and cleared up much early confusion.[8] Yet while these tests helped show what knock was not, they did not reveal what it was, nor what caused it.

Kettering, though he always downplayed the role of theory in engineering, was never without a theory himself, and his method was actually quite different from the cut-and-try method he often espoused. Like most researchers, he began with analogies. To make sense of his early data, he compared combustion to a problem in cooking. Fuel molecules, like potatoes, came in various shapes and sizes. And so two fuels, like two bushels of potatoes, could be put in the same "oven" and yet cook differently because while they might have the same mean weight, their compositions could be very different.[9]

Such analogies led Kettering to rank fuels by physical characteristics—composition, specific gravity, boiling point—to see how these corresponded with knock tendency. However, the engine trials showed no consistency to such rankings.

Kettering then turned in another direction. He noticed that fuels less prone to knocking, like high-quality gasoline, seemed to be more volatile than ones that knocked badly. Perhaps, he reasoned, nonknocking fuels evaporated easily and completely in the engine and formed a homogeneous mixture with the air, and so burned smoothly.

Knocking fuels, on the other hand, could remain on the cylinder walls in the form of tiny droplets. After the spark, as the piston began to recede, these droplets—exposed to the high temperature and pressure—could burn spontaneously and cause knock.[10] Kettering relayed his idea to Midgley, who, also working by analogy, from plants that send up red leaves in the spring to gather more sunlight and warm themselves, guessed that adding dye would absorb radiant energy, vaporize the droplets, and smooth combustion.

In his eagerness to test the theory Midgley rushed to the laboratory one Saturday to run a trial with iodine, the only gasoline-soluble dye he could find on short notice. To his delight, the iodine actually worked, though subsequent tests with other dyes showed no effect on knock. At this point Kettering and Midgley displayed the flexibility and insight that would ultimately lead to success. Rather than assume that the analogy was more than that and not merely a convenient framework for a later theory, they were able to isolate the significant fact in the experimental failure—that a chemical additive had reduced knock—and discard the rest.[11]

The constant interplay between analogy and evidence led to a new theory. While observing combustion through a spectroscope, Kettering thought he noticed a high concentration of acetylene. That observation led him to suspect that certain fuels were breaking down into secondary explosive compounds which then caused the knock. Chemical additives like iodine worked, he speculated, by holding the maximum temperature in the combustion chamber below some minimum needed to create these secondary compounds.[12]

Most of Kettering's chemists took issue with this idea, and doubted the Boss had even actually observed acetylene. However, the theory did offer an appealing link between knocking and preignition. Carbonized engines were known to knock more than clean ones, and Kettering's theory explained why: carbon insulated the combustion chamber, kept the temperature higher, and formed the explosive secondary compounds. So the search was on for an additive that would keep combustion temperature low.

In detail, each of Kettering's theories was wrong. But in a fundamental sense he was on the right track. For all these theories focused, in one way or another, on the relationship between the chemistry of a fuel and how it was affected by chemical additives or "dopes." This was not at all obvious; it grew directly out of Kettering's idea that knock had something to do with the specific properties of the fuel. So as the chemists tested one compound group after another looking for an antiknock additive, always with an anxious Kettering peering over their shoulders with his inevitable question—"What's new? What's new?"—they were guided by more than a hunch. Each theory, though primitive, gave meaning to the results of the engine trials. Kettering liked to call this a "scientific foxhunt."

Not long into the chase, Thomas Boyd stumbled upon the knock-suppressing qualities of aniline in his investigation of nitrogen compounds. Its effects were so much more impressive than any previous compound that after comprehensive engine tests, Kettering sent a sample to the Hudson Motor Company for independent evaluation. When Hudson confirmed the laboratory's results, Kettering patented aniline as an antiknock additive. [13]

Though aniline was hardly marketable at this point, its announcement as an antiknock additive caught the oil establishment by surprise. Having neglected fundamental research for so long, the major oil companies faced a possible coup led by a virtually unknown automotive engineer. Frank Howard, a patent attorney in Chicago, won himself a job as head of research for Standard Oil of New Jersey by warning one of its vice-presidents about Kettering's patent: "Unless the fuel producers themselves get into this work of investigating the properties of their fuels, there is a good chance that they may have to pay tribute to others." [14]

Kettering's breakthrough also attracted attention from his new partners at Du Pont. Du Pont was lukewarm to the idea of producing aniline itself. Several chemists pointed out that the price of aniline was closely tied to the cost of dyestuffs, and would soar under pressure from automotive use. Further, Du Pont knew Kettering was at work on substitutes which might leave it at any time with a huge commitment to an obsolete product. But Charles M. Stine, Du Pont's research director, was anxious to cooperate on a longer-range effort. Several trips back and forth between Dayton and Wilmington, Delaware sealed the bargain and divided spheres of responsibility. For his part, Kettering realized that the capability of producing a liter or two of antiknock additive in the laboratory was vastly different from profitable, large-scale chemical production, and was equally eager to cooperate.[15]

Aniline was costly, smelled horrible in the exhaust, corroded most engine metals, and gummed up nearly every device used to inject it into the engine. Under other circumstances, Kettering would never have seriously considered marketing it. The fuel crisis, though, demanded action, and while he instructed Midgley and Boyd to look for something better, Kettering prepared to exploit the only remedy discovered so far. With aniline additives, compression ratios could be raised and precious fuel saved.

To build a broader base for his idea, Kettering began promoting it within the automobile industry. His first prospects, naturally, were his new associates in the General Motors divisions. He sent samples to various divisional engineers. Cadillac's technical manager, E. C. Garland, reported aniline's effects on one bad knocker as "little short of magic,"[16] leading its promoter to exclaim, "I am sure that in the development of these anti-knock injectors, we have opened up a new phase of the internal combustion engine."[17] But despite such enthusiasm, no one was willing to underwrite the commercial development of aniline, and Kettering had to return to the laboratory to look for something better.

Kettering continued to broadcast his basic message to the technical community at large, speaking before the American Petroleum Institute, the SAE, and similar professional gatherings.[18] His humorous, fast-paced lectures amused and enlightened his audiences. Even people who had heard the same stories several times chuckled at the third and fourth retelling. But behind the humor was a serious and timely theme. If the oil and automotive companies did not move quickly to stem the fuel crisis, disastrous economic and social consequences would surely follow.

These speaking engagements offered splendid opportunities for Olive to sample the social delights of New York City and relieve the boredom of an empty Ridgeleigh Terrace. Meetings and business conferences kept her husband occupied most days, but there was always shopping and the theater in company with other corporate wives such as Helena Raskob. For such an ardent fan of Broadway, the New York excursions were particularly welcome. During one week she attended no less than six performances. On those rare evenings when business did not interfere, her wandering spouse joined her for dancing, one of their few shared amusements. Olive looked forward to these evenings for weeks, and as she once confessed to J. J. Raskob, "I sincerely hope we can have some dancing as I am sure you enjoy 'tripping the light fantastic' as much as I do." [19]

Meticulous in his work, Kettering was rather casual when it came to social obligations. He often found himself without a wallet and had to ask his fellow executives for a short-term loan. After one particularly embarrassing episode, Olive explained to Raskob, "I am mortified to 'pieces' to think Mr. Ket didn't settle for those tickets you kindly secured. Will you please send me the amount and I will pay it." [20] Kettering's personal secretary finally squared the matter, writing to Raskob, "At Mrs. Kettering's request I am enclosing Mr. Kettering's check for $73.00 to refund you money spent, I believe, for theatre tickets. Mrs. Kettering asked me to tell you that the children would have to go without shoes but this bill be paid. She also said something about having to have a new fur coat." [21]

Professional meetings kept Kettering in touch with a worldwide network of researchers working on the fuel problem. In England, a small band of consulting engineers led by the eminent Harry Ricardo was pursuing a line of inquiry quite different from the General Motors effort, attacking the puzzle with mechanics instead of chemistry. Through a careful study of spark plug placement and valve position and close attention to combustion chamber design, they developed a "turbulent" head which swirled the charge and reduced knock significantly. [22]

Interestingly, both Kettering and Ricardo dropped the knock investigation, at least temporarily, in favor of an alcohol will-o'-the-wisp. At almost precisely the same time, both researchers settled on alcohol as the key to unshackling the internal combustion engine from nonrenewable fossil fuels. Ethanol never knocked, it could be produced by distilling waste vegetable material, and it was almost pollution free. Ricardo compared alcohol fuel to living within a man's means, implying that fossil fuels were a foolish squandering of capital. Echoing these sentiments, Kettering wrote, "vegetation offers a source of tremendous quantities of liquid fuel, the utilization of which awaits only a proper cheapening and simplification of the process of converting cellulose to a liquid suitable for motor fuel."[23]

Ricardo convinced the British government to undertake extensive research into the conversion of molasses to ethanol, to alleviate a domestic fuel shortage and bolster the declining market for West Indies molasses in Prohibition America. Kettering spoke out against taxes on alcohol as an impediment to fuel research, talked with several dealers selling a mixture of alcohol and gasoline called Alcogas, and designed a special carburetor to accommodate the alcohol fuel.[24]

The popular press snapped up such prophecies and widely predicted that the conversion of waste to motor fuels would rejuvenate the depressed family farm. But as Kettering foresaw, alcohol needed a vastly cheaper and more energy-efficient production process before it could be practical.

The details of integrating the Dayton companies into the General Motors family and organizing the copper-cooled engine project began to occupy most of Kettering's time, and he became a less frequent visitor to the antiknock laboratory in Moraine City. But at least every other day while he was in town, the Boss poked his head into the doorway of the laboratory and sat down with Midgley and Boyd for an hour or so to discuss recent progress.

Their reports, though, were far from encouraging. After a year of virtually no improvement, Kettering called his fuel section together for his version of a pep talk. "By God, if you don't come up with something within the next three to six months you're all fired," he announced. And as Hochwalt, who had recently joined the staff full time, recalled, "he meant it!"[25]

Since the nitrogen compounds were obviously going nowhere, Midgley shifted the research to another compound group. One promising group was the organometallics. Several of these metal-carbon bonds suppressed knock well, though not as well as aniline, and

Midgley hoped that a thorough investigation of organometallics might yield a superior antiknock additive. Hochwalt devised a zinc ethyl alkalating technique for synthesizing the compounds, and the investigation was under way. They caught fire in air, however; the reaction was so hazardous that for a time Hochwalt refused Kettering admission to the laboratory. "I wouldn't have allowed him in the laboratory, then," he recalled, "because he'd have killed himself."[26] Some of the new additives did suppress knock fairly well, though not spectacularly, and at least the work again appeared to be heading in the proper direction.

The project's chemical sophistication was rapidly outrunning its sponsor's ability to keep abreast of its progress with his semiweekly chats alone. Still, Kettering was an eager student, and Boyd and Hochwalt were able to teach him enough chemistry so that he could contribute some important suggestions. On a train ride home from New York in April 1921, according to his own account, Kettering noticed a newspaper story about a University of Wisconsin professor and his newly discovered selenium compound. The researcher claimed that selenium oxychloride was a universal solvent, leading several chemists to ask jokingly what he planned to keep it in. Kettering seriously doubted its powers as a solvent, but he recognized that the compound closely resembled the organometallics Boyd was testing.[27] On a hunch, Kettering told the researchers to try selenium oxychloride as an antiknock agent. None of the chemists expected much success, for both oxygen and chlorine were known knock inducers, but to humor the Boss they tried it. On April 6, 1921, Boyd's first engine test revealed an astonishing knock resistance.[28] His trial also vindicated the discoverer's solvent claims; the selenium oxychloride quickly ate away the engine's metal parts.

Two days later Hochwalt prepared an organic derivative of tellurium, a neighbor of selenium in the periodic table and one the researchers hoped would prove less corrosive. Indeed, not only was tellurium easier on engine parts; it suppressed knock five times as effectively as selenium. An excited Thomas Midgley fired off a letter to Charles Stine at Du Pont saying, "we have recently discovered an anti-knock material which is twenty-four times as strong as aniline volumetrically. This material looks very, very practical, and I feel sure that this is going to radically change our previous plans, obsoleting the injector; in fact, obsoleting the use of aniline, or tar products, in any way, shape, or form."[29]

These various new antiknock additives did suppress knock well and allowed the researchers to raise the compression ratio of a test Chevrolet from 4.1:1 to 7.0:1, but they did not behave nearly as well as Midgley's report implied. After a brief road trial of the Chevrolet, the testers dubbed it "the Goat" for its hill-climbing ability and its horrible-smelling exhaust.[30] This evil odor, smelling suspiciously of garlic, left such a residue on anyone nearby that the researchers called it tellurium poisoning. Boyd later remembered, "In those days everyone in the laboratory carried an atmosphere with him, and his coming was announced before he fully arrived. . . . Some of the boys would walk a mile rather than subject themselves to the ordeal of riding on a street car."[31] Deluged with complaints from angry wives and informed that Raritan Copper Works, the nation's largest supplier of tellurium, could provide only 30 tons a year, enough to treat only a small percentage of America's annual gasoline consumption, Kettering called off this branch of the investigation.

During the next months, the researchers attempted to put a little more science in their trial and error. They thought one important step in this direction would be finding a more reliable measure of knock. In the prospecting stages, the "listening" method was one they tried. The observer merely listened to the ping and tried to describe it in some sort of qualitative way, for instance "slight pinging," "decided detonation," or "very violent knock." Pressure-volume cards helped somewhat, but their impressive graphs were scarcely more accurate than a human ear. Other indicators they used measured the temperature of the cylinder wall, for knock was known to cause overheating, but heat was only one of many symptoms of knock and not a very reliable one.[32]

Midgley and Boyd finally devised an instrument to match the increasing chemical sophistication of the antiknock project, the "bouncing pin" indicator. A small rod on the top of the test engine cylinder head was jostled by knock and completed an electric circuit.

The circuit then caused a sulfuric acid and water solution to emit hydrogen that was collected in a graduated cylinder. Thus the chemists could compare quantitatively the effectiveness of different dopes.

A pattern slowly emerged from the mass of data. In July 1921, Boyd noticed an unusual and potentially significant relationship between known additive compounds. When he arranged the elements of the periodic table in ascending order of atomic number and checked off the elements that formed molecules of more than one atom in the gaseous phase, a pattern of triads appeared. The first group, after hydrogen, included nitrogen, oxygen, and fluorine. Arsenic, selenium, and bromine comprised the second triad; antimony, tellurium, and iodine the third. A closer look at the triads revealed a remarkable coincidence. Within each group the lightest element reduced knock the least and the heaviest element suppressed knock the most.[33]

Other periodic table arrangements disclosed further "coincidences." The most interesting was the grouping of antiknock elements under a novel periodic table assembled by Robert Wilson of MIT. Using Irving Langmuir's studies of valence and atomic structure, Wilson ordered the elements by the number of vacant spaces in the outer electron shells. When Boyd and Midgley marked the antiknock elements (or more correctly the elements composing antiknock additives), they found that they were all located in the same corner of the table.[34]

For five months, Hochwalt prepared organometallic compounds of these elements. Boyd dutifully tested them with the new indicator. Kettering, who according to one of the researchers hardly knew the difference between organometallics and aniline, watched the work with continuing financial and spiritual support. "He was the inspiration of the group and also got the money, which was the important thing, to carry on the work," another researcher recalled.[35]

Actually, Kettering contributed much more than money and moral support. His broadmindedness and vision frequently overcame his shortcomings in specific chemical knowledge. Under the tutelage of Hochwalt and Boyd, he had learned quickly and offered some surprisingly good insights and suggestions. "He would bring out things in an individual just by his talking," Hochwalt later said. "He looked at the total picture and we were so intense on our specific little spot that we were working on . . . that there was a tendency for us to become a little narrow." [36]

In late November, one of Kettering's literature searches uncovered an obscure organometallic lead compound called tetraethyl lead (TEL). On December 8, Hochwalt prepared a few cubic centimeters of TEL by dropping zinc ethyl onto lead chloride. [37] The next morning Boyd tested the compound in one of the laboratory engines. His laboratory notebook recorded a knock-suppressing tendency fifty times as effective as aniline. A series of dilutions still could not blunt its ability. Even one part in 1,300 parts of gasoline suppressed knock completely.

The commercial possibilities of the compound were immediately obvious. The laboratory sent a telegram to Midgley, then in New York. Two days later Kettering returned from a business trip. Everyone met in the Boss's office. Midgley extended his hand to Kettering and shouted, "Shake! We really have uncovered something now!" and scratched out Boyd's data on the blackboard. Within minutes, the Boss assembled everyone within earshot for a lecture on the importance of the discovery. [38] Yet he never attributed any flash of genius to this moment. Reviewing the episode in later years he said, "It would be difficult to go back over the years of research on tetraethyl lead and find out just what time such a 'flash' came, because it was just a succession of failures, with just enough success to keep us going." [39]

Devising an economical way to produce TEL proved nearly as arduous as discovering it. Hochwalt's procedure yielded only one liter at a time, and even this tedious process relied as much on luck as on science. When Kettering shifted the fuel section into more spacious quarters at the Moraine plant and the researchers reassembled the chemical apparatus, the genie in Hochwalt's equipment suddenly disappeared. No amount of coaxing and readjustment could entice it back. Finally, Kettering demanded a detailed written account of the move in fifteen-minute intervals from everyone involved. Careful cross-checking uncovered the substitution of a glass funnel broken in transit with a copper one. The tiny bit of copper washed into the batches from the funnel had poisoned the reaction.[40]

On another occasion, the chemists nearly destroyed the new laboratory in an attempt to speed the reaction. They mixed ethyl nitrate with a sodium lead alloy and placed it in a pressure vessel. Slowly at first, then with alarming swiftness, the pressure rose. Before they could release the safety valve the autoclave exploded, shattering glassware and smashing fifty windows. Miraculously, no one was seriously injured.[41]

In searching for the key to production of TEL in large quantities, the chemists tried half a dozen reactions, but found none better than Hochwalt's original process. Robert E. Wilson, director of MIT's Research Laboratory of Applied Chemistry and one of Kettering's many academic contacts, visited the Dayton laboratory in early February 1922. After extended discussions with Kettering on the TEL production process, Wilson returned to Boston with a $2,400 contract for applied research on the problem. At the same time, Pierre du Pont began asking some hard questions about the commercial future of the $120,000 research investment at Dayton.[42]

Throughout the spring of 1922, chemists at Du Pont, MIT, and General Motors looked for what they all knew would be at the heart of a cost-efficient TEL reaction, a proper catalyst to cause ethyl iodide to react with sodium-lead. Midgley received an unexpected boost in this direction in a chance conversation with Charles H. Milligan at the spring meeting of the American Chemical Society in April 1922.[43] When Midgley told him about the frustrating trials with TEL, Milligan suggested a series of normal propyl compounds to add stability to the reaction. Following Milligan's advice, the Dayton chemists successfully synthesized the first one-gallon batch of TEL on May 5, after a twenty-seven-hour vigil attended by nearly everyone at the laboratory, including Kettering. The new process speeded reaction time, increased yields, and reduced cost so significantly that by May the fuel section had expanded production to several gallons a day.

Encouraged by these developments, Kettering revived the promotional campaign he had abandoned during the bleaker days of aniline. He outlined the advantages of TEL in a letter to Pierre du Pont and encouraged him to support an experimental production plant.[44] He also shared the General Motors catalyst breakthrough with du Pont. To free the Dayton chemists from the demands of chemical engineering, Kettering and the chairman devised a scheme whereby the Du Pont Company would manufacture the raw TEL and Kettering's chemists would focus on applications research, that is, how the additive would behave in an automobile. Early testing on leaded fuel in several company cars produced unexpected spark plug corrosion and exhaust valve unseating, difficulties that would take Kettering and his men several years to eliminate.

Meanwhile, Kettering developed a new system for delivering the TEL to the gasoline tank (at a squeeze from the driver a hand pump discharged enough additive to treat five gallons) and planned the construction of a pilot blending plant in Dayton. By August, raw TEL was arriving at the Dayton blending plant in fifty-gallon batches from Du Pont.

To spur further interest in his new product, Kettering sent samples of TEL to several influential oil company executives. Lacking even a rudimentary knowledge of antiknock additives, these amateur testers badly abused the product. One executive, not bothering to consult with his chemical experts, poured the diatomaceous earth packing into his tank instead of the TEL and promptly clogged his fuel line. Another put the TEL in dirty storage tanks where the antiknock additive sank below a small pool of water and failed to mix with the gasoline. Naturally he found no difference between leaded and unleaded gasoline until a personal visit from Midgley unraveled the mystery.[45]

News of such an important discovery spread quickly through the automotive world, giving rise to all sorts of wild speculation. Kettering liked to demonstrate the additive's potency for laboratory visitors by sprinkling a few drops near the carburetor of a badly knocking engine. Midgley offered the first public demonstrations of TEL at the SAE summer meeting in 1922. The work so impressed the American Chemical Society that it later awarded Midgley its Nichols Medal for his contributions to the campaign. Journalistic interest also ran high, and to suppress irresponsible rumors Kettering invited an editor of the *National Petroleum News* for a private interview.[46]

The resulting story quieted speculation well enough, but it recounted the development so accurately that several General Motors executives openly feared that the secret was in jeopardy. Patent Department head James McEvoy was so alarmed that he complained to vice-president Charles S. Mott, pointing out that several innovations, including a fan-belt design for the copper-cooled engine, had already been stolen from the laboratory. When the story finally reached du Pont, he confronted Kettering.[47]

Lashing out at his accusers in a scathing letter to the chairman, Kettering pointed out that the gossip was completely unfounded. "The seriousness of Mr. McEvoy's letter, as I have mentioned before, lies in three points," Kettering countercharged. "(1) Mr. McEvoy apparently knows nothing of patents and patent laws nor the method in which inventions are generated: (2) he has not had any experience at all in the processes of research: (3) he has not given you the actual facts at all in making his statements and the conclusions which he has drawn from his presented facts are not consistent with them." He then closed with a thinly veiled threat of resignation. "If you insist upon McEvoy's handling our patent work," he wrote, "you will have to reorganize the research laboratory completely."[48]

This would not be the last of Kettering's temper tantrums, though Pierre du Pont eventually managed to smooth his ruffled feathers this time. McEvoy continued to head the Patent Department of General Motors for many years with the utmost competence, and no one ever stole the secret of TEL. The incident served principally to remind everyone that Kettering ran research pretty much as he liked, exploiting his highest corporate connections when he felt strongly about something and venting his fierce temper at anyone trespassing in his domain.

On February 1, 1923, a new sign in Willard Talbott's service station in Dayton advertised "Ethyl" gasoline at $.25 a gallon, Regular for $.21, High Test for $.25, and New Navy Benzol Blend for $.27. Kettering had coined the Ethyl brand name himself and convinced Talbott, a personal friend, to carry the experimental gasoline. By ten o'clock Talbott had not sold a single gallon of leaded fuel, and several embarrassed researchers observing the historic moment decided to promote the product more vigorously. They approached each customer, "not exaggerating the benefits they would derive" they later told Kettering, and peddled seventy gallons during the next three hours. A newspaper supplement in the afternoon inspired a steady stream of customers, and by closing Talbott had sold 310 gallons of leaded gasoline.[49]

For the next two months, Talbott marketed Ethyl fuel under the close scrutiny of Kettering and the chemists. In early April, Sloan and Kettering met to plan a new corporate home for this successful product. They agreed that a new company, the General Motors Chemical Company, should be established to blend and market TEL and that it should be housed within the Research Corporation until it was capable of standing on its own. Nonetheless it would keep its own books and be expected to operate on a profit-and-loss basis like any other corporate division. Kettering became president of the company and Midgley vice-president.[50]

By accepting the presidency of the General Motors Chemical Company, Kettering moved into an unusually active managerial role. Midgley supervised day-to-day operations. But to Kettering fell the responsibility for negotiating sales territories, apportioning research on chemical engineering and applications, and deciding how the company could best exploit its new chemical discoveries and patents.

A scramble for spheres of marketing influence by the major oil companies presented the new president with a managerial challenge. Although he hardly qualified as a seasoned corporation politician, Kettering did surprisingly well in his first diplomatic mission to the oil industry. He met with representatives of the major companies;W. L. Mellon, president of the Gulf Oil Company; Frank Howard, vice-president of development for Standard Oil of New Jersey; and Robert Wilson, new research director of Standard Oil of Indiana. In allocating exclusive territories among them, Kettering weighed research commitment and patent position heavily. Consequently, Jersey Standard won the eastern market on the strength of a recently patented high pressure and temperature production process for TEL.[51] Wilson and his company secured an exclusive license in eleven midwestern states. Mellon went home disappointed.[52] So did Kettering's brother Adam, who tried to obtain a license for his Chevrolet dealership in Ashland, Ohio.[53]

President Kettering worried about the limited capacity of the Dayton blending plant. Negotiations with Jersey Standard over a combined manufacturing and marketing effort dragged on through the fall and winter of 1923 and left General Motors Chemical with a serious backlog of orders.[54] Pressed by increasing demand for leaded gasoline, General Motors finally committed itself to union with the oil company after more than a year of wavering. Each corporation subscribed to one-half of a stock offering in a new company, Ethyl Corporation.[55] Kettering was elected president of the new corporation; Frank Howard and Thomas Midgley were elected vice-presidents. Ethyl then shifted all blending operations from Dayton to Jersey Standard's plant in Bayway, New Jersey.

Success had temporarily diverted the research staff from the unresolved health hazards posed by TEL. Lead compounds, especially in an oil-soluble state where they could be absorbed directly into the skin, were known to be poisonous. To prevent accidental contamination, the fuel section workers had donned rubber coats, boots, and gloves, and had exercised extreme caution in handling the substance.

Despite the precautions, Midgley and Hochwalt, who had been working with TEL longer than anyone else, began complaining of lead poisoning as early as January 1923. "After working with the concentrated materials for a year," Midgley told Kettering, "I find myself to have suffered to some extent from organic lead poisoning. . . . I am forced to take a short vacation in order to throw off the toxic effect of the lead compounds."[56] At Midgley's urging, Hochwalt extended his February honeymoon to six weeks for the same reason.[57] And health conditions in the Dayton blending plant were much worse than in the laboratory. By June 1924, 2 men had died and about 60 others had been seriously affected.

Kettering recognized that the health issue could significantly undermine his nationwide marketing effort. To settle questions that had been raised, he hired two medical consultants, Robert A. Kehoe of the University of Cincinnati medical school and R. R. Sayers of the U. S. Bureau of Mines, to evaluate the safety risks of TEL, both in manufacturing and in general use. Sayers looked into the effects on test animals of leaded gasoline exhaust at various concentrations; Kehoe examined about 20 garage mechanics and drivers who had been exposed to TEL over the past two years. Neither found any evidence of lead contamination in their subjects, and recommended only better safety precautions within the blending plant.

Yet only weeks after getting this report, Kettering faced a major crisis with Ethyl. An accident in the new Standard Oil TEL blending plant in Bayway, New Jersey killed 10 men and sent 50 others to the hospital with acute lead poisoning, many in straight jackets to control their delirium. Headlines dubbed leaded gasoline "Looney Gas," and shocking cartoons depicted Ethyl as a greedy giant squeezing blood from an innocent public. Even medical experts contributed to public alarm with published interviews claiming, among other things, that "if an automobile . . . using this gas should have engine trouble along Fifth Avenue and release a quantity of gas with the lead mixture, it would cause gas poisoning and mania to persons along the avenue."[58] New York City quickly, and understandably, passed an ordinance prohibiting the manufacture, sale, and use of leaded gasoline. Shortly thereafter, Ethyl shut down its production plants and stopped marketing leaded gasoline in most parts of the country.

The suspension of manufacturing knocked the wind from Kettering's otherwise full sails. His drives to Detroit with young colleagues lost their spark. Rather than entertaining his companions with marvelous tales, the Boss just glowered and sped down the road muttering about government interference and public ignorance.[59]

In contrast to his private silence, Kettering became more active as a public spokesman. Speaking to influential business and professional groups, he warned that an innovation crucial to the economy and the military must not be halted by public hysteria, especially since the health hazards were as yet unsubstantiated. Health risks were simply an inevitable part of progress, he said. Unless Americans were willing to forgo the car, which Kettering thought inconceivable, gasoline extenders like TEL would have to be tolerated. "Many years of research may be necessary before the actual development of such a [petroleum] substitute can start," he told the American Chemical Society. "More years of development may be necessary before practical results of a quantitative nature are obtained." So until that time, he suggested that the benefits of TEL far outweighed its risks.[60]

Meanwhile, the Surgeon General's office opened an investigation into the TEL affair, and invited representatives from Ethyl, General Motors, and Standard Oil, the companies' medical consultants, and medical experts in industrial hygiene from leading universities.[61]

The participants met on May 10, 1925. From Kettering's opening remarks on the history of TEL, in which he stressed the economic importance of his innovation, the conference was sharply divided. On one side were industry representatives who argued that the social benefits of TEL outweighed its possible, and unproven, risks. On the other, spokesmen for the Harvard School of Public Health and labor organizations contended that health issues were paramount. Several independent researchers attacked the studies by Kehoe and Sayers, pointing out flaws in methodology and sampling. Both sides claimed to speak for the public interest; they disagreed on what that interest might be, and where the burden of proof should fall. Frank Howard spoke for Kettering and the industrialists, claiming, "Our continued development of motor fuels is essential to our independence. . . . It must be not fears, but facts that we are guided by. . . . This development must be stopped, if it is to be stopped at all, by proof of the facts." Industrial hygiene experts protested that by the time all the "facts" were in, it might be too late. "It seems to me that it must first be proved that it is not poisonous, because of the tremendously diffuse results that this amount of lead scattered in fine powder over a long period might cause," noted one physician from Harvard University.[62]

Public opinion and expectations were on the side of industry this time, and the burden of proof fell on TEL's critics. The Surgeon General organized a follow-up study to settle the health question definitely, and asked an independent panel of experts to conduct it. The study looked at 250 men, half of whom had worked with TEL for at least three years. By later standards, the analytical techniques would be judged crude, and by any standards the sample was small and the time frame rather short. Nonetheless, when the committee presented its report in January 1926, it felt confident in recommending only better industrial safety standards, and concluded that "there are at present no good grounds for prohibiting the use of ethyl gasoline of the composition specified as a motor fuel, provided that its distribution and use are controlled by proper regulations." Kettering felt vindicated. A short while later Ethyl was back in business, and the health issue forgotten, at least until the 1960s. [63]

Shortly after, Kettering surrendered leadership of the Ethyl Corporation to Earle Webb, the former general attorney for General Motors. While he continued on for many years as a valued director, competing automotive projects were more compelling.

The drama of the health issue tended to overshadow an equally important campaign against the mechanical side effects of TEL. Kettering's first road tests in 1922 had disclosed an annoying tendency for the fuel to form a litharge, or glaze, in the combustion chamber. This lead coating fouled spark plugs, unseated exhaust valves, and disabled an otherwise healthy engine after a few miles. [64] Confident that if chemical correctives could cure knock, they could also cure the side effects of lead, Kettering asked Boyd to undertake another scientific foxhunt for a cure. With a combination of chemical insight and intuition, Boyd narrowed the search first to halide compounds. Carbon tetrachloride, he found, combined with the lead and carried it out the exhaust. Unfortunately, carbon tetrachloride could become perilously explosive. A container sent to Pierre du Pont blew up when a servant unwittingly left it too near a steam pipe. Another can went off in J. J. Raskob's garage, burning it to the ground. [65] Obviously, the chemists needed a more stable corrective.

A comprehensive study of the other possibilities undertaken jointly by the laboratory and several chemists on retainer at MIT discovered that ethyl bromide was a stable replacement for the explosive chlorine compounds. Road tests of a fleet of Dayton Power and Light Company trucks in the fall of 1923 confirmed the superiority of bromine correctives. [66]

Unfortunately, bromine was rare and expensive. In January 1924, Kettering and Midgley visited the Dow Chemical Company of Midland, Michigan, the nation's only large supplier of the substance, and received the gloomy news that Dow could promise only enough bromine to treat a small percentage of America's annual gasoline consumption. Kettering envisioned a market of something like 2 billion gallons a year and promptly halted the negotiations when he found Dow could not deliver.[67] Instead he hired a Cornell chemist, Wildner D. Bancroft, during the summer and set him to work looking into other correctives. Bancroft's suggestion—copper and sulfur compounds of chlorine—did not work nearly as well as bromine.

A bit discouraged, Kettering returned to Midland with Midgley and a representative of Jersey Standard in August. While President Herbert Dow still could not promise to meet the demand, he suggested seawater as a possible source of bromine. The element existed in great abundance there, though in very low concentrations.[68] On trapping and concentrating the bromine, Dow could offer no advice except pumping seawater into evaporating tanks and then extracting the element from the brine. "I suggested that we might consider this problem to be merely the pumping of the Pacific Ocean over the Rocky Mountains and letting it dry out," Midgley wryly recalled, "to which he replied that was just about what it amounted to. . . ."[69]

Kettering never accepted expert opinion as final, and on the train ride back to Dayton he and Midgley began discussing seriously the seawater extraction of bromine. Perhaps, they decided, a method of extracting the bromine directly could be devised. Back at the laboratory Kettering set Graham Edgar, another recent academic acquisition (University of Virginia), to work on the project.

In November 1924, Kettering left for Europe and North Africa to escape the pressure of the TEL affair and search for new sources of bromine in the event Edgar's research was not successful.[70] He brought Olive with him and put her up in the Ritz Hotel in Paris while he conducted business. She shopped, frequented the opera and symphony, and thoroughly enjoyed the role of a wealthy American abroad. He toured the French bromine mines of Ain-es-Serah in Tunis. Upon his return to Paris, he received a telegram from Jasper Crane, the European representative of Du Pont. Crane had heard rumors of a competing antiknock additive being developed in Germany and wanted Kettering to investigate. Kettering toured the production facility and watched a demonstration of the product, though the German chemists would not, of course, disclose its contents. Kettering strongly suspected that the additive was iron carbonyl, a remedy abandoned by General Motors because of its harsh treatment of spark plugs. (His suspicions were later confirmed. The German company eventually filed for a European license for TEL, though it marketed iron carbonyl in Europe for some time.) On the return voyage Olive caught "laryngitis and was unable to talk part of the way, which was quite a punishment for her," Kettering joked to one of his friends.[71]

Back in Dayton, Edgar had devised a promising method of extracting bromine from seawater. By adding chlorine and aniline, he obtained tribromoaniline, which could then be chemically induced to surrender its bromine. The Du Pont Company succumbed to Kettering's sales pitch for harvesting the seas, and put up $40,000 for the commercial development of the extraction process. The first pilot plant foundered on the shores of Maryland, a victim of excessive sand and suspended particles in the intake pipes.[72] On Irénée du Pont's advice, the plant was then squeezed aboard a converted lake steamer rechristened the *S. S. Ethyl* and sent to sea on March 20, 1925.[73] For two weeks, the craft plied the Gulf Stream waters two hundred miles off the Virginia coast, sucking the bromine-rich waters into the miniature chemical factory and trapping the precious element. One hundred thousand pounds of bromine later, the *Ethyl* steamed into Wilmington to cries from the press of "robbing Father Neptune" and wide predictions of harvesting gold from the seas.[74]

None of these fanciful dreams came to pass. The *Ethyl* never sailed again, though her maiden voyage convinced Herbert Dow that seawater extraction of bromine was possible and profitable. Dow offered a lower price on bromine and began a research effort to reduce cost and increase yields even further. Later, Ethyl and Dow Chemical joined in constructing a major bromine extraction plant near Kure Beach, North Carolina, thus assuring an adequate supply of halide corrective as sales of leaded gasoline took off in the 1930s.

To all this work Kettering lent an inquisitive mind and frequent fruitful suggestions. His familiar greeting in the laboratory signaled the beginning of yet another round of intense, probing questions. He dissected every aspect of every experiment down to unanswerable queries on the nature of catalysts, or friction on a molecular level.

His analyses were sometimes surprisingly fertile and kept up the spirits of his researchers during the dark days of repeated failure and public suspicion.

Only occasionally did Kettering's confidence sag privately. On a drive back from Detroit with Frederick Hooven, then a young mechanical engineer in the laboratory, he confessed, "Well, all I am is nothing but a goddam salesman." [75] Yet this self-appraisal, so negatively uttered, actually pointed to a strength of vital importance in the next phase of the TEL project. The success of the product would rest as heavily on Kettering's promotional abilities as it would on the chemical expertise on his staff.

From the beginning, promotional gimmicks marked the campaign. Boyd had very early suggested a red dye for TEL, not only to prolong shelf life but to distinguish leaded gasoline as a unique, and by implication better, product.

Bruce Barton, something of a gimmick himself, organized the formal advertising campaign. As a partner in Batten, Barton, Durstine, and Osborn, one of New York's most progressive agencies, Barton had made a name for himself peddling a form of pop religion as well as more prosaic material goods. In Barton's scheme, religion was a business and Jesus a master salesman. Kettering, whose own religious convictions tended toward agnosticism, felt a certain sympathy for Barton's God but very little for his copy. "I am extremely disappointed," Kettering wrote after seeing the first Ethyl advertisement in the *Saturday Evening Post*. "It looks as though it had been set up by a Chinaman." [76] After adding half a dozen suggestions for improvement he concluded with a sarcastic flourish, "You take any *Saturday Evening Post* and look through it and our stuff will grade about third rate. Of course, that may be all right; we may be a third rate concern, but I do not like to advertise it to the public, especially when you are supposed to have a first rate advertising agency." [77] When the dust settled, the copy had been revised and Kettering had once again demonstrated that he paid close attention to an area often overlooked by other technical men.

The General Motors divisions turned out to be harder to convince than the public. Kettering began fighting the production engineers even before TEL reached the market, and wholesale distribution only intensified the struggle. Wary of valve and spark plug trouble, the divisions preferred to let someone else take the commercial risk. They refused to redesign their engines to accommodate the leaded fuel and would not recommend leaded gasoline to their customers.

Tetraethyl lead could help remedy petroleum shortages only if automobile compression ratios were raised to increase fuel economy. That, unfortunately, required modifications and a degree of commitment the divisions seemed determined to avoid. "If we expect to capitalize upon the development of this material [TEL], we must be willing to make such changes as are necessary to adopt our motors to Ethyl Gas," Kettering impatiently reminded Buick's chief engineer.[78] Facing a stone wall of resistance, Kettering turned to divisional manager, E. A. DeWaters, pleading with him to "do a little something to slow down the negative attitude which Buick Service people are taking towards Ethyl gasoline."[79] He outlined the many advantages of leaded gasoline, reminding DeWaters that "the basis of Ethyl gasoline was not a fuel so much for present motors as it is the great benefits which the industry can hope to secure from the use of high compression engines. As soon as we get wide distribution, we can begin to raise the compression of our motors." Kettering even threw out the challenge of competition, hoping to inspire the divisions, by noting that "some General Motors competitors are now getting ready to give optional heads with their motors." Despite these sound arguments, DeWaters would not change his mind. Divisional decisions were frequently based on short-term demand, something Kettering refused to recognize.

Oakland also resisted high-compression engines. The production engineers experimented with a Ricardo-type head developed by the Research Corporation in 1925, but Patent Department fears of infringement discouraged further study.[80] In response to Kettering's nagging, Oakland's general manager declared, "we cannot list any very great advantages that our dealers will derive from the use of Ethyl gas until our compression is raised."[81] Yet he would not adopt the new heads.

Finally, in October 1926, Kettering organized a special engineering seminar on the problems of adapting engines to leaded fuels. One of the Buick automobiles tested at that time displayed every customer complaint from stubborn valves to lead contamination of the lubricating oil, and even the research engineers had to admit that divisional complaints had some merit.[82] After another six months of intense study, the laboratory developed a new high-compression head acceptable to the divisions.[83] In July 1927, more than five years after the initial road tests of TEL, the divisions circulated a bulletin to their dealers advising them to withdraw any objections to leaded fuel.

Theoretical issues, so important in the early going, had largely been pushed aside in the rush to perfect and sell leaded gasoline. As the furor of the initial campaign quieted, theoretical matters again rose to the fore. Two fundamental questions interested Kettering— the difference in physical and chemical properties between knocking and nonknocking fuels, and the relationship between TEL and knock suppression.

To attack the first issue, he gathered a team of three young chemists—Thomas Boyd, John Campbell, and Wheeler Lovell—and had them investigate the knock-resisting abilities of various hydrocarbon constituents of gasoline. He hoped that detailed knowledge of the relationship between molecular structure and knock might reveal a technique for rearranging fuel molecules into knock-free structures. That is, he believed that a smart chemist ought to be able to synthesize appropriate hydrocarbons without waste of either material or energy, a process later called isomerization.[84]

Through a comprehensive investigation of different hydrocarbon families—paraffins, naphthenes, aromatics—the researchers determined that the tendency toward knock increased with long, straight, carbon chains and decreased with compact, branched, ones. Despite many differences in other kinds of performance, this result proved surprisingly constant.[85] And while the secret of cost-efficient isomerization eluded the team, their published results helped lay the foundation for later commercial processes developed by the oil industry.

In the spring of 1927, Lloyd Withrow, an academic recruit from the chemistry department at the University of Wisconsin, began a study focusing on the physical and chemical effects of TEL on combustion.[86] Kettering, like nearly everyone else at the time, supposed that TEL acted as a catalyst, and he wanted Withrow to find out if this was so. Withrow doubted the catalyst theory, and samples snatched from an operating test engine with a sampling valve confirmed his suspicions. TEL seemed to decompose completely before the oxygen concentration of the samples began to decrease, suggesting that the lead was not itself a catalyst, and perhaps merely a means of introducing some unknown catalyst.

To investigate this phenomenon more closely, Withrow mounted quartz windows in a test engine and photographed the combustion process stroboscopically. In a paper prepared for publication in April 1930, he reported "that the effective anti-knock agent in the engine is not the lead alkyl itself, but a decomposition product of it." In addition, Withrow concluded that knock was a violent, spontaneous inflammation in the last part of the charge accompanied by a sharp rise in pressure.

Next, Withrow teamed with GM physicist Gerald Rassweiler to study knock spectroscopically. Their investigation of the light absorption of combustion in knocking and nonknocking engines convinced them that some sort of chemical reaction was occurring in the fuel-air mixture in the last part of the charge.

Kettering showed particular interest in this phase of the work, and it inspired another of his deductive theories about knock, the radiation theory. According to this hypothesis the light emitted by the flame front itself was absorbed by the last portion of the charge, raising its temperature prematurely and causing detonation. TEL prevented knock, then, by acting as an optical screen, keeping radiation from reaching the last part of the charge. Withrow's early observations fit in so neatly with Kettering's prejudices that his work received top priority even in an austere depression budget. Later, Withrow found that the flame front emitted light in the visible range while absorption occurred in the ultraviolet range, casting considerable suspicion on the radiation theory.

During the mid-1930s, Withrow and Rassweiler's work contributed important data to the understanding of combustion and detonation. In normal combustion, their research indicated, the fuel-air mixture released its chemical energy through the flame front, which then emitted light characteristic of CH, C_2, and OH radicals. Knock resulted from a spontaneous explosion ahead of the flame front, showed different emissions, and therefore seemed related to preflame chemical reactions. Apparently TEL inhibited the preflame reactions and thereby prevented knock.

Concurrent with these findings, Kettering and his researchers also played a vital role in standardizing knock measurement. In an attempt to develop a reference fuel, the researchers compared fuels of unknown knock resistance to a standard mixture of kerosene and aniline, awarding an "aniline equivalent" to each sample representing the amount of aniline needed to bring the test fuel up to the knock resistance of the reference.[87] Harry Ricardo later refined this idea by replacing the aniline scale with one based on a comparison with varying mixtures of two pure fuels, one of high knock resistance and the other of low. A test fuel thus received a number corresponding to the percentage of knock-resistant fuel in a mixture of the known fuels equal in performance to the unknown sample. In 1926, Graham Edgar of Ethyl Corporation perfected the present octane scale by substituting isooctane (a very effective antiknock fuel) and normal heptane (a poor antiknock fuel) for Ricardo's standards. The octane number thus represented a knock resistance equivalent to that percentage of isooctane in an isooctane/normal heptane solution.[88]

The combustion studies originally grew out of Kettering's interest in the petroleum shortage of the early 1920s. But while the glut conditions of the late 1920s and 1930s diverted most automotive engineers in other directions, Kettering never lost sight of fuel economy as a primary goal of the automobile designer. At the fall meeting of the American Chemical Society in 1925, he unveiled what might have passed for the "car of the future" decades later.[89] Acknowledging that present sources of petroleum were in no imminent danger of exhaustion, he nonetheless argued, "every gallon of petroleum taken out of the ground leaves one gallon less to be taken out in the future, and some day—no one knows just when—our petroleum reserves will have diminished to the point where we can no longer supply our motorists with a sufficient quantity of cheap, volatile motor fuel from this source." Noting, too, that economical substitutes lay far in the future, he urged automotive engineers to start designing more fuel-efficient cars immediately.

To start them thinking, he offered his own version of such a hypothetical vehicle. First, it would cut gasoline consumption with light weight, a short wheel base, and streamlining. Second, a factory-set carburetor and spark advance automatically corrected for load and speed would increase efficiency. Finally, low-drag brakes, a four-speed transmission with overdrive, and an economical rear end would complete the efficient little automobile.

Bringing the audience back to reality, Kettering reminded them that while such a car was well within the current capability of the automobile industry, very likely no one would buy it. It would not climb hills or accelerate quickly in high gear, and "it lacks that reserve power so much desired by the motoring public."

Nonetheless, after a series of technical distractions in the late 1920s, Kettering returned to his "light car" design in 1932. It began as an effort to exploit what Kettering perceived as a major weakness in the contemporary automobile market—the lack of a true "economy car." As he later reminded Sloan in reviewing the project, "we started out to produce a car that would have a reduction in weight of one-third its counterpart of conventional design, and would give at least 40% better fuel economy over all driving conditions."[90] The new automobile was also designed to reduce both initial and operating costs, "an economy car which would sell for less than $500, without a corresponding sacrifice in comfort and utility." Kettering did not underestimate the difficulty of the task. He recognized that to save that much weight and achieve that kind of performance would require a radical departure from traditional design.

First came the design of an ultra-light, two-stroke engine in 1932. It was a twin-cylinder, valveless design in which exhaust gases left through ports at the lower end of one cylinder while a fresh charge entered a similar port in the other. This eliminated all valves and would potentially give smoother performance. The common combustion chamber of the twin cylinders was U-shaped, and gave its name to the engine.

A prototype for Buick returned 174 horsepower on the test stand at an incredible 4.3 pounds per horsepower. Standard engines then weighed in at 7 or 8 pounds per horsepower.[91] But despite an impressive power-to-weight ratio, the little engine seemed beset with a number of troubles. It ran roughly at part throttle and at speeds from 2,000 to 2,500 rpm. It dieseled badly, continuing to run after the ignition was cut off. The exhaust had a terrible smell and irritated the eyes. And most distressing, fuel economy failed to come close to predesign predictions. Investigations with a modified sampling valve revealed that the hot scavenging gases produced irregular flame propagation, contributing in part to rough performance.[92] Extensive studies of the engine's exhaust by B. A. D'Alleva of the fuel section concluded that much of the air-fuel mixture was being carried out by the exhaust. "As high as 40.7 percent of the total fuel input to the engine is being lost in this manner," he reported to Kettering. "This fuel loss was lowered by decreasing the blower speed ratio so that a smaller volume of the air-fuel mixture was taken in by the cylinders per stroke. However, the power also decreased when this was done."[93] Further attempts to quiet the engine and reduce fuel consumption exacerbated the problems, and only later did the researchers discover that by cleaning out the carbon deposits and running the engine on unleaded gasoline they could eliminate rough performance.[94]

Meanwhile, Kettering pushed for higher compression in regular four-stroke engines. In reply to an inquiry from Sloan about the wisdom of raising compression ratios on General Motors products, he assembled testimony and data from several top assistants that indicated boosts of 5.25:1 to 8.0:1 resulted in mile-per-gallon gains of 60 percent at 10 mph and 40 percent at 40 mph, with increased power, acceleration, and top speed.[95] One of Kettering's responses unwittingly revealed both the future course of the light car and the reasons for its ultimate demise: "The gain from high compression will be more desirable to the car owner if it is taken largely in performance rather than in less cost per mile for fuel."[96]

As the light-car program proceeded, it expanded to include not only the engine but an equally innovative chassis and suspension. To save weight, the project engineers combined the body and chassis into one unit, employing a tubular "fuselage" construction which was then "translated" into pressed sections, covered with sheet metal, and welded. The entire automobile weighed in under 2,000 pounds. A modified Dubonnet suspension achieved the low rate of spring motion needed to insure proper stability and comfort.

E. V. Rippingille, a key engineer in the program, gave Kettering extremely optimistic reports on both chassis and engine, echoing the Boss's own words when he said, "the shortcomings of the two-cycle engine are not inherent except to the extent that we do not yet know how to overcome them." Reminding Kettering of the engine's relative youth, Rippingille continued, "Low speed performance, acceleration, and stability have been no easy task for the four-cycle engineers, and it is from this extreme fineness of performance that a great sacrifice in economy has been made. It is little wonder, therefore, that we find this a problem in a type of engine which has only four or five years of development behind it, compared with twenty-five years of four-cycle experience." Indeed Rippingille's only fear was the notorious tendency of research engineers to concentrate on purely technical problems instead of focusing on commercial development. "This deficiency is due to the very attribute that makes good Research men—the ability to evolve new ideas," he mused. "They get them so fast they are always thinking ahead of the job at hand, which is, therefore, obsolete before it is completed."[97]

Development of the light car continued throughout the late 1930s, closely watched and jealously guarded by Kettering himself. While his engineers battled technical obstacles of poor handling, faulty lubrication, improper cooling and unsatisfactory low-speed performance, the Boss fought the administrative wars. In one letter to Sloan, he pointed out once again that such an innovation should not be subject to the usual corporate constraints. "The Corporation today has marvelous accounting systems, fine manufacturing establishments, with good engineering and sales departments, for handling the work of manufacturing products which have been in production for some time and in which the details have been well worked out," he noted. "These procedures of mass-production are almost diametrically opposite to those which are essential in the development and early production of a new product." Therefore he recommended an entirely new plant for the light car, headed by sympathetic research engineers, so that General Motors would "not have to repeat the great waste of time, money and human effort in trying to overcome these normal fixed-mind conditions."[98]

Kettering kept refining the light car engine until war postponed further development. As an experimental prototype, the tiny, two-stroke engine performed superbly. It weighed several hundred pounds less than standard automobile engines and delivered substantially more horsepower from a mere 160 cubic inches. Fuel economy averaged 20–25 percent better than comparable four-stroke engines, sometimes more.[99] Yet changed market conditions after the armistice shelved the power plant, as American consumers worried less about economy and more about power. Faced with a very different kind of consumer demand, Kettering salvaged the project's best ideas for new high-compression and high-performance engines. The small-engine, light-car concept would wait many years before another energy shortage revived it.

By the 1930s, buoyant optimism had replaced the pessimism of the decade before. New oil strikes in the Persian Gulf and the commercial adoption of high-compression engines and antiknock fuels dispelled fears of a fuel shortage. Even Kettering, who looked at the problem over a very long range, stopped talking about a crisis. In answer to an inquiry from the chief economist of the Federal Trade Commission, he replied, "There doesn't seem to be any question about the adequacy of the sources of energy that could be used for automobile power. Entirely aside from the question of how long petroleum will last, it seems assured that enough motor fuel could be gotten from oil shale to last a great many years; enough from coal by some of the newer [distillation] processes that are in the offing to last for thousands of years; and enough from vegetation to last just as long as the sun shines. So, although the price of automobile fuel may go up a great deal, the likelihood of the motor car ever having to be curtailed on account of the lack of energy to run it is quite remote indeed."[100]

He matched this incredible foresight with a personal commitment to forestall the day of economic reckoning by helping organize the Cooperative Fuels Research Council. Whenever possible, he used his influence to encourage cooperation between research facilities in the automotive and oil industries, fostering a tradition of sharing that would have far-reaching results for fuel and engine efficiency.

Kettering's contributions to coping with the fuel shortage—recognizing the crucial problems, asking the right sort of questions, organizing the researchers and keeping them headed in the proper direction, aggressively promoting the end solution—had a significant, if unexpected, impact in the short run. As compression ratios and automobile efficiency and economy gradually increased, so did consumer expectations. New sources of petroleum and better ways of using it encouraged a new profligacy. Instead of the frugal, efficient power plants of Kettering's dreams, high-performance fuels and engines brought in their wake larger, more powerful engines no more fuel conserving than their predecessors. Americans used Kettering's innovations not so much to conserve fuel as to expand their use of the automobile. Tetraethyl lead and the engine improvements that it allowed led ultimately to a more rapid depletion of petroleum resources and the gradual disappearance from the industry of Kettering's original vision of conservation.

While the fuel research did not lead exactly where Kettering had originally intended it would, his foresight was unmatched in his day. As far back as the thirties he promoted fuel efficiency as a crucial component of automotive design and spoke of a potential 450 miles in a gallon of fuel, if only engineers could learn how to tap it. And if the fuel-saving innovations and improvements that he presided over in those years failed to inspire his contemporaries, they were of paramount importance to the next generation.

8 / KEEPING THE
CUSTOMER DISSATISFIED

Pausing to chat with reporters after one of his annual tours of European automobile shows in the 1920s, Kettering summed up the reasons for the success of General Motors. "What interested me most of all in Europe," he said, "is the fact that most of its people have the horse and buggy idea. If only the people of the shops and farms could be stimulated to be dissatisfied they would all have cars, phonographs, radios, and what not; but if they are satisfied, then they want nothing. Our own prosperity and the progress of our automobile industry are due alone to the fact that an American is never satisfied."[1]

Many engineers, particularly those in Europe, disdained this frankly commercial approach to engineering. They claimed that Kettering had reduced automotive engineering to the least common denominator of cost. Kettering once admitted to Sloan that "there are certain points which we can always learn from the European engineer for the reason that he approaches his problem entirely independent of the commercial phase of it."[2] Nonetheless, sophisticated engineering for its own sake was, in his view, a luxury the American automobile industry would have to forgo.

Kettering's revolutionary innovations often overshadowed his equally important incremental contributions, the innovations that kept American car buyers dissatisfied. The success of Alfred Sloan's new marketing strategy—a car for every purse and purpose—depended on Kettering's ability to deliver the right kind of automobile. For only when this year's model was significantly more convenient, comfortable, and appealing than last year's could Sloan entice the American consumer onto the treadmill of the annual model change and the full model line.

This was a different kind of challenge, one requiring a progression of developments rather than revolutionary change at each step. Aware of these new circumstances, Kettering paid close attention to engineering trends throughout the industry and relied more than ever on the talents of specialists, the college-educated experts he said he disliked. Kettering himself could not always master the technical details of each investigation, but his grasp of engineering fundamentals and his uncanny sense of technological direction allowed him to contribute crucial ideas at the right time. Many researchers would participate, but Kettering's ideas really charted the automobile's progress through the next decade.

Perhaps symbolically, these innovations came out of Detroit and not Dayton. Kettering's previous innovations had enhanced the Research Corporation's importance to General Motors, but gradually the distance between Detroit and Dayton was viewed as a problem by top management. Kettering spent hours driving or riding the train between conferences, and lines of communication were often strained. In July 1924, Sloan finally told the Technical Committee, "For the purpose of better coordination with other General Motors activities, the research activities of the Corporation, heretofore conducted as General Motors Research Corporation, have been transferred from Dayton, Ohio to Detroit, Michigan, and effective August 1, 1925, these activities will be designated—Research Section, General Motors Corporation."[3]

As before, Kettering opposed the move for personal and professional reasons. Olive was active in cultural and social affairs in Dayton and had no desire to live in Detroit. But this time the transfer was inevitable. Olive compromised by agreeing to a suite of rooms at the Book-Cadillac Hotel in downtown Detroit, with the intention of returning to Dayton at every opportunity. Kettering furnished the suite in grand style and even installed an organ to remind his wife of home. He also kept another elegant suite at the Waldorf-Astoria for business trips to New York. They never considered either place home. As Kettering often said, his home was in Dayton, but since he could not find a job there, he had to work in Detroit.

Kettering's engineers showed no more enthusiasm for the move. Carroll Hochwalt and Charles Thomas, one recently married and the other under the spell of a new fiancée, quit the laboratory and founded a research laboratory of their own, which later became part of the Monsanto Corporation's research division.[4] After the move was completed in November 1924, F. O. Clements expressed Kettering's feelings as well as his own when he wrote, "Quite recently we moved our Laboratories from Dayton to Detroit and it has much handicapped our own work, upsetting our program a full six months. Furthermore, we lost quite a part of our personnel with the move."[5]

Still, research flourished at the new location, and Kettering even grew to like the new quarters. Within four years the laboratory outgrew the first facilities and moved into a huge new building across the street.

Improved corporate testing facilities came with the new laboratory. Located in a rural area west of Detroit, the Proving Grounds substituted scientifically designed banks, gradients, and measuring instruments for the drama of open road trials, providing far more accurate gauges for assessing Kettering's innovations. This kind of testing was unique in the industry, but with economies of scale, the cost was only about thirty cents a car.[6]

The laboratory was housed in a new eleven-story brick building downtown. Kettering had his office on the tenth floor. It was huge— about thirty feet on a side—and its layout and furnishings set the tone for the work he directed. On each outside wall Kettering installed double-paned windows imbedded in glass brick for insulation. In the ceiling he put some of the first commercial fluorescent lights and an electric heating system controlled by a thermocouple on the desk. Even the upholstery was experimental. All the furniture was made of rubber, without springs but comfortable. In the corner, to remind him of his commitment to practicality more than anything else, Kettering had a work bench with a vise, calipers, pliers, and other tools. On the wall he had a plaque reading, "Any problem, thoroughly understood, is fairly simple." [7]

Kettering's staff grew along with the laboratory facilities. When the lab moved to Detroit, Kettering led a total staff of 260. By the 1930s that number had increased to almost 400, and by the end of the decade it was 500. The scientific and technical component of the staff kept pace, from about 50 in the mid-1920s to 100 in 1938, representing 18 chemists, 4 physicists, 9 metallurgists and 69 engineers, many with doctoral degrees. [8]

Similarly, the budget increased steadily from around $375,000 a year in the 1920s to about $2 million by the late 1930s. On paper, that budget was divided three ways. About 40 percent went toward consulting work for the manufacturing divisions, day-to-day complaints about better brake drums, faulty fan belts, and the like. Another 40 percent was targeted for advanced engineering, finding a better gear metal or an improved lubricant. Finally, 20 percent was given to more fundamental studies, things like infrared spectroscopy and the molecular composition of fuels. [9]

Organizationally, the laboratory was little different from what it had been in Dayton. The actual sections were virtually unchanged except for an occasional name change and the addition of new divisions like organic and electrochemistry to reflect new Kettering interests. However, Kettering did make some significant changes in the administrative area. He created a new post of assistant general manager to relieve business pressures on the technical staff, and more important, he set up a Technical Data section to edit and send reports of laboratory work to other parts of the corporation. Its function was chiefly public relations, making the laboratory visible. As Kettering put it, after learning himself the hard way, "Getting the maximum benefits from research involves selling the results to the operating divisions or to the manufacturing departments. . . . It is all very well to make discoveries in the laboratories, but if these do not find their way into processes and products, then the research was wasted."[10]

A new headquarters, a bigger staff and budget, and more formal organization did little to change Kettering's informal style of running the laboratory. It was still "900 percent Charles Franklin Kettering," noted a business analyst from *Fortune* who visited. "This laboratory might make sense without him, but it is hard to picture how."[11] Indeed, while others did the interviewing and hiring, Kettering put the recruits wherever he pleased. To the first-time visitor the place looked chaotic—in one corner a researcher with a stroboscope studying and recording gear-tooth contact at full load, next to him someone watching a knocking one-cylinder engine and recording pressure-volume cards, not far away someone else checking paint durability with a testing wheel and an ultraviolet light. The reporter from *Fortune* claimed he could scarcely tell the department heads from the technicians, or from the mechanics in the GM garage downstairs, for that matter.

Kettering kept things that way because he hated overspecialization. The problem had to be the boss, he liked to say, and the person who was going to solve it had to "run errands for it." Any researcher who worked for him, he said, "has to be whatever he has to be to solve the problem, because the problems are not specialized, they are what they are."[12] Consequently, Kettering put a knowledge of fundamentals ahead of specialized training. For him, the problem and the person who had to solve it counted most. As he put it, "we allocate the work by the capabilities of the individuals rather than by the titles of the sections to which they are assigned. We are not at all confused when someone calls our attention to the fact that carburetion comes under the Electrical Section while pistons are under Engineering Tests instead of Power Plant."[13] Kettering recognized that the problems his men were working on cut across the lines of traditional scientific and technical disciplines, and therefore let flexibility and common sense be his guides. He admitted that "there is no definite way in which you can draw departmental lines of research because they shift with every product."[14] So it was not uncommon to find chemists, metallurgists, and electrical engineers working together on one project. When questioned about this arrangement, Kettering replied, "The great difficulty is the transition from the individual as an inventor to the group as an inventor, that is what I was trying to develop—group invention rather than individual invention." [15]

Kettering gave all the research under him his personal stamp. As in Dayton, he arrived at the laboratory late in the morning, usually after breakfast with someone at the Book-Cadillac coffee shop. Important or interesting guests he brought to the office; the rest he dispatched. After looking over the mail, and checking with Clements on appointments and other pressing matters, he headed off for his daily rounds. At each stop he talked with the men, looked over their notebooks, slid under a chassis to examine things for himself, or just chatted. Sometimes he stayed a few minutes, other times all afternoon. If a particular project really caught his fancy he invited the lucky assistant to lunch. Rarely did he leave a station without a suggestion or two and a few words of encouragement.

Because Kettering dominated research just as he dominated conversations, his men got an undeserved reputation as yes men. Undeniably, he left his mark on them. "You can't help noticing how the department heads fall unconsciously into his ways of speech and constantly quote his aphorisms," noted one amused visitor. "It is doubtful if even the strongest-minded engineer could work for him without showing it. Sometimes, when in a vein of iconoclastic preaching, the Boss reminds you of an old-womanish Abe Lincoln. At others, when he is tinkering with a stroboscope or drawing graphs on his big office pad, he looks like a young and impish Ichabod Crane." [16]

When asked about his chief responsibility at General Motors, Kettering once replied, "Well, it is supposed to be running the laboratories, but the main problem we have, of course, is the selection of the proper research problems. That is really the most important thing we have to do." [17] And while Kettering did much of the choosing himself, into the decisions he made went mountains of information collected and condensed for him by a network of correspondents and contacts.

Some good ideas (and many not so good) came to the laboratory from independent inventors. The automobile was still young in the 1920s and a popular field for backyard mechanics. Kettering was a well-known advocate of untutored ingenuity, and many inventors took him at his word. His morning mail often brought several letters from hopeful amateurs with ideas. The most persistent made the pilgrimage to Detroit personally and waited outside the office door to see the great engineer himself to try to interest him in their inventions. Clements got rid of most callers, but Kettering sometimes took time to speak with them, and he frequently read over their written suggestions. He even set up a New Devices Committee under J. H. Hunt to consider outside ideas.

Some farsighted notions on automotive lighting reached Kettering this way. One enterprising inventor sent an idea for reducing headlight glare by incorporating rare earths into the headlamps and windshield glass. The glass would absorb certain wavelengths and decrease driver eye fatigue. Kettering followed up the suggestion as far as writing the National Research Council, which informed him that the glass would severely reduce visibility in fog. Another man suggested to Kettering the first electrical signaling device for an automobile, a neon sign in the shape of a hand. Uncharacteristically, Kettering did not appreciate the significance of the idea, and never pursued it. [18]

Such suggestions did inspire Kettering to try out some of his own ideas for automotive lighting. He rigged the clock on his car (one of the first automotive timepieces) to the taillights to switch them on automatically at dusk, and tried to patent the idea. [19] He also developed a double-filament, deflecting headlamp. Apparently, other drivers were less pleased than the inventor was with the lights. "Quite a percentage of people shout at me as they go by," a test driver reported. [20] Kettering replied that nothing was wrong with the headlamp; the public just needed a little driver education, which it got when the headlights were introduced on the 1925 Cadillac and Buick.

Kettering frequently took an active role in evaluating these outside inventions. One inventor, trying to interest General Motors in a rubberized fabric disc for a universal joint, recalled that while some engineers were testing the device, "Kettering came along in an old slouch hat and wanted to know what we were doing. After being told, he proceeded to slide under the car on one of those small wheeled skids and observe the action as the engine was accelerated and decelerated."[21]

Occasionally, even the Boss let a good one get away. The New Devices Committee initially rejected the quarter window for the front door, and then had a hard time tracking down its inventor when they decided they wanted it after all.[22] More often, Kettering and his engineers saw what the amateur inventors who brought them the ideas could not. One demonstrated a new truck suspension, was politely rebuffed, and then rudely surprised four years later when General Motors introduced an upgraded version on its passenger cars. The inventor was hardly bitter, though, and years later looked on Kettering's "borrowing" with more admiration than anger.[23] Other would-be royalty collectors took their lessons about divulging inventions to clever researchers less gracefully. After an interview with the New Devices Committee, one commented it seemed "a place where sheep were sheared."[24]

Random ideas from outside could never satisfy the laboratory's need for innovations, and Kettering had to keep in touch with technical developments in other ways. One good source was the laboratory's library, which Kettering built to 23,246 volumes and 1,398 scientific reports during his tenure. However, personal contacts were even more important. The automobile, it was often said, was European by birth and American by adoption. While American engineers had taken the lead in later years, Europeans could still claim a number of innovations. To keep track of them, Kettering stationed a network of correspondents abroad and attended the annual European automobile shows almost without interruption until the end of his career with General Motors.

One of the best innovations to come from a European source was four-wheel brakes. Charles Short, Kettering's chief European contact, told him that some sixty foreign manufacturers were displaying front-wheel brakes at the Paris Automobile Show in 1922.[25] On the strength of this recommendation, Kettering purchased a Rubay car and shipped it to the laboratory. Upon inspection, he found the car too "Frenchy" for American tastes, though he did concede that it "carries with it a fundamental idea that might bring forth pretty good results."[26]

Indeed, the Rubay sparked a laboratory investigation of four-wheel brakes that by 1927 led to the universal adoption of the system by all the General Motors divisions. This impressive result was not accomplished without some clever promotion on Kettering's part, however. As an inducement to customers, he suggested that General Motors offer four-wheel brakes as a free option the first year, and write off the expense to advertising. The divisions followed this advice and the demand for the brakes subsequently soared.[27]

Power brakes also came to General Motors through the European connection. In a Christmas greeting thanking a British acquaintance, W. O. Kennington, for a toy top and a soap bubble kit, Kettering included some important remarks on the power brake question. "Albert Champion was in yesterday, and was telling me about riding in a Buick equipped with vacuum Servo," Kettering explained. "We are keeping alive here the idea of Servo operated brakes. While up to the present time the chief engineers of the different divisions have not been interested in Servo, we think that with the new brake development, the thing might come. I wonder if you would send us a sketch of this mechanism, and then we can at least have it on file with sketches of other mechanisms, since we are making a complete study of the whole brake problem."[28] Although power brakes did not become standard on General Motors automobiles until the 1950s, Kettering did keep the file active over the years.

Developments in the automotive industry were not, of course, independent of technological changes in the industries that supplied vital materials and parts. For instance, since the automobile annually consumed about 80 percent of the nation's rubber, mostly for tires, and about 75 percent of the plate glass, Kettering kept a close watch on technical developments and potential supply problems in these industries.

The rubber industry had steadily improved the tire's fabric, the quality of the rubber, and the traction of its tread, but Kettering pushed for more rapid progress. When a new Goodyear tire lasted an impressive 5,000 miles in a test, Kettering still wrote the company's president complaining, "From my point of view, today the tire is by all odds the weakest thing in the automobile."[29]

The balloon, or low-pressure tire, was a major breakthrough. Kettering kept the divisions up to date on the changes, and praised the new tires' virtues, including "the cushioning effect given to a car equipped with these tires in traversing rough roads, thus giving greater comfort to the occupants."[30] In his efforts to speed up acceptance of new things, Kettering sometimes encountered unexpected political complications. While balloon tires were still experimental, he publicly predicted they would soon replace their high-pressure competitors. The statement was safe enough technically, but risky from the standpoint of corporate relations. Sloan reminded his enthusiastic head of research:

It is most dangerous at the present time for any important officer of the Corporation to mention the question of balloon tires, for the reason that the whole picture is chaotic, as we know, and even a mention of the thing, no matter how carefully guarded, may give the impression that we are about to go in production or something of that kind and force the situation on the manufacturers and ourselves, which, to say the least, would not be constructive.[31]

Nevertheless, by 1925 balloon tires were standard on all General Motors cars.

Disturbed by accident statistics on passenger injuries caused by hitting the windshield, Kettering also devoted some time to developing safety glass. And by the mid-1920s this lifesaving feature was also offered on most General Motors models.

Kettering liked to investigate these innovations himself, and would occasionally overrule the specialists he brought along to evaluate them. When one assistant criticized a new type of universal joint that a supplier was trying to sell to General Motors, reciting a litany of reasons why it was no good, Kettering retorted, "But, George, the damn thing works," and bought it anyway.[32]

Another important source of ideas for the laboratory was the Du Pont Company, which had already contributed so much to the success of TEL. While Kettering was working on the copper-cooled car, Pierre du Pont was also toying with the idea of a "garageless car." As he pointed out to Kettering, "A closed car covered with weather proof material . . . could be left at the door at any time, thus proving much more useful to the average owner of a small car than the apparatus which must be carefully housed against the weather."[33] But Kettering answered that the real challenge was "largely a question of paints," not the fabrikoid du Pont had in mind, and that any work that could be done "on the paint subject . . . would surely be of great value."[34]

What made paint a vital issue was not only quality but time. Paints took so long to dry, required such expensive hand finishing, and tied up so much floor space in inventory that General Motors faced a real crisis. The introduction in the early 1920s of closed body designs with even more area to paint made matters even worse. The short-term solution was a black baking enamel that could be oven dried in a fraction of the time and cost. It was this economic reality, and not some concession to the sober tastes of the common man, that had inspired Henry Ford's famous quip about giving the customer any color he wants, so long as it was black. For the Model T, basic black was somehow appropriate and adequate. However, for General Motors, which depended on its aristocracy of styling to distinguish models that were assembled in exactly the same way and with essentially the same materials, it would not do. General Motors needed a fast-drying colored paint.

Fortunately for Kettering, Du Pont chemists had just developed a fast-drying pyroxylin lacquer and were looking for a market. Thanks to the corporate connection, the two parties got together early in 1922. Kettering reported:

Our Du Pont friends are sanguine of ultimately producing a new type of dope that will carry the pigments required to make a satisfactory enamel. They are not too willing to talk about this yet, since it is in the laboratory stage. However, it looks very promising. If a new material of this type could be adopted, it would do away with all necessity of heat whatsoever.[35]

During the meetings with the Du Pont chemists, Kettering agreed to let them concentrate on chemical composition, while his researchers would look into the details of application, drying time, temperature, adhesion, and durability. He particularly pointed out to them the special requirements of automotive paints, warning that the "build" or color intensity was crucial, and that matching the new paint to old undercoatings might be difficult. [36]

Kettering's caution was well justified. Outdoor exposure tests did show the durability and fade resistance the Du Pont researchers claimed for their paint. [37] In the laboratory, however, it was hard to apply and left a dull, lackluster finish. Kettering blamed Du Pont for what he felt was an unsatisfactory paint, arguing that the chemists did not appreciate the subtle points of automotive finishing. [38]

To test the experimental paint, now called Duco, under closer to actual conditions, Kettering fished two hundred car bodies out of an old stone quarry in Pontiac, banged them out and sandblasted them, and applied the finish. Within a few weeks the Duco softened the undercoating and the finish peeled off in huge strips. [39]

Gradually, Kettering's chemists, headed by Harry Mougey, learned how to work with the Duco—to bake the undercoating to stop the softening process and to prefinish the steel bodies in acid baths. [40] But even though Duco promised to eliminate weeks of puttying, varnishing, baking, air drying, and polishing, Kettering had a hard time convincing the divisions to try it. H. H. Rice of Cadillac summed up divisional anxieties when he explained to Kettering:

I think one of the most dangerous things the Corporation could do would be to adopt, generally, the new method of painting before it had been tried and in every conceivable fashion. I can conceive of a bad engine or other mechanical fault in a car which would do less damage, from an advertising standpoint, than poor paint. [41]

One division had no choice. Oakland was in desperate financial shape and badly needed some outstanding selling point. So in the spring of 1923 it agreed to let Kettering remodel the finishing department.

The new finishing schedule began in August. Instead of the usual two or three weeks for finishing, the new Oaklands required just two days. Where 170 men once finished 200 bodies a day, twenty fewer men now finished twice as many. Division manager A. R. Glancy estimated that labor costs in the finishing department dropped nearly half during the first month.[42]

There were also a few problems, though. The paint came in one color only, light blue, and would not take a proper sheen, leaving instead a dull, eggshell finish. Kettering argued resourcefully that these apparent liabilities should be converted into assets by advertising the distinctive appearance of the new paint.[43] His strategy worked. Customers, lured by the novelty and expected durability of the paint, waited in long lines for the "True Blue" Oaklands, and many canceled orders rather than accept a standard finish.[44]

The successful sales campaign even healed some old wounds between Oakland and Kettering left over from the copper-cooled episode. Glancy requested Kettering's photograph for his office. "I don't know why you should want to spoil an otherwise perfectly good office with my photograph," Kettering teased, "but I am very glad to send you one."[45]

Oakland's booming sales forced other divisions to take a second look at Duco. Buick sent an engineer abroad in search of new colors for Duco to match the shades of exclusive European designers.[46] By the next model year every division offered at least one model in Duco. Color, once an unimportant aspect of the automobile, now assumed a primary place in the customer's mind, confirming what Sloan had told Kettering only a year before: "I am of the opinion that the sale of our lower priced cars will be much enhanced if we bring them out in colors."[47]

The commercial adoption of Duco actually drew Kettering closer to the technical side of the venture, and he continued to personally investigate the durability of the paint. His winter vacations to Florida offered an ideal opportunity for this. While Olive enjoyed the social life of Miami Beach, he escaped to a small shack near Coral Gables to observe the effects of the harsh Florida sunshine on test panels of Duco. With instruments of his own design, and the able assistance of Earl DeNoon, he measured the amount of sunlight and dew reaching the panels and discovered that dew was actually more destructive than sunlight.[48]

Kettering also found time to study Duco in the field. He visited used car lots and talked with owners, and found that alcohol spills badly damaged the finish. The potential for disaster was alarming, since alcohol was the principal antifreeze in those years. So he urged the divisions to switch to glycerine/ethylene glycol antifreeze, which did not affect Duco, or failing that, to pay closer attention to radiator construction to prevent spills.[49]

Duco, besides eliminating an expensive bottleneck in the manufacturing of automobiles, helped transform the low-priced car from a strictly utilitarian vehicle into something more. The new finish became one more advantage of the increasingly carefree, convenient, and comfortable automobile Kettering was creating for the American consumer. As he told the Association of National Advertisers at their annual convention in May 1927, "Your advertising used to be just what the automobile used to be, the simple moving from one place to another. But now with the motor car developed to a work of art, competition is making it the survival of the fittest, which, in both cases, is getting the attention of the public long enough to make it interested in what is being offered and then giving the buyer more than he expects."[50]

By the mid-1920s Kettering was so well known as one of America's pioneers in industrial research that he was invited to join an informal group of industrial research directors. The first meeting was held on February 15, 1923 at the University Club in New York. Among the other initial members were Frank B. Jewett of Western Electric, Willis R. Whitney of General Electric, C. E. Kenneth Mees of Kodak, and Charles L. Reese of Du Pont. About once a month the group met to talk over philosophies of industrial research.[51] The personal contacts also helped the members solve particular technical problems.

For instance, when General Electric patented a new oilless bearing material called Genelite, a matrix of metallic oxides mixed with carbon that held a lubricant within the bearing and gave it self-lubricating properties, Whitney promptly sent a sample to Kettering to solicit his opinion on its possibilities in the automotive market. Kettering replied that the material was too weak, brittle, and expensive. But privately he saw an opportunity to improve the material's performance while getting around the General Electric patent.[52]

With metallurgical expert Harry Williams, Kettering tried replacing the Genelite oxides with powdered metals. After some work they developed a sintering process—pressing and heating the mixture at a temperature below melting—that scattered the carbon particles throughout the mixture and provided tiny pores to draw oil to the bearing's surface. Within a year Kettering had a workable oilless bearing material that he called Durex.[53]

When word of the discovery leaked, General Electric wanted a cross-licensing agreement that would assign the automotive applications to General Motors and preserve the electrical market for itself. Kettering felt that he had a commanding technical lead, and had "much more to give them than they have to give us . . . [since their] patents are undoubtedly more or less worthless." Yet he also knew that openness with other research laboratories could pay off in the future, and therefore counseled "good fellowship and feeling between the two laboratories."[54]

Kettering invited General Electric engineers to the laboratory for a look at the bearings and even told them the formula. The details of the manufacturing process he kept secret, realizing that process could often count more than product. As he told the Patent Department, "We should keep to ourselves the details of the automatic machines designed to do away with undue labor and necessary to produce these bushings and bearings in quantity until such time as patents are granted."[55]

Kettering eventually set up a pilot plant for Durex in the laboratory, where he supervised the working out of special installation techniques for the fragile material and resolved preproduction bugs.[56] Later the project was transferred to the Moraine Products division where it became a commercial success. A number of research engineers who had become involved with the venture were also allowed to move, another way Kettering kept his "boys," as he called them, contented, and ensured a smoother transition from laboratory to market.

Other metallurgical ideas came to Kettering through his visits to other laboratories and manufacturing facilities. A visit to the Holley Carburetor Company plant, for example, opened his eyes to the benefits of permanent molding, a way of replacing open sand molds with light, cast-iron ones that speeded the production process considerably. Holley's breakthrough was to control the transfer of heat from the casting into the mold by protecting the mold with a layer of fireclay covered with a film of carbon smoke to prevent actual contact between molten metal and the surface of the mold.[57]

Kettering temporarily filed this information away, pursuing more favored projects instead, until Clements warned him, "There are two or three concerns getting very active on this phase of work, and unless we move rapidly our efforts will be completely lost."[58] It was at times like this that Clements' meticulous organization proved its worth, spurring development in the right direction at the right time.

Kettering immediately sent out feelers to the divisions. Several of them expressed an interest—Chevrolet for cylinders and tappets, Buick for pulleys, Oldsmobile and Cadillac for assorted odds and ends.[59] Next, he set out a three-tiered approach to the research program: "first, a machine upon which the various molds are mounted; second, the molds themselves, which will mean various kinds of materials for different kinds of work; and third, the metallurgy of the changing mixtures which are poured into these molds and the treatment given them after they are removed."[60] Finally, to ensure that the efforts of the metallurgists would be properly rewarded, he contacted McEvoy for a complete analysis of the patent situation, urging him to search for patentable ideas in the manufacturing process even if the basic idea was covered.

The major breakthrough came when metallurgist Alfred Boegehold discovered that the addition of silicon cut annealing time from nearly 100 hours to less than 4 and also yielded a tougher product.[61] But this became only one of dozens of incremental improvements that gave Kettering the kind of permanent molding system he wanted, a system he then could successfully sell to several divisions.

While Durex and permanent molding were never widely appreciated outside the automobile industry, they did significantly lower production costs for many items, and both joined the growing list of "invisible" improvements produced annually by the laboratory. As Kettering boasted to Sloan about the molding process, "In the same floor space and with the same amount of labor, you can produce about ten times as much work." [62]

Kettering often said he wanted to keep his customers dissatisfied by improving each year's model. Some customers, of course, were dissatisfied with the General Motors cars they already owned. However, Kettering gathered suggestions on how to upgrade the automobile from this source too.

Throughout the early 1920s, Kettering received periodic letters from owners of General Motors automobiles who complained that their oil was losing viscosity or that their timing chains and other engine parts were broken or badly pitted. [63] Kettering knew that the problem was crankcase dilution, and that it was caused by poor-grade gasolines (common in those fuel-short years) that sneaked past the piston rings and into the crankcase. He also knew how serious it was. "The fuel problem is the greatest one we have," he told Sloan, "and by this I mean the condition of our present gasoline which makes for carbonization and crankcase dilution; meaning in the end increased cost of operating a motor car by having to clean carbon and throwing away lots of unused oil." [64]

As he surveyed the technical literature on lubrication, Kettering discovered that no one had systematically attacked the problem of crankcase dilution. With the specialized talents at his command, and his own ability to balance cost against efficiency, he knew he was in a better position than other automotive engineers to exploit the situation profitably.

In the summer of 1923 Kettering assigned Caleb E. Summers, a young assistant, to the crankcase dilution study. What Kettering wanted was a thorough search and evaluation of the existing state of the art. First, Summers built a "refinery" device borrowed from a design in the *SAE Journal*. Essentially, the system drew the oil into a small reservoir where the exhaust manifold distilled the gasoline off from the oil, and then returned each component to its proper place. Summers installed the units on four Cadillacs owned by General Motors executives. After lengthy road tests and a conference with the owners, he told Kettering that while the experimental system reduced dilution to about 16 percent under normal conditions, it did not work well until the car was completely warmed up, and the warm-up period was when dilution was worst.[65]

Kettering next asked Harry Mougey to look into the abrasion side of dilution—how dirt and dust affected an engine with diluted lubrication, and how these effects could be reduced with better filtering.[66]

Eventually, Kettering put nine engineers on the project, divided between Summers working on dilution and Mougey on abrasion. He pressed them on with constant reminders that several competitors were already moving quickly in this area and that General Motors would need an offsetting sales weapon.[67] Summer's team came up with an improved distillation system that circulated the oil through a still heated by exhaust gas and controlled thermostatically to overcome the problem of slow warmup.

Mougey's work led in some surprising directions. Alerted by complaints from owners using high-sulfur fuels and aided by Kettering's sharp eye for the literature, Mougey discovered that sulfurous fuels, under the right conditions of dilution, could produce a sulfuric acid that ate tappets, piston rings, and other engine parts. Apparently water vapor was the villain, for it caused the reaction.[68]

Mougey published his findings and presented them to the 1924 summer meeting of the SAE. Concurrently, Kettering had one of the men author a popular pamphlet summarizing what Summers and Mougey had learned, both to help drivers better understand lubrication and to cultivate a market for the laboratory's innovations.[69]

That fall, Mougey and Summers put together a simpler "blow-through" ventilator and oil/air filtration system that could eliminate abrasion, dilution, and acid wear. Kettering then dispatched his engineers to sell the idea. Typically, each division greeted the proposal differently, from Cadillac, which enthusiastically endorsed it, to Chevrolet, which worried about the cost.[70]

Cadillac, with the most convenience-conscious customers, brought out the ventilators in 1925 to excellent reviews. "No corrosion troubles have been encountered this winter," Mougey told Kettering. "Water had been practically eliminated; dilution kept within reasonable limits." His exuberance temporarily clouding his judgement, Mougey predicted that "the present combination of ventilation and filter will maintain the oil in a condition in which it will never have to be changed at all."[71] Kettering still advised drivers to change their oil every three to six months, for he knew ordinary drivers did not care for their engines the way Mougey did.

Despite Cadillac's success, most cost-conscious divisions were difficult to convince. Oakland was particularly unyielding. Manager Glancy argued that "these two accessories are sales talking points only," and that "if General Motors stood as a unit without these accessories, a great deal of money would be saved and no sales lost."[72] Kettering had to exploit his highest corporate connections to push the innovation through. "It seems about the only way cooperation can be worked out with them is by an Executive Order," he complained to Sloan, and sent along a number of laboratory tests to support his arguments for the ventilators. As usual, Kettering won, and Sloan did issue an executive order.[73] Within a year, ventilators and filter systems became standard features on all General Motors cars, and the annoying troubles of corrosion and abrasion vanished dramatically.

Kettering fully recognized the value of these incremental refinements to General Motors' products. Reviewing the corporation's position for Sloan, he commented, "These very important developments [in crankcase ventilation and filtration] which are inexpensive in the long-run, certainly give us a tremendous advantage over our competition. We are not running neck and neck with any of our competitors from an engineering standpoint at all, because I think we know more about this subject than anybody else."[74]

Some customers' complaints counted more than others, particularly when the customer was P. S. du Pont. After driving his new Cadillac, du Pont wrote that he noticed a vibration period at about 35 mph so severe he could scarcely make out the blur of his hat in the rearview mirror. "I can easily imagine that the above trouble causes ill comments concerning Cadillac cars," he said.[75] Indeed, other Cadillac owners had already complained that at 18 and again at 35 mph the car developed a loud hum accompanied by a vibration. Cadillac's solid reputation and traditionally luxurious appointments made this fault obviously unacceptable.

A complete analysis of engine vibration required mathematical sophistication beyond Kettering's abilities. More than once he had dismissed computations with the comment that if all the slide rules swelled and stuck, engineers would be better off. Actually, though, he was well versed enough in the mechanics of engines to orchestrate the more finely tuned efforts of the engineers he needed for the project.

As always, Kettering first outlined the problem. Engine vibration, as he understood it and explained it to his staff, resulted from three interrelated forces—forced vibration, caused by out-of-balance machine parts; torsional vibration, caused by the twisting deflection of parts such as the crankshaft; and harmonic vibration, a resonance caused by the natural pendulum-like oscillations of engine parts.[76]

Next he consulted his network of correspondents to find out what had already been done. One European source replied that F. W. Lanchester, the same eccentric British inventor who had helped inspire the copper-cooled engine, had recently developed a torsional vibration damper, a small flywheel connected to the crankshaft through a slipping clutch that compensated for the torsional wind-up.[77] Kettering purchased one of Lanchester's dampers but found that it wore quickly and was hard to adjust. His investigation suggested that there was lots of room for improvement, perhaps even patentable improvement, and so Kettering began assembling a staff to study the vibration problem.

From the outside he hired Theron Chase, an engineer from Hudson who had previously worked on vibration problems. From the inside he tapped Caleb Summers, who in addition to his work on dilution had a strong background in mathematics. Kettering then gave them a list of ideas for reducing vibration and set them to work on a Cadillac engine. However, after Kettering's light-weight aluminum pistons and improved engine mounting did not do the job, the Boss admitted it was time to try something else.[78]

That something else became a way of dividing the inertial forces of the eight-cylinder crankshaft with equal but opposite components which would then cancel each other. Kettering explained the genesis of the development to the Patent Department:

When we developed the 90 degree crankshaft [with the throws 90 degrees apart instead of on a single plane] for the Cadillac Motor Car Company, we did it by taking their original shaft and twisting it on a large bed plate which we had in the laboratory at the time. This shaft was too light and when it was put in the motor we had eliminated all of the centrifugal forces but it did leave the torsional periods quite prominent. In order to get a satisfactory demonstration on this job we improvised a friction balancer on the outside. We then gave this thing some thought because we knew it would be impossible to build motors with such an improvised arrangement. We then began to study what we could do in the way of a torsional vibration device, provided we could make the Cadillac crankshaft stiff enough to not cut it.[79]

One way to eliminate the torsional vibration was to license the Lanchester patent, which Kettering did. But at the same time he tried several ways of getting around the patent. One idea was an electrical vibration damper which would electromagnetically absorb the vibration into specially tuned circuits in the generator. For a time this was Kettering's pet project. He and J. H. Hunt actually came up with a workable system, but the cost of the special low-frequency circuits was too high.[80]

Another approach resulted in the harmonic balancer, a device that mounted on the crankshaft with a flexible leaf-spring coupling, and that oscillated out of phase with the natural period of the shaft to dampen excess vibration. Kettering admitted to the Patent Department that "we did not feel that we had contributed a new idea to harmonic balancing," but he did believe the work had developed a device that "took up very much less space, weighing much less, and could go on the cheeks or throws of an ordinary shaft" and that "had contributed detailed structures which would adapt these balancers to every particular use."[81]

Naturally, Kettering had to promote the balancer. Cadillac was eager to try it, but other divisions were more cautious. Kettering invited the Oakland manager to test-drive a Cadillac and witness for himself "what it has been possible to do by a complete analysis of crankshaft forces."[82] He sent Summers on several technical missions to other divisions. And he knew success was assured when the chief engineer of Chevrolet finally acknowledged what Kettering had been saying for years:

We must recognize that we have raised the standard of quality on our car, outside of the engine, quite materially this year, and that the public is going to ultimately demand that the engine result be improved to correspond both as to durability and smoothness. . . . Further, there is no question but that the public is going to be stimulated to expect more smoothness out of a Four, when Six-cylinder smoothness is available pretty close to our price.[83]

Prodding his "boys" for even more cost-efficient vibration control, Kettering stirred the imagination of yet another NCR expatriate, Thomas Van Degrift. From lengthy chats with Kettering, Van Degrift put together an idea for dynamically balancing machine parts on an instrument that looked deceptively like a drill press. When the balancer spun a crankshaft or other engine part, it revealed otherwise hidden flaws in balance and took much of the guesswork out of design correction.[84]

By the fall of 1925, Kettering had assembled an impressive array of talent devoted to vibration studies. Under his guidance and inspiration they had developed better crankshaft designs, harmonic balancers, preassembly balancers, and such cost-efficient techniques that Kettering promised the divisions that he could eliminate vibration for only $1.50 a cylinder. That kind of figure made a smoother ride something every division could afford.[85]

Henry Ford made the mass-produced automobile possible because instead of tooling up a cheap car, he designed a car suited for the mass market and then figured out how to manufacture it cheaply. Kettering democratized automotive luxury in a similar way. While attacking first the problems of convenience and comfort on more costly cars, he always developed and refined his ideas for the less expensive models. The result was a generally egalitarian technology within the system of status and style crucial to Sloan's overall strategy.

Scarcely any possible incremental improvement escaped Kettering's view. He pushed unglamorous projects as hard as any others. When insurance underwriters complained of increased automobile theft, he began a study of locking mechanisms which ended in an imaginative steering column lock.[86] To prevent windshield icing, he developed and patented a way of electrically heating wiper blades and experimented with chemical deicers.[87]

For engines too, Kettering recognized the importance of incremental change. "With a change in muffler design we have been able to increase the high speed horsepower [on a Cadillac] 7 or 8 percent. With different methods of carburetion we have been able to raise the low horsepower as well as high horse power 7 or 8 percent," he told Sloan. "While we are spending large sums of money in the redesign of engines I feel that these small things which influence power per pound are not getting all the consideration they should receive."[88]

Not every incremental improvement came out as Kettering thought it would. He put one engineering team to work on a slide-valve engine, which he hoped would eliminate the timing troubles of poppet valves. It idled beautifully but tended to seize at full throttle. Kettering, though, loved the elegance of the design, and soon the engineers were afraid to tell him about the engine's drawback. The Boss was known to fire men who were not making progress in the right direction. "It got so they wouldn't open up the throttle," one of the assistants recalled. "Every time the Boss would come around to see how things were going why they'd turn this thing on and let it idle and let him marvel at how quiet it was." Only after a year of deception did they summon the nerve to break the news to Kettering, who finally ended the project.[89]

Occasionally, Kettering's passions grew into major corporate commitments. One of his favorite personal projects during these years was the development of a better bus. Even in the early 1920s he saw that expanding urban populations and the growing highway system had created a demand for a new kind of "deluxe" long-distance bus. He and Pierre Schon of the GM Truck division agreed that a light-weight bus might sell, especially since truck sales were off and the "additional profits derived from the sale of buses would be a life saver for many 'G.M.C.' dealers."[90]

Sloan was less enthusiastic than Schon. As he told Kettering, "I am getting letters from one person after another almost daily who feel that we ought to be in the bus situation and yet when it comes down to a showdown nobody has interest enough apparently to say let's go ahead and do it."[91] Kettering had the interest and the resources, and undertook the project.

Some corporation executives urged Kettering to acquire an existing bus manufacturer and avoid some of the inevitable and costly mistakes of development. Kettering expected mistakes, since he had no experience with buses, but knew he would learn from them and ultimately do a better job. He preferred to start from scratch.

By the summer of 1925, he was ready with a prototype front-wheel-drive bus with a Cadillac engine, four-wheel brakes, and an automatic transmission. He christened it "Miss Ohio." To test his bus he boarded son Eugene (now sixteen), his young friend Adam Schantz, Charles Mott, and Bill Chryst for a western tour. For a month the group imitated the famous Edison, Ford, and Firestone excursions, camping under the stars and swapping tall tales. They all complained about Kettering's driving, but after 8,000 miles of rough roads, the Rocky Mountains, the deserts of New Mexico, and endless greasy spoon restaurants, the party returned, sure at least of the bus's reliability.[92]

The Yellow Coach division carried on from there, with over a hundred of Kettering's research men for assistance. Building on this foundation, General Motors later became a leader in bus design and manufacture.

Alarmed by the increasing numbers of cars rolling off American assembly lines, thanks in part to Kettering's success in changing consumer tastes, some social critics began to question the wisdom of allowing such a potent economic and social force to grow anarchically. Would not prudence dictate a slower, more controlled course, they argued, giving the country more time to adapt to the innovation with less disruption?

Kettering had an answer for them; let the free market make the adjustments. "Some one will ask, where are all the automobiles going to find room if we continue to add thousands of automobiles each day to the 12,000,000 or more motor vehicles now in the United States?" he asked. He found it strange that more thought had not gone into building more roads. "As long as motor car transportation is worth more than it costs, the questions of providing highways will be taken care of."[93] The benefits of the automobile were so obvious in his view that the nation would simply have to accommodate itself to its demands.

On May 31, 1927, the last Model T rolled off Henry Ford's assembly line, a victim not only of Sloan's organizational and marketing strategies but of changing American tastes so brilliantly stimulated by Kettering's unceasing campaign to upgrade the comfort and convenience of the automobile in a cost-efficient manner. While Ford worked out a replacement for the Model T, Chevrolet entrenched itself as the nation's best seller, and General Motors assumed the leadership of the automotive industry.

That event marked a watershed for the industry. The American automobile had come of age. Thanks to Kettering's ability to see the technological future and to select the men and ideas needed to make it happen, the automobile had changed more radically in the previous decade than in any other part of its history. The innovations pioneered and perfected in the General Motors Research Laboratory had transformed the car from a plaything and a workhorse into a convenient necessity of everyday life.

Of course, this upgrading had dramatically increased the cost of car ownership. Even Sloan was shocked to learn the cost of owning and operating a 1927 Chevrolet. Relaying his surprise to Kettering, he exclaimed, "The thing that strikes me is the average cost per car, including depreciation. When you consider the millions of people who operate cars in this country on the income they must have, it is hard to see how they could set aside this relatively large amount of money to maintain a car."[94]

Kettering was not surprised. He, perhaps better than Sloan, appreciated how attached to their automobiles Americans had become. And he knew how important technological innovation would be in extending the affair. In one of his typically homespun but insightful stories, Kettering explained the strategy. Select the best example of the automotive art and seal it in a glass case, he suggested. Then put the price in gold letters on the front. Check each year and see if the posted price isn't too high. "And what do you think you can get for that car at the end of fifteen years?" he asked. "It will be just as good as it was when we put it in the case, but the only man who will buy it is the junk dealer. Why? Because the car depreciated? No . . . because through the appreciation of new car designs, the eyes on the outside looking in have changed. . . . What we did do was appreciate your mind. We simply elevated your mental idea of what an automobile should be."[95]

9 / THE CHALLENGES OF MANAGEMENT

General Motors' success earned Kettering a salary well into six figures a year and stocks and investments worth millions; he owned 450,000 shares of General Motors common stock alone, yielding an annual dividend of about $700,000. But this wealth did not embarrass him. To his scientifically oriented colleagues at the American Chemical Society meeting in 1927 he said, "I was taught that a scientist is a man who works at his subject for the sake of the subject alone, and that a man who works on a scientific project with the idea of selling it has no right to be associated with science. I have since learned that a bank account in the black is the popular applause of a scientific accomplishment." [1]

Kettering could certainly measure his scientific success by the "popular applause" of a well-stocked bank account. For some of the men he managed, though, science was more than a path to profitable technology. It was a special community with goals and rewards quite separate from his world of engineering and profit. Innate curiosity and professional ambitions drove these researchers just as strongly as profit drove other corporate players. To meet their professional needs and to channel the talents of his more scientifically inclined researchers in corporate directions was one of the major challenges of Kettering's career. Ironically, it was the same challenge that he often presented to his own superiors.

Thomas Midgley personified the dilemma. For two decades, he and Kettering collaborated on some of the laboratory's most profitable chemical research. Yet Midgley's own proclivities inclined him toward scientific theory and away from problems of practical application. In later years, Kettering found it increasingly difficult to focus Midgley's attention on commercial innovation.

Nearly a decade after their last important work together, when Midgley's research had become almost entirely theoretical and he had achieved prominence in the chemical establishment, he made a speech that strikingly illuminated the philosophical rift that had grown between himself and Kettering. On May 22, 1942, the Chicago Section of the American Chemical Society gave Midgley its Willard Gibbs Medal for outstanding achievement, adding a final triumph to his professional career. Harry Holmes, national president of the society, introduced the honored recipient and recounted his exploits in the chemistry of motor fuels and refrigerants. In his acceptance speech, however, Midgley did not discuss his commercially successful discoveries. Instead he talked about his studies in rubber chemistry, work respected within the profession but scarcely known outside it. To justify his choice of subject, Midgley explained that this work was more "scientific" than his earlier research. "Perhaps I consider the work on synthetic rubber more scientific," he continued, "because nothing commercial ever came of it." [2]

Kettering never doubted that his job as research director was to provide the corporation with profitable innovations. As he put it, "the man responsible for the laboratory must never lose sight of the fact that research work done with corporate funds must justify itself economically." At the same time he showed an appreciation for other points of view, and a knack for selecting projects as interesting in a theoretical way to his best chemists and physicists as they were commercially appealing to GM.

As research director, one of Kettering's important responsibilities was to keep an eye on technical developments and potential supply problems in industries that GM depended on, such as the glass and rubber industries. As the price of natural rubber, spurred by wartime shortages and a British-led cartel, climbed sharply in the 1920s, Kettering asked his chemists to investigate synthetics.

Synthetic rubber was not a new idea in the 1920s. As early as 1909, German chemists demonstrated the possibility of converting isoprene—a volatile liquid produced by fractional distillation of rubber, or more important, derived from coal or petroleum—to a synthetic rubber capable of vulcanization. The finished product did not polymerize properly and it lacked sufficient tensile strength and elongation. It was also unstable.[3] Despite these handicaps, a slightly modified methyl isoprene rubber proved a boon to a resource-starved Germany during the war. For tires, cables, and especially for submarine storage batteries, the substitute was invaluable.[4] After the war, when the price of natural rubber returned to normal levels, the future of synthetic substitutes looked dim. As one executive from B. F. Goodrich put it, "the world has little to expect, and the planters nothing to fear, from synthetic rubber. . . ."[5]

Yet in some ways the commercial prospects for synthetic rubber still looked promising. Data uncovered by the indefatigable Boyd revealed that the cost of rubber had increased from only 23 cents a pound in July of 1924 to 90 cents a year and a half later.[6] A British Far Eastern rubber restriction scheme threatened to push the cost of rubber even higher, perhaps past wartime levels. Since an automobile tire was about 50 percent rubber, the implications for General Motors were enormous.

Little more than a literature search came of GM's first efforts in this direction, however, because the price of rubber leveled off just after the lab started work. Yet Kettering concluded that "there have been some advances made in this thing since the last time I made a study of it." As he reported to Alfred Sloan in 1925, the polymerization problem appeared resolved, and the only remaining stumbling block was a commercially feasible process for producing isoprene. "It looks as though, with the immense amount of work we did with Ethyl Gas in connection with organic compounds, that there is a very good chance to make isoprene synthetically."[7] During the

Christmas holidays in 1925, the two executives met in New York to discuss the possibilities of a synthetic rubber investigation at General Motors.

Kettering wanted Midgley to head this research, even though the chemist was no longer actually a GM employee. Like several other top researchers, Midgley had chosen not to move to the new Detroit laboratory in late 1924. Instead, he remained in Dayton to continue his responsibilities as vice-president of Ethyl Corporation and to set up an independent consulting practice. Now Kettering saw an ideal opportunity to learn something about rubber chemistry that might be commercially important, and at the same time to put Midgley's talents back to work for GM. Kettering arranged a special subsidy so that Midgley could pursue his rubber research at the Hochwalt and Thomas laboratory in Dayton, which was housed in the old Ludlow Mansion that had served as the Dayton Metal Products lab during the war. When Kettering approached Midgley with the idea, the chemist was delighted. Sloan offered a budget of $60,000 for the first year of study and Midgley began the project in January 1926. To keep an eye on the work and to ensure that it continued in the best interests of General Motors, Sloan asked Kettering to "look after it," which he did through frequent, informal visits.[8]

Kettering held Midgley's research abilities in high regard, but he also recognized that synthetic rubber presented a difficult challenge. Nonetheless, he was convinced that "while we may not be able to make an absolute substitute for rubber . . . we will get something which will be of very great value."[9]

He also saw in the synthetic rubber project an opportunity to lobby for more funds for other research efforts. Kettering pointed out to Sloan that "to have an appropriation of this size made entirely outside the control of the Laboratory naturally meets with a certain negative reaction with some members of the organization." Kettering suggested, of course, that Sloan therefore increase appropriations for other research projects also. "Some of our important research problems are being handicapped here by our being a little hard-boiled on the amount of money we have allowed on them," he noted.[10]

The Patent Department of General Motors failed to share Midgley's and Kettering's enthusiasm. Only weeks after the rubber research began, George Lovett, once in charge of the chemical division of the United States Patent Office and now a member of the corporate patent division, arrived in Dayton to check on Midgley's work. He was not impressed. A patent search had disclosed the extreme difficulty of the undertaking and had also indicated that the most feasible processes were already covered by German patents.[11] Midgley had expected the project to take about three months, but two of those months were already gone, with few concrete results. "I do not mean to say that the solving of the problem is an impossibility," James McEvoy wrote to Sloan after reading Lovett's report, "but I do feel that, unless Midgley knows of some absolutely revolutionary and unknown method of turning Isoprene into rubber, his work should be stopped."[12]

McEvoy felt that Midgley had grossly underestimated the extent of the undertaking and had not studied the literature sufficiently. "I do not believe that he has made any real effort to study the subject as he was totally ignorant of most of the patents and articles mentioned by Mr. Lovett to him," McEvoy remarked.[13]

McEvoy based his pessimistic report on observations of Midgley's early efforts to make isoprene from cracked petroleum. In the course of this work, Midgley developed several promising techniques for converting petroleum products, by distillation and treatment with special magnesium and sodium compounds, into polymers much like isoprene. But the more difficult procedure of turning isoprene into synthetic rubber eluded him.[14]

Despite the Patent Department's pessimism, Sloan decided to continue the rubber investigation. Fortified by Kettering's optimism and confident of Midgley's capabilities, he chided the patent group, "I think, considering Midgley's past performance and the confidence that we all hold in his research ability, that we ought not to dictate too closely because it is important to keep up his morale and all that sort of thing." Success might seem far away, but the project had cost relatively little so far, and as Sloan reminded the patent men, "sometimes the most surprising things come out of developments of this character."[15]

Midgley's rubber research continued slowly throughout 1926, and he periodically reported the results to Kettering and Sloan. When time allowed, Kettering stopped by the Hochwalt and Thomas laboratory for personal visits and discussion. No real breakthrough had been achieved, but as Midgley continually argued, much of the work done on synthetic rubber up to this time was confused and contradictory. He was not even sure that isoprene was the best original material. The synthesis of other hydrocarbons seemed to promise a better synthetic product.[16]

Midgley also encountered a common frustration. "With this work half completed a monograph . . . was discovered to contain a report of some work on synthetic rubber which amounted practically to having done the same piece of research which we were pursuing, founded upon the same initial discovery which we had made ourselves . . . ," Midgley lamented.[17] That was part of the cost of following Kettering's advice about ignoring the "experts," a cost McEvoy found unacceptable. Still, with this and other setbacks, the project progressed, and at a meeting at the end of the year Kettering and Midgley agreed that it would be a great mistake to cancel funding after such a promising start. Kettering prodded Sloan into providing $50,000 for another year of study.[18]

Less easily swayed by "possible" results and "hoped-for" breakthroughs, Sloan sought an outside opinion on the investigation from Lammot du Pont, president of the Du Pont Company and a chemical expert.[19] Lammot agreed with the General Motors Patent Department. He advised that while good fortune and serendipity quite obviously played a role in research, one could not always count on them. "It is true that discoveries do not always come from the sources to be expected, but again, judging from what I have heard of synthetic rubber and the work that has been done, its development is not going to be a *discovery*, but more likely a painstaking search for the right method (probably already known) for doing each of the several steps required."[20] He further advised Sloan against producing raw materials and urged General Motors to stick with the fields it knew best and leave organic chemistry to others.

But with Kettering still convinced that the project would result in something profitable, Sloan held firm despite Lammot's pessimism. Several other factors also weighed in favor of continued support. For one, of all the outside supplies purchased by General Motors, the rubber tire was the "most unsatisfactory from the standpoint of erratic costs out of line with the real economics of the case."[21] For another, past research efforts whose ultimate success was equally despaired of had resulted in handsome profits for the corporation. Perhaps, he thought, synthetic rubber would prove as rewarding. After all, as Sloan pointed out in a letter to Lammot, General Motors spent only $375,000 a year on research, and a good deal of that was for practical engineering and therefore was really for "engineering that is properly a part of the cost of sales."[22] Certainly a corporation doing a billion dollars of business a year could afford to gamble a few thousand dollars in hopes of a lucrative return.

A final reason for Sloan's support was his keen appreciation of the need for good researcher morale. "I know of many instances where certain of our people become greatly interested in a certain idea, the value of which perhaps they over-estimate, if they are prevented from developing those ideas, in a way, it has a reactionary influence," Sloan told Lammot, thinking of his own experiences with Kettering. "On the contrary, if they are encouraged, even if it results in some cost to the Corporation, it has a beneficial influence on the entire picture."[23]

Sloan's boldness and generosity rested largely on his faith in Kettering, for the rubber investigation had already far exceeded his limited knowledge of chemistry. He confessed to one of his confidants, "Frankly, I know very little about chemistry and have very little appreciation of what they are trying to do or what progress they may have made. I must, therefore, rely upon Mr. Midgley and Mr. Kettering."[24] Actually, Kettering was no expert on rubber chemistry himself. He too was operating primarily on faith, based on long experience with industrial research in general and Thomas Midgley in particular.

Midgley's background in mechanical engineering gave his synthetic rubber chemistry an unusual mechanical perspective. He thought that natural rubber got its elasticity from the mechanical properties of its structure. That is, he believed isoprene acted something like matted coils or springs, while the sulfur molecules so crucial in vulcanization were a bit like stitches which knit the coils together and preserved their elasticity. The trick to synthetic rubber, then, was to find something else to replace the isoprene "coils" and sulfur "stitches." Midgley felt certain he could find them, and that when he did, he could put together better kinds of rubber.[25]

Without a more detailed knowledge of the structure of natural rubber, however, Midgley could not hope to duplicate these properties synthetically. So he undertook a series of experiments designed to unravel rubber's structural secrets. He learned a lot about the position and strength of bonds in rubber, about how and where rubber molecules join to sulfur during vulcanization, and about rubber's molecular weight. He discovered that rubber consisted of two distinct compounds with different physical properties. And he investigated the importance of protein in natural rubber and identified its amino acids.[26]

While these experiments added a great deal to the theoretical knowledge of rubber chemistry, they did not help Midgley with the original problem, and he was still unable to synthesize more than tiny amounts of artificial rubber at very high cost. Of more concern to Kettering and Sloan was Midgley's increasing interest in fundamental studies and his apparent disregard of commercial results.

Sloan's strong defense of the rubber appropriations was actually the beginning of the end for the project. Sloan had defended the investigation on psychological grounds, not because he anticipated commercial success from Midgley's project. "It was no more than fair, when he became tremendously interested in the problem under discussion [synthetic rubber], to at least spend a little money to see what he could make of it—not with the hopes that anything could be accomplished, but because in a way, dealing with big things, he was entitled on account of his previous record, to a reasonable amount of consideration," Sloan remarked to Lammot.[27]

Commercial application looked very far away, and Sloan decided to terminate the venture. In February 1927 he wrote to J. Brooks Jackson, business manager of the Research Corporation, notifying him that the synthetic rubber project had funding until the end of the year but no further. "If at that time there are no very definite developments which indicate a more hopeful outcome," he told Jackson, "I shall certainly feel that Midgley has had his chance, and irrespective of the argument that will, of course, be advanced at that time, that further work will bring the result, in view of our more or less secondary interest in the proposition, I will be inclined to recommend that we discontinue."[28] From past experience, Sloan was well acquainted with the favorite arguments used by researchers to ensure additional funding and he was prepared to resist them.

He did not share his doubts with Midgley, however. In March, Sloan wrote the chemist a letter of support. Money was not a problem, he said, and if some experts were skeptical, that was only a natural reaction in an untried area of research. "As long as you and Mr. Kettering feel that we are making progress," Sloan told him, "I am perfectly willing to continue the activity for a reasonable time anyway in order that we may exhaust those ideas which you have in mind."[29]

Kettering, a veteran of similar campaigns, knew exactly what Sloan was saying. After candid discussions with Sloan on the future of the venture, he realized that corporate support was crumbling. He agreed that progress had been slower than anticipated but argued that most research was like that. "There is no reason on earth why we cannot go through with this job," he told Sloan. "I would personally be very willing to bear the expense involved should we reach a point where the corporation would not want to finance it any longer."[30]

Pressures for termination mounted throughout the year. By the end of 1927, McEvoy and the Patent Department were less hopeful than ever of commercial success. McEvoy strongly urged Sloan to end the project, for he believed that Midgley still knew "nothing whatever about the subject except what has been disclosed by other people."[31]

Discontinuing an unfinished project required delicate maneuvering. As Kettering himself once remarked, "the laboratory head—in addition to his scientific equipment—must have an equipment of sound sense of values. He must be able to direct the main lines of each research which his assistants are carrying on, and he must help them choose which side lines are likely to yield profitable results. He must know when to leave a side line and return to the main line. And, most important of all, he must know when to stop."[32] Kettering knew terminating this project was going to be difficult, for by this time Midgley had a substantial commitment to rubber chemistry. He had already prepared several papers for publication and presentation before the American Chemical Society. Fundamental questions beckoned, tempting him far from the problems of immediate application.

To retain Midgley's talents for the corporation and redirect his enthusiasm to more promising ventures, Kettering worked out an unusual scheme. He arranged for further funding of Midgley's fundamental studies while he cast about for another stimulating project. In May 1928 Kettering even sent Midgley off to Cornell University so that he could pursue his studies there for a time.[33] Kettering kept a close watch on this work, corresponding with Midgley frequently and visiting him occasionally.

Midgley's rubber research became his lifelong obsession. He published most of his results in the ACS *Journal* from 1928 through the late 1930s. These studies brought their author the professional recognition he coveted, though as Sloan and Kettering had feared, nothing commercial ever came of them. But then Midgley was in good company. Just as General Motors began phasing out its rubber investigation, Ford Motor Company and Firestone Tire and Rubber Company advanced Thomas Edison nearly $200,000 for a similar venture. Edison, then in semiretirement on his Florida estate, spent two years seeking a new source of natural rubber. After examining some 14,000 varieties of plant and trying endless experiments on the composition of new rubbers, all Edison had to show for his work was a fourteen-foot hybrid goldenrod and a large investment in Georgia real estate by Henry Ford.[34] Even Wallace Carothers, Du Pont's nylon inventor, had no success synthesizing rubber.[35]

The lack of practical results hardly bothered Midgley, who by this time was completely engrossed. "The theoretical investigation of rubber which I elected to pursue, is continually broadening in its aspects and it may be some little time before we have obtained any commercial results, if ever," he wrote from Cornell in the fall of 1928. "However, it is work that needs to be done and we are having a good time doing it." [36]

It was not long, though, before a new refrigerant study would offer enough theoretical interest to lure Midgley back into corporate ventures, at least for a time.

General Motors was in the process of consolidation and organizational change under Sloan's early leadership. Some divisions, such as Samson Tractor Company, were trimmed or eliminated. Others were added or reorganized. In the winter of 1927, the Frigidaire Company was on the critical list. While the company had improved on the disastrous record of its first years, it had not proved as profitable as top executives had hoped. Only some great change, technical or otherwise, would fortify its position within the corporation.

Frigidaire had a short and checkered career. Alfred Mellowes, a mechanical engineer from Detroit, originally founded the Guardian Frigerator Company in 1916. For two years, he built and serviced the products himself. And though he only sold thirty-four refrigerators during his first years in business, he built a loyal following of customers who invested heavily in his enterprise. They fared better as customers than owners, though, and lost most of their investment.

William C. Durant brought the sagging company into United Motors in June 1918 as a hedge against the possibility that the government would curtail automobile production; devices to conserve food were considered essential goods. When the war ended five months later, Durant sold the company to General Motors at the original purchase price of $56,366.50. [37]

General Motors had no more success than Mellowes in making the venture profitable. The bulky and unreliable units defied every effort to make them cheap and dependable, and the company continued to lose money. By April 1921 Frigidaire had accumulated $2.5 million in debts, and General Motors was ready to jettison its unfortunate purchase. [38] Only Kettering's intervention saved it.

Kettering's interest in refrigeration stemmed from the war. Early in 1918, he had commissioned an informal investigation of the subject at the Dayton Metal Products laboratory. Like Durant, he wanted a new product for the postwar market. In November of that year R. H. Grant, sales manager of the Domestic Engineering Company, suggested another reason for studying refrigeration carefully. Nearly half of the Delco-Light owners in the south could be sold a refrigerating option, he calculated.[39] Kettering became intoxicated with the notion of a huge tropical market for refrigerating and air conditioning. "To the eye of the Lord I suppose a Mexican is a precious human soul. But what good is he to an American industrialist who has radios and washing machines and vacuum cleaners and automobiles to sell? He is almost zero," said Kettering. "But what will this tropic man be, both as a competitor and a purchaser, when he begins buying temperature just as he buys water and light? . . . The possibility of this simple idea is so great that we can hardly begin to visualize the changes it will make."[40]

In 1921, Sloan transferred Frigidaire from Detroit to Dayton and combined it with the Domestic Engineering Company. This corporate realignment thus brought together all General Motors' interests in refrigeration and at the same time offered Kettering an opportunity to expand his research in the field.

Kettering paid close attention to the market in planning his strategy of innovation. Contemporary refrigerating systems were complex and expensive, typically with a water-cooled refrigerator in the basement and the cabinet in the kitchen upstairs. Kettering therefore thought that the first priority should be "finding out what can be done in the matter of cost, and the simplification of the apparatus."[41] What he had in mind was a self-contained unit that could be unloaded from the delivery truck and plugged into a socket in the kitchen.

To eliminate the bulky circulating pumps and cooling tanks of the competition, Kettering drew on his automotive experience, transplanting air-cooling simplicity from the automobile, where it had failed, to home refrigeration, where it would succeed. Throughout the early 1920s, he worked with a team of Frigidaire engineers to perfect an air-cooled compressor, introduce asphalt and cork sealing, and reduce the size and weight and increase the dependability of the company's offerings.[42]

Of course, Kettering did not expect these improvements to sell themselves. He urged Frigidaire to put out a promotional booklet outlining the advantages of air-cooled refrigeration. To Frigidaire general manager E. G. Biechler he suggested, "The right kind of advertising program would help you in establishing greater confidence with the people than you now enjoy."[43] This combination of technical innovation and aggressive marketing put Frigidaire into the black for the first time by 1925.

Kettering took a particularly keen interest in the service aspects of marketing. When the Frigidaire unit in his Detroit apartment broke down, and defeated the efforts of several service men to fix it, Kettering hauled two Frigidaire executives into his office for a stern lecture on the importance of good customer relations.[44]

Kettering also prodded Frigidaire into new marketing areas that competitors had overlooked. He fought hard for a research program in mechanical dehumidification at a time when most engineers were looking toward chemical answers. And to emphasize his point that the key to effective air conditioning was humidity control, he urged all Frigidaire engineers to wear lapel buttons proclaiming, "I am a wet ball thermometer!" He took an active role in an experimental program of air-conditioning railroad cars. "On several occasions, he joined us riding in the car, observing the tests, reading the instruments, and taking as intimate an interest in what was going on as any of the younger engineers whose direct job this was," said one project engineer.[45]

Kettering continued to keep one eye on technical developments in the unsettled home refrigeration market too. By the mid-1920s there were two competing types of mechanical refrigeration, each with a crucial weakness. Both utilized the same thermodynamic principle, that a liquid absorbs heat as it evaporates, but in very different ways. Compression refrigerators employed a small, motor-driven pump to maintain the pressure differences crucial for the cycle. Absorption units, on the other hand, used a heat-driven percolator (or absorber) to accomplish the same end. Compression units suffered primarily from toxic and flammable refrigerants; absorption refrigerators were handicapped by inefficient absorbers.

Kettering recognized that the best alternative was far from obvious. He attended professional meetings and conventions, talked with leading experts, and bought several different refrigerators to see how well they worked. What he learned was that neither system had an overwhelming technical advantage. Absorption units used about three times more power but cost less to manufacture.[46] The flux of the market encouraged him. As he wrote to Biechler, "since there is no basic patent situation in any of the work which we have started, our organization should be able to develop these machines into practical form for household work and get considerable patent protection." As to the ultimate outcome, he had no doubt: "I think you must figure on taking a place in the field within the next two years which will absolutely dominate the situation."[47]

To best exploit the abilities of his laboratory chemists and the first-hand experience of the Frigidaire engineers, Kettering set up a cooperative research program that included representatives of each. Kettering himself provided the conduit of information between the two groups. Late Friday afternoons he drove home from Detroit. Edward Newill, chief engineer at Frigidaire, recalled:

My door would swing open and Mr. Kettering, completely unannounced, would walk in about nine o'clock on Saturday morning. His invariable greeting was, "Hello Ed. What's new?" So, that started the conversation and we would gather two, three, or four of the Frigidaire engineering people, primarily the research group, and head for the laboratory to show Mr. Kettering what we had done since the last visit. Of course, the net result of this was that we would talk to Boss Ket during the first hour or hour and a half, bringing him up-to-date on our projects, and then we spent the rest of the morning listening to Mr. Kettering telling us the interesting things that he had been doing in this same period.[48]

Initially, Kettering's researchers looked into the absorption cycle. They discovered that the open door for technical innovation was the absorbent itself. Water worked well enough under normal conditions. But in hot climates (where Kettering expected the best market for home refrigeration) the temperature of water rose too quickly and reduced its efficiency as an absorber. Consequently, Kettering bought an absorption machine and had his chemists replace the water-ammonia solution with other absorbents.[49] Among other things, they uncovered several interesting solid absorbents that became liquid after absorbing ammonia and were therefore suitable for absorption refrigeration. They also explored some promising new refrigerants like methyl chloride as possible replacements for the ammonia. None of this was entirely unknown in the chemical community, but as Kettering shrewdly observed, "when specific application is made of these compounds, certain rearrangements of apparatus will have to be made, which will constitute patentable features."[50]

Kettering's researchers did come up with three interesting new absorption refrigerators. One used calcium chloride as a solid absorbent, and though relatively simple and cheap, it required alternate heating and cooling of the absorbent which reduced thermal efficiency. A similar prototype replaced the calcium chloride with lithium nitrate, which improved efficiency somewhat. The third used a continuous absorption process, electrical heating (instead of gas flame), and an air-cooled engine.[51]

Kettering put much faith in the third option. He told Biechler:

We are laying out a machine now . . . that represents the best that all of us know in connection with a continuously operated, dry, absorbent, air-cooled machine, which has all the installation advantages of our present compressor type machines. It is too early yet to make any statements as to the costs of this machine, but it looks very much as though it would not cost any more than a corresponding compressor machine.[52]

His expectations were not fulfilled. Wheeler Lovell, a chemist in the Research Laboratory who concentrated on theoretical studies of combustion, worked on the absorption machine under Kettering's watchful eye for some time. Lovell did manage to increase the thermal efficiency of the machine almost 30 percent. But minor troubles plagued him. After a year and a half of battling stubborn circulating fans, absorption tanks clogged with viscous lithium nitrate, poor cooling, and slow absorption, he gave up. Only one new Frigidaire absorption machine actually made it to market (in late 1926) and that was a stopgap version of the calcium chloride unit.[53]

Baffled by an inability to overcome the obstacles of perfecting a practical absorption refrigerator, Kettering turned to improving the compression refrigerator. Again, familiarity with the market gave him the edge. A series of highly publicized accidents with toxic and flammable refrigerants focused his attention on refrigerants. Only a very few substances met the exacting requirements for pressure and temperature, and all of these were either poisonous or flammable. Common refrigerants included methyl chloride, butane, and ammonia. Frigidaire, and some of its competitors, used sulfur dioxide. About the only advantage of this poison gas was its penetrating and irritating odor that gave potential victims some warning. Whenever a Frigidaire refrigerator was defrosted, there was a chance the ice pick would slip and cause a dangerous leak. Several Frigidaire customers, in fact, had died this way, so the need for a better refrigerant was obvious.[54]

Besides the commercial prospects, Kettering saw in the refrigerant work an ideal opportunity to lure Midgley away from the rubber studies. A series of literature searches by Boyd indicated that the refrigerant project might lead to some questions of great fundamental interest.[55] And it looked to Kettering like the kind of project that would best utilize Midgley's broad perspective on chemical problems.

At first, Midgley resisted Kettering's overtures. But by the end of the summer of 1928, Midgley agreed to leave Cornell and go to work on the refrigerant project.[56] He still declined the offer to join the Research Laboratory in Detroit, however, so Kettering once more arranged a special subsidy so that Midgley could pursue the work in Dayton and at Ohio State University.

Kettering's role in the early going, as usual, was to chart broad directions. At one of the first meetings with Midgley, the laboratory chemists, and the Frigidaire engineers, Kettering laid out what he considered the key requirements of the new refrigerant—a suitable boiling point, nontoxicity, noninflammability, and relatively low cost.

Of course, setting criteria was one thing and finding a compound that satisfied them quite another. However, Midgley soon narrowed the search to a small set of compounds. Working from Robert Wilson's periodic table, which he had used so effectively in the search for an antiknock compound, Midgley noticed that all the elements of sufficient volatility appeared in a cluster on the right-hand side of the table. After he dismissed the ones he thought too unstable, only a handful remained. Every known refrigerant consisted of some combination of these elements. Even more remarkable to Midgley was the order of the group. When he compared physical properties of these elements, he noticed a pattern—flammability decreased from left to right on the periodic table, while toxicity decreased from bottom to top.[57]

Midgley presented his findings to his colleagues at a dramatic meeting in the Hochwalt and Thomas Laboratory. "We took the wallpaper off an old dining room and we papered it with white paper and we drew the coordinates in there of all the critical pressures and temperatures of all known gases used in refrigerators," Kettering recalled. Exactly in the middle, where an ideal refrigerant should be, was the element fluorine. Most of the chemists were skeptical about fluorine as the basis for a refrigerant because it was known to be poisonous and corrosive. However, someone (almost certainly Midgley's assistant Albert Henne, who had recently completed a doctoral dissertation under Frederick Swarts, the acknowledged expert on fluorine chemistry) suggested that fluorine substitutions on chlorine compounds might yield a suitable refrigerant. The others strongly disagreed. At this point, Kettering interceded with his usual plea for empiricism. "Well, I don't know, I think we ought to try it."[58]

Midgley and Henne went back to the laboratory to try. "Plottings of boiling points, hunting for data, corrections, slide rules, log paper, eraser dirt, pencil shavings, and all the rest of the paraphernalia that takes the place of tea leaves and crystal spheres in the life of the scientific clairvoyant, were brought into play," Midgley remembered.[59] The blackboard work narrowed the search to a few promising candidates. One synthesis led to dichloromonofluoromethane, another to dichlorodifluoromethane, the real breakthrough. From there Midgley and Henne put together a whole family of fluorinated hydrocarbons which later became known as the freons.

No one at first grasped the significance of these compounds. When Kettering first learned about them, and their surprising fire-extinguishing properties, he thought they might be useful as fire inhibitors rather than refrigerants.[60]

Even as the potential of the freons as refrigerants became obvious, the chemists remained skeptical about corrosion and toxicity. But as Kettering had suspected at the beginning, experiment put the lie to theory. None of the metals commonly used in refrigerator construction showed any reaction to the freons.[61] Preliminary animal studies by Robert Kehoe at the University of Cincinnati indicated that the fears about toxicity were similarly groundless.[62] Kehoe, who had played a key role in the health studies of TEL, now headed an industrial hygiene laboratory funded by, and named for, Kettering himself. But whether or not the sources of funding influenced the research in any way, Kehoe's tests on monkeys, dogs, and guinea pigs were vital in winning eventual approval for the new refrigerants. In any case, no later investigations contradicted Kehoe's original conclusions.

As excitement mounted in the laboratories, so did expectations in the boardroom. The freons looked like the ideal antidote for Frigidaire's uncertain market position. By July 1929, the chemists' enthusiasm had filtered through Kettering to the upper management levels. Frigidaire's general manager began to push for pilot production. "One thing is certain," he wrote to John Pratt, General Motors vice-president in charge of the accessory manufacturers. "If the problem is as near solved as it looks like it is, the quicker we can determine we have the right thing, the better off we will be. Nothing would please me more than to spring a thing like this on our most radical competitor, and I wish we had it today rather than waiting six months or a year."[63]

Preproduction details delayed the start-up of a pilot plant until the fall and winter of 1929. By then, Du Pont Company chemists were also active in refrigerant research, introduced to the subject by the General Motors chemists. Several Frigidaire managers worried that Du Pont would upstage their efforts with an announcement of the discovery.[64]

Midgley and Henne also pressed Kettering to unveil the research before their hard work was overshadowed by a Du Pont release. In the spring of 1930 he relented, and at the April meeting of the American Chemical Society in Atlanta, the chemists introduced freon.

Midgley, who delighted in the theatrical, breathed in a bit of the compound on stage and slowly exhaled it to surround and extinguish a candle flame, demonstrating both the nontoxicity and the noninflammability of the refrigerant. The audience was amazed.[65]

The chemical community greeted Midgley's research with acclaim and enthusiasm. The American Chemical Society *Journal* and *Industrial and Engineering Chemistry* published the results. Midgley's position in the scientific world was further enhanced that spring by his election to the Board of the ACS, a post he would hold until his tragic and premature death fourteen years later.

Kettering's team now faced the inevitable challenge of developing a cost-efficient manufacturing process. Despite its obvious advantages, freon would still have to compete with other refrigerants, particularly in commercial markets. Boyd studied ten basic reactions in hopes of finding a high-temperature process combining carbon tetrachloride with cheap, easily obtained fluorine compounds like sodium fluoride, calcium fluoride, and potassium fluoride and appropriate catalysts.[66]

Despite some success in perfecting fluorine reactions, a full-sized production plant did not lie in General Motors' future. Sloan believed that the most profitable course for General Motors lay in capitalizing on known manufacturing skill, not striking out into unknown markets. Remembering the success of Ethyl Corporation, and reluctant to commit the corporation to full-fledged chemical production when Du Pont already had chemical engineering experience, Sloan and Pratt began negotiations with the parent organization.

On August 27, 1930, the two companies formed a joint stock corporation to manufacture and market freon. Du Pont, in recognition of its chemical knowhow, received 51 percent of the new Kinetic Chemical Company stock. General Motors held the remaining shares and received a substantial royalty for its initial development and patent position.[67] For his work, Midgley was rewarded with a vice-presidency.

Until the final phases of the commercial negotiations, Kettering played an active role in managing the project. His forceful intercessions in the councils of finance kept open the funding channels. Just as important, he bolstered the researchers' morale with friendly encouragement and frequent conferences. When Frigidaire executives worried that Midgley's late and erratic hours would cause security problems, Kettering arranged for a new laboratory just outside the plant fence.[68] To demonstrate his personal faith in the product, he converted the refrigerating equipment at Ridgeleigh Terrace and on his yacht to freon.[69]

Du Pont's intervention and the forming of Kinetic Chemical quickly redefined Kettering's role as manager and Midgley's role as chemist. In June 1930, when talk of a joint manufacturing effort was still tentative, word filtered down that all further research would be cleared through Dr. H. W. Elley of Du Pont.[70] Later directives further restricted General Motors' part in the project, transferring the study of manufacturing processes and composition to Wilmington and limiting General Motors' chemists to "finding more gas detectors for leaks," an important if uninspiring assignment.[71]

The exciting challenges of pioneering research gradually gave way to unglamorous, if crucial, problems of balance, noise, and lubrication. Midgley soon realized that he could advance in his field only by moving on to other projects. Kettering was preoccupied with a concurrent project on the diesel engine and had no new chemical investigations to offer his friend. Midgley returned to his rubber studies and used his position as vice-president of the Ohio State University research laboratories to begin a series of fundamental studies that would engage him until his death in 1944. He rose rapidly to the top of his profession and was president of the American Chemical Society when he died. Though Midgley retained close ties to General Motors through Kettering and his Ethyl and Kinetic Chemical board memberships, he never again participated in any of their commercially directed research projects.

Struck with a rare form of adult polio in 1942, Midgley nonetheless gamely pursued his chemical research. A mechanical engineer at heart, he developed a system of ropes and pulleys to enable himself to move about his bed more easily. During one of these maneuvers, he became entangled in the ropes and accidentally strangled, a tragic victim of his own ingenuity. His death upset Kettering greatly. After the burial, Kettering penned an eloquent eulogy for his friend. "At his funeral," Kettering wrote, "the minister read the familiar verse, 'we brought nothing into this world, and it is certain that we can carry nothing out.' It struck me then that in Midgley's case it would have seemed so appropriate to have added this: 'but we can leave a lot behind for the good of the world.' "[72]

General Motors profited handsomely from Midgley's brief association with the refrigerant project. Despite a relatively high cost, the freons proved so superior to their competition that within five years they became the standard refrigerant in domestic use and were licensed to most of Kinetic's competitors. Coupled with Frigidaire's other advances in technology and marketing, the freons raised the company to a leading role in the industry and divisional status in the corporation. New uses for the product, chiefly as a spray propellant for insecticide during the war, built a firm foundation for a major industry.

Kettering's contributions to these chemical projects were many. With an eye for the technical future and the men who could make it, he chose the synthetic rubber and refrigerant projects and research teams and sold General Motors on both. Steering toward projects theoretically interesting to the chemists and financially appealing to the accounting and patent departments, he did much to steady the innovation process, bringing men of science and men of business together for their mutual benefit.

Too often, research projects were divided into groups, "pure" and "applied." Kettering wisely rejected this artificial distinction, recognizing that every project contained elements of both. By emphasizing the fundamental questions implicit in even the most commercially oriented projects, he was able to hold on to as outstanding a chemist as Thomas Midgley.

To assist the professional ambitions of his chemists, he encouraged publication and active participation in professional societies. He also answered the criticism of skeptical patent experts and stingy corporate vice-presidents. For the very best researchers, he offered special accommodations and even his personal financial support. If a project turned sour, he served as mediator, finding new fields of research for the scientists and smoothing ruffled feathers all around.

Kettering lacked Sloan's organizational talents. But his feel for handling researchers did perhaps as much for the corporation as Sloan's managerial strategies. Because Kettering understood and accepted the special needs of industrial researchers, chemical endeavors flourished at General Motors.

10 / THE DIESEL AND THE DEPRESSION

Frederick Hooven, one of Kettering's close associates on a number of technical investigations, once said of him that "he had the vision to see which way things ought to go and then the uncanny ability as a salesman to push them that way."[1] Never would Kettering put these skills to better use than in his development of the light-weight, two-stroke diesel for General Motors.

The compression-ignition power plant was Rudolph Diesel's idea. As early as the 1890s, Diesel predicted that his engine would replace the steam engine and revolutionize the power field. In the years following this bold claim, the use of his machine in merchant ships, submarines, switching locomotives, and stationary power in factories and for electrical generators seemed to support the prediction. However, the diesel was still a rather slow, heavy engine, which created obvious difficulties where speed and weight were critical considerations. Kettering and his General Motors engineers would carry out the final phase of the revolution and make the diesel light and flexible.

Surprisingly, the revolution involved little truly revolutionary engineering. It required only imaginative adaptation of existing technology and appropriate managerial innovations. Kettering's contributions to the new diesel, both technical and promotional, were crucial. Alfred Sloan once said, "In a large organization like General Motors it is seldom possible to assign to any one person the credit— or the blame—for initiating some major undertaking. But in the case of the diesel, Charles F. Kettering comes very close to being the whole story." [2]

The diesel attracted Kettering because it promised far better fuel economy than conventional gasoline engines. A diesel draws in plain air, instead of a mixture of air and gasoline, compresses it to very high temperature and pressure (about 16:1), takes in a charge of fuel oil or some other heavy hydrocarbon, and ignites it with the heat of compression alone. Among its advantages is that it uses higher compression (for more power and thermal efficiency), it can use cheaper fuel, and it needs no electrical ignition system. However, to withstand high compression, it needs a stronger, and more expensive, construction, and tends to be relatively heavy and slow compared with a gasoline engine. [3]

A number of prominent engineers looked to the diesel as a possible solution to the fuel crisis of the 1920s. Elmer Sperry tried his hand at improving the diesel, and often told Kettering about the potential thermal advantages of the diesel. In 1920 he wrote Kettering, "Instead of going down the street gasping for breath and suffering tremendous fuel economy losses and thereby having about 5% thermal efficiency to the back axle, we can do the same thing at an enormous fuel savings [with an automotive diesel]. . . . Why aren't you the logical fellow to take the next step with me and put this thing into service?" [4] Kettering pointed out that while the diesel did seem to have a promising future, the engine would need some radical modifications before it would be useful in an automobile.

Kettering kept up with the technical work in progress on the diesel, particularly developments in Europe. He sent letters to leading German and Swiss firms, and learned that most of them saw a strong market for the diesel in the stationary power field and for marine uses but did not foresee practical applications in the rest of the transportation industry. [5]

Several mechanical engineers that Kettering talked to within the

Research Corporation were more encouraging. Charles Short, who had worked with diesels at General Electric before he joined General Motors, told Kettering that in his opinion, some of the drawbacks of the contemporary diesel, its great weight for one, resulted from poor design and were not inherent handicaps of the engine. Said Short, "It is not necessary, as is almost universally believed, that the heavy oil engine be built more robust than the standard [gasoline] engine."[6]

By the late 1920s, other engineers were also taking a closer look at the diesel. The SAE devoted its 1927 meeting of the Midwest Section to technical developments in diesel trucks and locomotives. C. Lyle Cummins, active in the diesel truck field, gave a paper on his new fuel-injection system. An engineer from the Baldwin Locomotive Works, an established steam engine company, presented a study on a "diesel-electric power unit for locomotives" undertaken with General Electric. Kettering sent one of his research engineers to the meeting, but the representative returned with the opinion that, at least for the moment, the diesel was still too slow and too heavy, and that barring a severe fuel shortage, its liabilities would more than offset any gains in fuel economy.[7]

Kettering supported diesel developments with his private investments. Along with Carl Fisher, a wealthy friend and Florida land developer, he invested substantial sums in the Trieber Diesel Company, a small New Jersey research and development firm headed by O. E. Trieber. Kettering's interest caused a considerable stir both within the company and in the larger engineering community. After a meeting of the three principals in Miami, Fisher told Trieber that Kettering "was very anxious to see you as he has finally decided that he wants to get in some manner into the Diesel picture. I think he is entirely sold on you and certainly this is a blessing and we want him with us."[8]

In the spring of 1928, Kettering started his own study of the diesel. On the advice of several friends and associates, he commissioned the *Olive K*, a 105-foot yacht, from the Defoe Shipbuilding Company of Bay City, Michigan. For its power plant he selected a 175-horsepower, four-stroke diesel.[9]

Olive decorated the yacht herself, and found it perfect for entertaining. She organized frequent dinner parties and cruises on the Great Lakes, formal affairs catered by tuxedoed stewards. Olive did not like waves, and on her instructions the vessel was kept close to shore. On one memorable occasion, though, the wake from a lake steamer shook the boat and sent the chief steward and his pudding tumbling down the galley stairs.

For Kettering, the *Olive K* was primarily a floating laboratory which offered him a chance to tinker with the diesel. He spent most of his time on board in the engine room, accompanied by his male guests. The engine did require fairly constant attention but not so much as Kettering gave it. Fred Hooven, a frequent guest on the summer cruises of 1928, recalled that most of the time Kettering was just fiddling with nothing particular in mind.[10]

Although the engine experiments were mostly for fun, they taught him some important lessons about diesels. The erratic performance of the fuel injector suggested to Kettering that a better design was needed. He told Carl Fisher, "It looks to me as though this whole problem of Diesel engines gets back to the injection system."[11]

Another valuable lesson was the potential of the two-stroke cycle. Looking for better performance from the engine, Kettering met with William Jackson, a consulting engineer from Detroit. Jackson told him that a four-stroke engine would never deliver good performance. "The logical choice when considering the correct design of an oil engine is the two-stroke cycle," said Jackson. "By adopting this cycle we double the number of power impulses per cylinder and this naturally permits our using a smaller number of cylinders than we would have to do if we directly compared such an engine with a four-cycle . . . type."[12] Jackson offered his patents, and himself, to General Motors in return for a "substantial salary," but after conferring with the legal department, Kettering wanted only the patents.[13]

By the fall of 1928, it was obvious that Kettering had adopted the diesel as his current pet project. The family cat was even named "Diesel Dust." One potential application of the diesel that excited him was in the sluggish railroad industry. He complained about the railroads' lack of interest in technological innovation:

In the Pullman car, I think—a slot for razor blades, a slide in the window and a coat hanger have been the entire increments of progress over the last twenty years. . . . The Diesel engine has some great possibilities in connection with railway operations. I have often felt that I would like to build a train for some railroad. . . . I would make it very quiet and in other words, do to the railroad what we have tried so hard to do in automotive practice.[14]

Kettering had some bold plans for the marine market too. He thought about building another yacht with advanced diesel power plants, and incorporating an idea for synchronizing them electrically to eliminate the vibration typical of marine diesels. He wrote Fisher, "I am figuring a little bit now on having a boat built about 165 to 170 feet long, more or less as an experiment to see if it is possible to build a Diesel but that will not have a lot of noise and vibration about it. Certainly I have never seen one yet but was full of vibration. I would like to build a boat so that you would think you were being towed."[15] But distractions at the Research Laboratories and a lack of interest in the idea by outside companies delayed his plans.[16]

Finding a suitable engine to drive the proposed yacht was not easy. Kettering wrote to most American diesel builders, but found none of their engines appropriate. The president of the Winton Engine Company of Cleveland promised to build Kettering "the finest Diesel Engine produced in this Country."[17] Kettering ripped the design to pieces.

This proposal does not interest me in the least. The reason it does not interest me is because . . . I do not believe your organization is sold on the solid injection engine, in order to be a trustworthy concern to build these. I do not believe that you can chain drive these generators but believe they have to be made integral with the main engine shaft. It seems to me, that with the present development in Diesel engines, a man would be foolish to install these tons of cast iron when we are right on the eve of a transition in which we can get horse power without so much weight. I have just about decided to drop the question of a new boat until I can really see some prospect of getting a power plant that would represent what I think it is possible to do.[18]

Kettering finally decided that if he was to get a better diesel engine, the Research Laboratories would have to build it. Fortunately, at the same time, other top corporate executives were looking for a new product line to fill an expected gap in the automobile market. Alfred Sloan recalled dropping by the Research Laboratories in Detroit one day and asking Kettering why the diesel, despite its efficiency, had not found much of a market. He came away from Kettering's lecture convinced that General Motors should be in the diesel engine business.[19]

In September 1928, Kettering met formally with Sloan, John Pratt, and Fred Fisher (of Fisher Body), to discuss a major diesel investment by General Motors. Kettering's enthusiasm had its usual impact. After the meeting, John Pratt told him, "Mr. Sloan and Mr. Fisher were very much impressed with what you thought were the future possibilities of the Diesel Engine." The committee asked Kettering to keep on top of technical developments in the field and gave him a half-million-dollar budget for experimental designs.[20]

However, Kettering was a long way from building any engines. First he wanted to study the various components of the diesel carefully. The diesel had a long technical history, particularly in Europe, and Kettering knew from experience that a good engineer never ignored the work of others. Moreover, he knew that successful innovations were usually imaginative adaptations of earlier ideas: "it may be that all we need to do is pick out all the important factors which are fairly well developed," he wrote Pratt. Still, he had no doubts about the ultimate outcome. "I think we have a wonderful opportunity of going out and doing a real job here and the whole internal combustion engine problem has opened up in such a way that I feel we should be the leaders of every phase of it."[21]

The next year was a significant one for the future of Kettering's diesel. On June 19, 1929, the Research Laboratories were moved into new quarters across the street from the old location. Kettering presided over the housewarming and led his guests on a guided tour of the facility, which included an illustrated lecture on diesel research.[22]

Concurrently, General Motors began negotiations with several firms active in diesel development and manufacturing. Sloan once told Kettering that "it is always cheaper to buy . . . things partly developed than it is to start at the beginning and go through everything, making mistakes which are always costly and over a period of years represent an extraordinary sum of money, usually greater than it takes to buy out something even if you pay something for the goodwill."[23] Kettering generally preferred to make his own mistakes. But the diesel was an established industry with tight patent protection, and even Kettering agreed that buying existing companies might give General Motors a better chance at the business.

Many companies were active in the field. Most, at least in Kettering's view, were not worth very much from a technical standpoint. The Trieber Company, for instance, had produced nothing of importance despite Kettering's investment, and was eliminated from consideration. The decision left one of Kettering's friends, Henry B. Joy, out in the cold. He complained to Kettering, "The best thing I ever had a chance to get going right, since the 'Packard,' has been canned by . . . General Motors." But Joy accepted his loss with a bit of humor. With the letter to Kettering, he enclosed a newspaper clipping about a German plumber who claimed he could convert lead into gold. "Why bother about making motor cars or Diesels," Joy teased. "Get busy and make the money direct!"[24]

Another possible acquisition was Cummins, makers of automotive diesels. Kettering invited C. L. Cummins out to the laboratory one evening in order to test Cummins' engine. "Ket and I sat in the car," Cummins remembered. "We gradually increased the throttle speed until the engine roared at capacity r.p.m. Suddenly a tremendous flash nearly blinded us. Smoke billowed through the laboratory. I shut off the engine as Ket and I leaped from the car." The diesel exhaust had violently reacted with a compound in the flexible pipe used to expel exhaust gases from the laboratory. Despite this mishap, Kettering wanted to buy Cummins, but Cummins' partner would not sell out.[25]

An even more interesting property was the Winton Engine Company, the Cleveland firm that Kettering had criticized for the too-heavy marine engines. Automobile magnate Alexander Winton had founded the company in 1912, and it had been building marine diesels for more than a decade. Kettering was especially interested in a type of fuel injector Winton then had on the drawing board. The other General Motors executives involved with the diesel investment went along with Kettering's recommendation to buy out the firm.

Pratt wrote to Sloan, "The purchase of this company will give us a while for capitalizing the development of our research organization along engine lines and will assist materially in keeping us abreast of Diesel engine developments. The business should be reasonably profitable, and if expansion continues, as most of our engineers believe it will, we should ultimately make a good return on the investment." [26]

In addition to Winton, Kettering had his eye on another Cleveland firm, the Electro-Motive Company. This small consulting company was one of Winton's customers and specialized in locomotive engine installations. In recent years, business had dropped off considerably, and the firm's present assets consisted primarily of its chief engineers, Richard Dilworth and Harold L. Hamilton. After extended negotiations, made difficult by fluctuating stock values, the Executive Committee of General Motors voted to acquire the two companies. On June 30, 1930, Winton officially joined the General Motors family, and on December 31, Electro-Motive followed.

Meanwhile, Kettering purchased a new yacht with Winton engines, intending once again to add personal evaluation and experience to the corporation's diesel program. The ship was designed by the renowned New York naval architects Wells, Cox, and Stevens, and built by the Defoe Boat Works. Kettering sold the original *Olive K* at the end of August 1929 and accepted delivery of the new boat on September 5. A party of General Motors associates helped him celebrate the christening of the second *Olive K* in Bay City, Michigan. [27]

The new *Olive K* cost almost half a million dollars, was 170 feet long, and combined the finest in marine architecture with sumptuous decor. Olive selected the interior furnishing, including a black walnut dining room ensemble, a taffeta and velvet embroidered piano cover, an electric fireplace, a well-stocked library, and antiques in the parlor. [28]

Kettering limited his suggestions to technical matters. He designed and installed a central phonograph and radio system that gave each of his guests individual listening choices. He purchased a Sperry gyroscopic stabilizer to steady the vessel in rough seas, and even found time to work out a practical electrical engine synchronizer.

The synchronizer was particularly ingenious. Normally, as the yacht pitched from side to side, one propeller dug deeper into the water than the other, increasing resistance on one side and setting up a noticeable vibration. Kettering overcame the problem with a system of alternating-current generators that balanced the speed of the two diesels and kept vibration to a minimum. They also provided a convenient source of alternative electrical power for the boat.[29] Kettering thought so much of the synchronizer that he asked James McEvoy to patent three of its special features.[30]

In January 1930, Kettering organized a six-week cruise aboard the yacht for several of his close friends. After a shakedown cruise in Lake Huron, the *Olive K*, under the command of Captain F. F. Tabeling and a crew of twenty-two, headed south to Miami for a rendezvous with the Ketterings and their guests John Pratt, Bill Chryst, Julius Stone (a Dayton banker and industrialist), Gar Wood (a famous boat racer), Roy McClure (a Detroit physician), and Eugene Kettering and his friend and classmate, Virginia Weiffenbach.[31]

Eugene was included because he had recently dropped out of Cornell University and had nothing better to do. Kettering had always hoped that his son would follow in his footsteps as an engineer. Eugene did show natural aptitude for practical mechanics, like his father, but he had little grasp of abstract concepts, particularly mathematics. He gained admission to Cornell, and enjoyed an active fraternity and social life there. He did not do well in the academic subjects. In April 1927, in the middle of his freshman year, Eugene told his father:

I have been spending all my time on Calculus but I don't see it like I should and the reason is because I don't have the high school work clear enough in my mind. I don't seem to be able to remember a thing I had in high school. I knew I was dumb but I didn't know it was as bad as it is. I can't grasp things like the rest of the fellows can. I wish I could because I am interested in things like physics and electricity. . . . The only thing I seem good for is to drive a taxi or something like that. I think I would understand things a lot better if I had practical or more common examples instead of reading out of a book that something was so. I guess as a student I am a total loss. Never the less I'm not going to give up as long as I can still kick. [32]

Kettering helped his son as much as he could. He read Eugene's textbooks, worked through some of the problems, talked with the Cornell professors, and arranged for private tutors. More to the point, perhaps, he urged Eugene to pull himself up by the bootstraps.

In the first place, you have to add as we do in business—your debits and credits, or assets and liabilities. In the first place, you are very much interested in engineering—you have no difficulty in seeing through mechanisms and knowing what to do to fix them. You do not have to worry as I did— about your finances—so all this has to be stacked up against the liability of your dislike for the particular kind of mathematics that seem to be essential in the modern engineering school before you can take these things which directly interest you. . . . If it is necessary for you to get a tutor that will help you in your mathematics, do that—and then for the summer maybe the best thing to do is to come to Detroit and we will get some fellow, who is a good mathematician, to spend a certain amount of time with you each week and go and review all of your past mathematics.

There is no job that you ever strike, no matter in what line, that is all to ones liking. . . . I know that you enjoy working around mechanisms and have a natural talent for engineering matters. I would like to help you in every way possible to get as much of a technical foundation as possible. [33]

But even Kettering's best efforts could not get Eugene through the tough Cornell curriculum. Eugene left school for the cruise in January and never returned. On board he proposed to his tall, blond, high-school sweetheart. Both families had long assumed that Virginia and Eugene, friends since childhood, would marry. Their April 1930 wedding ceremony at the Dayton Westminister Presbyterian Church was an elaborate social event. [34] After a two-month honeymoon in the West, Eugene settled down to a solid, if undistinguished, career with Winton and Electro-Motive arranged by his father.

The *Olive K* left Miami on January 6. On the second night out the stabilizer broke down in heavy seas, and the entire party became seasick. Mrs. Kettering and Miss Weiffenbach got off in Havana, and the men continued on to Panama and the Pacific Ocean.

Kettering relished the all-male company. He strolled around the deck in his underwear, explored lava beds on the volcanic islands in the Galapagos, chased sea turtles, and caught red sand crabs on the beaches. He did not have much luck with fishing at first. But when he "couldn't get anything on his new pole, [he] took Gar's old one, and landed a fine bonito," and later caught a large shark.[35]

He also spent a lot of time below deck in the engine room. The Winton diesels acted up constantly. "I do not think we ran at any time over twenty hours without breaking [a nozzle]," Kettering wrote to Deeds, back in Dayton. He added that there would be little trouble overcoming the problem, but the *Olive K* had to be docked for valve grinding and other engine repairs.[36]

The trip left a vivid impression on the guests. McClure recounted:

So unique a host was Kettering that I constantly felt like calling him Captain Nemo, for *Twenty Thousand Leagues Under the Sea* was in my youth a favorite. Captain Nemo is not in the same class as Kettering. . . . Captain Nemo never had such music as we had. . . . Ket had it arranged so that we not only could dial from our phones any other phone on the boat, but any one of the twenty-four phonograph records . . . the programs each day being changed and placed by each phone. Also while in the North any one of ten radio broadcasting stations when dialed would automatically tune in. . . . Of course, Ket called this an experimental boat and spent a great deal of time in the engine room and back of the radio cabinet.[37]

While Kettering was away on his extended vacations and business trips in Europe and the South Seas, his engineers kept on top of the diesel situation. The more they observed, the more confident they became. One of the research men told Kettering:

The G.M. Research organization is in a favorable position to carry on an investigation of the problems of increasing the speed and M.E.P. [mean effective pressure] of oil engines in spite of our lack of previous experience with existing types of engines. The problems to be solved are the mechanics of the injection system, the processes of combustion, and the design of light, high-speed engine structure. Our experience with the high speed valve gear, and such instruments as the electrical stroboscope places us in a position to attack the injection problem that is not likely to be found in the existing Diesel engine industry.[38]

At the first opportunity upon his return, Kettering plunged back into the diesel project. He met frequently with his new partners at

Winton and Electro-Motive. Hamilton, Electro-Motive's president, recalled, "He and I had many talks together with our feet on the chair some place thrashing around the problems that went along with the job we were talking about, taking the weight out of the diesel and reducing the weight of the reciprocating parts and getting some snap to it." [39] Late into the night the two engineers shared ideas and dreams. Kettering became more and more excited as the discussions wore on. "It was like ringing a bell to a fire horse; he wanted to get into that act quick," said Hamilton.

Fuel injection was still a major problem. Stationary diesels used compressed air both to inject the fuel into the dense atmosphere of the combustion chamber and to give the charge the necessary turbulence. The weight of the compressor was the drawback. Solid fuel injection—injecting the fuel without first mixing it with air—was another possibility. Winton had employed this system on its diesels (including the ones on the first *Olive K*). But while this "common rail injector" (so-called because it supplied fuel to all cylinders through a single, low-pressure pump) cut weight, it frequently gave one cylinder more fuel than another, with erratic, smoky performance.

One Winton engineer, Carl Salisbury, had worked out an improvement, a "unit injector," in which he combined the fuel reservoir, pump, and injector into a single unit mounted directly on the cylinder head. His prototype was huge, two feet long and three inches in diameter, and far from practical, but it piqued Kettering's interest. "It is not unlike the Bosch system, only the pump is built as part of the injection nozzle and operated from an overhead rocker arm," he explained to Eugene. [40]

Kettering invited Salisbury to the Research Laboratories to explain his idea to the engineers in the power plant section. After the meeting, F. G. Shoemaker noted in his log book, "Kettering suggested using injection valve to do away with the carburetor [common rail injector]. Engineers from Winton Company presented drawings of new fuel valve which incorporates a pump in each nozzle assembly." [41]

Kettering bought a set of Salisbury's injectors for the *Olive K*. After a few trials, he told his engineers that the nozzles clogged frequently and that combustion was poor. Also, the units seemed quite sensitive to changes in engine temperature. Kettering suggested that one reason for the poor performance was the dampening effect of friction on the cylinder walls, which lowered turbulence and prevented a good mixture of fuel and air.[42]

After much work, the engineers in the power plant section discovered that the real secret to an improved unit injector was high pressure, which in turn required extremely close production tolerances. With pressures of 4,000 psi, a clearance between the injector plunger and its cylinder of 30/1,000,000 of an inch, and a hole in the injector tip of no more than 6/1000 of an inch in diameter, the clogging, dripping, and smoking stopped.[43] The engineers managed also to reduce the size of the injectors considerably. While these were only incremental improvements on a well-known idea, the combination of parts was novel enough to deserve a patent.

The two-stroke cycle was another step toward a better diesel. Kettering, of course, was familiar with the basic idea. In the fall of 1930 he and George Codrington, president of the Winton division, toured European diesel manufacturing firms for a closer look at foreign design. The men met with several leading diesel engineers, including Robert Sulzer, president of the Sulzer Brothers Company in Switzerland. Sulzer was a major producer of diesel switching locomotives, and Kettering was impressed with their designs. Codrington said of their meeting, "If you can imagine two farmers out on a good time together that would about describe the two men."[44] Sulzer strongly recommended a two-stroke diesel design.

When Kettering returned from Europe he had the Research Laboratories purchase a number of diesel engines of various designs. Subsequent trials confirmed that the two-stroke engine was indeed simpler, lighter, and more powerful than similar four-stroke versions.[45]

The two-stroke cycle's great advantage was that it offered a power stroke on every revolution of the crankshaft, or twice the power for the displacement of a four-stroke cycle. But it was hampered by inadequate scavenging; that is, the engine could not completely expel exhaust gas, draw in a fresh charge, and compress it all in a single stroke; some of the waste gas inevitably remained, decreasing efficiency and fuel economy.

To improve scavenging, the power plant section engineers bought several commercial blowers designed to force out the exhaust gases, and then experimented with different modifications. They blew smoke through wooden models of two-stroke engines and studied the air flow characteristics.[46] Eventually, they came up with an important innovation, a blower with helical instead of straight blades, which they called "uniflow scavenging." The system reduced both pulsation and noise, an advantage Kettering was particularly interested in. "One of the most important problems we have in connection with the design of our new Diesel," he told one project engineer, "is the elimination of noise."[47] In operation, the blower pushed air into a special reservoir surrounding the cylinder, from which it entered the cylinder through a series of ports cut in the wall, and exited through poppet valves in the top of the cylinder head. The blower charged the cylinder at slightly greater than atmospheric pressure for completer scavenging.

The new blower and uniflow design improved performance dramatically. A small prototype test engine pulled 100 horsepower at 750 rpm, about double the expected power of a four-stroke diesel of the same dimensions. Just as important, the two-stroke ran cooler and smoother.[48]

Concurrently, the laboratory conducted other related studies of light-weight alloys for a stronger, lighter, design, high-temperature pistons and valves to handle the special demands of a diesel, and better bearings, connecting rods, and lubricating oil.

Kettering kept abreast of the developments in unit injection, uniflow scavenging, and two-stroke designs partly in person, and partly by letter, but much of his attention was focused elsewhere—travel, speaking engagements, professional meetings, and writing.

Each fall, Kettering took his annual tour of automobile shows. Even the birth of his first grandson, Charles Franklin II, in August 1931, did not delay the fall sailing.[49] Olive usually went along. She loved the shopping and sightseeing, and frequently took side tours without her husband. In 1927 she and Virginia Weiffenbach toured

England and France, and in 1929 and 1934 she cruised the Mediter-
ranean with Mrs. A. R. Maynard, a wealthy friend from Dayton.
Kettering made sure fresh orchids were delivered each night Olive
was on board, and he even sent a Rolls Royce and chauffeur to London so that she could get around the city in style.[50]

Kettering preferred his vacations aboard the *Olive K*, where he could
relax with his male companions. In January 1932, he gathered the
old Galapagos gang for a second Caribbean cruise. He led his friends
through the Mayan ruins at Chichen Itza, and marveled at the
acoustics of the ancient handball courts.[51] Again, the Sperry gyroscopic stabilizer broke down, and the guests suffered from seasick-
ness. "We have had this in operation now almost two years and have
made just two trips on which the stabilizer did not break down,"
Kettering wrote the manufacturer. "It seems to me when a customer
pays you in the order of $50,000 for a piece of apparatus, that he has
a business, as well as a legal right to expect that the piece of apparatus
will perform somewhere near what the maker told him upon purchasing that it would do."[52] Characteristically, he offered a few specific technical suggestions to improve the stabilizer. He told Sperry
to increase the size of the brakedrum and to modify the cooling system.

Edgar Guest wrote a poem to commemorate the second voyage.

Once in an idle moment I remarked;
"I own a yacht to sail the southern seas,
And when upon that vessel I've embarked
I live a life of luxury and ease."

Two weeks this year upon the Olive K
The steward stood to heed my beck and call
The port we sought lay many miles away.
Said one, "You do not own that ship at all
'Tis known the Olive K belongs to Ket
'Tis so recorded in the book marine."

"That's very true," I answered him, "and yet
I think you fail to grasp just what I mean.
Since I've his friendship, by his own design
I share with him adventure's glorious thrills.

Once I'm on board, the lovely ship is mine
With this exception—Ket pays all the bills."[53]

A banking crisis in Dayton also kept Kettering busy. Among his other offices and civic responsibilities, he was chairman of the board of the Winter's National Bank, a largely ceremonial post until the banking failures of 1931. In September, the Union Trust Company, the Winter's main competitor, went bankrupt, and many financial experts expected the repercussions to include a run on the Winter's.

Before the bankruptcy was publicly announced, George Smith telephoned Kettering, then in Europe, and told him the news. Kettering cut short his trip and sailed for New York, where a car was waiting to take him to Dayton. On October 13, 1931, Kettering met with the Winter's officers in an all-day session. The board scrutinized the bank's fiscal condition and the possible effects of the Union Trust Company's failure. Later that evening, the group met with officials of the Union Trust at Ridgeleigh Terrace to discuss a possible merger. Kettering and Smith opposed the merger, and after a heated debate that lasted until dawn, the talks broke down.[54]

The next morning, the state superintendent of banking officially closed the Union Trust, which set off the expected run on the Winter's. Kettering and his son stayed on the floor of the bank from early morning until late at night, talking with customers, trying to reassure them. He even arranged an emergency loan from the Federal Reserve, but it was unnecessary. Kettering described the day for his English friend W. W. Constantine:

I have been trying to get a chance to write you ever since I returned but I have had an extremely hectic time owing to the bank situation in Dayton. The largest bank closed its doors on Saturday after I arrived home, which threw almost the entire banking burden on our bank. Through the assistance of a lot of good friends we were able to handle this thing very nicely and I think that now everything is in pretty good shape.[55]

Eight months later, the Winter's Bank took over the remnants of the Union Trust. Kettering's part in the crisis gave him quite a reputation in the banking world, and he later spoke to many bankers' meetings about his philosophies of finance, including his somewhat vague contention that the key to good banking was research.[56]

A rare pose in the office at the Dayton laboratory in 1924.

The Kettering family ready for a trip west in the experimental bus in 1923. From left to right: Eugene Kettering, C. F. Kettering, Olive Kettering, and one of Eugene's friends.

The GM Research Laboratory in Detroit, 1929.

Making a few notes on Wheeler Lovell's fuel experiments in 1928.

An experimental prototype of the two-stroke diesel engine.

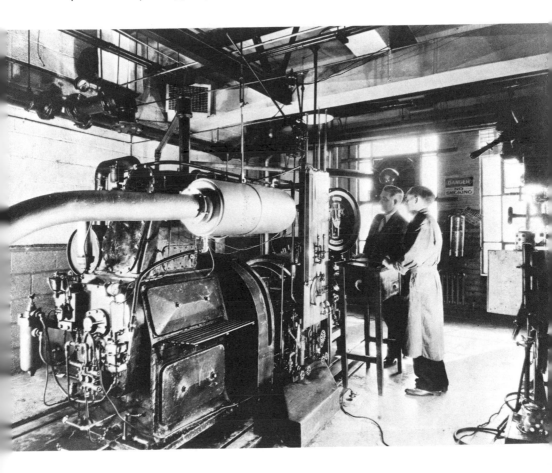

Kettering's yacht, the second Olive K, *at anchor.*

Looking over one of the streamlined Burlington Zephyr locomotives powered by GM diesel engines.

The Kettering fever cabinet, for treating venereal disease.

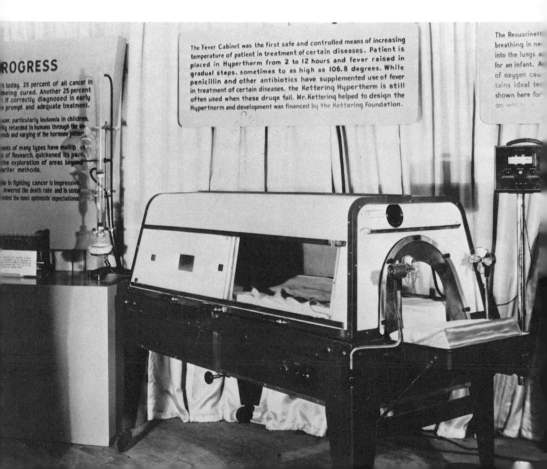

ROGRESS

today, 25 percent of all cancer in
being cured. Another 25 percent
if correctly diagnosed in early
prompt and adequate treatment.

cer, particularly leukemia in children,
retarded in humans through the u-
nds and varying of the hormone patter

ents of many types have multip
of Research, quickened its pa
the exploration of areas beyond
rlier methods.

le in fighting cancer is impressiv
lowered the death rate and in som
eded the most optimistic expectation

The Fever Cabinet was the first safe and controlled means of increasing
temperature of patient in treatment of certain diseases. Patient is
placed in Hypertherm from 2 to 12 hours and fever raised in
gradual steps, sometimes to as high as 106.8 degrees. While
penicillin and other antibiotics have supplemented use of fever
in treatment of certain diseases, the Kettering Hypertherm is still
often used when these drugs fail. Mr. Kettering helped to design the
Hypertherm and development was financed by the Kettering Foundation.

The Resuscinett
breathing in ne
into the lungs a
for an infant. A
of oxygen cau
tains ideal te
shown here for
on whi

Poking under the hood of a high-compression engine prototype in 1947.

Cutting his seventieth birthday cake in Loudonville, Ohio.

Beside his private seaplane, The Blue Tail Fly, *just after retirement in* 1947.

Inspecting the new Corvette at the opening of the Parade of Progress in 1954.

The Dayton banking crisis was only a tiny part of the worsening economic situation throughout the country that followed the stock market crash of 1929. The depression gave Kettering, and his work, an entirely new philosophical dimension, and made him into something of a celebrity.

Along with his colleagues in the engineering and business communities, Kettering had grown accustomed to taking credit for the economic miracle of the 1920s. This seemed only natural, for the automobile industry was perhaps the outstanding example of economic growth during the decade. But in the 1930s, the situation was reversed, and many social critics saw the ailing automobile industry as a harbinger of widespread worker alienation and general economic collapse. Even President Herbert Hoover, the engineer-politician who had promised scientific efficiency in government, came in for bitter criticism. Kettering had little interest in politics, but he had supported Hoover (and won a bet with John J. Raskob over Hoover's nomination), and was disillusioned by the President's failure to forestall recession.[57]

While Kettering became increasingly conservative during the depression, he did not support Technocracy, the only ultraconservative doctrine in those years that attracted members of the engineering community.

"I recently read some articles on 'Technocracy,' " he told the American Association for the Advancement of Science. "The only thing I have to say is that I wish those fellows were my competitors." He then went on to relate one of his favorite stories about the car in the glass case and how it depreciates because innovation changes the customers' expectations.[58] Though he showed little understanding of Technocracy's intricate economic proposals or its intellectual roots, the idea that businessmen and engineers were irreconcilable adversaries he felt was utter nonsense. After all, he personified their mutual interest.

Kettering believed engineers should act through the inventive and economic processes rather than politics. He insisted that traditional capitalistic institutions were the best means of channeling innovations into the social mainstream; democratic, because the wants of each consumer could be tallied by dollar votes; efficient, because the price system allowed gradual accommodation to changing consumer demand. He saw no reason to tamper with the status quo. And he refused to blame engineers for technological unemployment. "I don't feel that the engineer is to blame . . . at least if there is any blame attached it is for what the engineer did not do, not because he did too much," he wrote.[59]

Kettering defended his views in a series of popular articles. In his first piece, published in the *Saturday Evening Post* in December 1930, he offered an engineering analogy to explain the business cycles of capitalism. He dictated the article, as he did most everything he wrote, and then had it rewritten by the public relations department of General Motors. But the ideas were all his own. The economy, Kettering said, was like an automobile engine. It had natural, and unavoidable, fluctuations. Engineers could dampen the vibrations in a crankshaft, and economists should be able to similarly adjust economic oscillations. "In our engineering and scientific work we know of no way of holding a thing on a perfectly defined course," he wrote. "The only way you can regulate is to restrain the swings on one side and reduce them on the other and try to produce out of the average of these continuing oscillations a fairly straight line or a fairly even motion." When the economy got another "big job," something like the automobile industry in the 1920s, it would quickly pull itself out of the depression.[60]

Yet within a year, Kettering's confident prognosis gave way to alarm. In an article entitled "Industry at the Crossroads," he reflected on the deepening crisis and expressed his frustration with the business community's inability to turn things around. He asserted that American business had temporarily abdicated its historical dynamism in favor of safe investments. "Instead of studying human needs and finding new ones, the accepted practice was to let mass production go on supplying the old and the obvious needs," he said. "We trusted to the magic of advertising to sell goods in markets already saturated."[61] In Kettering's view, only industrial research could put the nation back on its feet, by creating new industries, jobs, and wants.

He presented his case for industrial research directly to businessmen and engineers whenever he could. At the annual meeting of the Advertising Federation of America in June 1931, he complained, "Never has it been so difficult to sell an idea as it is today. We are suffering with industrial stagnation and that is all that is wrong with us. If you want to kill any idea in the world today, get a committee working on it to pick out the flaws. Why? Because there is not one man in a thousand who has any imagination." [62]

To fellow engineers he gave the same message. He urged them to pay more attention to practical problems, and pleaded for closer co-operation between scientists and engineers in meeting commercial needs. Speaking to the American Association for the Advancement of Science, he said:

We have gone so far in scientific development and especially in mathematical science, that we have lost connection with the industrial relationship, and, hence, we find in our industrial scientific organizations today that we must have a number of people whom we call translators. These attempt to translate from the modern science back into the technology and material relationships in which we are working. [63]

Kettering had not lost faith in American knowhow, though. "I have absolute faith in what can be done because we haven't exhausted the smallest percentage of our energy and resources," he said. [64] He periodically forecast an imminent upturn in the economy, led, naturally enough, by the automobile industry. "In the present situation," he said, "the automobile people, at least, feel that with new and better cars they can charm many dollars of cash out of their hiding places and back into circulation." [65]

They were wrong in that prediction. In 1932, automobile sales dropped to 1,100,000, down from 4,140,000 just three years before, and for the first time the number of registered cars declined absolutely. The industry's misfortunes only seemed to enhance Kettering's personal prestige, and his Research Laboratories looked more important than ever. On January 9, 1933 *Time* featured his long, thoughtful face on the cover. The inside story outlined his legendary career, with special focus on the place of research in the past, present, and future automobile industry. "He is GM's visionary magician, perched on a high stool whose legs have grown longer and larger as the business has expanded," wrote the reporter. "His fluency of speech and his position as No. 1 engineer of the biggest company have often made him the spokesman for his profession."[66]

In some quarters, the cover touched off more interest than the story. An advertising manager for the American Optical Company spied Kettering's wire-rimmed glasses, and pointed out the irony to Kettering's advertising friend, Bruce Barton: "Something like a million people will see Mr. Kettering wearing old fashioned glasses and extolling on the importance of new things."[67] Barton suggested a new set of frames to Kettering, who missed the point completely, and replied with unintended irony, "There is nothing that I am able to gather . . . which shows that these glasses would improve vision at all. Perhaps the reason that I don't understand is that I have always been accustomed to looking ahead and therefore have not been conscious of the side bars of my glasses."[68]

Kettering's message of recovery through research won him a large conservative backing. He became a popular speaker at rotary clubs, chambers of commerce, and other business meetings. The members of these groups, worried by the proposed reforms of the New Deal, applauded Kettering's more conventional cures. "Yours was the outstanding address of our meeting and we just want you to know that the whole gang appreciated it," wrote the chairman of the Michigan Banker's Association after the annual meeting.[69] The famous and politically influential Committee of 100, a group of conservative millionaires who gathered each winter in Miami Beach, elected Kettering a member. Even a few liberals saw merit in his ideas. When liberal senator Robert F. Wagner met Kettering on a cruise to Europe in the thirties, they compared notes on causes and cures for the economy's problems. Despite a few jabs from Kettering, who teased Wagner that at least he had actually put men to work, while the Labor Relations Act was only paper, the senator agreed that Kettering's scheme of employment through research made good sense.[70]

Kettering's talent for putting his doctrines into practice did not go unnoticed in the engineering world. The Franklin Institute of Philadelphia, one of the country's oldest engineering societies and a leading promoter of industrial research, awarded Kettering the Franklin Medal for his contributions to automotive engineering. What the institute most appreciated was his commercial results. The plaque noted that, thanks in part to his innovations, the automobile "has grown [into] the greatest industry in this country, the manufactured product of which has, in only a quarter of a century changed the face of the civilized world."[71] The recipient of the honor seemed so appropriate, given Benjamin Franklin's similar combination of practical wisdom and scientific curiosity, that some journalists tried to link the institute's namesake with Charles *Franklin* Kettering. The Washington Award Commission of the Western Society of Engineers selected Kettering for its special honor for "high achievements in guiding industrial research towards the greater comfort, happiness, and safety of mankind in the home and on the highway." The National Academy of Sciences made him a member in 1928, and five years later, the chairman of its Division of Engineering and Industrial Research. From this post Kettering pushed cooperative research between universities and industry, "to bridge the gap between fundamental research in the universities and applied research in industrial labs."[72] He also collected honorary doctorates of science and engineering from New York University, Brown, Northwestern, and several others, including his alma mater, Ohio State.

The government too paid close attention to Kettering's ideas. He was appointed honorary chairman and toastmaster of the Centennial Celebration of the American Patent System, and took the opportunity to praise patents as a way of fostering inventiveness. Noting the distinguished company of government officials and businessmen, he kidded that the occasion was "quite a promotion for us inventors."[73]

More seriously, he was called as a witness by the Temporary National Economic Committee in its investigation of the concentration of economic power. The committee suspected that large corporations collected patents to suppress competition, and that this was one cause of the depression. Hence many corporate witnesses came in for tough questioning. Kettering, however, was a different story. "Babes in the woods of discovery and invention, the TNEC was fascinated by the rambling eloquence of 'Boss' Kettering. . . . The committee seemed to sense his attitude of good-natured indulgence towards its stuffy questioning," reported one source.[74] Sitting around a table with six congressmen and their aides, Kettering explained his philosophies of industrial research, economics, and assorted other subjects. He downplayed the role of patents in his work. Patents were valuable, he said, primarily as a psychological incentive for younger researchers ("It is just like a diploma to those boys; we like to see them get them") and as a defensive weapon against competitors, to keep them from securing the patents themselves and then charging General Motors royalties.[75]

Kettering's most entertaining observations were on how to apply his philosophies to social problems. He advocated an experimental approach, trying out social programs on a small scale. Falling back on one of his favorite metaphors, he explained, "You must be patient, because we must learn how to set up a one cylinder government and try it out."[76] The committee members all agreed that Kettering's testimony was a highlight of the hearings, and as he left he was one of "those whose faces gleamed most frequently in the glare of the photographers' flashes."[77]

The articles, speeches, awards, and newspaper reports brought Kettering more national attention than any engineer since Thomas Edison. A serialized biography by friend Paul de Kruif appeared in the *Saturday Evening Post*, and added to the growing Kettering legend.[78] Kettering himself had little interest in his public image, and called yet another biography "A good job with a poor subject." His sister Emma resented de Kruif's references to the family's humble origins. "It makes me cross to have him class you as a 'hillbilly,' " she wrote her brother. "Our family had as much class as anyone in those days and the hill-billys lived south of town."[79]

Common folks lionized Kettering. A high-school student sent a penciled sketch of his hero for a personal autograph, and though Kettering did not like to give autographs, in this case he obliged.[80] Several high schools and colleges organized "Kettering Clubs," and one even arranged a telephone interview with the great man himself.[81] Through it all, Kettering kept the common touch. On the way home from Columbia University, where Kettering had received an honorary doctorate of science, Olive bubbled over with stories about the celebrities and the elegance of the affair. The driver listened patiently. When she had finished, Kettering leaned forward, put his arms on the back of the front seat and grinned, "It was a high-toned occasion indeed for us bread and egg people from way out west."[82]

Celebrity seekers besieged his Detroit office for interviews or at least a glimpse of the engineer. Bolder suitors waited in ambush at the Book-Cadillac Hotel. Kettering occasionally invited a lucky caller to breakfast, but almost no one got into the office. Most of these visitors came for more than a casual chat. "Untold numbers come to our office specifically with the desire in their heart to see Mr. Kettering. They seem to think that he can find some way to rectify their troubles," Clements once complained to George Smith.[83] The answer they usually suggested was money.

Kettering was more than generous with his close relatives. When Emma wrote asking him to find a job "for your only nephew ready for work," he found the young man a position at the Flxible Company.[84] He paid thousands of dollars in medical expenses for his sisters, and sent $2,000 to cover the bills for his brother David's funeral. But his charity had its limits. He thought the "dole," as he called it, only encouraged laziness. Finally, after a flurry of requests for money from some distant cousins he had never met, he told George Smith, "If it is a matter simply of providing some fundamental things like chickens, eggs, false teeth, etc., I think we might be able to help them out. Of course, it has been my experience that these things once started never have any stopping place."[85]

Generally, his financial advisers vetoed his basically generous impulses. William Durant, when old and penniless, asked Kettering for a $2,100 "loan" for a mining venture. Kettering was inclined to go along, out of pity for an old friend. But his financial advisers said no. "We know Mr. Kettering would personally like to comply with your request . . . but this cannot be done and be consistent with the financial program we have laid out," they told Durant. "For this reason we are overruling Mr. Kettering's wishes and requesting that you do not expect the check to be sent by Mr. Kettering."[86]

In the spring of 1933, Kettering published an article in the *Satur-*

day Evening Post entitled "America Comes Through a Crisis." Though it had much the same message as the rest of his popular depression pieces—that only industrial research and enlightened business could put the country back on its feet—a new optimism appeared.[87] Kettering predicted that with the right mental attitude, recovery might take only a matter of months. He considered attitude so important that he told the members of the American Chemical Society, only partly tongue in cheek, "As we think, so we are, and if we can modify that thinking by chemical processes, let us get at it tomorrow."[88]

Kettering had higher hopes for his diesel engine as an aid to economic recovery than he did for chemical mood modifiers. In early 1933 it looked to him as if the diesel was on the threshold of commercial success, with automotive, marine, and locomotive applications.

From Kettering's point of view, the automotive diesel looked the least likely. Since the early 1920s, he had been telling anyone who would listen that the automobile diesel was not the easy solution to petroleum shortages that some hoped for. Kettering thought the high initial cost of diesel engines would outweigh any gains in fuel economy. Even if that obstacle could be overcome, he predicted that "if by magic one-half of all the automobiles could be instantly thrown over to the diesel cycle, there would be only a fraction of a cent difference in the filling station price of these fuels."[89]

More promising, in his opinion, were marine diesels. The slow-speed diesels of the 1920s had already worked a minor revolution in shipping, and Kettering expected to complete it with the innovations from the Research Laboratories. By the end of 1932, a joint engineering program of Winton and the laboratories produced some marine prototypes with two-stroke cycles, unit injectors, and uniflow scavenging. The Research Laboratories built the specialized parts—the blowers, injectors, crankshafts, pistons, and connecting rods—and the production men in Cleveland fitted them to modified six-cylinder Winton blocks.[90] In December, Kettering announced, "We are coming along very nicely with the new engines over at Winton and I think we will have the first of the eight cylinder ones running about the middle of February."[91]

The intended market for these engines was military, not civilian. In March 1933, Harold G. Bowen, assistant head of the Navy Bureau of Engineering, invited Kettering to Washington for a confidential interview on the two-stroke marine diesel. Bowen, an Annapolis graduate with advanced degrees in mechanical engineering from Columbia, was keenly interested in new technology for the navy. He had played a vital role in the transition to high-pressure steam power, and when he heard about Kettering's work, he recognized an innovation with equally revolutionary implications.

Diesel engines had been used by the U. S. Navy since the last war, especially for submarines. But these were slow, four-stroke engines, and the submarines they powered could not keep pace with the rest of the fleet. Bowen told Kettering that the navy was looking for a lighter, faster diesel, and Kettering replied that Winton and the Research Laboratories could supply it. Bowen then secured a $500,000 appropriation to study high-speed marine diesels.[92]

Winton submitted a 12-cylinder prototype to the trials. The design was competing against five conventional diesels sent by leading German and American firms. The Winton performed well in the tests at the Engineering Experimental Station in Annapolis, and pulled 950 horsepower at 750 rpm. But the officers in charge of the trials, unaccustomed to the unusual design, picked one of the competitors instead. Nevertheless, Bowen contributed an enthusiastic minority report and convinced his commanding officer to also give Winton a contract for experimental diesels.[93]

After Kettering examined the completed engines, he exclaimed, "The new engines are such a tremendous advance over anything that anybody ever suspected in diesels that we are anxious to get a pair of them in actual marine service under our own supervision."[94] His optimism was rewarded. They later powered the *U. S. Shark*, the first of the navy's high-speed diesel submarines. Modified versions of the original design were used in mine sweepers, landing craft, submarine chasers, and tugboats. Although Kettering did not spend much time with the Winton engineers designing these engines, he did attend many of the official trials and he promoted the diesel vigorously.[95]

Kettering had other ideas in mind for the new diesel also. To one of his business associates, he wrote:

What I have in mind is this: I have discussed with you from time to time the possibilities of using the diesel engine in a wider range of activities. From some very careful data which we have collected here, based upon careful experimentation, it looks as though it would be possible to make generating sets up to at least 400 k.w., now, that could be installed, I believe for under $50.00 per k.w. . . . You can see at once that if you could get low cost fuel that power could be developed on location for equal to or better than the best super power rates. We are making the same studies now in connection with the possibilities of building locomotives that would use diesel engines.[96]

On the matter of decentralized power generation, Kettering was wrong; diesels would have only a minor role in the power industry. However, his predictions on locomotive diesels were quite accurate. About the same time, Kettering told Pierre du Pont that with new developments in scavenging, injection, and alloy parts, "good reliable diesel engines can be built at around 20 lbs. per horsepower," or about one-third the weight of other diesels. He invited du Pont for a firsthand look at the diesel research, "as we have some exceedingly interesting things here which I think have a tremendous commercial value."[97]

Surprisingly, Kettering spent a lot of time trying to invent his way around an electrical transmission for his diesel. Electrical transmissions had been thoroughly tested by this time, and offered full power across the whole range of engine speed. But Kettering seemed to prefer a mechanical system. He told one of the consulting engineers with whom he worked on the problem, "I should judge from your letter that you have no more love for an electric drive than I have and I should like to sit down and talk to you about railroad requirements and therefore, when you come to Detroit, I would like to discuss this whole subject as we have given it considerable thought."[98]

In the end, Kettering's mechanical substitutes were not successful, and he returned to the electrical transmission.

The Century of Progress World's Fair of 1933 gave Kettering opportunities for a dramatic introduction of the diesel. Set in Chicago, the Century of Progress was intended primarily as an exercise in the power of positive thinking. It was sponsored and assembled by a business community trying very hard to take the public's mind off the present and focus attention on the possible miracles of the future. The fair's president, Rufus C. Dawes, set the tone for the exhibition when he proclaimed at the opening ceremonies, "Here are gathered the evidence of man's achievements in the realm of physical science—proofs of his power to prevail over all the perils that beset him. Here in the presence of such victories men may gather courage to face their unresolved problems."[99] The ceremony itself typified the fair's preoccupation with form rather than substance. At a signal from Dawes, four beams of light captured by four American observatories were focused on a photoelectric cell that in turn tripped a set of relays and lit up the fair grounds, to the delight of some 200,000 spectators.

Kettering was not above a little popular salesmanship either. He talked General Motors into including an exhibit of research tools along with the regular corporate display, including such instruments as a stroboscope and an induction furnace to help the public appreciate the scientific side of General Motors' work. When the research department mounted the exhibit with complicated explanations and boring titles, Kettering came back with "Frozen Motion" for the stroboscope and "Magnetic Stove" for the furnace. Later, Kettering took the show on the road as the Parade of Progress and personally performed experiments at the opening in Lakeland, Florida.

Chevrolet's exhibit was a working model of an automobile assembly line powered by Kettering's experimental diesels. In April 1933, two Winton diesel engine blocks had been sent to the Research Laboratories in Detroit. The power plant section had outfitted them with the latest injectors and blowers, and in dynamometer tests they yielded 1,000 horsepower from a total weight of 11,000 lbs., though the working horsepower was closer to 600, for a true weight-to-power ratio of about 20 lbs. per horsepower.[100] On May 19, Kettering shipped these engines to Chicago, where a team of engineers from Winton, led by Eugene, installed them in the Chevrolet exhibit.[101] They were displayed in the open, behind glass shields, and attracted sizable crowds.

One visitor to the diesel display had more than a passing interest in the engines. He was Ralph Budd, president of the Burlington Railroad. At that moment, Budd was under intense pressure to come up with something that would lure passenger traffic back to the railroad. One of Burlington's major competitors, the Union Pacific, had recently commissioned a streamlined, gasoline-electric passenger train that was attracting considerable public attention. Budd needed something like it, and thought Kettering's diesels might be the answer.

Kettering told Budd that the engines on display were only prototypes, cooled with water pumped directly from Lake Michigan, never tested in service, and prone to frequent breakdown. Eugene Kettering often said about the only thing on the engines that did not need constant repair was the dipstick. Nonetheless, Budd persisted. After a couple of meetings, Kettering agreed to deliver two workable, 8-cylinder locomotive diesels. On June 17, 1933, Budd ordered the engines from General Motors.[102]

Winton had responsibility for the blocks, the Research Laboratories would supply special parts (e.g., injectors and blowers), and Electro-Motive the transmission and final installation. The E. G. Budd Company of Philadelphia would build the train itself, to be named the "Zephyr" after the god of the west wind.

Ralph Budd described the proposed train for his board of directors on July 11, 1933:

Order has been placed for a Diesel-driven stainless-steel train capable of traveling at a speed of 120 miles per hour. The train will comprise three cars built as an articulated unit along aerodynamic lines, will weigh about 169,000 pounds, and have a total seating capacity of 70. The first car will contain the motor, baggage and mail compartment; second car, baggage and express, with a buffet and smoking compartment in the rear to seat 19 passengers; third car will be entirely devoted to seating space with a capacity of 51, which includes 12 parlor chairs. The overall length of the train will be approximately 196 feet, and the estimated cost $200,000.[103]

Kettering spent the fall in Europe and missed some of the frustrating development work. The research engineers had discovered an ominous amount of cylinder wear in the Century of Progress diesels. They learned that the high-sulfur fuels were combining with water in the engines and forming corrosive acids. By adding a chemical base to the lubricating oil and raising the water jacket temperature, they eliminated the corrosion. "We know that there is nothing about the engine to make it wear faster than others," one of the men wrote Kettering, who was always anxious to keep abreast of things by mail.[104] On his return from Europe, Kettering still had to cancel his annual Florida vacation in order to hurry the project to completion, and he sent Olive on alone. Yet he found time to attend meetings of the Railroad Advisory Board of the National Research Council, a good place to keep in touch with technical and business aspects of the railroad industry.[105]

After several delays, the Zephyr was finally unveiled in Philadelphia in April 1934. Alfred Sloan gave the keynote address on national radio. The train toured the eastern seaboard for two weeks and then headed west to Denver and a race to Chicago against the sun.[106]

On May 26, at 5:05 A.M., the streamliner left Denver for a nonstop run to the opening of the second year of the Century of Progress. The train was packed with corporate officials, journalists, and the Burlington mascot, a mule named "Zeph." Crowds gathered at small town crossings all along the way to witness the historic event. A hundred thousand people were waiting in Chicago thirteen hours later, when the Zephyr broke a tape stretched across Halstead Street and set a world speed record. The train had covered 1,071 miles at an average speed of 78 mph, about twelve hours faster than the standard run. And the fuel bill, according to Budd, was only $14.64. "It was a thrill of a century for me to be at the controls of the Zephyr," said J. S. Ford, the train's engineer.[107]

Kettering capped the day with a speech to an overflowing crowd in the General Motors Hall of Progress. He talked about the importance of industrial research as a national resource, and took a few jabs at the New Deal. Automotive pioneer Charles Nash spoke for most of the audience when he told reporters afterwards, "I think men think

'Boss' Kettering should be listened to rather than some young men who never earned a dollar in business in their lives."[108]

The Zephyr's tremendous promotional success convinced General Motors to look at the diesel as a serious commercial product. In June 1934, a small group of top executives met to discuss corporate strategy. The committee included Kettering, George Codrington from Winton, Harold Hamilton from Electro-Motive, and Alfred Sloan and Charles E. Wilson from the Executive Committee. Kettering pushed for a total commitment to the locomotive diesel. He said $500,000 would be enough to put General Motors into the business. Sloan suggested that such a sum was too modest, to which Kettering replied, "I know, but I figure if we spend that much, you'll come through with the rest."[109]

After the meeting, Sloan wrote Kettering a letter expressing his unqualified support: "I feel very strongly that there is a tremendous opportunity here. It will certainly be a great reflection upon us if we do not prepare to capitalize that opportunity in a broad and aggressive way."[110] Of course, Kettering was ready to move immediately, even if the market for diesel locomotives was hardly proven. "You are always too late with a development if you are so slow that people demand it before you yourself recognize it," he said. "The research department should have foreseen what was necessary and had it ready to a point where people never knew they wanted it until it was made available to them."[111] Kettering got the appropriation, and in January 1935, the Executive Committee voted to spend $6 million for a locomotive production plant for Electro-Motive to be located in La Grange, Illinois.

Several technical obstacles still separated the prototype Burlington diesels and a commercial product. Most of these were minor—clogging fuel injectors, weak exhaust valve springs. But one serious problem stood out—cooling. "The fundamental principle in the development of the two-cycle uniflow engine is proper cooling of the piston and this, so far as durability of the engine is concerned, is No. 1 consideration," Kettering told Charles Wilson.[112] Kettering set out a five-stage research plan he thought would accomplish this objective of improved cooling: increase the temperature of the cooling water at or near the top end of the piston stroke; reduce the temperature of the pistons themselves; increase the hardness of the cylinder lining; increase the corrosion resistance of the liners; and reduce the acidity of the lubricating oil.

Kettering had outlined the project; other engineers carried out the work at each stage. A team of engineers at the Research Laboratories discovered ways of reducing cylinder wear by using materials from lead-copper bearings, and learned to improve the flow of cooling water in the jacket.[113]

Eugene Kettering redeemed himself in his father's eyes by working out a new technique for cooling the pistons with a stream of oil shot through small holes in the connecting rods. And with another Winton engineer, Eugene invented a "heat dam," a thin plate mounted between the piston head and the ring belt which kept heat from cooking the oil around the rings.

By the end of 1934, Kettering had already told a close friend, "The diesel engine development is coming along in very fine shape. We feel now that we have made the preliminary step whereby the diesel engine business can be what it should have been a long while ago."[114]

Unfortunately, technology was never the whole story of a General Motors innovation. Management also had its place, and in this case, good management was sorely missed. As the diesel expanded from research project to full-scale corporate commitment, inevitable tensions arose between the widely scattered teams of engineers. For instance, the Research Laboratories in Detroit manufactured the unit injectors and sent them to Cleveland or La Grange where they were fitted onto the engines. When something went wrong with the temperamental units, it was hard to assign the blame. The research engineers naturally suspected the production men of not understanding the delicate nature of the systems, and the production engineers accused the research men of overly complex design. This round went to the researchers. "We have been working on the design for the 11×13 injector for Winton: they say they now understand that they will have to build the cylinder head around the injector—not visa-versa as in the past. Here's hoping it works out," said one.[115] Kettering's men also grumbled about the unwillingness of Winton to share problems openly with the Research Laboratories and accused them of deliberate secrecy.[116]

At least in part because of this atmosphere of mistrust, the prototype Burlington diesel did not work very well. At times, things got so bad that Kettering suggested closing down Winton completely until better communication could be established.[117]

In the summer of 1935, the engines for the second Burlington Zephyr were finally ready. J. C. Fetters, an engineer on Kettering's staff, accompanied the train on its maiden run from Chicago to Denver and back. He carefully monitored the engine's performance and fuel consumption. He found that the diesel, though appreciably smaller than a regular steamer, was nearly as fast and powerful. It had lower fuel cost, reduced exhaust emissions, required no water stops, and gave a noticeably smoother ride. "I would say that, in general, the railroad men were giving the locomotive a very sound and careful appraisal," he reported.[118]

Frequently, Kettering went along on the test rides, to evaluate his engines but also for the publicity. When the public relations men dozed off, he headed for the cab to join the engineer and the fireman. On one trip from Texas to Chicago, he kept the crew spellbound until dawn with tales of fever therapy, magnetism, photosynthesis, and his other current interests. None could recall a more fascinating night.[119]

The Sante Fe Railroad took delivery of the third General Motors' passenger diesel, the "Super Chief," on September 14, 1936. The art and color department of General Motors unveiled a stunning color scheme for the locomotive of black, cobalt, sarasota blue, golden olive, and pimpernel scarlet for the occasion.[120] The Super Chief cut fifteen hours from the regular schedule, and set a speed record, on its first trip from Los Angeles to Chicago. However, on the return trip it caught fire in the New Mexican desert and limped into California behind a steam locomotive.[121]

Despite organizational and technical problems, and disparaging remarks from steam-locomotive builders about reliability (a vice-president of Baldwin Locomotive Company predicted, "Some time in the future, when all this is reviewed, we will not find our railroads any more Dieselized than they are electrified"),[122] the diesel rapidly gained respectability. Though initial costs were higher, when fuel and water savings, maintenance charges, and other costs were figured in, the diesel was actually cheaper. By the late 1930s the diesel, and the streamlined trains it powered, had restored passenger revenues significantly.

At the end of 1935, the Executive Committee took important steps to rationalize the diesel program at General Motors. All locomotive work was transferred to the new Electro-Motive plant in Illinois, and a production plant was established for diesel switchers. The committee assigned exclusive production of marine diesels to Winton and cut out the Research Laboratories' diesel production altogether by setting up the Detroit Diesel Engine division for the manufacture of unit injectors. Kettering liked the new arrangement, and wrote to a friend after the final meeting of the joint diesel engineering staffs, "The work in general on engines is coming along at a very fine pace and it looks as though at least in another year the production of diesels would be getting on somewhat of a commercial basis."

Again, Kettering's crystal ball was accurate. The two-stroke diesel, modified for endless applications but still the same basic design, became the backbone of a profitable line of General Motors products, from freight and switching locomotives to submarines and small electric power plants. Much of the credit for such commercial success belonged to John Pratt, who applied automotive marketing techniques to the diesel—long-term financing, standard designs using common parts and technology, factory-trained maintenance men. But Kettering and his staff deserve equal credit for developing such a flexible and economical power plant.[123]

Only in the field of automotive diesels did General Motors fall behind, and there most of the blame must also rest with Kettering. He did some work with a two-stroke diesel truck engine. But he could never accept the idea of a four-stroke automobile diesel. He let himself be so blinded by this prejudice that when Harold Hamilton came back from an SAE meeting with a glowing report on the Cummins truck engine, Kettering told him, "Knowing Mr. Cummins very well, I should not attach too much importance to anything that he might say on the Diesel engine subject. Mr. Cummins' article impresses me as one in which the writer was almost 100% ignorant of the fundamentals of the engineering problems involved." [124] Cummins went on to develop a very successful line of four-stroke truck and automotive diesels, but through the 1950s Kettering consistently killed any General Motors' projects with four-stroke diesel design.

Alfred Sloan marked the end of Kettering's direct involvement in the diesel project with a celebration at the Waldorf-Astoria Hotel on October 28, 1937. Sloan invited several hundred prominent railroad and automotive executives, top engineers, editors of technical journals, and university and government transportation experts to celebrate the diesel's fortieth anniversary and its successful debut on the railroad. [125]

Characteristically, in his address that night, and in later talks with reporters, Kettering tended to exaggerate the opposition and apathy he had faced from business. "Think of what it would mean to the country if we could take our financial leaders and infect them with this vision virus," he told journalists, "and find them suddenly expanded mentally and spiritually, men with the imagination that Wall Street needs so badly." [126]

Privately, Kettering acknowledged his debt to the progressive management of General Motors. He also thought that the earlier failure of the diesel had been the result of trying to force it down an unnatural evolutionary path. In a little sketch of the diesel's history that he wrote for Sloan, Kettering explained his idea. The diesel, he argued, had been invented by men familiar with the steam engine, and when they designed the diesel, they built it just like the engines they knew best. Naval engineers too followed the steam model closely, and ended up with a diesel engine too much like the contemporary marine steam engine. The story was the same in automotive engineering. Said Kettering:

Later on, an attempt was made to use the Diesel for automobile work. I have followed the developments in Europe quite closely for a long while and in almost every case it again was a condition of making the Diesel like something else. In other words, they tried to make the Diesel engine like the gasoline engine so that the gasoline engine could be taken out and the

Diesel put in its place without any change in the mechanism. The delay of the Diesel has been due to its higher weight and faulty engineering in attempting to make it fit in where it did not naturally belong.[127]

Kettering believed that he succeeded because he recognized the separate path of the diesel, and guided it that way. "I feel that the new engineering which we have done gives us a greatly reduced power weight ratio and opens up the field so that we may expect a very large advance in the use of this type of power-producing apparatus," he concluded.

The diesel was an extremely profitable innovation for General Motors. The corporate flexibility that Kettering and his Research Laboratory offered proved invaluable in adjusting to the ever-changing market for goods and innovations the giant corporation faced year after year. In his testimony to the Temporary National Economic Committee Kettering had bluntly predicted that future breakthroughs in the automobile industry were unlikely: "I don't see how . . . [a] revolutionary thing could happen, especially in a highly developed art like automobile manufacturing. You just can't flash one of those things out. We have made about 45,000,000 automobiles now and the engineers have scraped those bones pretty carefully,"[128] But Kettering's laboratory could keep the innovations coming, if not in automobiles, then in something else.

On August 24, 1939, Kettering sold the second *Olive K* to the New Jersey Sandy Hook Pilots Association for $107,000 and cut his last personal ties to the diesel study. Justly proud of the project but ready to move on, Kettering wrote to a friend: "We are getting unbelievable durability out of these jobs now together with good fuel and oil consumption, so I think that all the ghosts have now been laid to rest and the light weight Diesel engine is an assured success."[129]

11 / SOME BIOLOGICAL DIVERSIONS

Despite a crushing schedule at General Motors, Kettering found time in the 1920s and 1930s to sponsor and participate in some interesting studies of medicine and biology which intrigued him. Funded out of his own pocket, these projects gave freer rein to the idiosyncratic side of his research personality. That had its drawbacks. Kettering's legendary persistence, an asset when held in check by shrewd managers like Alfred Sloan, sometimes became a liability. His distrust of expert opinion, often crucial in his automotive successes, occasionally led to dead ends in unfamiliar fields. Too many commitments robbed him of the chance to educate himself thoroughly. Infrequent weekend chats scarcely gave him enough information to keep abreast of current research in areas outside his corporate work, much less equip him to direct it.

Yet Kettering still contributed in surprising ways to medical instrumentation and photosynthesis research. Perhaps he best revealed the style that sometimes let him turn the tables on the professionals in something he said to Paul de Kruif: "Do you know what an incurable disease is? It's one the doctors don't know anything about. The disease has no objection to being cured at all."[1] That was Kettering—irreverent, incisive, unstoppable.

Kettering did not expect immediate, profitable results from this work. Indeed, he told an early group of collaborators on a photosynthesis study, "I want you all to get married and have a lot of children because I think this is about a three generation job."[2] However, he did expect each step of the research to have a definite objective, an independent stand at a time when many researchers were leaning the other way. To critics of this mission-oriented approach he replied that unexpected discoveries would be just as likely whether one did or did not have some specific goal. "I cannot see any difference in importance between digging out a fact when you need it and digging it out when you don't need it," he said.[3] And anyway, he reminded the critics, the goal kept things moving, kept people motivated. The movement was the important thing:

Nobody ever stumbled [on something] while he was standing still. You only stumble when you are moving. So we always had it a rule in our organization when we lacked intelligence we speeded up motion, because the chances of stumbling infinitely increased.[4]

One of Kettering's first outside research interests was homeopathy, a brand of medical heresy he picked up from his family physician. It had a controversial history dating back a century and was based on two key ideas: that a patient was best treated with substances that produced symptoms of the disease in healthy patients, and that the more dilute the therapeutic agent, the more potent the cure (the law of infinitesimals). Despite opposition from traditional medicine, homeopathy had slowly made some inroads until by the turn of the century, it was accepted almost as an equal partner.[5]

Homeopathy attracted Kettering because it emphasized the cause of disease, not just the treatment of symptoms. Its search for the "catalytic reactions" supposedly responsible for the law of infinitesimals particularly intrigued him because it fit so neatly with his belief that the key to scientific understanding was the study of fundamentals. Beneath the distracting metaphysics of homeopathy Kettering thought there might be a comprehensible science.

To support the study of "catalytic reactions," he donated $500 to the Ohio State University College of Homeopathic Medicine in April 1916. He followed this initial gift with a more sizable contribution of $8,000 six months later.[6] The next spring, Kettering found himself in a far better position to support homeopathy, both financially and as a public spokesman. His Ridgeleigh Terrace neighbor, Ohio governor James M. Cox, appointed him to a seven-year term as a trustee at his alma mater.

In early 1920 Kettering initiated what became a series of contributions to the Homeopathic College. In February he donated 60 milligrams of radium, valued at $7,200, for experimental treatments of cancer. Then in late spring he offered the university 1,000 shares of his new General Motors stock, with a par value of $100 a share, for the exclusive support of the homeopathic program.[7]

That July the American Institute of Homeopathy invited Kettering to address the annual meeting in Columbus, Ohio. His speech encouraged exploration of medical fundamentals. "When you get down to that you can do wonderful things in medicine," he told the homeopaths. "The only reason I felt like putting my support back of the Homeopathic School was because they seemed to be the most willing to go ahead and do these things."[8]

Kettering's generous offer unexpectedly set off a major campus controversy. Although Kettering was not aware of it, Ohio State's two medical schools, homeopath and allopath (traditional), were locked in a bitter internal dispute over priority and prestige. The allopaths, on the strength of the recent Flexner Report on American medical education and growing progress in conventional therapies, were gaining the upper hand, and Kettering's gift threatened to tip the balance the other way. The allopaths objected to any strengthening of the rival school and were determined to thwart Kettering's charity.

Kettering, whose concurrent work on the copper-cooled engine suggested a lack of insight into institutional politics, was oblivious to the conflict. He never imagined that his gift would be considered part of the competition between the factions.

Dr. Thomas Mendenhall, a quarrelsome allopath and a member of the university's Board of Trustees, launched the first attack. Addressing the other board members, including Kettering, he argued, "In modern scientific medicine there can be no lasting difference of opinion any more than there can be no lasting difference as to the effect of a certain fertilizer on a given soil, or as to the cube root of a number or the co-efficient [of expansion] of a metal." Then, referring obviously to Kettering's gift, he added, "the lure of a large endowment must not cause us to forget that this is the twentieth, and not the eighteenth, century."[9]

The board stood with Kettering. The resolution to accept the gift passed with Mendenhall's single dissenting vote. On June 16, 1920 the university publicly announced Kettering's contribution, and a few weeks later construction of a $200,000 research building for the Homeopathic College began.[10]

Mendenhall and the allopaths retreated. However, as head of the university's committee on medical education, Mendenhall had ample opportunity to lobby against the homeopathic center. The professional tide seemed to be running with him, and after two years of collecting data and talking with administrators and faculty, Mendenhall felt that he had sufficient strength to challenge Kettering.

Kettering knew about the impending assault. With troubles enough at the Research Corporation he had no desire to become entangled in any campus disputes. On March 20, 1922 he wrote friendly board member Judge B. F. McCann, setting forth his position. "If the Trustees decide to abolish the College of Homeopathic Medicine or to unite it with the other College of Medicine," he said, "I should be entirely at peace if they abolished the whole business from a to z. . . . If the College of Homeopathic Medicine cannot be maintained, then I have no particular interest in maintaining the other college."[11]

At the next board meeting Mendenhall proposed that Kettering's gift revert to the university and that the two colleges of medicine be combined. "The face of CFK, who was sitting opposite, got red as fire," one of the participants recalled, "and he looked as though he was going to explode with a blast of the strong language of which he was well capable at that time. But instead, he did not say a word." The vote deadlocked. Kettering, McCann, and another trustee opposed the motion; Mendenhall and two other trustees supported it. On June 19, Mendenhall forced another vote on the issue. Kettering was absent this time, apparently because he did not wish to escalate the issue, and the measure passed three votes to two.[12]

Kettering's expected resignation did not follow. University president W. O. Thompson offered to resign in protest unless the trustees rescinded the vote, and other trustees and officials promised support. Kettering refused their backing. "Very much as I would like to be relieved from my position on the Board of Trustees, I am not the kind of fellow that believes in running away at a time like this," he told Thompson. "And I think you would be making a great mistake just now to present your resignation."[13] The university returned Kettering's money and his radium.[14] Both Kettering and Thompson retained their positions.

Though he made no further efforts to revive the Homeopathic College at Ohio State, Kettering still hoped that his views on homeopathy would one day be vindicated. From time to time, he received letters from scientists and doctors interested in the art. His replies showed an unwavering faith in the homeopathic principles, and a growing certainty that the medical community would never properly appreciate his ideas. "I have found that the medical profession in general has been very adverse to anybody offering any suggestions along their line," he wrote one physician asking about catalytic reactions. "This is why your letter is so much appreciated. Anybody who has given this subject any consideration, whatever, will recognize that the fundamental laws of physics and chemistry are exactly the same in the human system as they are in any other organism. I should like to see a medical research organization worked up [to] approach this question from the same standpoint as we approach an engineering problem."[15]

What he envisioned was a medical laboratory much like the Research Corporation, where teams of experts could explore the human body in the same way that mechanical and chemical engineers at the laboratory dissected the automobile. The results of their work would then filter down to ordinary physicians who could perform the more mundane tasks of diagnosis and treatment, much as the divisions took care of the practical problems of automotive engineering.

Kettering would later sponsor an innovative medical research center based to a certain extent on this vision, but for the moment the disappointments of the homeopathic episode dampened his enthusiasm for the project. Misunderstanding, jealousy, and tradition—the same human weaknesses that had destroyed the copper-cooled engine—seemed to be at work in the medical profession too. As Kettering explained to one correspondent, "Such a laboratory would not require any great amount of money and its staff could be readily picked from within the medical and engineering professions today, but the limitations of your profession have made it impossible for the men who I would pick, to do perhaps the kind of work that I suggest in any other but their kind of organization." [16]

Plans for an interdisciplinary medical research laboratory began to take shape four years after the homeopathy fiasco. In June 1927, Kettering and his financial advisor George B. Smith incorporated the Charles F. Kettering Foundation for the support of worthy but unprofitable research. [17] One of its goals was to bring together various medical specialists to study certain critical problems.

Through the health tests on TEL and various professional affiliations Kettering had established a network of medical acquaintances. These friends often gathered at Ridgeleigh Terrace on Sunday afternoons for informal discussions of current medical issues. A common complaint voiced at these sessions was the difficulty of keeping abreast of current research in an era of rapidly expanding knowledge. Everyone agreed that it was becoming increasingly difficult to practice medicine and at the same time keep up with the many new developments.

Kettering found this situation deplorable, for from experience he knew the importance of keeping up with research. After several meetings with delegations from nearby Miami Valley Hospital, he proposed sponsoring a formal series of bimonthly medical conferences on contemporary issues. To coordinate the meetings and head the pathology and clinical laboratories at Miami Valley Hospital, the

Kettering Foundation hired a young pathology specialist from Johns Hopkins University named Walter Simpson, a rough-talking type to whom Kettering took an immediate liking.[18]

In the winter of 1930 Simpson had a visit from Paul de Kruif, a friend and popular writer on medical subjects. De Kruif had recently returned from an interview with Julius Wagner von Jauregg, a Viennese physician who had discovered an artificial fever therapy for paresis, a frequent complication of advanced syphilis, and he told Simpson about it. Simpson correctly guessed that Kettering would be interested, and introduced the two by long-distance call to Cleveland. Kettering talked to de Kruif for nearly an hour and then invited him to New York for further conversation the next week. Kettering kept the writer in his suite from lunch until late afternoon, exhausting him with endless questions on the possibilities of fever therapy.[19]

When Kettering returned from his Florida vacation in the spring he asked Simpson out to Ridgeleigh Terrace, and for an entire weekend he questioned him on the history of fever therapy. Kettering was particularly intrigued to hear that Willis Whitney of General Electric had mechanized the treatment with a shortwave oscillator he called a radiotherm, which Simpson had actually seen in an experimental version at the Albany Medical College.[20]

Only days after the meeting, Kettering wrote Whitney and asked if he could buy a radiotherm for the Miami Valley Hospital. Whitney candidly replied that the machine was still experimental, and questioned whether the Miami Valley staff would even know what to do with it. Kettering answered each of Whitney's objections and added, "I would like to enter an order for one of these pieces of apparatus either directly to you or through your Dayton representative." As a personal favor Whitney relented, and by the time Kettering returned from his European tour in the fall, Simpson had already set up the radiotherm purchased by the Kettering Foundation for $1,000.[21]

Knowing that Whitney would be anxious to check the results personally, Kettering invited him to visit Dayton to meet the researchers and observe the treatments. Kettering assured Whitney that Simpson and his assistant Fred Kislig "are both very fine high grade fellows, entirely different from the usual M.D. type."[22] What he meant was that they were willing to do things his way. Kettering's distrust of the medical profession lingered, and he preferred to call the shots as long as he paid the bills. Mrs. de Kruif once scolded Simpson and her husband, "It's always, 'Yes, Boss, that's right Boss.' You both act like he was God."[23] The Boss, however, never objected to their attentions.

Simpson's initial trials revealed one of the reasons for Whitney's original reluctance to sell Kettering the radiotherm. The beads of sweat that gathered on the fevered patients were heated by the short-waves and caused serious burns.[24]

Informed of the problem, Kettering suggested a simple but effective cure—pass a column of hot, dry, air over the patient to evaporate the perspiration. He installed a bank of high-voltage light bulbs in the cabinets and a fan to circulate the air over the heater and the patient. The improved system eliminated much of the discomfort of the therapy.[25]

For the next few months, Kettering talked of nothing but fever therapy. Yet after a year's work with Frigidaire's Edwin C. Sittler modifying and adjusting the units, and despite some promising results in the treatment of general paresis and arthritis, he was not satisfied with the cabinets. The therapy was still uncomfortable and frightening from the patient's point of view. One of Simpson's reports described a typical case: the patient "remained asleep for the first eleven minutes. He then awoke suddenly, let out a terrific whoop and just raised hell for the next twenty minutes, when we were forced to abandon any attempt to raise his temperature above 101."[26]

In May 1933, a chance discovery significantly altered the future course of fever therapy. During the treatment of a fifteen-year-old boy admitted to Miami Valley for congenital syphilis, the shortwave unit broke down. Yet, the boy's temperature climbed to 106° F in the usual fifty minutes.[27] Hot air alone could apparently induce a fever as rapidly as radio waves.

Kettering immediately asked Simpson to carefully compare the radiotherm and conditioned air treatments. Simpson could not find any differences and admitted that the latter "is a much simpler, much safer and much less expensive method."[28]

A few serious complications remained. Patients suffered severe dehydration and various side effects, from vascular collapse to kidney damage. With close monitoring of body functions and liberal doses of salt water laced with peppermint, the fever researchers learned to control the problem and ease the five-hour ordeal.

Simpson later told the American Medical Association that after four years of therapy on 384 subjects and 2,844 sessions, not one serious complication had developed, and successful remission had occurred in many cases of gonorrhea, syphilis, rheumatic fever, chorea, and arthritis.[29] The report naturally created considerable interest in the treatment. A physician from the University of Pennsylvania inquired about using the technique for treating human cancer.[30] One enterprising veterinarian even asked Kettering if he thought the idea might be useful for dogs. Kettering replied that while he had not thought of that application, he was confident that fever therapy could indeed be extended to animals.[31]

With the device seemingly on the verge of acceptance by the medical profession, Kettering began negotiations with Frigidaire for limited manufacturing. Frigidaire eventually built thirty cabinets and Kettering loaned them to medical research centers like the Mayo Clinic and the Henry Ford Hospital.[32]

Widespread use of the treatment resulted in further technical refinements to the cabinets and brought recognition to Kettering and Simpson. Dayton hosted a national conference on fever therapy in 1935. International recognition came two years later. Charles de Fontnouvelle, Consul General of France, presented Kettering and Simpson with the Chevalier Legion d'Honneur, the country's highest civilian award and a rare honor for foreigners, at the First International Congress on Fever Therapy in New York in May 1937.[33]

Fever therapy remained a valuable therapeutic tool until the discovery of chemotherapeutics like penicillin during the war, though as Simpson freely admitted to Kettering, the "whole treatment is 40% the doctor, 50% the nurse, and 10% the machine."[34] In the meantime, Kettering won fame and respect from a profession he had often maligned.

Kettering's engineering expertise aided in the development of another impressive diagnostic tool. Roy D. McClure, chief of surgery at Henry Ford Hospital and a frequent guest on Kettering's yacht, and a colleague named Frank Hartman were exploring the relationship between anoxemia (a deficiency of oxygen in the brain) and anesthesia during surgery. Beginning in 1938, they experimented with several instruments designed to monitor oxygen levels in the blood, hoping to perfect a reliable and simple diagnostic unit. They succeeded in modifying an existing German instrument so that they were able to read oxygen levels photoelectrically through the web of a patient's hand, but the device was stubborn and temperamental.[35]

Kettering first saw the machine at a luncheon meeting with the physicians at the hospital in 1938. "We showed this apparatus one sweltering hot summer day to our long-time friend Charles F. Kettering," McClure remembered. "Off came his coat and on hands and knees he explored the inside workings of the box. He came up with the statement that the feeble impulses through the photoelectric cells could be amplified in a different way to greatly simplify the process."[36]

During the next year, Kettering adapted for the oxyhemograph an amplifier developed by E. J. Martin of the Physics and Instrumentation Section of the laboratory. What seemed a minor modification transformed McClure's instrument from a primitive experiment into a reliable clinical tool. After the original trial of the modified device in February 1940, McClure told Kettering, "yesterday, for the first time, and again today, with the assistance of your men and the apparatus of the Ford [Hospital] men, we were able to run continuous curves of blood oxygen content in the Operating Room. It looks as though this present apparatus is very successful. . . . We got quite a thrill out of this today."[37] The air force later used the device to measure the blood oxygen levels of pilots to prevent dangerous high-altitude anoxemia.

Not all Kettering's medical investigations were as serious or productive as either the fever therapy research or the oxyhemograph. When Listerine first came on the market, Kettering was curious about its effectiveness and asked Simpson for an opinion. Simpson recommended instead "our old friend 'salt solution' " as a reliable and cheap substitute.[38]

Innovative education as well as innovative medical research won Kettering's support. His sponsorship of Antioch College (in nearby Yellow Springs, Ohio) gave new life to the financially troubled school and provided a home for his imaginative studies of photosynthesis.

When Arthur Morgan began to revitalize Antioch College in 1920, Kettering, as a partner in the progressive Moraine Park School, naturally attracted his attention. Morgan left his post as head of the Miami Conservancy District to accept the presidency of Antioch in 1920. He brought the programs, and financial supporters, of Moraine Park with him. He planned to institute a unique curriculum combining liberal and vocational training which, like Moraine Park's, would prepare young men and women for the tasks of small entrepreneurship. He expected each student to spend about half the time working in a real business, and the other half studying traditional subjects on campus.[39]

Kettering was a wholehearted supporter of cooperative education. He had followed Herman Schneider's pioneering programs at the University of Cincinnati for years and personally aided the venture by hiring many of the graduates.[40] "What gives cooperative education its strength is that it lap-welds theory from the classroom with practice on the job," Kettering wrote, using a typical engineering analogy. "It creates a weld that is much stronger than the butt-welding of a college degree followed by employment, the two touching at one line of contact."[41]

Kettering's friendship with Morgan and his ideological commitment to work-study programs cemented his allegience to Antioch. Beginning in 1925, he contributed substantial sums to the college and undersigned several large loans. Two years later his foundation awarded Antioch $200,000 for a new natural science building.[42] And though he eventually spent $375,000 on the construction and another $375,000 on upkeep,[43] he would not even allow the college to name the building after him. His no-nonsense approach to science was reflected in the functional brick architecture and in a simple photograph with the inscription, "This is a place to work not a monument to anybody."

In the same years that he contributed so generously to Antioch, he also laid the foundation for the photosynthesis project it would one day house. The petroleum crisis and the alcohol fuel investigation at General Motors led him to consider the possibilities of converting organic materials directly into automotive fuels. Of one of these fuels, alcohol, he mused, "I would say it would be a gallon of last summer's sunshine—but a lot of people would call it moonshine."[44] He thought that photosynthesis could unlock the secrets of more direct conversion processes.

Seeing far beyond most of the engineering community, Kettering urged his colleagues to study alternative fuel sources immediately. At a meeting on fuel supplies in Dayton in 1920, he outlined his ideas at a luncheon conference with some of his top engineers. Enjoying bean soup, he related a little parable:

You know, fellows, a bean is pretty smart. Nature provides the bean with a quantity of nourishment to keep it going until it gets a start in life. When planted in the ground, it sends up a sprout to take a look around. There it could say, "I'll just grow in this lovely sunshine and put out a lot of leaves. I have plenty of bean meat to keep me going for a while." But the bean, being smart, does no such thing. Instead, it uses its store of nourishment to send roots deep into the earth. Only then is it ready to put out leaves in the sunshine. Now, the petroleum you have been talking about is nothing but 'bean meat' to keep us going until we can get a good start. If we are as smart as the bean, we will, while petroleum does last, dig into the secrets of nature. If we do that, we will find other sources of energy to keep us going after petroleum has been used up.[45]

Because his botanical work had no immediate commercial objective, and because Sloan would not fund such speculative research, Kettering housed the project in a greenhouse at the foot of Ridgeleigh Terrace and paid the expenses himself. For several years, he and two young chemists carefully monitored the growth of certain plants. They planted disinfected seeds in sterilized flowerpots and controlled the plant's food intake by dripping a standardized nutrient solution through the sand. They compared plant diets during different stages of growth, collecting and analyzing the unused nutrient. Most plants, they noticed, changed their appetite during blossoming and when fruit began to appear. By varying the concentrations and timing of the feeding, Kettering grew flowers on immature plants and "cucumbers so large that I didn't dare tell about them because everyone thought I was lying." Later, he told a friend why nothing came of the project. "After several years of work and due to the fact that my time was so completely taken up in the development of some of our industries at that time, I was unable to get the kind of technician I wanted and we discontinued the work for some time."[46]

During the middle 1920s, he limited his botanical research to collecting literature and writing popular articles explaining what was then known about the subject. He often challenged his audiences with a question most people thought they could answer: "Why is the grass green?" Many even took the time to reply.

A vacationer in the Adirondacks wrote with the results of his "research":

Five years ago in an article in the *American Magazine* during an address on a technical subject you parenthetically asked the question, why is grass green? Enclosed herewith is the answer . . . as I have been five years on the trail of the answer, please guard it quite carefully.[47]

The "answer" was only a reprint of a short Luther Burbank article on chlorophyll. Kettering wrote back explaining that the issue was really more complex:

The question we have been asking is why it is that the green color is essential to this change. The writer is quite familiar with the nature and offices of chlorophyll in the plant life, but we want to go one step further and find out why it is that the particular wave length of green is the one that the plant rejects in its work. In other words, we are asking what the mechanism is by which chlorophyll is able to separate the oxygen from the air and put it into chemical combination.[48]

Kettering liked to tell another story about a golf course owner in Arizona who wrote to tell him, "I don't know what you have in mind, but out here the only thing that makes grass green is water."[49]

Professional audiences were reminded of Kettering's obsessive interest in the subject, and sometimes in surprising ways. During an important meeting in Detroit called to unveil the new General Motors diesel engine, Kettering mounted the speaker's rostrum, looked out over the anxious assembly, squinted over his thick glasses, and exclaimed, "I'll bet you expected to hear all about the two-stroke diesel. Well, you're not. I'm going to tell you why the grass is green."[50]

Despite Kettering's frequent publicizing, the work failed to generate much interest. The scientific community almost completely ignored the project. Kettering read what he could find on the subject, though, and brought up the idea whenever he could. By the summer of 1929, he was beginning to see the photosynthesis question as a crucial link in the fuel problem. "In thinking this matter over," he wrote to Clements, "a probable theory has presented itself to me; that the work of plant growth has perhaps been from samples and that the chlorophyll on the leaf of the plant contains the pattern and the absorption of certain radiant energy and transmission of certain others determining the construction of the final molecules in the plant. . . . I am led to believe that in a similar way organic compounds or especially isomeric compounds, can be produced one from the other by supplying the energy of combination of the compound to be changed."[51]

That is, photosynthesis might somehow select between several possible reactions, or a particular kind of radiation might induce a specific chemical reaction involving chlorophyll. Perhaps, Kettering reasoned, a similar process could be applied to fuel molecules. By using the proper wavelengths of light, chemists might be able to assemble hydrocarbons of a desired structure and performance. A simple light screen might provide an unlimited supply of fuel molecules.

This study, he believed, would once again demonstrate that research with a definite goal might have great impact in seemingly unrelated areas. Finding out why the grass was green might reveal the fuel source of the future. "The importance of this work is so great," he told his researchers, "that any constructive criticisms or suggestions should be brought to bear upon it at the earliest possible date so that active Laboratory work can be commenced at once."[52]

Because he felt the project had such an obvious and direct bearing on the fuel question, Kettering began the new study at the Research Laboratory in Detroit under General Motors' sponsorship. Following several of his suggestions for unraveling the mystery of the controlling factors in chlorophyll reactions, the Fuel Section investigated a series of well-known photochemical reactions. They discovered, among other things, a colorless nonelectrolyte that converted to a colored electrolyte in the presence of light in an alcohol solution. After achieving several variations of this reaction, however, they reported that the idea, while interesting and full of potential, looked out of the question commercially, at least for the moment. "Identification, isolation, or analysis of the many different isomers for a single halo-genation would involve months of work," they glumly concluded. [53]

Undaunted, Kettering looked for a new opportunity to expand the research. After a series of talks with Dr. O. L. Inman, a dean and head of the biology department at Antioch College, Kettering offered the school $2,000 from his foundation for a long-range study of photosynthesis. [54]

As in medicine, he sought to apply the successful techniques of industrial research in the studies. He insisted on a staff of diverse backgrounds, to avoid what he considered to be the sterility of narrow specialization. His original memorandum on the proposed staff recommended a chemist, a biologist, a physicist, and a director "able to draw upon specialized knowledge in (1) physical chemistry and radiochemistry; i.e. all relations between matter, chemical energy, and radiant energy; (2) organic chemistry, and (3) biological chemistry, being especially conversant with the physiology of plants." [55]

Perhaps placing personal preference and willingness to follow directives ahead of the criteria in his memorandum, Kettering chose Inman as director. For a chief assistant he wisely selected Paul W. K. Rothemund, a former student of the brilliant German chemist Hans Fischer. Fischer's work on the constituent components of chlorophyll earned him a Nobel Prize in chemistry in 1930, the same year Rothemund came to Antioch. Rothemund had received a solid background in the field from Fischer's teaching.

Despite the noncommercial orientation of the photosynthesis investigation up to that time, Kettering's first instructions to the Antioch staff in the fall of 1930 told of his expectations. "It should be stated, however, that even at the outset a considerably larger staff of researchers could be put on definite problems with immediate profit and the entire undertaking organized similar to the one which Dr. Haber developed for the nitrogen fixation problem in Germany," he explained. "There are in fact many points of similarity between the problem of nitrogen fixation and that of carbon fixation."[56]

Kettering usually visited the Antioch staff one or two weekends a month, chatting about the latest developments for six or seven hours. Sometimes he suggested specific instrumentation, for instance the Raman spectroscope that had proved so useful in the combustion studies at the laboratory, and other times he recommended an experiment or two, like an investigation of the chlorophyll in red cabbage.[57] Generally, though, he offered advice only on the overall direction of the project. Inman noted in one of his letters to Kettering, "It seems to me you will be in the best position to see that we don't lose sight of the broader aspects of the work."[58]

Occasionally Kettering's style irritated some of the less imaginative biologists. His interests were so broad, and the questions that occurred to him were so wide-ranging, that he wanted to talk about everything at once. Some researchers considered the sessions a waste of time. Rothemund recalled one meeting when Kettering discussed Spanish moss in Georgia, oats, hydrocarbon research in Memphis, methylene blue pigment in algae, and the use of X-rays in the study of fruitfly mutations.[59] His mechanical analogies also bothered some of the staff. He insisted on mechanical explanations for photochemical reactions, which most of the scientists did not like. However, contemporary journals of physics thought enough of his ball and spring models for the bending and stretching forces of organic molecules to publish them.[60]

The Antioch project struggled with quite an assortment of issues the first year. Inman and Rothemund directed studies of the interrelationship of chlorophyll, water, carbon dioxide, and radiant energy in the photosynthetic process. They cracked chlorophyll molecules with acids, alkalies, and enzymes and slowly unraveled the structure of the mysterious compound. They also transferred chloroplasts from one cell to another to study the effects of different kinds of chlorophyll. By observing the decomposition of the compound in the bodies of rabbits, goats, and guinea pigs, they learned about the relationship between animal health and chlorophyll.[61]

After a year of work the researchers had to admit that progress had been slow. "I am not surprised that so many men have worked on this field and found it difficult," Inman wrote to Kettering. "It is probably simple as done in nature but difficult because of our methods of attack. It is our aim to continually explore new ways of approaching this problem."[62]

The 1930s were exciting years in chlorophyll research, both at Antioch and elsewhere. James B. Conant at Harvard University deduced some of the chemical connections in the molecule, and in Munich, Rothemund's old teacher Fischer synthesized the first porphyrins from hemin and chlorophyll. Rothemund himself synthesized the porphines, the ringlike building blocks of the molecule.[63] Inman enthusiastically echoed one of Kettering's favorite statements in reporting to him on photosynthesis study progress. "I believe we have in this way spread the news that the world is not finished," he said, "and that there are many worth while things to be discovered or invented so that no young person need think that all he should do or will be permitted to do will be learn what other people have done before him."[64]

In line with Kettering's philosophy of research goals with commercial ends, the Antioch researchers focused considerable attention on practical projects. Inman reassured his patron, "We are trying to keep a good balance between our practical work and our experimentation."[65] They developed several techniques for storing green feed without losing vitamins and essential plant hormones. They also investigated different methods of freezing and storing orange juice.[66]

In plotting the course of this research, Kettering followed his own instincts and had little patience for objections from long-time photosynthesis researchers. When several of the Antioch chemists opposed Kettering's plan to study radiation chemistry in seawater as a possible model of prebiological chemistry, Kettering reproached Inman:

The very fact that your scientific people don't want to do this means nothing at all. For ever and a day the technical man has fought against experimental work—always wants to sit around and philosophize and the philosophy always arrives at the point that the experiment isn't worth doing. The thing we have to do is to make up our minds that we have brains enough to do this job and to start a broad line of experimentation with the idea that this is not really as complicated as we have been led to believe.[67]

Kettering was satisfied with the progress being made by the researchers he was funding, but reports of radicalism on the Antioch campus worried him. The New Deal had weakened his populist sympathies, and by the mid-1930s he was squarely in the Republican camp. Once, Kettering even offered his resignation in a disagreement over a faculty member whose liberalism he thought was giving big business a "black eye."[68]

Radical views continued to flourish on the Antioch campus, particularly support for the Soviet experiment, and in December 1933 George Smith sent Kettering a communist sheet published at Antioch under the editorship of Ernest Morgan, son of the college's first president, Arthur Morgan. Kettering, though he hardly agreed with the paper's revolutionary aims, attributed its sentiments to the exuberance of youth and not to deeply anticapitalistic intent on the part of the students involved. "I would not pay too much attention to the Brass Tacks," he told Smith, "though I think it is perfectly silly for Antioch to allow anything like this to go out over the name of Antioch College."[69] When Morgan's son wrote a personal letter of apology, he let the matter drop.[70]

The increasingly radical spirit of the campus started to threaten the photosynthesis research by the approach of the war, however. Kettering stood behind the character of the scientists and their students, but he distrusted many of the other students and the new president, Algo D. Henderson. At first, Kettering merely urged Henderson to soften the faculty and students' attacks on big business, to "rub off the sharp edges because we have to depend on industry for our cooperative work."[71] Later, Henderson's tolerance of radical professors and students drew Kettering's real scorn. "I don't think Antioch has any future unless you lay down what you stand for and quit trying to be all things to all people," he warned him. "Michigan has made it absolutely impossible for a known Communist to enter the University of Michigan. Until you people quit playing around with your pink teas I don't want anything more to do with you."[72]

Fortunately for Antioch and the photosynthesis research, the impending war diverted Kettering's attention to more compelling technical projects. With Inman making progress, the foundation continued to provide funds to the college. Inman collaborated with the Research Corporation to develop fluorescent identification techniques for chlorophylls, and to investigate primitive algae in hot springs.[73] Kettering followed this work closely from a distance and often circulated Inman's reports to outstanding researchers for comment.

Rothemund and Inman did not achieve any dramatic breakthroughs; they did, however, contribute some important data to an active and expanding scientific field, laying groundwork for the successful synthesis of chlorophyll after the war by researchers at Harvard and the Technische Hochschule in Munich.

With his personal funding of biological research, Kettering emerged from the anonymity General Motors' other top executives preferred. Although his philanthropy occasionally attracted the scrutiny of official auditors—the Securities and Exchange Commission included him as a subject in its investigation of private wealth and public power, and a congressional committee on tax evasion cited his private incorporation as an undesirable legal loophole[74]—it also won him influential friends in science and business.

Reporters looking for colorful copy sought him out. Kettering's aphorisms, anecdotes, and advice regularly appeared in newspapers and magazines, and seemed to bear endless repeating. "If there had been letters of appraisal written every New Year's Day through history," he told a group of journalists covering his fall sailing to Europe in 1937, "they would all read the same. 'I swear I don't know how grandfather and great-grandfather got along on what they had; and now I don't know what else there is for me to do.' To the unimaginative the world is always finished."[75] Nearly every interviewer mentioned his large, calloused hands, constantly moving, reinforcing some point or other, clarifying ideas with quick scrawls on his ever-present pad of graph paper. [76]

Scientific audiences too thought Kettering a delightful speaker. He could not possibly have accepted all the offers for speaking engagements he received from professional groups. The lucky few were never disappointed. His clever metaphors and stories lingered with his audiences long after the halls and dining rooms had emptied. At the New York World's Fair in 1940, he joined a distinguished panel of scientists gathered to field questions from scientifically inclined college students. Even in this sober assembly his wit and humor came through, and put everyone at ease. When asked by one young man if it was still possible to jump several rungs on the corporate ladder by marrying the boss' daughter, he replied, "I don't think you'd want to jump too many rungs or the rung you land on might break." [77]

The biological research showed Kettering's ingenuity and eccentricity in almost equal measure. Though his approach was frequently unconventional, his imagination and willingness to try new things partially atoned for his lack of professional depth. On the other hand, his unwillingness or inability to restrain this stubborn independence when it came to administrative politics sometimes hindered otherwise promising projects.

Tying together this diverse research was Kettering's conviction that, properly directed, science would give rise to useful technology, raise new enterprises, increase employment, and lead to a better lot for humanity. Social salvation through research was not entirely popular among scientists, but Kettering's beliefs were unwavering. "Research is industrial prospecting," he told one depression-weary audience. "We believe that there are still things left to be discovered. We have only stumbled upon a few barrels of physical laws from the great pool of knowledge. Some day we are going to hit a gusher that will keep us industrially busy for a long time to come refining the new oil of knowledge and making it into useful new products. Men will be back to work and all of us will live a fuller, more useful life as a result." [78]

12 / WORLD WAR II

Speaking to a conference of automobile company executives in 1940, Kettering reminded his colleagues that the nation was poorly prepared for war. No one appeared to have learned anything from the last war, he said, and once again everyone predicted an easy transition from civilian to military "knowhow." No such miracle would be forthcoming, he warned his audience. "I have been asked whether if ten men could dig a certain length of ditch in a day, twenty men could dig twice as much," he said. "My answer is that perhaps they could, but if a hen can hatch a brood of chicks in three weeks, it does not follow that two hens can hatch broods in a week and a half." The conversion would take some time, no matter how many economic and intellectual resources were devoted to it, for as he told the listeners, "We are in the egg-hatching rather than the ditch-digging period." [1]

Between the wars, the automobile industry had shown almost no interest in military matters, maintaining few direct links to military engineering. Kettering was an exception. He kept in touch with military requirements through his membership on various technical committees. Through his service as a consultant on marine power plants for the Science Advisory Board of the National Academy of Sciences, and through his contact with several naval departments as part of his work on submarine diesels, Kettering was better informed about military engineering than most civilian engineers.

He had continued to work on the aerial torpedo in the 1920s under the sponsorship of the army, until an economy move suspended the project after five years.[2] In 1939, with war breaking out again in Europe, Kettering wrote Henry H. Arnold, a young colonel stationed in Dayton during the first trials of the "bug" and now a general and Chief of the Air Corps, and offered to bring the torpedo out of moth balls.[3] Arnold was interested. However, he expressed some reservations, reminding Kettering that "our failure in the past to follow up in logical manner the knowledge gained on early experiments was due in part to the tendency to experiment for the sake of research, thereby losing sight of the original concept of the aerial torpedo which demanded that it be capable of being produced cheaply and quickly."[4]

Kettering had to agree; after all, he had joined the development program in the previous war because he felt that the Sperry torpedo was too expensive and too complex. He wrote back to Arnold pointing out some weight- and cost-saving improvements he planned to incorporate in any new "bug," including a monoplane design and a magnetic compass, and distance control in place of the costly and heavy gyroscope and generator. "In quantities of 10,000 or more, a quite satisfactory cost figure could be obtained," he assured the general, "and we are absolutely in sympathy with your point of view that it must be good and low priced."[5]

Important Washington contacts made it relatively easy for Kettering to obtain funding for the torpedo. William Knudsen, a colleague at General Motors for two decades and president since 1937, was chairman of the Council for National Defense and in charge of military aircraft production. He helped Kettering secure a $250,000 appropriation from the air corps for the project.

Kettering took an active interest in the design and construction of the new torpedo, perhaps too active. In fact, many of the engineers felt his constant suggestions simply got in the way. "In this kind of situation, the Boss was awfully hard to work with, and I think that he defeated his own purpose here by insisting that we do things in a certain way," one of them recalled. "If he had come back once a month instead of twice a day, I think things would have gone much better."[6]

Obsessed with cost, he may have handicapped his assistants with too great an emphasis on cost efficiency at the expense of performance. On the vital control system he set a price ceiling of only $35 a piece, and kept to it, even in the face of obviously deficient performance. "Kettering thought the magnetic compass, or some modification of the magnetic compass, would be the cheapest way to indicate direction and he was very insistent this was the way we ought to do it," said one of the staff members. Unfortunately every variation of the magnetic compass they tried suffered from "north turning error," a false reading caused by the earth's magnetic field that sent the torpedo into a spin. No amount of arguing could convince Kettering to replace the faulty magnetic compass with a more expensive but better performing gyroscope. When the men showed him a textbook pointing out the dangers of north turning error, Kettering simply dismissed the source: "Oh yes, I know the fellow who wrote this book. You know, I taught him all he knows about blind flying."[7]

Ultimately, the assistants did force some improvements past the Boss, but not without quarrels and hard feelings. By the end of 1941 Kettering and his men had developed a 200-horsepower, two-stroke radial engine that weighed less than 1½ lbs./hp, and workable directional controls. They subcontracted for a sleek monoplane body with a 500-pound payload capacity from Cessna Aircraft Company.[8] Even Arnold congratulated Kettering on the torpedo's progress: "I am very pleased that you are getting along so fine and look forward with a great deal of interest to seeing the completed article."[9]

Flight tests in December 1941 confirmed the significant progress they had made. Unlike the discouraging Florida trials on the original torpedo, these tests demonstrated considerable accuracy up to 200 miles. Kettering told his military sponsors, "We have proven that the plane will fly, that it is strong enough to carry the desired load, and that the engine is quite reliable. It has also been proven that controls can be made to work satisfactory."[10]

All this looked good on paper, but European geography was another matter entirely. With a range of only 200 miles, the torpedos would get no further than targets in captured enemy territory. Germany was far out of range. Meeting at the end of December, Arnold, Knudsen, and Kettering discussed the bug's fate. In its favor were low cost and rapid deployment, plus a lower risk of casualties (bomber crew losses were expected to average about 25 percent). Against these advantages, Arnold pointed out, limited range and uncertain effectiveness had to be weighed. Arnold convinced the others that a heavy bomber program was the better bet, and all three agreed to scrap the aerial torpedo.[11]

Resourcefully, Kettering investigated other possible applications, even for the civilian market. "A great deal of interest has been shown in the structural features of our little plane which we have designed here at the Laboratories," he told Sloan. "It is perfectly apparent to us that with proper study, a four-passenger airplane with a cruising speed of 150 miles per hour could be built in reasonable quantities and sold for approximately the same price as a Buick automobile."[12]

The torpedo never did become a successful weapon, nor was it to be a private airplane. It did foreshadow the most terrifying weapon of the European war, the German buzz bomb, and later the cruise missile, a subsonic, self-guided aerial torpedo of infinitely greater sophistication but similar conception. Arnold may have guessed at the possibilities, writing to Kettering at Christmas 1944, "It is a long way from the flying bug of '17 to the buzz bomb of '44 and from the colonel you knew in those days to the general of today. A lot of water has gone over the dam but looking back I recall with greatest pleasure our early associations and I know we were on the right track."[13]

Aerial combat had changed dramatically between the wars, but the basic problem of matching fuel to engine remained. To this field also Kettering hoped to make important contributions. Fortunately, the between-the-wars neglect of the torpedo had not extended to fuel research, and Kettering did not have to convince the military of its value. The importance of even small horsepower increases for combat airplanes was well recognized.

Kettering's plans revolved around a chemical curiosity known as triptane, an ultra-high-performance fuel that chemists at Ethyl Corporation and in the fuel research section at General Motors had discovered between the wars. It resisted knock twice as well as any known fuel, and blends of triptane and TEL could withstand compression ratios of 15:1 without knocking. What made it so important from a military standpoint was that blends of triptane and leaded gasoline, in high-octane aviation engines, offered the possibility of fantastic supercharging pressures, which would help takeoff of heavily loaded aircraft. The potential power and efficiency gains appeared to be limited only by the strength of aircraft engine design and the availability of the fuel.[14]

To tackle the availability problem, Kettering met with corporate executives and selected military officials in the fall of 1942 to discuss plans for a triptane pilot plant.[15] Kettering thought General Motors should fund the plant itself. Because triptane offered such high compression ratios, he saw it as a possible gasoline extender for the postwar market, or perhaps ultimately as the fuel for a high-compression postwar automobile engine. Sloan concurred, and told Kettering that triptane was just the sort of investment General Motors should be making to ensure its long-term profitability. The corporation invested half a million dollars in the plant.[16]

In October 1943 Kettering outlined the objectives of the pilot plant for his chemists: "1. To make a quantity of triptane, enough to permit a thoroughly comprehensive evaluation of its worth in practice to be made, 2. To get information on the reaction of the reactor, so as to be able to proceed to the development of a continuous reactor."[17]

Kettering's chemists encountered several obstacles on the way to quantity production. Lovell and Campbell experimented with various reaction times and temperatures, catalysts, and raw materials in order to cut costs and increase output. But while their work did increase production substantially, they were not able to lower the cost much.[18] Their engine tests also revealed that triptane was more sensitive to changes in mixture temperature, air-fuel mixture, and spark advance than other fuels.[19]

By February 1944, Kettering had the pilot plant synthesizing about 500 gallons of triptane a day, and his enthusiastic tours convinced even the skeptics from the Petroleum Administration that things were moving smoothly.[20] Yet the cost issue continued to trouble Kettering, particularly as he looked ahead to the postwar market. As Campbell correctly pointed out, "At a price above $.60 per gallon the extension of triptane production must still be based on its utilization as a super fuel which cannot be matched by lower cost fuel. Under these circumstances it is important to find some sound basis for evaluation of triptane in such applications."[21]

Where could Kettering find such a market? Military aircraft offered one possibility, though with the war drawing to a close, not a very likely one. Kettering had another idea, long-distance commercial aviation, where fuel efficiency would really count. "There is no question in my mind that the whole subject of long-range aircraft will be completely changed if we can get the high compression engines and the proper kinds of fuel," he told one associate, "and it looks as though triptane is at least among the best for this particular purpose."[22] Cost estimates around a dollar a gallon for postwar production were discouraging, but he had overcome more difficult initial problems.

Kettering never got a chance to test his price calculations. For once, he failed to anticipate the speed of technological advance. The rapid evolution of civilian and military jets eliminated the two most promising markets for triptane, and the expected postwar fuel shortage never materialized. Consequently, triptane went the way of other promising but unprofitable wartime innovations, into lab notebooks and memorandums but never into production.

Kettering had gone his own way in technical matters for a long time. In fact, as he got older, he sometimes acted as if he believed that good solutions could only come from areas where no one else was looking, a prejudice which certainly had its disadvantages. Some of these became obvious when he turned in a completely different direction from engineering colleagues who were developing radar and sonar to detect and track submarines, to fashion his own system.

Kettering focused on a weak point of the submarine that research rivals in places like the MIT Radiation Laboratory had overlooked, the diesel engines that he had invented. The engines made an excellent heat target on a cool night when the submarine surfaced to recharge its batteries. And the heat scope, unlike sonar or radar, cost relatively little and emitted no telltale signals of its own.

Starting on a very small scale, Kettering first tried using a handheld mirror to focus infrared rays on a thermocouple. He aimed this primitive device at ships passing outside his window at the Shoremead Hotel in Miami, but background thermal interference and a lack of sensitivity in the instrument always spoiled his results. Gradually, though, he made improvements, adding a better focusing mirror and upgrading the amplifier.[23] After his first successful trial in February 1941, he telegrammed an assistant back in Detroit, "Infrared just set up. Weather has been very bad over the weekend. Can pick up ships I think up to ten miles. Have new idea on scope which will eliminate the effect of wind. Believe scope can be greatly reduced in size."[24]

Kettering next told his navy contact, Admiral Bowen, about it. Bowen sent a British technical delegation to Florida to talk with Kettering and test the instrument. They returned quite impressed with the potential of the heat scope.[25]

Unfortunately, its inventor could not contain his enthusiasm for the instrument within strictly military circles. At a National Association of Manufacturers dinner in Detroit four months later, he inadvertently revealed something of the invention to a group of journalists. Asserting that the submarine menace was not as bad as it seemed, he said, "All you have to do is locate him when he's on the surface at night, and you've got him." When a sharp science writer guessed that Kettering must be working on a heat detector, the next morning's headline of the *New York Times* read, "Kettering Asserts Device Will Drive U-Boats From Sea." The story then went on to speculate further about Kettering's invention.[26]

That kind of publicity never bothered Kettering but it irked the security-conscious military. Admiral Bowen immediately wrote to Kettering, "our Naval Attache in London was quite worked up about the article in the press ascribed to you." Detailing the alleged indiscretion, Bowen demanded an explanation from the loose-lipped researcher so that "the Navy Department will be able to reassure its representative in London that there are no leaks in the Navy and in the corporations with which the Navy is accustomed to work."[27] Kettering complied, but grumbled that press speculation was "just another of those things which there does not seem to be any method of preventing."[28] Bowen accepted the explanation and dropped the matter.

The press, however, had more to say on the subject. Newspaper columnist Henry McLemore cruelly lampooned Kettering in an essay on the "Office of Blabbing and Popping Off," a ficticious government agency devoted to divulging military secrets to the enemy. "This refusal to keep anything secret is sporting," wrote McLemore. "It wouldn't be quite cricket, would it, to keep a new device to combat submarines up your sleeve? Some fine Axis U-boat commander might be knocked off before he had a chance to wreck a convoy."[29]

McLemore and his readers need not have worried; the heat scope was still far from combat ready. Kettering told Bowen at the end of July that the scope faced several major technical obstacles: "One has been mechanical portability so the apparatus will stay together under any conditions of vibration and motion. This, we feel, is completely licked." Another "was the effect of moving wires in the earth's field," which disrupted the sensitivity. "We have made a lot of progress within the last two weeks in the elimination of the so-called background effect," Kettering explained, "and all our boys here are enthusiastic over it."[30] Finally, the amplifier needed work. With Gerald Rassweiler, Kettering achieved a breakthrough with the "chopper" amplifier, which could amplify the weak direct current signal. Kettering explained the technical details to Bowen:

The system we are now using is a commutator which converts the thermopile into a square wave alternating current. This is put through a step-up transformer and then through an alternating current amplifier. The output from this amplifier is brought back through a synchronous rectifier and then read on the zero micro ammeter.[31]

By late 1942, Kettering thought the scope was ready for an official navy trial, and he convinced General Motors to fund the construction of half a dozen prototypes. Kettering instructed the project engineers to keep the scope as light as possible for aircraft as well as marine use. They got the weight down to eight pounds in the final version.[32]

Most of the technical troubles that Kettering had originally anticipated showed up in the official trials. The shock mountings for the amplifiers proved inadequate. The slightest jar caused unacceptable voltage fluctuations and interference. More critically, the heat scope's best performances occurred in a range of only a mile, and sun interference was often so bad that daytime use looked out of the question. Finally, the vertical range was so narrow that the airplane test pilots had to have a perfectly level course or the units would not work.[33]

When the government did not award a contract, many of the General Motors' engineers suspected political intrigue. Recalling their suspicions, one corporate veteran said, "We had several of these competitions and we were always better, and in many cases theirs wasn't even operating. But the Navy kept saying, 'Yes, but it [the competition] will be better. When it is completed it will be better than yours.' Really the problem was that they [the navy] were putting money into the other systems. They wanted to justify the money they had spent."[34]

Actually, for a variety of reasons, the competing shortwave radar rapidly surpassed the heat scope. By early 1943, the heat scope was obsolete, at least for antisubmarine warfare. In accuracy, range, and consistency, the heat scopes could not match the improved radar systems. For a time there was talk of using the heat scopes to detect surface ships from submarines, but nothing came of it. Government-sponsored engineering, big, rich, and scientifically sophisticated, simply overwhelmed the Kettering group which somehow continued to operate independently and perhaps eccentrically within the largest civilian manufacturing corporation in the world.

Nevertheless, Kettering continued to search for some application for the detectors, coming up with some rather interesting ideas. He thought about using them to find and track airplanes by focusing on their engines, anticipating heat-seeking weapons decades before their appearance. Late in the war he even tried the heat scopes as detection devices for men. He set up a scope on a private runway in Florida and had Earl DeNoon cross a line in front of it at one-hundred-foot intervals. DeNoon, dressed in a gray suit, coat, and vest, left clear signals up to 3,000 feet. "I want to write you the details of the test," Kettering told an associate, "because I think that this detector is of far greater importance than we realize."[35] He was right, although his claim would not be proven true until the jungle war in Vietnam, a generation later.

If Kettering's wartime innovations did not always make it to the front lines, many of the ideas he had perfected before the war did. Kettering once wrote that in modern warfare, "horse-power is war power,"[36] and the two-stroke diesel supported the assertion. The diesel was used in mine sweepers, submarines, and tugboats. One unusual variation, the "pancake" engine, marked something of a milestone in diesel design. To meet special requirements of low weight and bulk, the Research Laboratories developed a radial diesel—a central crankshaft surrounded by four banks of four cylinders each—with an output of 1,200 hp from less than two and a half tons. Its squat, cylindrical shape looked like a stack of pancakes, and the name stuck.[37]

Some of Kettering's other prewar work also paid surprising wartime dividends. The little exposure laboratory in Coral Gables which had provided so much data on paint deterioration was put to work studying material weathering. Instruments once used to measure the effects of sun, rain, and dew on Duco turned out to be just as good for things like canvas, army uniforms, and rubber boots. "A great many of the theorists felt that our work was not practical," Kettering boasted, "but during the War the Quartermaster Department sent us a great many samples of materials which we exposed to the weather and they said we were the only people who could duplicate ratings . . . and that our ratings were the direct indication of their service in the field."[38]

Wartime conditions, with traditional markets and sources of supply disrupted, also forced Kettering into an unusually active policy-making role in General Motors. Executive decisions dealing with potential supply problems and the probable course of the market relied heavily on Kettering's technological predictions.

Government restrictions on raw materials were one obvious difficulty confronting General Motors. Early in 1942, the federal government curtailed all new car manufacturing to conserve steel, rubber, and alloys, and a few months later when the Japanese occupation in Asia almost completely cut off natural rubber imports, it imposed a ban on all nonmilitary uses of rubber.[39]

With stockpiles of natural rubber low, and synthetic substitutes still in the experimental stage, General Motors faced a staggering inventory problem. It held nearly 600,000 automobiles in 1942, and Kettering scarcely needed reminding that these could not be sold until potential customers could be reassured about replacement tires. Therefore, he launched a comprehensive study of the tire and rubber situation, and concluded that proposed mechanical substitutes—such as spring wheels and fabric-cushioned wheels—would never work. "I doubt whether the average person realizes that he will not be able to get tire replacements," he told Sloan. "A great many people say that they will find some way of getting around this when the time comes. What we are trying to do is to disillusion people that there is some magic thing coming along to take the place of the pneumatic tire."[40]

To cope with the harsh realities of the situation, Kettering recommended a program of synthetic rubber research as well as nationwide rationing. He helped organize an SAE committee on rubber substitutes and did some work with Thiokol and Flexon, two cheap grades of synthetic rubber. On the advice of the SAE committee and other interested groups, the government lowered the speed limit to forty miles an hour, and later to thirty-five. The government also funneled $700 million into synthetic rubber research, which eventually yielded 700,000 tons of styrene rubber a year by 1945. However, as Kettering predicted, no magic replacement for the pneumatic tire appeared, and most Americans simply got through the war years with retreads and balding tires.[41]

Before the war, Kettering had only rarely bothered to attend General Motors' board meetings, and when he did, rarely ventured beyond purely technical matters. As the war progressed, however, he began attending regularly, taking a real interest in the Post-War Planning Group. Sloan, surprised and impressed with the change, nominated him for a spot on the Policy Committee, the group responsible for overall corporate strategy. "As one of the largest stockholders—a man of tremendous capacity, especially along the lines on which our success or failure depends—he would, if he would take a broad interest in our problems, be, for many years to come, a useful contributor to our policy phase of the Corporation's activities," Sloan wrote in support of Kettering's election.[42] Other members of the committee vetoed the nomination, however, fearing that Kettering would dominate these meetings, as he did most others, with stories, endless anecdotes, and sheer force of personality. Even Sloan had to admit, "He is so engrossed with technical matters and has been relatively little interested in matters of general policy that through his personality and the interest that he can always develop, the meetings become one of listening rather than doing business. It is probably good for all of us and we profit thereby, but business must be carried on."[43]

Kettering had other ways of making his voice heard within policy circles. He, almost alone among corporate officers, talked directly to Sloan. Accurately he told him to look ahead to rapid technological progress in the postwar world: automatic transmissions; automobile air conditioning; low cost aviation engines; high-powered diesels; and two-stroke automobile engines "lighter in weight, more economical to manufacture, better in every respect to the user, that will revolutionize the motor car industry after the rearmament program is over."[44] Consequently, among automobile makers, General Motors was perhaps best prepared for the many challenges of changing technology and markets.

The commercial success of Kettering's innovations and his visibility as a public spokesman for industrial research led many people to consider him for high public office. "I have already nominated you to President Roosevelt as a one-man head of his preparedness program," wrote one admirer.[45] Kettering got his chance when Roosevelt, pressured for some visible sign of the nation's readiness, named him to the head of the National Inventors Council (NIC) in July 1940.[46]

The NIC had its roots in the previous war when Thomas Edison and Josephus Daniels, the Secretary of the Navy, had put together the Naval Consulting Board, which solicited independent ideas for the war effort. It had come up with almost nothing of military value, and in the intervening years most professional engineers had concluded that such ventures were a waste of time.

Kettering, however, still appreciated the potential of the lone inventor. As something of an independent inventor himself, albeit with a university degree and an industrial research laboratory, he respected the fresh outlook and supposedly unprejudiced ideas of the amateur, which often compensated, in his view, for any lack of specialized training. Consequently, among top-level professional engineers, he was perhaps the only one who would accept the post.

Kettering had several other qualifications for the job. In evaluating independent inventions for the New Devices Committee, he had learned to recognize the central concept from sometimes confused descriptions. Further, he had an exceptionally broad background in fields as diverse as chemistry, aviation, and electronics. Most important, though, he was famous. As a celebrity well known for pronouncements on the place of the individual inventor in an age of corporate research, he was the natural choice for the position.

Kettering set up the NIC along the same lines as the New Devices Committee. Inventive suggestions that came in were reviewed by a technical staff which selected the most promising and passed them along to a committee of elite scientists and engineers. Some of these inventions were then sent to the technical staffs of the armed forces, which could use them or not as they saw fit. No NIC committee members, including Kettering, received any pay, though individual inventors could be compensated by the armed forces if the idea was thought to merit it.[47]

During the first year Kettering and the NIC received 40,000 suggestions. Only 25 of these seemed worthy of further study.[48] Kettering himself had to deal with many of the disappointed contributors, who frequently took their complaints of unfair treatment to friendly politicians and to the press. Kettering's limited patience was sorely tried at times by the stubborn arrogance displayed by some of the unsuccessful. One inventor submitted an utterly fantastic scheme to defeat the submarine menace by spanning the entire North Atlantic with a web of undersea listening cables. He would not rest until Kettering personally reviewed the proposal and wrote him a detailed critique.[49]

Of the 91,000 suggestions received by August 1942, only a handful had merited even a second glance, and the news media began asking probing questions about the validity of the venture. Kettering replied to critics that the very small percentage of innovations developed from a large number of suggestions was normal in industrial research. "You only need one [invention], you know, to win a war, if it's good enough," he reminded them.[50]

Nor was this strictly public relations. Privately, Kettering expressed equal confidence. In a conference with Sloan and other General Motors' executives in 1941 he said:

Now, I happened to be in Washington yesterday at the monthly meeting of the National Inventors Council and it is very encouraging to sit around the table and see how everybody is looking towards new things. This War has completely changed the attitude of our armed forces as to what is important, and they frankly say now the reason that they are coming to the Inventions Council and asking these things is because this is an amateur's War and one amateur is just as good as another, and that they have got more than three times as many suggestions for the Army and Navy in the first year of operation of our Council as they had in the entire duration of the Old Naval Advisory Committee.[51]

To refute the cynics and publicize some of the actual successes, Kettering organized a celebration commemorating the second anniversary of the NIC. Besides notable speakers, Kettering arranged for a display of ten successful innovations developed from NIC contributions, including an amphibious tank and a flying suit filled with milkweed floss instead of kapok, a raw material cut off by Japanese occupations. As he toured the auditorium with the press, Kettering reminded the reporters that each of the items exhibited had begun as an amateur inventor's idea which had "proved fruitful and of practical use."[52]

Lack of focus was probably the major reason why the NIC was not more effective, in Kettering's opinion. American ingenuity, though rich and imaginative, could not solve military problems unless it was

steered in the proper directions. In peacetime, the profit motive chan-
neled creativity; wartime required another kind of management.
Consequently, in May 1944, Kettering prepared a list of critical objectives for amateur inventors. By asking his contributors for solutions
to particular problems—flamethrower protection, self-inflating life
jackets, etc.—he hoped to marshal American knowhow and keep it
on the right course.[53]

Despite the almost overwhelming obstacles of bureaucratic confusion and limited time, the NIC did furnish several important innovations for the war effort. A land mine detector invented by a radio
mechanic from Florida and a heliograph signal mirror submitted by
an inventor from Washington were used widely and saved many
lives.[54]

Kettering personally played an active role in the NIC. He attended
most of the meetings, and led field trips to factories to give committee
members a firsthand look at manufacturing problems. Over lunches
with key congressmen and military officials, he promoted the NIC's
work. He became so popular that an Alabama representative at one
NIC dinner in Washington even "nominated" Kettering for the presidency of the United States, much to the embarrassment of real presidential hopeful Henry Wallace, who was also in attendance. Kettering deftly sidestepped the awkward moment and replied,
"Congressman, I reject the nomination because the only engineer
who was ever President of the United States didn't do a very good
job" (Herbert Hoover). [55]

So successful was the NIC, as a promotional tool and as a bridge
between the military services and important private contractors, that
Kettering, with Roosevelt's active support, planned to extend it past
the armistice. "We plan to continue working as long as they need
us," Kettering announced.[56]

During the war Kettering had an equally important public relations
role as a radio announcer. In 1943 General Motors took over the
sponsorship of the NBC Symphony of the Air. To give the program
a patriotic flair, Allen Orth, head of public relations for General Motors, nominated Kettering as master of ceremonies. Kettering's distinctive voice, widespread reputation, and the enthusiasm and inter-

est he brought to scientific and technical subjects made him the ideal candidate for delivering the patriotic messages Orth thought appropriate for the intermission programs.[57]

For the rest of the war, Kettering gave a weekly Sunday talk with a patriotic twist on science and invention. Orth actually wrote the speeches, but by working closely with Kettering, and including some of the engineer's favorite anecdotes and illustrations, Orth gave the talks Kettering's own flavor.

These "short stories of science and invention," as they were called, included a mixture of history, appeals to national pride, and corporate relations. Usually Kettering began with an illustration from the past, perhaps Eli Whitney and the invention of interchangeable parts, or Walter Reed and the fight against malaria during the building of the Panama Canal. Then, he related the story of the war effort, how American knowhow in mass production was winning the struggle to convert from civilian to military technology. At other times, Kettering's messages were more subtle. Praising George Washington for his foresight in supporting the first patent law, he told his audience, "Our outstanding position today can be attributed to the opportunity and incentive offered to inventors by a sound patent system," restating for the public what he had recently told a congressional committee investigating patent reform.[58]

Kettering's most consistent message was his optimism about the future. Beyond the horrors of war, he assured his listeners, were "Frontiers Unlimited." "We should all be greatly concerned about the future and try to make it the best possible," he observed. "For as I have often said, it is where we are all going to spend the rest of our lives."[59]

The short stories of science and invention generated a steady stream of fan mail and reprint requests. They reached a tremendous audience and helped make Kettering perhaps the best-known engineer since Thomas Edison.

The war years completed Kettering's metamorphosis from independent inventor, to entrepreneur, to manager of corporate research, to technological philosopher. His awards and honors reflected this transformation. In 1943, the joint engineering societies presented him with the John Fritz medal for "notable achievement in the field of industrial research, which contributed greatly to the welfare of mankind and of the nation." [60] The medal recognized his specific contributions to the field of engineering, but more symbolically, it honored his lifelong campaign on behalf of research and development as the key to progress. An even greater honor came to him on December 19, 1944, when the American Association for the Advancement of Science (AAAS) elected him president. [61] This singular distinction owed little to his technical achievements and nothing to his often idiosyncratic science. Rather, the election acknowledged Kettering's unwavering devotion to research as a philosophical principle.

Despite his thorough knowledge of government-sponsored research and his personal contacts with high-level military technicians, Kettering's innovative contributions to the war were limited. The years had not so much diminished his genius as locked him in an outdated inventive style. His military innovations—the aerial torpedo, the infrared detector, triptane—were curious mixtures of foreshadowing and obsolescence. In some important respects they anticipated later developments in guided missiles, the various uses of infrared radiation, and the restructuring of synthetic materials for specific adaptation. Yet they bore the distinctive stamp of Kettering's own past, the idea that innovation rested fundamentally on low cost and mass production. Modern engineering was moving toward jet and rocket propulsion, atomic energy, and advanced electronic radar—expensive, high-performance solutions to the same technical problems. Perhaps Kettering's ideas suffered even more from his unwillingness to join with the rising force in the technical community, the scientifically oriented teams of government researchers. Seeing no need to adapt to the changing times, Kettering isolated himself from the important technical developments around him and doomed his ideas to promising but limited starts.

These setbacks did nothing to diminish Kettering's energy or his enthusiasm, and when the war ended he was anxious to apply its technical lessons to a wide range of peacetime problems. In the philosophical style that was becoming his trademark, he told his fellow engineers at the SAE, "The only danger I think we have in the postwar era will be a lack of understanding between engineering and management as to the essentials of long-range research. If you can get people to take a long-range look at what can be accomplished through research and engineering and you can get an understanding between management and research, you can write your ticket for almost any kind of a world you would like to have, and I think you will get it."[62]

13 / THE LAST HERO

Upon his retirement from the presidency of the AAAS in December 1946, Kettering delivered one of his most thoughtful and enlightening speeches. Addressing a packed house of scientists and engineers in Boston, he congratulated the members on their many recent contributions to the war effort—penicillin, radar, the atomic bomb. He then reminded them that these achievements rested on a long tradition of accumulated wisdom. "Research is more a process of evolution than of revolution," he emphasized. "Progress is slow and occurs in small increments, and long periods of time are involved in new discoveries. The time to lay the foundation for future technical developments is now." [1] At an age (seventy) when most men are thinking about retirement, and in a time of much disillusionment, Kettering looked ahead eagerly to the postwar world, a cheerful philosopher in a troubling time.

Before he retired, Kettering wanted to make one more evolutionary contribution to the internal combustion engine, to cap his own impressive technical career and open a new chapter for a younger generation of automotive engineers. Three decades of dedication to the fuel/engine problem had already resulted in TEL, triptane, the two-stroke diesel, and a better understanding of combustion on a molecular level. Now Kettering was proposing what seems to be the logical culmination of these studies—a truly efficient, high-compression gasoline engine.

Just at the end of the war, Kettering presented his second seminal paper on the fuel/engine question to the SAE. He traced the history of the internal combustion engine and noted that the two key factors in improving it had been better fuels and higher compression. As Kettering saw it, rising octane numbers had finally hit a stubborn law of diminishing returns, and further gains in this direction would not be economical. What was needed, he said, was an ultra-high-compression engine (about 12:1) that would not need high-octane fuels. "Engines are all made out of metal and brains," he told the skeptics, "and what we want to do is put in as much of the latter as possible. When that is done we get the most and cheapest power out of a pound of fuel."[2]

For the next year Kettering and his power plant engineers struggled to design such an engine, one that could withstand high compression and deliver the same horsepower across the same speed range as a normal engine, yet with far less displacement and weight. Ultimately, they put together a six-cylinder version with a "square" (bore = stroke) design which, at 180 cu. in., had the power of a standard 257 cu. in. engine.[3]

Many of Kettering's researchers were surprisingly cool toward the project. E. V. Rippingille, second in administrative command, opposed the idea vigorously, though not openly, and called it "humoring the Boss." Even Kettering seemed reluctant to commit himself totally to the venture. Several researchers found his usual enthusiasm flagging whenever talk arose of a formal debut, and on one occasion, complaining that the engine was too heavy, he insisted on a complete design overhaul.[4]

But after the first road tests of the little engine in the fall of 1946, Kettering regained his optimism. "The consensus of opinion both from the standpoint of the oil industry as well as the automobile industry is that high compression engines are rough, their friction is high, and they are very hard on fuels," he told Sloan. "Now, like many of these things, this popular opinion is just 100% wrong as our engine is not rough, it has less friction than the average automobile engine, and it is very easy on fuels." Anticipating the usual resistance from the production engineers, Kettering added, "I know of nothing that is as important at the present time, from the General Motors standpoint, to get all of our engineers to understand that the compression ratio limits that we should design for any new engine is between 12 and 13 to 1."[5]

Kettering unveiled his new engine at the June 1947 SAE meeting held in French Lick, Indiana. While curious oil company executives, automotive engineers, and journalists crowded around, Kettering explained that the deceptively small engine in an otherwise standard Oldsmobile could average a then amazing 26.5 miles a gallon on experimental 85 octane gasoline (a standard Oldsmobile of the same power averaged about 18 miles a gallon). But lest anyone think that the prototype was ready for mass production and sale, he reminded his audience, "this isn't going to come tomorrow or the next day—in fact we're way ahead of the industry—possibly in a few years we'll improve the gasoline engine like we have the Diesel engine."[6]

Actually, the high-compression engine came much more quickly than Kettering expected. Oldsmobile developed a V-8 version and had it on the market within a few years. The other divisions rapidly followed suit. Oldsmobile wanted to name theirs the "Kettering Engine," in honor of his many direct and indirect contributions, not least of which was helping convince the oil industry to develop better fuels for the engine. The Boss would not hear of it, and Oldsmobile settled for a bronze plaque on the production facility reading "Kettering Engine Plant."[7]

Kettering himself did not see the high-compression engine through development and marketing. Feeling that he had carried the burden of automotive research long enough and confident that his work at least pointed the way toward future improvements (and under some pressure from formal retirement guidelines to step down), he announced his retirement at the French Lick meeting on June 2, 1947. Charles L. McCuen, a capable if undynamic engineer who had worked his way through the ranks at Oldsmobile, succeeded, but could not replace him. And though seventy years old and officially retired, Kettering agreed to keep his Detroit office and secretary and serve as a technical consultant to General Motors.

After revealing his retirement plans, he told the meeting, "The forward looking work on fuel and engines could not be in better shape than it is now. Engineers everywhere are thinking now in the right direction. I don't care how long it takes to gain the full advantages of high compression. Any rate of progress is all right, just so long as we are headed in the right direction."[8] The future seemed to be in capable hands. To close friends, though, Kettering looked tired and a bit discouraged, and he commented privately, "Well, the balloon is up; we will see what happens."[9]

Kettering did offer some support for the opinions of those who doubted that the profession's most distinguished and active participant would actually retire. "Retire?" he teased reporters, "I wouldn't fool around with that sort of thing."[10]

One thing more Kettering wanted to leave General Motors—a first-rate research center. Since before the war he had been pushing for a new laboratory and engineering facility, for research operations were spread throughout Detroit, housed in overcrowded or temporary quarters. He discussed the issue with Sloan many times and got him to admit that such a facility was needed, especially to maintain the "marvelous balance between the scientific and the engineering side" of General Motors' work.[11]

General Motors chose Eliel and Eero Saarinen as the architects, precipitating a feud between Kettering, who feared that artistic considerations would be favored over functional engineering, and other top executives. Kettering's opposition was so strong that after a series of showdowns between him and the Saarinens, the corporation decided to postpone the plans until after his retirement, and the funds were invested elsewhere.[12]

When word of the plans leaked, however, the Technical Center became a matter of public discussion. One professor of sociology asked Kettering if he intended to pursue questions in the social as well as physical sciences. Kettering answered that he could not see "how you can apply the so-called scientific method to what we call the social sciences," but he did concede that society itself was a sort of laboratory for these questions. Said Kettering, "The whole subject of history is the laboratory results of what has happened and I have always thought that the causes of history is one of the most important sources of information that we have leading up to the general problems which you mention."[13]

General Motors finally completed the Technical Center a decade later. Kettering attended the dedication on an unexpectedly cold, windy day in May 1956. After a parade of other speakers, the audience of five thousand leaders of industry, science, and education watched the man who had started it all so many years before in a barn slowly ascend the podium. The old engineer looked out across the twenty-two-acre artificial lake, the broad lawns, carefully landscaped fields, and low, handsome buildings of glass and glazed brick, and compared it all to an intellectual golf course. "Here in this institution we have the place where we can make indefinite practice shots and the only time we don't want to fail is the last time we try it," he said. "I've been an inventor all my life and of course a great many people think of inventors as screwballs or longhairs. I can't claim the last," he added, stroking his bald head, "so I will put on my hat."[14]

Kettering did not fit very well into this world of white-coated technicians and advanced university degrees. The academic scientists, the successors to men like Boyd, Midgley, and Hunt whom he had brought into General Motors, had transformed the place, made it their own, and left little room for a "screwdriver and pliers man."

Still, he frequently visited both the Detroit laboratory and the new Technical Center during his retirement years. He never rode the elevators (too slow) and never stayed in his office (too isolated). He poked around the laboratories as in the old days and surprised nervous young doctors of physics with his tall presence and probing questions.

To one young physicist he confided that he would gladly trade his years of achievement for the challenge of a new generation.[15] But the opportunities open to the young physicist were very different from the kind of challenge Kettering preferred. Much of the pioneering of the automobile industry was over. The heyday of automotive engineering had given way to a refinement and specialization poorly suited to Kettering's talents and temperament. He had faced the young physicist's choice many years ago at NCR, and he had traded the security of an established industry for the excitement of the new. He had cast his lot with the automobile, had grown old with it, and had contributed more than anyone else to its development. Now, some thought, both were old and tired.

Yet there were still fresh fields to conquer, even for a man in his seventies. One challenge was cancer. Since the 1930s, he had provided financial support for research at the Barnard Free Skin and Cancer Hospital in St. Louis.[16]

Kettering was never shy about telling the researchers he funded how to go about their work. In this case he felt that the research had veered too far from scientific fundamentals and too close to traditional medicine. "I am very much interested in this work at St. Louis," he told one of his photosynthesis researchers at Antioch. "I think we really have some chance of helping these boys get some of this cancer difficulty ironed out. They have been treating this too much as a medical theory and not enough from a chemical standpoint. I have felt all along that cancer was a chemical disorder and not a bacterial one, although bacterial upsets in some of the ductless glands might be the cause of the chemical change."[17] When the researchers shifted to a study of chemical carcinogens, the patron was happier, and predicted that this approach would let the researchers "get ahead of the disease rather than behind it."[18]

When a neck tumor claimed Kettering's sister Emma in December 1944, the cancer project suddenly changed from a scientific puzzle to a personal crusade. Kettering was stranded by a snowstorm and could not even attend the funeral services. "The storm came up so unexpectedly that it was impossible to get the roads open," he told his brother Adam. "We tried both ways and were not able to get through."[19]

Six months later Kettering got a chance to broaden his role in cancer research when Sloan asked him to support a major effort at New York City's Memorial Hospital. Sloan proposed giving $2 million for a building and $2 million more for ten years of research. He wanted Kettering's name and his advice, not his money.[20]

On August 7, 1945, they unveiled the Sloan-Kettering Institute to the press. Their announcement unexpectedly coincided with and was overshadowed by the bombing of Hiroshima. However, the few science writers who bothered to attend the news conference were treated to an excellent sampling of Kettering's philosophy. Seizing the most appropriate and topical of analogies, he told them, "Mr. Sloan and I over the years have worked together on many apparently hopeless industrial problems which today seem so simple that I am inclined to feel we can apply some of these time-tried techniques to this age-old problem. Very rapid progress against this mysterious scourge could be made if the problem got the same amount of money, brains, and planning that was devoted to developing the atomic bomb."[21]

The Ketterings spent most of the next winter in Florida. For Kettering these days were a welcome vacation from other obligations, though he often relaxed with a pencil and graph paper. Early in January 1946, during their stay at the Surf Club, Olive began to tire easily and appeared to be suffering from jaundice. At the end of the month Kettering took her back to Detroit, where she entered Henry Ford Hospital for exploratory surgery. "The doctors told me after the operation that she could live no longer than three months," Kettering wrote a close friend.[22] The diagnosis was pancreatic cancer. He said nothing about the prognosis to his wife. For Olive's friends he also kept up the front: "The operation came along very well but she got an intestinal infection which set her back quite a little. I think now she is definitely on the way to recovery. She is walking a little bit every day and was better this morning than she has been yet."[23] Only to his closest friends did he admit the truth. And when he told Hugo Young in Loudonville about Olive's condition, Hugo recalled that Kettering cried openly. "Oh, how he sobbed."[24]

For the next few months Kettering cut back his work schedule drastically and spent nearly all of his time with Olive in Detroit. On the days he did go to the laboratory, he always called his wife exactly at noon. They passed their last weeks together in relative peace and happiness, and on the last day of April she died. Kettering then began the sad task of informing their friends. "We had a wonderful life together and I, of course, miss her more than words can tell," he wrote an old Ashland acquaintance. "She died from cancer of the pancreas but did not know what was wrong. She did not suffer and was active and working up until a few days of her death. She had day and night nurses but went out for a ride every day and worked around the apartment."[25]

Olive's death left Ridgeleigh Terrace an empty, lonely place. No more luncheon parties or organ concerts to fill its halls with sounds. Only a few servants remained. Eugene and Virginia spent most of their time in Hinsdale, Illinois, near the Electro-Motive plant. For company in Dayton, Kettering insisted that the pilots of his two private planes live at Ridgeleigh Terrace when he was in town. Other nights he passed watching televised boxing with the night watchman at the Winter's Bank.[26]

The three grandchildren provided some distraction. When each of the grandchildren was born, their proud grandfather put them through a fascinating little ritual. Placing the baby on his lap he would say, "Now your hands, God gave you these to be used and no matter how much you have in your head, it will be of no use to you whatsoever until you learn how to use your hands and to know what your hands are for."[27]

Kettering enjoyed spoiling them just a little. When Chuck graduated from high school, his grandfather took him in his private seaplane, *The Blue Tail Fly*, for a fishing trip to the Georgian Bay. Later, he spoke at each of the grandchildren's college graduations. Susan, the youngest, was perhaps his favorite. As a child she was a faithful correspondent and filled her grandfather's days with stories of Chuck's talking crow, Jane's academic achievements, and the pet cat's attack on their mother's fur. She called her grandfather Babo and he called her Tuny.[28]

Kettering also lost himself in the cancer research. He personally financed a major effort at the Southern Research Institute in Birmingham, Alabama, gave generously to the Sloan-Kettering Institute, and supported other cancer research as well, to the tune of several hundred thousand dollars a year.[29]

Typically, Kettering devoted a great deal of thought to the practical ends and attainable progress of cancer research. As he pointed out to one investigator, "Every problem has to be approached from the standpoint of the prospector and the miner. Some people like to prospect but all the prospecting in the world will not bring the ore to the smelter. So you have to, some place along the line, begin to work the claims. . . . It is my impression that today we have too many prospectors in the cancer research field and not enough miners." [30] As in his automotive work. he wanted research focused on immediate goals.

Despite all the funds, and the efforts to transplant industrial research methods into cancer research, the work did not get as far as he expected. He attributed this failure to "prejudice and jealousy" on the part of many of the researchers and to a lack of willingness to follow his philosophies more closely. [31]

Such setbacks never completely dampened Kettering's hopes for a cancer cure, and he passed both his optimism and his spirit of generosity on to his son and grandchildren. "You have contributed so very much, both physically and spiritually, to the work of this institution for which we never cease to be grateful," C. P. Rhoads, director of Sloan-Kettering, told him. "It was heart-warming indeed, to receive a cheque for $5,000 from your grandson, Chuck, at Christmas-time and to know that he, too, shares the Kettering interest in the welfare of the Sloan-Kettering Institute." [32]

Another venture that increasingly occupied Kettering's time in retirement was the photosynthesis work. "We have the scientific knowledge to provide an adequate diet for every one of the 2,000,000,000 inhabitants of the globe if the information were properly applied," he told one audience with more hope than conviction. [33] He told another that because of the potential of solar energy conversion, "the American public has nothing to worry about in either fuel or food supplies." [34] To make such boasts reality, he devoted himself to Antioch and the photosynthesis research.

Unhappily, a conflict of personalities nearly destroyed the entire program in the years following the war. Algo Henderson's liberalism offended Kettering's conservatism even more in those days of cold war. Kettering accused Henderson of "harboring an undercurrent of communism in your organization which has a shaded green light from the executive office." Reminding Henderson who was paying the bills, he warned, "Now, our Foundation has a very large investment in Antioch, but as things stand . . . they would be willing to sell out very much below par."[35]

Kettering's politics affected the scientific aspects of the photosynthesis research too. His biweekly visits tapered off to once a month and then stopped altogether in the spring of 1947. Rothemund and others detected an irascibility that often flared into open anger in their meetings on campus. Consequently, they started visiting him in Dayton instead, but the old enthusiasm seemed to have disappeared.[36] In May, Kettering wrote Henderson that "at a meeting of the C. F. Kettering Foundation in Dayton it was decided to discontinue any further support to Antioch College and to arrange to remove the photosynthesis work as soon as practicable."[37]

Before the fateful order could be carried out, Henderson resigned and was replaced with a more pro-business professor of industrial relations from MIT. Not all the damage could be undone, however, for Kettering had already begun setting up another photosynthesis laboratory in the basement of Ridgeleigh Terrace, far from the corrupting influence of the campus.

The rooms of the mansion's basement soon buzzed with unaccustomed activity as a new group of researchers brought life to the almost deserted house. Howard Tanner, William Trehame, and a handful of other workers began just where the earlier studies had begun, trying to find out why the grass was green, though with more emphasis than previously on photochemistry and the chemical processes of photosynthesis.

For several years the investigation proceeded informally and modestly. Trehame worked with photocells to improve the direct conversion of sunlight to electricity, and studied the reactions of plants under colored lights. Kettering enjoyed the intimacy of the small laboratory and often dropped in to collect data, turn a few knobs, or read a meter or two. Other times he simply tried out a few jokes on the researchers in preparation for a forthcoming lecture.[38]

In Florida too, Kettering continued his photosynthesis studies. He covered plants with selective filters to evaluate the effects of different wavelengths of light on growth and fertility. He worked out an aerial radiation counter for measuring the amount of sunlight falling on agricultural fields. And he personally collected seawater samples in the Gulf of Mexico and sent them back to Dayton, theorizing that since life originated in the oceans, the action of sunlight on organic material in seawater must hold the secret of life itself.[39]

Publicly, Kettering predicted great things from the little laboratory. "We must be able to eliminate the time-consuming problem of aging vegetable materials in the ground in the natural but centuries-long process of making coal and oil," he told one incredulous audience.[40] He even claimed that the photosynthesis study rivaled nuclear fission as a research project. In the long run he may have been right, but no amount of boasting could conceal the relatively primitive laboratory facilities and the youthful inexperience of the researchers. Against one of nature's most perplexing phenomena it was clearly an unequal contest.

In 1952, Kettering consolidated the Ridgeleigh Terrace laboratory with the ongoing project at Antioch. "We are building a new lab at Yellow Springs," he told his brother. "This will take most of the work from the house." He also mentioned an interesting trip to a missile base in Florida: "Tuesday we got up to Co-Co for several days at the Guided Missile Base. As you know I started this work many years ago."[41]

Kettering's renewed commitment to photosynthesis research at Antioch marked the beginning of a new period of close association with the college. In Samuel B. Gould, who took over the presidency in 1954, Kettering found a friend who inspired the trust and enthusiasm missing since the Morgan era.

Over the years Kettering and Gould became good friends, and in the Gould household Kettering found refuge from the loneliness of Ridgeleigh Terrace. On many evenings, just before dinner, his black Chevrolet would pull into the driveway and its owner would amble to the front door looking for a meal and some conversation. Gould and his wife always welcomed their half-expected guest and usually had a plate of Kettering's favorite corn fritters waiting.

Even the Gould's son looked forward to these visits and Kettering's clear and patient explanations of aeronautics and other scientific wonders. Still, the teenager was not afraid to challenge the old engineer. After one spirited debate over flight characteristics, Kettering invited his young friend to a demonstration in his private plane, and the following afternoon the young man received an unforgettable lesson in the importance of the experimental method. [42]

Gould also tried, when he could, to temper Kettering's political outbursts. One afternoon Kettering came over for the Army-Navy football game, and immediately launched into a tirade on the softness of American foreign policy. "I had never seen him so agitated before," said Gould, "in fact, he became so carried away that Mrs. Gould rushed down from upstairs thinking that we were having a fight of some kind." By the time Gould finally had him calmed down, the game was over. [43]

In general, Kettering operated his foundation on the belief that the man who gave the money should decide the policy. But Gould could be persuasive, and frequently loosened Kettering's financial grip. Thus, Antioch received a steady flow of funds. In 1955 Kettering donated $767,000 for a student union, and a year later he gave $750,000 for a library in his wife's name. [44] Gould would not go along with Kettering's proposal to modernize the grand romanesque Antioch Hall by removing its turrets, but usually college and patron saw eye to eye. Antioch even elected Kettering chairman of the board of the college he had once denounced as a seedbed of radicalism. His only request was that he be excused from having to attend the meetings. [45]

Two or three times a week Kettering visited his thirty researchers in the Solar Laboratory, a modest three-story brick building on the southwest corner of the campus. During the winter he telephoned from Florida just as regularly, always with the same message—"Send me the data!" [46]

The Solar Laboratory tackled a surprisingly diverse number of projects in those years, from prebiological chemistry and synthetic chlorophyll to the role of trace elements in photosynthesis and organic fuel cells. Characteristically, Kettering chose the problems himself. For instance, he left a note for the researchers, "Here's a field of corn growing in a sea of atmospheric nitrogen and unable to use any of it. How does nature convert this gaseous nitrogen to ammonia which plants can use?"[47]

Kettering liked the personal contact he had with the photosynthesis workers. Through long discussions, meter reading, and report reading, he kept in touch with the investigations and thoroughly enjoyed himself. Monday mornings young laboratory technicians frequently discovered sheets of graph paper with Kettering's weekend calculations. At any one time "he usually had some 'pet' project in the laboratory and he would spend a lot of time with the people who were working on that one project and pretty much ignore the rest of the place," one recalled. Which was just as well, perhaps, for with too many irons in the fire, Kettering could never manage to keep up with every aspect of every project. "He sometimes got left a little behind on the details," said one scientist, "and his solution was to go back to a place that he understood, so we sometimes found after we got a distance away from our beginning experiments, we were suddenly urged back to doing them all over again."[48]

Nonetheless, Kettering took good care of his "boys." He often took them out to lunch. True to his lifelong eating habits, he usually ordered a peanut butter and jelly sandwich for himself. Once a young student chef, not recognizing the donor of the building, told him his choice of sandwich was not available that day. Without protest, Kettering simply asked for something else. And William Treharne recalled that several times Kettering offered to buy lunch for the group only to find himself short of cash. The others anted up for the meal, though Kettering's chauffeur always repaid them promptly.

Other Kettering idiosyncracies became Antioch legend. Dr. Glenn Elmore, a young chemist at the Solar Laboratory, remembered Kettering's driving habits as an eighty-year-old man.

We had this consultant . . . who came up here about every six months. . . . Mr. Kettering was always interested in talking to him. One day he had his new Chevrolet with a fuel injection pump on it and he wanted to show us what pickup and speed it had. He said, "Well, I'll give you all a ride." First thing we knew, we were going eighty miles an hour. I already knew from taking [the consultant] back and forth to the airport that he didn't like to drive fast at all. Thirty-five miles [an hour] was his top speed. . . . [He] just sat there and was nervous, and then he said, "Does he drive this fast all the time?" Mr. Kettering just pressed on the gas and away we went.[49]

Occasionally, the photosynthesis research became physically demanding, but Kettering refused to make any concessions to his age. As a result, he gave a few good scares to the Antioch staff. On the roof of the Solar Laboratory he installed a small windmill, a way of capturing solar energy, he was fond of saying. The assistants held their breath every time he headed for the narrow stairway leading to the roof. One trip very nearly cost Kettering his life. It was a stormy afternoon, and the voltage regulator connecting the windmill to a bank of storage batteries failed. Kettering was halfway up the stairway when the batteries exploded. Acid splashed over his head and burned holes in his suit while he was trying to throw the switch and cut off the current. Meanwhile, several younger, and less courageous, researchers cowered in a corner.[50]

Another time, unable to contain his enthusiasm for a new X-ray tube, the intrepid engineer connected it to a transformer and held the unshielded, buzzing tube in his bare hands while the horrified staff took turns "running in the lab and trying to suggest that perhaps it would be better if we deferred the experiment for the time being."[51]

If the laboratory never did unlock the secret of photosynthesis, or find a cheap way to convert solar energy into food or fuel, it did contribute substantially to the literature. Until the end of his life, the Solar Laboratory remained a special source of pride and interest for Kettering.

Perhaps Kettering's most compelling ambition of his retirement years was achieving a position in the scientific world equal to his status in the engineering community. His election to the presidency of the AAAS and his achievements in the field of chemistry were unique and significant accomplishments for an engineer, but they represented his sponsorship and management of science more than his personal theoretical contributions. He still suffered from an inferiority complex in the presence of recognized scientists that was heightened by any real or imagined suggestions of his scientific ignorance. "Oh, yes, the auto mechanic," Albert Einstein is supposed to have remarked when introduced to Kettering at a Princeton commencement.[52] The implication wounded Kettering's pride, making him even more determined to cap his career with an important theoretical contribution to science.

Ironically, it was a belief he shared with Einstein that inspired Kettering's last, and perhaps most quixotic, quest. Both men were troubled by the rise of quantum theory, with its emphasis on probability and uncertainty. They preferred a strictly mechanistic interpretation of nature. Moreover, both believed that elementary natural forces were only different manifestations of one, predictable, force, what Einstein called unified field theory and Kettering less elegantly referred to as scientific monism.

The difference between Einstein's and Kettering's approach to the challenge of unified field theory reflected their different professions and inclinations. Einstein was a theory man, a scientist who worked with pure thought experiments. He spent the last half of his career trying to work out a general equation to link gravity and electromagnetism. Kettering never bothered with such mathematics; he preferred to test his ideas experimentally. Neither man found much support within the scientific community. Most physicists dismissed Einstein's quest as misguided. The few who knew of Kettering's work considered it preposterous.

Kettering's ideas of physics came from classic, and many would say outdated, sources—William Thomson, James Clerk Maxwell, and Michael Faraday. He was more at home in the world they had constructed of magnetic lines of force and mechanical cause and effect. He kept copies of their texts in his library and annotated them heavily. When asked by a reporter for a list of books he would take to a desert island, Kettering included Maxwell's treatise on electricity and magnetism.

Kettering also kept up with more recent studies, but he believed that most of these researchers were asking the wrong questions. For instance, next to a discussion of wave versus particle theory in a text by French physicist Louis de Broglie, in which de Broglie argued the difficulty of reconciling the dual nature of light, Kettering confidently scribbled, "should be no trouble," and quickly passed onto other matters.[53]

Kettering agreed with Einstein that the special properties of space were at the heart of physics. But there they parted company, and Kettering had his own theories on the subject. "All the forces across space, such as gravity and electrostatic and magnetic are space functions and are due to special configurations of space," he claimed. These configurations, in turn, depended on what Kettering called the "inertia" and "elastic" nature of space itself, which were created by the mass and velocity of something tangible. For Kettering, then, a magnetic field actually had mass and velocity, and had kinetic energy, though in a minute amount.[54]

From the 1930s on, he assailed anyone who would listen with his theories. On the Galapagos cruise, one of his guests recorded that he "had a most interesting long talk with Ket in the afternoon on his theory that all physical problems reduce to expressions of inertia and elasticity, especially about his belief that a magnetic field should affect the velocity of light."[55]

Kettering also devised some ingenious experiments to test his ideas. In one of these, he set out to detect and measure inertial changes in a magnetic field by trapping magnetic lines of force in a torodial coil (a doughnut-shaped electromagnet) and then reversing the flux. Instrumentation was the major obstacle, for the changes Kettering expected would be extremely small. With a young university-trained physicist, Gifford G. Scott, he set up some rather sophisticated instruments to detect inertial changes and to shield the experiment from outside interference—vibration, the earth's magnetic field, and iron deposits.[56]

While their methods became increasingly refined over the years, they were never able to detect the predicted effects. But Kettering refused to be discouraged. He surmised that the effects were too small to be picked up by their instruments, and sent Scott back to the laboratory with orders to produce more sensitive equipment. Some of these instrument problems turned out to be quite interesting, and Kettering frequently became involved in them. A friend who told him about some special aluminum wire he thought might be useful in one of the experiments reported that Kettering "beamed with the look and enthusiasm of a child who had just been given a coveted toy."[57]

If the equipment did not substantiate Kettering's theory, at least it was not wasted. Scott, who was more aware than Kettering of contemporary research interests in physics, adapted the instruments for a number of other studies, including a precise measurement of electron momentum in electrical carriers like copper and aluminum, and a new way of calculating the electron's mass/charge ratio.[58] This last experiment attracted considerable attention from the scientific community, and Robert Millikan congratulated Kettering on the ingenuity of the experimental method. Kettering was so flattered by the compliment from the Nobel Laureate that he called a special meeting of the laboratory department heads to tell them about it.

Over the years Kettering put together a succession of laboratories for Scott's magnetic studies, initially with General Motors funds and, when his own successor there scrapped the project, with his own money on a site near Ridgeleigh Terrace. To evaluate the venture and suggest possible new directions, Kettering hired an outside consultant, Samuel R. Williams, a retired physics professor with special expertise in magnetism. Kettering was surprised to learn from Williams' report that Scott's research, far from helping to prove the kinetic nature of magnetic flux, had actually offered convincing evidence to the contrary. Williams told Kettering, "I believe Mr. Scott has answered the question about magnetic inertia in an indisputable fashion and that the energy stored in a magnetic field is not kinetic energy. . . . These experiments of Mr. Scott's seem to me to set at rest this problem, which has been a headache for nearly a century, as to whether the energy of a magnetic field is kinetic or not." Williams then urged Kettering to make the best of the situation: "Now that we have established the fact that magnetic energy is not kinetic energy, we should turn to the other alternative that magnetic energy is potential energy. . . . We should see what happens there in all sorts of different media. The way in which various media affect the transmission of magnetic energy through space may open to us how it is transmitted through a total vacuum."[59]

Despite the good advice, Kettering never quite let go of his theory, nor of his hope that it might someday be vindicated and win him the scientific status he dreamed of. In fact, on the day before he died he was in the magnetics laboratory trying once again to prove the theory. In the end, the magnetics research yielded some good data, some improved analytical techniques and instruments, and thanks to Scott, some important work that interested more orthodox physicists.

Less scientific but perhaps even more important was Kettering's contribution to the one aspect of scientific research that could never be forgotten—financing it. He actively lobbied for government support of research, and testified on behalf of a bill creating the National Science Foundation. He told a friend afterward, "It is my impression that we will get a fairly sound Bill for Government controlled research. The educational institutions, of course, are whooping this up because they think this is their chance to get some Government subsidy." [60]

Well into his seventies, Kettering continued to view the world as a continuing challenge. If his pace slackened a bit, still he secured some additional patents, and generally disproved Midgley's frequently cited declaration that scientists and engineers should retire at age forty, after which he believed creativity evaporated. Two devices Kettering developed in his "retirement" were a humidity-sensitive starter switch for air conditioners and an instrument for detecting irregular heartbeats below the range of human hearing. [61]

Retirement also gave Kettering a chance to reflect on the broader significance of his career, and to share those reflections with students, businessmen, and engineers. His dry wit and colorful style endeared him to nearly every audience, and his eloquence and quotability made him the best-known engineer of his generation.

Distinguished universities vied with one another in awarding Kettering honorary doctorates in law, humanities, science, and engineering. He collected nearly forty such degrees recognizing him not only for the depth of his scientific knowledge and the breadth of his humanistic concern but, in the words of his Princeton citation, also for his "canny common sense." [62]

College audiences were delighted with his commencement addresses, even ones that were not, as on one extremely muggy George Washington University graduation, only five minutes long. Perhaps it is difficult, reading them thirty years later, to understand why they were so popular, since they consist of the usual exhortations to hard work and individualism. Even one of Kettering's friends complained, "Why, the man has one speech. It's a good speech, but I've already heard it ten times and I'm not going back."[63] But despite the high-pitched, twangy delivery and occasional fumbling, Kettering's conviction, his earthy humor, and the love of subject he conveyed overcame whatever formal flaws he had as a public speaker. Most considered him eloquent, and his faith in science and engineering struck a responsive chord with the college generation of the 1950s.

Younger audiences also appreciated his lively tales. Girls' conservatories and troops of Boy Scouts found him a willing and enthusiastic lecturer. The scouts awarded him the Silver Beaver and the Silver Buffalo for his contributions to "boyhood," though he had never been a scout himself.[64]

The technical community continued to applaud Kettering's philanthropic work. The six joint engineering societies created a special award named for him, and he won the Herbert Hoover Medal for "great, unselfish, non-technical service by engineers to their fellow man."[65]

Conservative business gatherings particularly appreciated his eloquent and often amusing defense of free enterprise. He once said that "if there is as great a gulf between practice and theory in Russian scientific education as there is in some other aspects of Russian life, the more engineers they turn out, the safer we shall be."[66] His suggestion that the medal he received from the American Petroleum Institute for doing more than any other individual to promote petroleum products belonged more properly to coal-mining strike leader John L. Lewis roused howls of laughter from the members of the Economic Club.[67] And the Committee of 100, the conservative group of businessmen who vacationed at the Surf Club elected him president of an organization he had once considered too reactionary to join.[68]

However much Kettering's conservatism pleased these audiences, his grasp of political realities must be judged shallow and naive. He seriously suggested to Arthur Morgan at one time that America should get out of Europe and let Russia take over so the people there would get a proper taste of communism and reject it once and for all.[69] Sometimes his antiradicalism carried him dangerously close to communist-baiting excess, as in this speech:

Since I have retired I have organized a couple of new companies. The first I have named the Utopia Transportation Company Limited. This is a non-profit organization to give free transportation. Its purpose is to give free travel tickets to those who get up in the public square and tell you this is a "lousy" country. It would give them travel tickets to where they want to go—not where you want them to go, but where they want to go. This company is called the Utopia Transportation Company, Limited—limited to furnishing transportation in one direction only. The other company I have organized to sell stock—stock in the greatest corporation the world has ever seen. This company I have called the United States Preferred.[70]

The ultra-conservative ideology did nothing to tarnish Kettering's image. In 1952 he won the Horatio Alger Award for personifying the American tradition of rising from rags to riches—an appropriate testimonial to a truly extraordinary career. Like Alger's fictitious heroes, Kettering was becoming something of a legend. One journalist covering the story of the award was so awed by Kettering's achievements that he credited him with "research on chlorophyll which resulted in its present widespread use."[71] No matter misstatement or misunderstanding. They knew a good man when they saw one.

Kettering's birthday celebrations became community and even national events. Loudonville hosted the seventieth, complete with a picnic luncheon at the Kettering homestead, a pageant of the life and times of young Charlie Kettering, and gifts including three local crows captured for his grandson Chuck, whose own pet crow had, ironically enough, been sucked into a speeding diesel locomotive.[72]

On his seventy-fifth birthday, the city of Dayton and General Motors joined forces to host a personal engineering retrospective. Kettering toured exhibits of his own work and stopped to pose beside some of his favorites with celebrities such as Arthur Godfrey. When asked about his plans for new revolutionary projects, he just grinned and replied, "There are no big projects. Pure research starts with small things—big applications follow."[73] Of the tall old man in the rumpled suit, the *New York Times* commented, "In a day when doubt and despair are abroad in the land, when even young men are uncertain of the future, it is good to be reminded by one of our sturdy citizens who has an abiding faith in a good tomorrow."[74]

The aging body could not always keep up with the youthful spirit, though. The endless parties, lectures, and travel sent Kettering into the Henry Ford Hospital for a prostate operation and a few weeks of recuperation shortly after the Dayton celebration. Ignoring his doctor's warnings, he maintained the hectic pace, hemorrhaged, and landed in the hospital again four months later.[75]

Even audiences far less sympathetic than the Boy Scouts and the Chamber of Commerce often wound up praising Kettering. In 1953 the Justice Department asked for his testimony in an antitrust suit against Du Pont and General Motors. For two days Kettering offered a lively presentation filled with fact, fancy, and humor which nonetheless scored some important points for the defense.[76] The government ultimately won the case on appeal, but Kettering went down on record as a fascinating advocate of industrial research. Subpoened documents revealing the executives' reluctance about putting Kettering on the Policy Committee because they feared that his rambling soliloquies would distract from important business only enhanced Kettering's public image. "Charles F. Kettering was as interesting as Scheherazade when he talked to the old policy committee of General Motors about scientific research," noted one amused source, comparing Kettering's ability to talk himself out of a term on the boring committee to the dancer's charming herself out of a death sentence with 1001 tales.[77]

Perhaps the most wonderfully appropriate of all the awards and tributes that came to Kettering in his later years was his election as the first president of the Thomas Alva Edison Foundation, a non-profit institution devoted to encouraging engineering education. Kettering greatly admired his illustrious predecessor, and was like him in many ways. They shared a rural upbringing, a pragmatic bent, a mild distrust of academic science that grew more intense with advancing years, and recognition as versatile, prolific, and heroic inventors. They displayed similar temperaments and eccentricities—persistence bordering on pigheadedness, colorful profanity, dietary fads, a fondness for cigars and for vacations in Florida where they each preferred experiment to leisure. Kettering's election provided one last similarity to Edison; it made Kettering a genuine technical hero, perhaps the last of his kind.

As head of the Edison Foundation, Kettering solicited funds to restore Edison's laboratory and library in West Orange, New Jersey, and began the herculean task of organizing Edison's voluminous notebooks. He told Harvey Firestone, Jr., the son of one of Edison's closest friends, "It seems to me we have a wonderful opportunity of utilizing the background of Edison's accomplishments as a means of teaching people how to do research and development work as well as showing the general public what it means to them."[78] Kettering planned a series of monographs on Edison's inventions, and co-authored a short, popular, history of technology under foundation auspices.[79]

Kettering also used his role as spokesman for the Edison Foundation to bemoan the disappearance of the independent inventor in an age of corporate research and academic specialization. His public criticism of the "experts" went back a long way. The record shows that he had always hired academics and funded university research. But in retirement his pronouncements, both in public and in private, became far more dogmatic. More than one distinguished academic squirmed under the inevitable question, "But how will you apply your theoretical research to man's needs?"[80] Kettering clearly enjoyed this sport, though his sarcasm often embarrassed his friends and associates, who tried to steer him away from direct confrontations. "Late in his life all his friends were afraid that he'd make a fool out of himself, he became so obsessed with this dislike of analysis," one long-time colleague remembered.[81]

Of course, not all these attacks on academic narrowness and arrogance were without merit, and it was not just nostalgia that committed him to his crusade. He reminded audiences that mathematical expertise and advanced training were not always the keys to engineering success: "If Thomas A. Edison, the Wright brothers, and Henry Ford had taken I. Q. tests, they wouldn't have gotten in the bleachers."[82] It was not that he believed inventors had to be born, though.

"Psychologists and psychiatrists to the contrary, I believe you can train fellows to be inventors," he said. "To make an inventor all you have to do is take his mind off the idea that it's a disgrace to fail. All you do is teach him to fail intelligently."[83]

The breadth of a modern engineer's responsibilities—entrepreneur, salesman, public relations expert, and manager—called for the broader experience of the old-fashioned inventor, Kettering felt. Speaking to a Columbia Engineering alumni dinner, he used an analogy to explain his position. Comparing American technical progress to an endless fabric woven on a loom of industrial research, he said, "The threads that run lengthwise in the loom represent the different sciences. They are the warp. These are the base of almost all our technical education. This type of education tends towards extreme specialization. The cross threads which tie the warp together and are put in by the shuttle represent the work of the inventor. These are called the woof. Some of our educators do not recognize this process at all. . . . they think an inventor is a 'screwball' because he is at right angles to what most people think is the basis of our scientific development." Lest some miss the point or think it should be otherwise, he urged them to try sleeping in a hammock woven with warp alone.[84]

All in all, he was much the same in his last years as in all the rest, always energetic, unfailingly enthusiastic. There was more time for research, board meetings, and awards. Kettering spent most of his time at Ridgeleigh Terrace to be closer to Antioch, the magnetics laboratory, and his remaining friends. He still passed the winters among the business titans of an earlier generation at the Surf Club. And the ladies still found him a spirited dancer and a shameless flirt. He occasionally entertained at the Moraine Country Club. Yet these were lonely years too, and friends would be surprised and a little embarrassed to find him having a Manhattan and dinner at the Country Club with only his pilots for company.[85]

For his eightieth birthday, on August 29, 1956, the town that had grown up around Ridgeleigh Terrace and had taken the name of its most famous citizen hosted "Kettering Honor Week," which featured special greetings from President Eisenhower and the mayor of Kettering, England, window displays, and a civic celebration.[86] "The record of your life is a blend of invention, research and production, all lifted by service to your fellowmen," the President said. "The contributions you have made to the development of the automobile industry, to the practical affairs of home and factory, to the security of America and to the health of all peoples, have brought you world renown, respect and gratitude."[87]

Kettering continued to air his favorite prejudices as pugnaciously as ever. A steady stream of awards and honorary degrees, including a particularly appropriate citation named for him and offered annually by George Washington University for work in patent, trademark, and copyright research,[88] offered splendid opportunities to express his opinions. Of the American failure to beat the Russians into space he said, "Plain political and administrative stupidity."[89] Of the malaise in American technical education he commented, "You can't do a new job with educated people. They want to do it the way they are educated."[90] Confrontations with academicians became more belligerent, and when Linus Pauling visited Antioch College in 1958 as the commencement speaker, the organizers took some pains to keep the two men apart. The enforced separation avoided a potentially explosive though possibly fascinating encounter.[91] Commenting on a typical Kettering speech given at the Engineers' Club in Dayton in 1958, a reporter said, "Ket tweaked the nose of the press, boxed the ears of professors and kicked the shins of 'slide rule engineers.' "[92] That was his style.

On the first of each month Kettering traveled to New York City for the board meetings of General Motors and Ethyl Corporation, and for meetings at the Edison Foundation. At marathon breakfast sessions at the Waldorf-Astoria, he entertained members of the press eager for colorful copy. The face might have looked older, but the eyes still gleamed behind the thick glasses, and the stories flowed as quickly as ever in the distinctive, shrill tones.

A breakfast meeting in late July 1958 left an indelible impression on a reporter from *Newsweek* who had managed to arrange an interview with Kettering while he was in New York on business.[93] Wearing a gray, single-breasted suit and a blue shirt with stiff, snap-on collar, the old engineer strolled into the Waldorf's coffee shop at precisely eight o'clock. With a quick greeting of "I'm a pliers and screwdriver man, not a theory man," he introduced himself and sat down to his usual meal of hot porridge with sugar.

George Probst, executive director of the Edison Foundation, joined them, and Kettering launched into a narrative punctuated with hastily drawn diagrams and eloquent gesticulation. Ranging over a wide assortment of current topics, he paused briefly to explain that atomic-powered automobiles had a doubtful future—"We had worked hard to get rid of the steam car; who wanted to go back to them with a nuclear reactor substituted for the firebox." He then offered a cheery prediction on solar energy—"We're close enough to the secret to imitate in the lab how leaves store the energy of the sun and hold it as food. But we're not ready to announce it yet. Think, using all that energy. Food for man . . ." As his voice trailed off the waiter reappeared and reminded the speaker of his next appointment. Quickly thanking the reporter for his patience, Kettering shook hands, said goodbye, and headed across the room in his loping stride.

His pace hardly slackened until the final week. Between meals at the country club and the regular banquets, he filled the hours with study at the photosynthesis laboratory and the magnetics center. Gould's resignation from Antioch at the end of September 1958, distressed him, for he could never understand flagging commitment, and Antioch's success was important to him.[94] Generally the last weeks were pleasant and productive. There were occasional warnings of overexertion, and even a slight stroke in the early fall, but nothing very unusual for a man of eighty-two.

Then on Friday, November 21, he collapsed after a retirement dinner for chief GM designer Harley Earl in Detroit.[95] He felt better after the return flight to Dayton, though he stumbled debarking from his airplane, and on Saturday he went to the magnetics laboratory. However, after another stroke on Sunday, his personal physician, Douglas Talbott, put him in an oxygen tent in Ridgeleigh Terrace and summoned Eugene and Virginia from Hinsdale.[96]

On Monday, he rested comfortably. Tuesday morning Gould called to tell Virginia that he and his wife were driving to Boston for the Thanksgiving holiday. Virginia told him that Talbott gave her father-in-law no better than two weeks. Gould then detoured the ten miles to Dayton before heading east. He found Kettering resting in his upstairs bedroom conscious but unable to speak. He held his friend's hand for a minute or two, and Kettering nodded a silent farewell.

No one spoke to Kettering again. Shortly after Gould's visit he lapsed into a coma. At 2:43 P.M. he died of a multiple stroke.

The body lay in state all day Thursday, Thanksgiving Day, in the Engineers' Club. Throughout the day a huge crowd passed the simple bronze casket and paid their last respects to the gaunt figure dressed in a charcoal gray herringbone suit, white shirt, and dark blue tie. Over the familiar owl-eyes were his trademark, the gold-rimmed glasses. His hands rested on an old beige blanket he had once used against the chill of *The Blue Tail Fly*. [97]

It snowed savagely on the day of the funeral, grounding scores of mourners in Detroit. A few hearty souls, including Alfred Sloan, braved the weather. Those who could not sent telegrams. After a short and simple ceremony at the Christ Protestant Episcopal Church, a black limousine, followed by a fleet of forty General Motors automobiles, carried him to his final rest beside Olive in the Woodlawn Cemetery. [98]

Not much of the $200 million fortune he left behind found its way into the hands of friends or family. Kettering had willed $25,000 each to his brother-in-law Ralph Williams and to a nephew and two favorite nieces. To the three grandchildren, Jane, Chuck, and Susan, he left the same amount. The remainder passed to the Kettering Foundation and Kettering Inc., a trust fund to be managed by Eugene. Ridgeleigh Terrace went to Virginia and Eugene. [99]

"Charles F. Kettering was one of the benefactors of our time, practical yet an idealist, indeed something of a philosopher but a cheerful one," said the *New York Times*, beginning the chorus of eulogies. "He called himself a mechanic, a 'pliers and screwdriver man.' He was always 'fixing' things. But his contribution of inventive genius, his passionate interest in research—automotive, medical, and in the field of solar energy—put the world in his debt for a better, more comfortable, life." [100]

What everyone remembered, of course, were the inventions. His self-starter put women behind the wheel ("Some would call that a mixed blessing," quipped one obituary); his Duco paint and his high-compression engine made the car a symbol of masculine power; his four-wheel brakes, crankcase ventilators, crankshaft vibration dampers, and the rest made the automobile so complicated that hardly anyone could understand it or fix it, and so easy to use that everyone did. In making technology simple by making it complex, not only for automobiles but for office systems, home refrigeration, and the railroads, he made convenience, comfort, and simplicity watchwords that forever changed American society.

Others recalled Kettering's philosophical side, his unwavering optimism and faith in man's ability to shape his own destiny. They found inspiration in a man who was such a tireless opponent of complacency, of sterile theory, of those who said that something could not be done without bothering to try. Kettering insisted that the past should not limit the future, or in his words, that the past must be a guidepost, not a hitching post.

Many eulogists sensed that Kettering's death marked the end of an era. The "last of the inventors," one called him; the "last of the pioneering automobile Titans," noted another. Certainly the chronology was right. Kettering was born in the same year as German inventor Nicholas Otto's four-stroke engine, and died at the zenith of the automobile age, in the year of tailfins and chrome. Kettering was also transitional in a more important way. Beginning his career as an inventor and entrepreneur and ending it as director of one of the nation's largest industrial research laboratories, he personally bridged the single most important development in twentieth-century technology, the transition from independent invention to scientifically oriented and corporately harnessed research and development.

Only the most perceptive observers of Kettering's career caught his real genius, though, his ability to sell research to an often skeptical business world. Maurice Holland, who worked with Kettering for twenty years on the National Research Council, called him "the greatest salesman of science this country ever produced." And Alfred Sloan, who also knew what he was talking about from firsthand experience, called his friend a "master salesman." In his commonsense way, Kettering did as much as any one man to convince a generation of American businessmen that "research is the most valuable insurance policy a company can have."[101]

Most commentators linked Kettering's name with two other giants of American history, Thomas Edison and Henry Ford, and not with Whitney, Jewett, Mees, and the other pioneers of industrial research. Kettering deserved that distinction. He belonged with a more independent, a more idiosyncratic, a more colorful fraternity of men. "His monumental accomplishments will obscure the fact that he was—almost incidentally—the largest stockholder in General Motors," predicted the Detroit *Times*. And the Detroit *Free Press* agreed that even General Motors could not seem to contain him: "He was as homely as the village tinkerer. The only difference was that the world—nay, the universe—was the village workshop of 'Boss Ket.'"

If some of the less fortunate implications of what he did escaped his notice, if he never foresaw that leaded gasoline and freon would have grave ecological consequences, that high-compression engines (with their nitrogen oxide emissions) and endless freeways would make American cities unlivable, and that annual upgradings of comfort and style could become as much consumer manipulation as progress, it was because he thought the benefits clearly outweighed any costs. Kettering never blamed technology for its social and environmental side effects. For him, technology was the solution, not the problem. He had no patience with those who wanted a moratorium on invention or in some other way wanted to put the genie back into the bottle. Paul de Kruif perhaps best caught that side of the Kettering philosophy:

You find any fact, says Boss Ket, and you cannot put it into oblivion. You cannot put the brakes on any discovery, not even that of the atom bomb, and you shouldn't try to; you've got to go on with it even if we're all blown to hell with it. What you should do is step up the study of human nature, you may even find a chemical, a vitamin, a hormone, a simple pill to take the devil out of human nature. . . . This is Boss Ket's faith and when you hear him give out with it, it is not bleak, there is religion, there is glowing hope, there is white-hot fire in it.[102]

As Kettering often said, "The price of progress is trouble and I don't think the price is too high." In that he spoke as much for a generation as for himself.

From posterity, Kettering wished only to be judged by his own standards. He once said of Thomas Edison: "Imagine that we were suddenly deprived of all the things for which he was responsible. What would we not give to have these things returned to us?" Kettering would have liked that epitaph.

NOTES

Frequently cited archival sources appear in the notes in abbreviated form. Below is a list of these codes.

AA   Antioch College Archives, Antioch College, Yellow Springs, Ohio.
AFM   Wright-Patterson Air Force Base Museum Archives, Dayton, Ohio.
DDE   Dwight D. Eisenhower Presidential Papers, Eisenhower Presidential Library, Abilene, Kansas.
DPL   Dayton Public Library, Dayton, Ohio.
EMHL   Eleutherian Mills Historical Library, Wilmington, Delaware.
KA   Kettering Archives, General Motors Institute, Flint, Michigan.
KA OH I, II Kettering Archives Oral History Projects
KF   Kettering Foundation Archives, Charles F. Kettering Foundation, Kettering, Ohio.
KMHM   Kettering-Moraine Historical Museum, Kettering, Ohio.
NCR   NCR Patent Archives, NCR Corporation, Dayton, Ohio.
RR   Records Retention Unit, General Motors Research Laboratories, Warren, Michigan.
TT   Trial Transcript of U.S. *vs.* E. I. Du Pont de Nemours, United States District Court, Northern Illinois District, Eastern Division, 1953.

1/The Early Years

1. Thomas A. Boyd, *Professional Amateur: The Biography of Charles Franklin Kettering* (New York: E. P. Dutton, 1957), p. 14.

2. Boyd, Interview with James P. Hunter (KA OH I); Rosamond M. Young, *Boss Ket* (New York: Longmans, Green, 1961).

3. Paul de Kruif, "Boss Kettering," *Saturday Evening Post* (July 15, 1933), p. 6.

4. W. Chalmers Fort to CFK, December 5, 1935 (RR).

5. De Kruif, "Boss Kettering," p. 6.

6. Boyd, *Professional Amateur*, p. 15.

7. Boyd, Interview with Alice White (KA OH I).

8. Boyd, Interview with Sarah Pippitt (KA OH I).

9. De Kruif, "Boss Kettering," p. 7.

10. *Ibid.*, p. 5.

11. Boyd, Interview with Adam Kettering (KA OH I).

12. Boyd, *Professional Amateur*, p. 21.

13. CFK to Guy M. Wilson, April 29, 1941 (RR).

14. De Kruif, "Boss Kettering," p. 7.

15. Boyd, Interview with Andrew A. Easly (KA OH I).

16. W. K. Eicher to CFK, July 19, 1933 (RR).

17. CFK, "Running Errands for Ideas" (KF).

18. Emma Culler to CFK, August 7, 1934 (RR).

19. "Catalogue and Prospectus, Summer School" (University of Wooster, 1900), p. 5.

20. Boyd, Interview with Lyman C. Knight (KA OH I).

21. Boyd, Interview with Earlis P. Snyder (KA OH I).

22. De Kruif, "Boss Kettering," p. 78.

23. Thomas A. Boyd, ed., *Prophet of Progress: The Speeches of Charles F. Kettering* (New York: E. P. Dutton, 1961), p. 205.

24. Boyd, *Professional Amateur*, p. 30.

25. Frederick Terman, "A Brief History of Electrical Engineering Education," *Proceedings of the IEEE*, (September 1976), p. 1401; Alexis Cope, *History of the Ohio State University, 1870–1910*, (Columbus, Ohio: Ohio State University Press, 1920), p. 55.

26. CFK, Official transcript, Ohio State University (KA).

27. *Ibid.*

28. Boyd, Interview with Harry F. Smith (KA OH I).

29. Thomas A. Boyd, *More Tales of Boss Ket* (Detroit: privately published, 1974), p. 10.

30. Boyd, Interview with A. D. George (KA OH I).

31. Boyd, Interview with J. H. Hunt (KA OH I).

32. M. D. Fagen, ed., *A History of Engineering and Science in the Bell System* (New York: The Laboratories, 1975), p. 482.

33. Boyd, Interview with CFK (KA OH I).

34. Boyd, Interview with Ralph D. Williams (KA OH I).

35. Boyd, Interview with H. A. Gehres (KA OH I).

36. De Kruif, "Boss Kettering," p. 68.

37. Boyd, *More Tales of Boss Ket*, p. 12.

38. Herbert Bostater to Arvid Roach, February 25, 1942 (RR).

39. CFK, C. Leibold, H. Bostater, "A Study of the Design of Certain Types of Telephone Apparatus" (Master's thesis, Ohio State University, 1904).

40. Boyd, *Prophet of Progress*, p. 125.

41. Michal McMahon, "Corporate Technology: The Social Origins of the Amer-

ican Institute of Electrical Engineers," *Proceedings of the IEEE* (September 1976), p. 1384; Photograph of OSU AIEE, 1904 (RR).

42. CFK employment contract with Edward Deeds and National Cash Register, April 20, 1904 (KA).

43. Bostater to Roach, February 25, 1942 (RR).

44. Boyd, *Professional Amateur*, p. 46.

45. CFK to Eugene Kettering, March 13, 1928 (KA).

46. Interview with William Trahorne (KF).

2/The Cash

1. *New York Times*, June 19, 1948, 19:1.

2. CFK patent agreement with National Cash Register (NCR); Stanley C. Allyn, *My Half-Century with NCR* (New York: McGraw-Hill, 1967), p. 25.

3. Isaac Marcosson, *Wherever Men Trade: The Romance of the Cash Register,* (New York: Dodd, Mead, 1945); Samuel Crowther, *John H. Patterson: Pioneer in Industrial Welfare* (New York: Doubleday, 1924); and Daniel Boorstin, *The Americans: The Democratic Experience* (New York: Random House, 1973).

4. Thomas G. and Marva R. Belden, *The Lengthening Shadow: The Life of Thomas J. Watson* (Boston: Little, Brown 1962), p. 62.

5. A. J. Lauver to Sales Department, May 24, 1904 (NCR).

6. A. J. Lauver to Employment Bureau, July 2, 1904 (NCR).

7. Boyd, Interview with B. M. Shipley (KA OH I).

8. Boyd, Interview with Richard H. Grant (KA OH I).

9. CFK, U.S. Patent 939,267, "Store-Service Credit System Apparatus," filed October 29, 1906, issued November 9, 1909 (NCR).

10. CFK, U.S. Patent 975, 533. "Store-Service Credit System Apparatus," filed December 14, 1904, issued November 15, 1910 (NCR).

11. CFK to A. J. Lauver, September 3, 1904 (NCR).

12. CFK, "Data for NCR, Inventions #4," January 19, 1905 (NCR).

13. Lauver to Factory Committee, August 22, 1905 (NCR).

14. CFK, "Data for NCR, Inventions #4," January 19, 1905 (NCR).

15. E. A. Deeds, Patent Log Model, "Motor Drive on #79 Principle Machines." (NCR).

16. W. A. Chryst, Patent Division Log (NCR).

17. CFK, U.S. Patent 910,690, "Driving Mechanism of Registering Machines," filed June 9, 1905, issued June 26, 1909 (NCR).

18. CFK, "Drawings of #79 motor," Inventions and Records Section, drawer 194 (NCR).

19. CFK, "Notes," 1905 (NCR).

20. CFK, "Electrical Indications" (NCR); CFK, U.S. Patent 910,690, "Cash Register," filed June 9, 1906, issued November 3, 1911 (NCR); Boyd, Interview with B. M. Shipley (KA OH I).

21. W. H. Muzzy to CFK, May 4, 1905 (NCR).

22. CFK, "Auditing System Specifications," February 7, 1907 (NCR).

23. *Ibid.*

24. Paul de Kruif, "Boss Kettering," *Saturday Evening Post* (August 12, 1933), p. 50.

25. Thomas A. Boyd, *Professional Amateur: The Biography of Charles Franklin Kettering* (New York: E. P. Dutton, 1957), p. 55.

26. CFK to W. A. Chryst, August 8, 1905 (KA).

27. CFK, "Monthly Report, Inventions #4," November 8, 1905 (NCR).

28. "Monitor Rating, Inventions #4," September 9, 1905 (NCR).

29. Isaac Marcosson, *Colonel Deeds: Industrial Builder* (New York: Dodd, Mead, 1947), p. 90.

30. E. C. Howard to W. H. Muzzy, July 13, 1905 (NCR).

31. Lauver to CFK, November 4, 1905 (NCR).

32. C. G. Heyne to CFK, January 3, 1906 (NCR).

33. W. H. Muzzy to CFK, February 21, 1906 (NCR).

34. R. H. Grant to CFK, April 17, 1906 (NCR).

35. Lauver to CFK, September 16, 1905 (NCR).

36. De Kruif, "Boss Kettering," p. 50.

37. CFK to J. E. Warren, July 9, 1906; Warren to CFK, July 16, 1906 (NCR).

38. CFK to C. G. Heyne, July 18, 1906 (NCR).

39. Warren to CFK, August 1, 1906 (NCR).

40. Heyne to CFK, August 1, 1906 (NCR).

41. Boyd, Interview with Chryst, Haas, Bradford (KA OH I); CFK, Patent Log, "Hotel and Restaurant Checking Machine" (NCR).

42. CFK, "Specifications for Restaurant Checking Machine" (NCR).

43. CFK to W. H. Muzzy, July 30, 1908 (NCR).

44. CFK, "Specifications for Restaurant Checking Machine" (NCR).

45. CFK to Muzzy, July 30, 1905 (NCR).

46. CFK, "Specifications for Restaurant Checking Machine" (NCR).

47. W. A. Chryst Diary, July 9, 1908 (KA).

48. CFK, U.S. Patent 959,059, "Adding and Subtracting Machines," filed August 31, 1908, issued May 24, 1910 (NCR).

49. C. A. Snyder to CFK, December 15, 1906 (NCR).

50. CFK to Synder, December 18, 1906 (NCR).

51. J. E. Warren to CFK and C. F. Raymond, August 16, 1906 (NCR).

52. CFK, "Mr. Kettering's Report of his Interview with Mr. Scott of Columbus" (NCR).

53. CFK to J. C. Gorton, January 2, 1907 (NCR).

54. *Ibid.*

55. *Ibid.*

56. Rough draft of same letter.

57. E. J. DeVille to CFK, December 24, 1907 (NCR).

58. Chryst Diary, February 15, 1908 (KA).

59. *Ibid.*, March 19, 1908.

60. *Ibid.*, April 23, 1908.

61. *Ibid.*, May 5, 1908.

62. E. J. DeVille to J. A. Oswald, June 9, 1908 (NCR).

63. T. J. Watson to DeVille, July 24, 1908 (NCR).

64. DeVille to CFK, August 5, 1908; CFK, Patent Department Log #1719, "Model of Crank Operated No. 1000 Machine" (NCR).

65. Watson to DeVille, September 3, 1908 (NCR).

66. Boyd, Interview with Chryst, Haas, and Bradford (KA OH I).

67. Chryst Diary, June 23, 1908 (KA).

68. Robert Conot, *A Streak of Luck: The Life and Legend of Thomas Alva Edison* (New York: Bantam Books, 1979), p. 398.

69. CFK, Inventions Record Section, "CFK Drawings: Motion Picture Machine" (NCR).

70. Chryst Diary, June 23, 1908 (KA).

71. Boyd, *Professional Amateur*, p. 59.

72. CFK to J. C. Gorton, January 2, 1907 (NCR).

73. W. H. Muzzy to Deeds, November 17, 1908 (NCR).

74. Deeds to Muzzy, December 3, 1908 (NCR).

75. CFK, "Description of the Bank Register" (NCR).

76. DeVille to CFK, September 1, 1909 (NCR).

77. T. J. Watson to DeVille, October 5, 1909 (NCR).

78. Muzzy to W. Pflum, March 2, 1910 (NCR).

79. Chryst Diary, August 10, 1908 (KA).

80. De Kruif, "Boss Kettering," p. 48.

3/*The Delco Years*

1. Kettering was not consistent on this point. See his testimony, U.S. Congress, Senate, Temporary National Economic Committee, *Technology and Concentration of Economic Power*, 77th Cong., 3d sess., 1939, pt. 30: 16294ff.

2. John B. Rae, *The American Automobile* (Chicago: University of Chicago Press, 1965), p. vii.

3. CFK, "History of the Self-Starter" (KA); Boyd, Interview with William Chryst, Nelson Haas, Zerbe Bradford (KA OH I).

4. Lynwood Bryant, "The Internal Combustion Engine," in Melvin Kranzberg and Carroll Pursell, *Technology in Western Civilization* (New York: Oxford University Press, 1967), p. 661.

5. Boyd, Interview with Chryst, Haas, and Bradford (KA OH I).

6. Isaac Marcosson, "The Story of the Self-Starter" (KMHM).

7. William Chryst Diary, August 12, August 13, 1908 (KA).

8. Thomas A. Boyd, *Professional Amateur: The Biography of Charles Franklin Kettering* (New York: E. P. Dutton, 1957), p. 62.

9. CFK to William Chryst, April 13, 1909 (KA).

10. Chryst Diary, May 18, May 19, 1909 (KA).

11. *Ibid.*, May 22, 1909.

12. Boyd, Interview with CFK (KA OH I).

13. Chryst Diary, July 20, 1909 (KA).

14. Personal communication from Ohio Secretary of State to author, March 7, 1980.

15. Boyd, Interview with Chryst, Haas, and Bradford (KA OH I).

16. CFK, U.S. Patent 1,037,491, "Ignition Apparatus for Explosive Motors," filed September 15, 1909, issued September 3, 1912 (KA).

17. CFK to Chryst, February 10, 1910 (KA).

18. *Ibid.*

19. Boyd, *Professional Amateur*, p. 66.

20. CFK to Chryst, February 10, 1910 (KA).

21. CFK, "Delco Ignition," July 28, 1910, p. 15 (KA).

22. Boyd, Interview with J. H. Hunt (KA OH I).

23. "A History of Delco Products" (mimeograph in public relations office, Delco Products Division, Dayton, Ohio), p. 9.

24. CFK and R. S. DeMaree, Sketchbook #1, p. 37 (KA).

25. CFK, "History of the Self-Starter."

26. C. E. Palmer, "Self-Starters for Automobiles," *The Horseless Age* (August 30, 1911); Harry Dey, "What There Is to Be Seen in Self-Starters," *The Horseless Age* (January 15, 1913).

27. "Boss Ket: Inventor and Visionary" (KF).

28. Thomas A. Boyd, *More Tales of Boss Ket* (Detroit: privately published, 1974), p. 126.

29. R. S. DeMaree to F. B. McNab, February 9, 1911 (KA).

30. CFK to J. B. Hayward, November 13, 1910 (KA); also cited in Robert Habingreither, "A Case Study of the First Successful Electric Self-Starting System" (Ed. D. thesis, University of West Virginia, 1978), p. 30.

31. *Ibid*; also Habingreither, "A Case Study," p. 32.

32. CFK to J. B. Hayward, November 13, 1910 (KA).

33. *Ibid.*

34. *Ibid.*

35. *Ibid.*

36. *Ibid.*

37. R. S. DeMaree to F. B. McNab, February 9, 1911 (KA).

38. CFK and R. S. DeMaree, Sketchbook #2, p. 113 (KA).

39. Chryst Diary, February 15, February 16, 1911 (KA).

40. Boyd, *Professional Amateur*, p. 71.

41. Boyd, Interview with J. H. Hunt (KA OH I).

42. Chryst Diary, April 13, 1911 (KA).

43. Habingreither, "A Case Study," p. 66.

44. *Ibid.*, p. 67.

45. Boyd, Interview with Chryst, Haas, Bradford (KA OH I).

46. "A History of Delco Products," p. 8.

47. Thomas A. Boyd, ed., *Prophet of Progress: The Speeches of Charles F. Kettering* (New York: E. P. Dutton, 1961), p. 54.

48. *Saturday Evening Post* (September 7, 1912), p. 29.

49. Boyd, Interview with J. H. Hunt (KA OH I).

50. Robert Conot, *A Streak of Luck: The Life and Legend of Thomas Alva Edison* (New York: Bantam Books, 1979), p. 382.

51. "A History of Delco Products," p. 9.

52. Arvid Roach, "Ket: America's Best-Loved Inventor" (unpublished MS, 1943) (KA).

53. Jay R. Nash, *Darkest Hours* (Chicago: Nelson-Hall, 1976), p. 406.

54. *New York Times*, March 26, 1913, 3:1.

55. Roach, "Ket."

56. George B. Smith, "Common Clay" (unpublished autobiography), p. 105 (KF).

57. Boyd, Interview with Chryst, Haas, Bradford (KA OH I).

58. Boyd, Interview with J. H. Hunt (KA OH I).

59. Roach, "Ket."

60. George Smith, "History of Activities of Charles F. Kettering, 1916–1939" (KA).

61. CFK and Edward Deeds, "A Message to the Workers," *Delco-Doings* (August 26, 1916) (KA).

62. E. A. Deeds to Alfred P. Sloan, June 16, 1916 (RR).

63. Rae, *The American Automobile*, pp. 43, 65.

64. Bernard Weisberger, *The Dream Maker: William C. Durant, Founder of General Motors* (Boston: Little, Brown, 1979), p. 209.

65. Alfred Sloan, *Adventures of a White Collar Man* (New York: Doubleday, Doran, 1941), p. 98.

66. Weisberger, *Dream Maker*, p. 213.

67. George Smith, "Common Clay," p. 118.

68. *Ibid.*

69. Weisberger, *The Dream Maker*, p. 213.

70. Smith, "History of Activities," p. 70.

71. *Ibid.*

72. Richard Hofstadter, *The Age of Reform* (New York: Random House, 1955), p. 32.

73. Boyd, Interview with Ernest Dickey (KA OH I).

74. Boyd, Interview with Chryst, Haas, Bradford (KA OH I).

75. Personal communication from Ohio Secretary of State to author, March 7, 1980.

76. CFK to L. Keilholtz, January 17, 1918 (RR).

77. CFK to R. H. Grant, August 10, 1918; W. H. Lodge to L. Keilholtz, May 19, 1919 (RR).

78. Dayton *Herald*, January 18, 1916, p. 5.

79. *Motor World* (January 1, 1919), p. 76.

80. Boyd, *Professional Amateur*, p. 95.

81. Smith, "History of Activities," pp. 9, 22, 23.

82. "Flxible Company Annual Report" (Loudonville, Ohio, 1963).

83. Smith, "History of Activities," p. 13.

84. "Flxible Company Annual Report."

85. Smith, "Common Clay," p. 124.

86. *Ibid.*, p. 125.

87. Stanwood Cobb, "A New Movement in Education," *Atlantic Monthly* (February 1921), pp. 227–34.

88. Smith, "History of Activities," p. 22; Smith, "Common Clay," p. 126.

89. Frank D. Slutz to CFK, June 21, 1922 (KA).

90. *Ibid.*

91. CFK to Eugene Kettering, August 7, 1922 (KA).

92. CFK to Eugene Kettering, August 17, 1922 (KA).

93. *Ibid*.

94. Slutz to CFK, July 12, 1923 (KA).

95. CFK to Slutz, September 27, 1923 (KA).

96. *Ibid*.

97. CFK to Chryst, February 10, 1910 (KA).

98. Scrapbook of Ridgeleigh Terrace in possession of Annebelle Owens, Dayton, Ohio.

99. Cleveland *Plain Dealer* (clipping, AA).

100. George Smith, "History of Activities," pp. 22–23.

101. Boyd, *Professional Amateur*, p. 71.

102. Charles H. Paul, *A Brief History of the Engineers' Club of Dayton* (Dayton, Ohio: National Cash Register Co., 1942), p. 3.

103. *Ibid*., p. 6.

104. *Ibid*., p. 8.

105. Boyd, Interview with Arthur Morgan (AA).

106. Paul, *Brief History*, p. 12.

107. Boyd, *Prophet of Progress*, p. 68.

108. *Ibid*., p. 75.

4/World War I

1. Grover Loening, *Takeoff into Greatness* (New York: Putnam, 1968), p. 98.

2. Personal communication from the Ohio Secretary of State to author, March 7, 1980.

3. CFK to Charles S. Coffey, May 28, 1918 (RR); Philip S. Dickey, "The Liberty Engine," *Smithsonian Annals of Flight* (Washington, D.C., 1968), 1(3):10.

4. *New York Times*, May 21, 1917, 1:8.

5. *New York Times*, July 1, 1917, IV, 1:1.

6. Dickey, "The Liberty Engine," p. 6.

7. U.S. Congress, Senate, *Congressional Record*, 65th Cong., 3d sess., 1918, p. 888.

8. U.S. Congress, Senate, Committee on Military Affairs, *Aircraft Production: Hearings Before the Subcommittee on Military Affairs*, 65th Cong., 2d sess., 1918, p. 276.

9. Roland V. Hutchinson, "Skylarking 1917–18" (unpublished MS, 1943), p. 5 (Kettering "Bug" File, AFM).

10. Senate, *Aircraft Production Hearings*, p. 284.

11. Hutchinson, "Skylarking 1917–18," p. 5.

12. *Ibid*., p. 10.

13. "Bulletin of the Experimental Department," Airplane Engineering Progress Report (June 1918) (RR).

14. Hutchinson, "Skylarking 1917–18," p. 35.

15. "Bulletin of the Experimental Department," Airplane Engineering Progress Report (August 1918) (RR).

16. Loening, *Takeoff into Greatness*, p. 102.

17. Hutchinson, "Skylarking 1917–18," p. 7.

18. *Ibid.*, p. 13.

19. George B. Smith, "Common Clay" (unpublished autobiography), pp. 133–37 (KF).

20. *New York Times*, July 31, 1918, 5:5.

21. *New York Times*, October 2, 1918, 13:3.

22. John Rae, *The American Automobile* (Chicago: University of Chicago Press, 1965), p. 72.

23. *New York Times*, September 13, 1917, 1:3.

24. Sloan to CFK, November 22, 1917 (RR).

25. Dickey, "The Liberty Engine," p. 34.

26. J. Edward Schipper, "Electrical Systems of the Liberty Engine," *Automotive Industries* (December 26, 1918), 39:1089–92.

27. J. H. Hunt to CFK, October 29, 1918 (RR).

28. Dickey, "The Liberty Engine," p. 51.

29. Louis Ruthenberg, "Ten Great Years with 'Boss' Kettering," *Ward's Auto World* (1969), 1:54; Thomas A. Boyd, *More Tales of Boss Ket* (Detroit: privately published, 1974), p. 67.

30. Senate, *"Aircraft Production Hearings,*" p. 276; James H. Perkins, "Dayton During World War I: 1914–1918" (master's thesis, Miami University, 1959), p. 43.

31. Thomas Boyd, "The Early History of Ethyl Gasoline" (unpublished MS), p. 8 (KA).

32. "Bulletin of the Experimental Department," Airplane Engineering Progress Report (July 1918), p. 154 (RR).

33. "Bulletin of the Experimental Department," Airplane Engineering Division, Special Fuels for Aviation Engines (December 1918), p. 54 (RR).

34. E. W. Dean and C. Netzen, "An Investigation of Airplane Fuels," *SAE Journal* (August 1919), p. 129.

35. Thomas A. Boyd, "Pathfinding in Fuels and Engines," *SAE Transactions* (April 1950), p. 182.

36. CFK, undated memorandum (RR).

37. Boyd, "Early History of Ethyl Gasoline," p. 10.

38. T. A. Boyd to F. O. Clements, September 21, 1918 (RR).

39. Boyd, "Early History of Ethyl Gasoline," p. 17.

40. F. O. Clements to L. H. Baekeland, February 23, 1918 (RR).

41. *Ibid.*

42. H. M. Rinehart to CFK, January 19, 1919 (RR).

43. Boyd, "Early History of Ethyl Gasoline," p. 14.

44. Thomas P. Hughes, *Elmer A. Sperry: Inventor and Engineer* (Baltimore: Johns Hopkins University Press, 1971), pp. 264–73.

45. "Resume of Aerial Torpedo Development," July 7, 1921 (Kettering "Bug" File, AFM).

46. C. Wiggin and H. Eisenberg, "Our 1918 Missile," *Saga* (August 1961), p. 18.

47. "Description and Partial History of the 'Kettering' Torpedo Airplane," p. 4 (Kettering "Bug" File, AFM).

48. Wiggin and Eisenberg, "Our 1918 Missile," p. 93.

49. Hutchison, "Skylarking, 1917–18," p. 31.

50. E. A. Sperry to CFK, June 24, 1918 (RR).

51. "Description and Partial History," p. 5.

52. Hutchinson, "Skylarking, 1917–18," p. 30.

53. Wiggin and Eisenberg, "Our 1918 Missile," p. 93.

54. Hutchison, "Skylarking, 1917–18," p. 91.

55. Bion J. Arnold, "Automatic Carriers, Flying Bombs," January 31, 1919, p. 5 (Kettering "Bug" File, AFM).

56. C. H. Wills to E. A. Sperry, October 7, 1918 (RR).

57. Arnold, "Automatic Carriers, Flying Bombs," p. 5.

58. Ibid., p. 11.

59. Ibid., p. 13.

60. CFK to W. C. Potter, November 19, 1918 (RR).

61. G. Morchae to T. H. Bane, June 13, 1919, and Morchae to Bane, August 19, 1919 (Kettering "Bug" File, AFM).

62. E. B. Harmon, "Memorandum," October 8, 1921 (Kettering "Bug" File, AFM).

63. "Log of Aerial Torpedo Experimental Work at Carlstrom Field, Arcadia, Florida," October 13–15, 1919 (Kettering "Bug" File, AFM).

64. Ibid., October 28, 1919.

65. Ibid.

66. Guy L. Gearhart, "Brief Trip of Air Torpedo Section to Carlstrom Field, Florida" (Kettering "Bug" File, AFM).

67. "Log of Aerial Torpedo," November 26, 1919.

68. New York Times, December 2, 1918, 4:6.

69. New York Times, July 20, 1919, 12:4.

70. CFK to J. J. Raskob, May 5, 1920 (RR).

71. CFK to Raskob, July 2, 1919 (RR).

72. CFK to William T. Magruder, January 9, 1917 (RR).

73. George B. Smith, "History of Activities of Mr. Charles F. Kettering from 1916 to 1938" (KA).

74. Mayer, Meyer, Austrian, and Platt, Corporate and Legal History of United Air Lines, 1925–1945 (Chicago: Twentieth Century Press, 1953), pp. 60, 160; Henry Ladd Smith, Airways (New York: Knopf, 1944), pp. 124–38.

75. New York Times, January 11, 1918, 24:1.

5/Joining General Motors

1. Thomas A. Boyd, Professional Amateur: The Biography of Charles Franklin Kettering (New York: E. P. Dutton, 1957), p. 102.

2. John Rae, "The Fabulous Billy Durant," Business History Review (Autumn 1958), p. 270.

3. Sloan to CFK and E. A. Deeds, July 2, 1917 (RR).

4. Alfred D. Chandler and Stephen Salsbury, Pierre S. du Pont and the Making of the Modern Corporation (New York: Harper and Row, 1971), p. 450 ff.

5. *Ibid.*

6. *Ibid.*

7. Alfred Sloan, *Adventures of a White Collar Man* (New York: Doubleday, Doran, 1941), p. 98.

8. O. F. Conklin to CFK, February 9, 1920 (RR).

9. CFK to Sloan, July 2, 1919 (RR).

10. Sloan to CFK, General Letter no. 13, June 16, 1919 (RR).

11. *Ibid.*

12. Sloan to CFK, undated (RR).

13. W. C. Durant to CFK, October 17, 1919 (RR).

14. Walter P. Chrysler, *Life of an American Workman* (New York: Dodd, Mead, 1937), p. 141.

15. Thomas A. Boyd, ed., *Prophet of Progress: The Speeches of Charles F. Kettering* (New York: E. P. Dutton, 1961), p. 84.

16. Arthur Pound, *The Turning Wheel* (New York: Doubleday, Doran, 1954), p. 184; *Moody's Manual of Railroads and Corporation Securities* (1920), 21:2.

17. Chandler and Salsbury, *Pierre S. du Pont*, p. 466.

18. CFK to J. G. Vincent, March 29, 1920 (RR).

19. Pound, *The Turning Wheel*, p. 449.

20. J. Edward Schipper, "The Central Research Laboratory of the General Motors Company," *Automotive Industries* (April 28, 1921), pp. 900–1.

21. John G. Frayne to Merle Tuve, November 25, 1923 (Merle Tuve Papers, Manuscript Division, Library of Congress).

22. CFK, "Engineering Topics for Technical Committee Discussion," October 10, 1920 (RR).

23. Schipper, "The Central Research Laboratory."

24. Interview with Carroll Hochwalt (KF).

25. CFK, "Trouble as an Approach to Research," in Malcom Ross and Maurice Holland, eds., *Profitable Practice in Industrial Research* (New York: Harper and Brothers, 1932), pp. 51–2.

26. Boyd, Interview with Mabel Clancy (KA OH I).

27. Interview with Carroll Hochwalt (KF).

28. Cleveland *Plain Dealer*, March 6, 1940 (clipping in Kettering File, DPL).

29. Boyd, *Professional Amateur*, p. 140.

30. Boyd, Interview with J. H. Hunt (KA OH II).

31. Sloan to CFK, September 13, 1920 (RR).

32. *Ibid.*

33. Reynold M. Wik, *Henry Ford and Grass Roots America* (Ann Arbor: University of Michigan Press, 1972), pp. 82–102.

34. Sloan to CFK and Deeds, March 17, 1917 (RR).

35. Sloan to CFK and Deeds, July 25, 1916 (RR).

36. Sloan to CFK, June 19, 1917 (RR).

37. Sloan to CFK, October 24, 1918 (RR).

38. C. M. Eason to CFK, December 17, 1921 (RR).

39. J. A. Craig to CFK, January 31, 1921 (RR).

40. J. A. Craig to CFK, March 31, 1922 (RR).

41. Sloan to CFK, June 12, 1922 (RR).
42. CFK to Sloan, August 28, 1923 (RR).
43. *Ibid.*
44. Chandler and Salsbury, *Pierre S. du Pont*, pp. 486–90.
45. *Ibid.*; John B. Rae, *The American Automobile* (Chicago: University of Chicago Press, 1965), pp. 83–84.
46. Chandler and Salsbury, *Pierre S. du Pont*, p. 492.
47. CFK to Pierre S. du Pont, December 18, 1920 (RR).
48. *Ibid.*
49. H. Bassett to CFK, February 19, 1921 (RR).
50. Sloan to CFK, September 13, 1920 (RR).
51. CFK to C. S. Mott, May 14, 1921 (RR).
52. *Ibid.*
53. CFK to C. S. Mott, February 22, 1922 (RR).
54. A. B. C. Hardy to Sloan, March 27, 1922 (RR).
55. Sloan to CFK, November 23, 1923 (RR).
56. CFK to Sloan, November 25, 1923 (RR).
57. *Ibid.*
58. Rae, *The American Automobile*, p. 242.
59. *New York Times*, November 13, 1925, 12:2.
60. CFK to Sloan, July 12, 1923 (RR).

6/The Copper-Cooled Engine

1. C. P. Grimes, "Air-Cooled Automotive Engines" *SAE Journal* (August 1923), p. 125.
2. Boyd, Interview with Fred W. Davis and R. V. Hutchinson (KA OH I).
3. *Ibid.*
4. Thomas Midgley to CFK, January 23, 1920 (RR).
5. Charles Lee notebook, "Automatic Fin Machine," February 26, 1920 (KA).
6. *Ibid.*, February 16, 1920.
7. *Ibid.*, "Commercial Furnace for Brazing Fins to Cylinders," January 27, 1921.
8. CFK to Sloan, July 12, 1923 (RR).
9. Boyd, Interview with John J. Raskob (KA OH I).
10. Boyd, Interview with John T. Smith (KA OH I).
11. Alfred Chandler and Stephen Salsbury, *Pierre S. du Pont and the Making of the Modern Corporation* (New York: Harper and Row, 1971), p. 517.
12. Alfred Sloan, *My Years with General Motors* (New York: Doubleday, 1963), p. 83.
13. Sloan to Fred Warner, December 27, 1920 (RR).
14. Sloan to CFK, December 27, 1920 (RR).
15. Sloan to Warner, December 27, 1920 (RR).
16. Boyd, Interview with Davis and Hutchinson (KA OH II).
17. Sloan to CFK, June 13, 1921 (RR).
18. Boyd, Interview with O. T. Kreusser (KA OH I).
19. Boyd, Interview with O. T. Kreusser (KA OH II).

20. Karl Zimmershied to Pierre S. du Pont, July 11, 1921 (RR).

21. *Ibid.*

22. *Ibid.*

23. Du Pont to Zimmershied, September 28, 1921 (RR).

24. Du Pont to CFK, September 28, 1921 (RR).

25. CFK, U.S. Patent 1,697,818, "Air-Cooled Engine," filed April 17, 1922, issued January 1, 1929 (KA).

26. Chevrolet Division publicity release (KA).

27. Boyd, Interview with Davis and Hutchinson (KA OH II).

28. L. R. Beardslee to CFK, October 27, 1921 (RR).

29. Sloan, *My Years with General Motors,* p. 88.

30. Du Pont to CFK, November 19, 1921 (RR).

31. General Motors Executive Committee, Advice of Action, November 30, 1921 (RR).

32. Louis Ruthenberg, "Ten Great Years with 'Boss' Kettering," *Ward's Auto World* (April–July 1969), p. 50.

33. CFK to du Pont, January 3, 1922 (RR).

34. CFK, "Minutes of Conference at Mr. Kettering's," December 19–20, 1921 (RR).

35. CFK, "Report of Conference Held Jan. 27, 1922" (RR).

36. William Knudson to CFK, April 1, 1922 (RR).

37. CFK, "Conference on C/C 4-cylinder," April 10, 1922 (RR).

38. CFK to O. E. Hunt, February 17, 1922 (RR).

39. CFK to du Pont, May 22, 1922 (Papers of Pierre S. du Pont, EMHL).

40. Du Pont to Sir Harry McGowan, July 21, 1922 (Papers of P. S. du Pont, (EMHL).

41. R. K. Jack, "Test of Copper-Cooled 6-cylinder Car No. 1," July 10–14, 1922 (RR).

42. CFK to du Pont, August 5, 1922 (RR).

43. CFK to du Pont, May 24, 1922 (EMHL).

44. CFK to George Hannum, undated (RR).

45. James McEvoy, "Copper-Cooled Car Patent Situation," August 28, 1922 (RR).

46. Chandler and Salsbury, *Pierre S. du Pont,* p. 530.

47. Boyd, Interview with Davis and Hutchinson (KA OH II).

48. Chevrolet Division memorandum, October 24, 1922 (Papers of P. S. du Pont, EMHL).

49. CFK to C. S. Mott, October 28, 1922 (RR).

50. *Ibid.*

51. CFK to du Pont, November 7, 1922 (RR).

52. Chandler and Salsbury, *Pierre S. du Pont,* p. 532.

53. *Ibid.*

54. Du Pont to Knudsen, November 10, 1922 (Papers of P. S. du Pont, EMHL).

55. S. D. Heron, "Some Aspects of Air-Cooled Cylinder Design and Development," *SAE Journal* (April 1922).

56. J. Edward Schipper, "Chevrolet Copper-Cooled Car Ready for Market," *Automotive Industries* (December 28, 1922), p. 1259.

57. *New York Times*, December 16, 1922, 16:3.
58. Sloan, *My Years with General Motors*, p. 98.
59. Boyd, Interview with O. T. Kreusser (KA OH II).
60. CFK to du Pont, October 19, 1922 (RR).
61. Boyd, Interview with Joseph Butz (KA OH I).
62. Alexander Laird to Frank McHugh, July 19, 1922 (Papers of P. S. du Pont, EMHL).
63. Du Pont to Knudsen, March 30, 1923 (Papers of P. S. du Pont, EMHL).
64. Du Pont to William deKrafft, March 30, 1923 (Papers of P. S. du Pont, EMHL).
65. DeKrafft to du Pont, June 1, 1923 (Papers of P. S. du Pont, EMHL).
66. J. B. Tyler to du Pont, April 6, 1923 (Papers of P. S. du Pont, EMHL).
67. Boyd, Interview with Joseph Butz (KA OH I).
68. *Ibid*.
69. Du Pont to Sloan, July 7, 1923 (Papers of P. S. du Pont, EMHL).
70. Du Pont to Knudsen, May 12, 1923 (Papers of P. S. du Pont, EMHL).
71. *Ibid*.
72. CFK to Sloan, June 30, 1923 (RR).
73. *Ibid*.
74. Knudsen to du Pont, September 1, 1923 (Papers of P. S. du Pont, EMHL).
75. CFK to Sloan, June 29, 1923 (RR).
76. Knudsen to du Pont, September 1, 1923 (Papers of P. S. du Pont, EMHL).
77. *Ibid*.
78. Ruthenberg, "Ten Great Years With 'Boss' Kettering," p. 51.
79. Sloan, *My Years with General Motors*, p. 87.
80. CFK to Sloan, June 26, 1923 (RR).
81. Sloan to CFK, June 29, 1923 (RR).
82. CFK to Sloan, June 30, 1923 (RR).
83. Sloan to CFK, July 2, 1923 (RR).
84. CFK, "Memorandum of Conference Held in Detroit," July 6, 1923 (RR).
85. CFK to Sloan, July 7, 1923 (RR).
86. CFK to Sloan, draft, July 12, 1923 (RR).
87. Sloan to CFK, August 24, 1923 (RR).
88. Du Pont to Colin Campbell, August 18, 1923 (Papers of P. S. du Pont, EMHL).
89. CFK to Sloan, November 23, 1923 (RR).
90. *Ibid*.
91. CFK to J. H. Davis, February 26, 1924 (RR); also C. R. Short to CFK, February 13, 1925 (RR).
92. Sloan to A.B.C. Hardy, March 13, 1924 (RR).
93. CFK to du Pont, September 28, 1923 (Papers of P. S. du Pont, EMHL).
94. Boyd, Interview with J. Brooks Jackson (KA OH II).
95. Sloan, *My Years with General Motors*, p. 123.
96. *Ibid*.
97. James Brittain, "C. P. Steinmetz and E. F. W. Alexanderson: Creative En-

gineering in a Corporate Setting," *Proceedings of the IEEE* (September 1976), pp. 1413–17.

98. Thomas A. Boyd, *More Tales of Boss Ket* (Detroit: privately published, 1974), p. 129.

7/Studying the Knocks

1. CFK, "SAE Presidential Address," *SAE Journal* (February 1918), p. 118.

2. Lynwood Bryant, "The Problem of Knock in Gasoline Engines" (unpublished MS, 1975), p. 1.

3. Thomas A. Boyd, "The Early History of Ethyl Gasoline" (unpublished MS), p. 73 (KA).

4. "How Long Will the Oil Last," *Scientific American* (May 3, 1919), p. 459.

5. Interview with Carroll Hochwalt (KF).

6. CFK, "Running Errands for Ideas" (KF).

7. Boyd, Interview with Arthur Morgan (KA OH I).

8. Boyd, "The Early History of Ethyl Gasoline" pp. 5–6.

9. CFK, "More Efficient Utilization of Fuel," *SAE Journal* (April 1919), p. 263. See Horace Judson, *The Search for Solutions* (New York: Holt, Rinehart, and Winston, 1980), p. 186, for a discussion of models and theories in science.

10. Boyd, "The Early History of Ethyl Gasoline," p. 6.

11. See Thomas P. Hughes, "Inventors: The Problems They Choose, The Ideas They Have, and the Inventions They Make," in Melvin Kranzberg and Patrick Kelly, *Technological Innovation: A Critical Review of Current Knowledge*, (San Francisco: San Francisco Press, 1978), pp. 166–82.

12. CFK, "Comments," *SAE Journal* (May 1919), p. 348.

13. Boyd, "The Early History of Ethyl Gasoline," p. 46.

14. Frank Howard to E. M. Clark, April 16, 1919 (TT).

15. CFK to John Marshall, August 15, 1919; C. M. Stine to CFK, February 2, 1920 (TT).

16. E. C. Garland to CFK, October 20, 1920 (RR).

17. CFK to Garland, October 28, 1920 (RR).

18. CFK, "Cooperation of Automotive and Oil Industries," *SAE Journal* (January 1921), p. 43; "SAE Fostering Research Work," *SAE Journal* (September 1919), p. 146.

19. Mrs. C. F. Kettering to J. J. Raskob, December 17, 1920 (Papers of John J. Raskob, EMHL).

20. Mrs. C. F. Kettering to J. J. Raskob, February 1, 1921 (Papers of John J. Raskob, EMHL).

21. M. L. Barringer to J. J. Raskob, February 9, 1921 (Papers of John J. Raskob, EMHL).

22. Bryant, "The Problem of Knock," p. 4.

23. Thomas Midgley and Thomas Boyd, "The Application of Chemistry to the Conservation of Motor Fuels," *Industrial and Engineering Chemistry* (September 1922), p. 850.

24. CFK to K. Zimmerschied, March 3, 1920 (RR).

25. Interview with Hochwalt (KF).

26. *Ibid.*

27. Williams Haynes, *American Chemical Industry* (New York: Van Nostrand, 1948), 4:204.

28. Boyd, "The Early History of Ethyl Gasoline," p. 78.

29. Midgley to C. Stine, April 15, 1921 (RR).

30. Boyd, "The Early History of Ethyl Gasoline," p. 90.

31. CFK and Allen Orth, *The New Necessity* (Baltimore: Williams and Wilkins, 1932), p. 77.

32. Thomas Midgley and Thomas A. Boyd, "Methods of Measuring Detonation in Engines," *SAE Journal* (January 1922), p. 7.

33. Midgley to Wilder Bancroft, July 14, 1921 (RR).

34. Thomas Midgley, "From Periodic Table to Production," *Industrial and Engineering Chemistry* (January 1937).

35. Interview with Hochwalt (KF).

36. *Ibid.*

37. CFK, "The Ethyl Gasoline Story," 1:2 (KA).

38. *Ibid.*, p. 3.

39. CFK, "Running Errands for Ideas" (KF).

40. CFK, "The Ethyl Gasoline Story," 2:3 (KA).

41. *Ibid.*

42. Boyd, "The Early History of Ethyl Gasoline," p. 131.

43. *Ibid.*, p. 134.

44. CFK, "Doping of Fuels," March 24, 1922 (Papers of P. S. du Pont, EMHL).

45. CFK, "The Ethyl Gasoline Story," 2:9.

46. James McEvoy to C. S. Mott, August 19, 1922 (RR).

47. *Ibid.*

48. CFK to P. S. du Pont, August 22, 1922 (RR).

49. Midgley to CFK, February 2, 1923 (TT).

50. Sloan to CFK, April 3, 1923 (RR).

51. Sloan to CFK, November 21, 1923 (RR).

52. W. L. Mellon to CFK, November 15, 1923 (RR).

53. CFK to Adam Kettering, May 31, 1923 (RR).

54. CFK to W. J. Davidson, April 11, 1924 (RR).

55. Sloan to CFK, June 23, 1924 (TT).

56. Midgley to W. D. Kennington, January 31, 1923 (RR).

57. Interview with Hochwalt (KF).

58. *New York Times*, October 31, 1924, 1:1; *ibid.*, October 28, 1924, 25:1.

59. Interview with Frederick Hooven (KF).

60. *New York Times*, October 25, 1925, IX, 14:2.

61. See Angela Young, "Interpreting the Dangerous Trades: Workers' Health in America and the Career of Alice Hamilton, 1910–1930" (Ph.D. diss., Brown University, 1982) for a perceptive look at the "conference system" in public health and how it affected the TEL investigation.

62. *Public Health Bulletin no.* 158, "Proceedings of a Conference to Determine

Whether or Not There is a Public Health Question in the Manufacture, Distribution, or Use of Tetraethyl Lead Gasoline" (Washington, 1925), pp. 72–73, 106; cited in Young, "Interpreting the Dangerous Trades," p. 184.

63. See Joseph Pratt, "Environmental Planning During the Ascent of Oil as a Major Source of Energy," *The Public Historian* (Summer 1980).

64. Boyd to CFK, July 26, 1924 (RR).

65. Midgley to J. J. Raskob, September 18, 1923 (RR).

66. Haynes, *American Chemical Industry*, 4:260.

67. Donald Whitehead, *The Dow Story* (New York: McGraw-Hill, 1968), p. 105.

68. Charles Stine, "Recovery of Bromine from Sea Water," *Industrial and Engineering Chemistry* (May 1929).

69. Whitehead, *The Dow Story*, p. 106.

70. Haynes, *American Chemical Industry*, 4:262.

71. CFK to Philip Chase, December 16, 1924 (RR).

72. Haynes, *American Chemical Industry*, 4:260 ff.

73. Stine, "Recovery of Bromine from Sea Water."

74. *New York Times*, April 5, 1925, X, 7:1.

75. Interview with Hooven (KF).

76. CFK to Bruce Barton, March 14, 1925 (RR).

77. CFK to A. E. Mittnacht, April 15, 1925 (RR).

78. CFK to W. J. Davidson, April 11, 1924 (RR).

79. CFK to E. A. DeWaters, September 3, 1926 (RR).

80. W. B. Earnshaw to CFK, January 31, 1925 (RR).

81. A. R. Glancy to CFK, July 11, 1927 (RR).

82. Boyd to CFK, October 13, 1926 (RR).

83. DeWaters to CFK, April 27, 1927 (RR).

84. Boyd, Interview with Wheeler G. Lovell (KA OH I).

85. Wheeler G. Lovell, John M. Campbell, and T. A. Boyd, "Detonation Characteristics of Some Paraffin Hydrocarbons," *Industrial and Engineering Chemistry* (January 1931), p. 27.

86. Boyd, Interview with Lloyd L. Withrow (KA OH II).

87. Lovell, Campbell, and Boyd, "Detonation Characteristics," p. 27.

88. Boyd, Interview with Lovell (KA OH II).

89. CFK, "Motor Design and Fuel Economy," *Industrial and Engineering Chemistry* (November 1925), p. 1115.

90. CFK to Sloan, March 11, 1937 (RR).

91. CFK to Sloan, July 19, 1932 (RR).

92. Boyd, Interview with Withrow (KA OH II).

93. B. A. D'Alleva to CFK, December 3, 1934 (RR).

94. Boyd, Interview with Withrow (KA OH II).

95. Boyd to F. O. Clements, June 19, 1935 (RR).

96. H. C. Mougey to Clements, June 21, 1935 (RR).

97. E. V. Rippingille to CFK, April 24, 1936 (RR).

98. CFK to Sloan, March 18, 1937 (RR).

99. Darl F. Caris to CFK, February 16, 1942 (RR).

100. CFK to Francis Walker, February 10, 1927 (RR).

8/Keeping the Customer Dissatisfied

1. *New York Times*, November 5, 1927, 4:3.
2. CFK to Sloan, November 28, 1927 (RR).
3. Sloan to CFK and General Technical Committee, July 31, 1925 (RR).
4. Dan J. Forrestal, *Faith, Hope, and $5000: The Story of Monsanto* (New York: Simon and Schuster, 1977).
5. F. O. Clements to W. M. Diddy, November 7, 1925 (RR).
6. O. T. Kreusser to CFK, "Monthly Report of Proving Ground Activities for October 1925" (RR); CFK, "Applying New 'Yardsticks' to Automobiles," *Scientific American* (January 1928), p. 22.
7. Lester Velie, "Kettering at GM," *Coronet* (September 1945).
8. C. Hull, "Industrial Research Laboratories of the United States," *Bulletin of the National Research Council* (July 1927), no. 60, p. 48; *ibid.* (January 1931), no. 81, p. 82; *ibid.* (December 1938), no. 102, p. 92.
9. CFK testimony, U.S. Congress, Senate, Temporary National Economic Committee, *Technology and Concentration of Economic Power*, 77th Cong., 3d sess., 1939, pt. 30:16294–16307.
10. CFK, "Trouble as an Approach to Research," in Malcom Ross and Maurice Holland, eds., *Profitable Practice in Industrial Research*, (New York: Harper and Brothers, 1932), p. 53.
11. "General Motors IV," *Fortune* (March 1939), p. 48.
12. CFK, "Running Errands for Ideas" (KF).
13. CFK, "Trouble as an Approach to Research," p. 53.
14. CFK testimony, *Technology and Concentration of Economic Power*, p. 16294.
15. *Ibid.*, p. 16293.
16. "General Motors IV," *Fortune*, p. 49.
17. CFK testimony, *Technology and Concentration of Economic Power*, p. 340.
18. L. Blackmore to CFK, March 16, 1923; CFK to Blackmore, March 20, 1923; K. Zimmerschied to CFK, September 16, 1920 (RR).
19. C. W. Adams to L. J. Stern, May 12, 1924; CFK to J. McEvoy, September 6, 1923 (RR).
20. J. H. Hunt to J. McEvoy, July 31, 1925 (RR).
21. Fred L. Haushalter, *Inventors I Have Known* (New York: Exposition Press, 1972), pp. 141–42.
22. *Ibid.*, p. 108.
23. Personal communication from Albert F. Hickman to author, June 22, 1981.
24. Haushalter, *Inventors I Have Known*, p. 112.
25. Charles Short to CFK, October 16, 1922 (RR).
26. CFK to Short, Clements, Lee, February 1, 1923 (RR).
27. CFK to Sloan, December 15, 1927 (RR).
28. CFK to W. O. Kennington, December 17, 1925 (RR).
29. CFK to Paul Litchfield, August 27, 1925 (RR); John B. Rae, *The American Automobile* (Chicago: University of Chicago Press, 1965), p. 90.
30. CFK to H. H. Rice, August 23, 1923 (RR).
31. Sloan to CFK, November 23, 1922 (RR).

32. Haushalter, *Inventors I Have Known*, p. 21.

33. P. S. du Pont to Irénée du Pont, August 11, 1921 (Papers of P. S. du Pont, EMHL).

34. CFK to P. S. du Pont, August 16, 1921 (Papers of P. S. du Pont, EMHL).

35. CFK, "Minutes," Committee to Study Enameling and Varnish Drying Practice, March 23, 1922 (RR).

36. J. J. Moosman to H. C. Mougey, March 14, 1922 (TT).

37. CFK, "Minutes," Committee to Study Enameling and Varnish Drying Practice, March 23, 1922 (RR).

38. H. C. Mougey to F. O. Clements, June 19, 1922 (TT).

39. CFK, "Running Errands for Ideas" (KF).

40. CFK, "Minutes," Paint and Enamel Committee, October 5, 1922 (TT).

41. H. H. Rice to F. O. Clements, February 23, 1923 (TT).

42. W. L. Carver, "Labor Costs Halved by Use of Duco in Finishing," *Automotive Industries* (September 13, 1923), p. 524.

43. Boyd, Interview with Fred Chase (KA OH I).

44. Clements to Sloan, October 29, 1923 (TT).

45. CFK to A. R. Glancy, May 12, 1925 (RR).

46. *New York Times*, January 9, 1927, IX, 1:1.

47. Sloan to Clements, February 4, 1924 (TT).

48. Boyd, Interview with Ralph Wirshing (KA OH I).

49. CFK to Sloan, October 15, 1925 (RR).

50. *New York Times*, May 10, 1927, 18:5.

51. Frank B. Jewett, "The Origins of the Industrial Research Directors Group" (unpublished, undated MS. sent to author by John M. Campbell).

52. CFK to J. McEvoy, undated (RR).

53. Boyd, Interview with H. M. Williams (KA OH II); CFK, "Engineering Data About Durex," undated (RR).

54. CFK to J. McEvoy, undated (RR).

55. *Ibid.*

56. Sloan to CFK, April 3, 1923 (RR).

57. "Casting Produced by Permanent Mold Process," *Automotive Industries* (January 31, 1924), p. 241.

58. Clements to CFK, December 17, 1923 (RR).

59. CFK, "G. M. Research Corporation, Tentative Budget for 1924" (RR).

60. CFK to Sloan, March 18, 1924 (RR).

61. Boyd, Interview with A. Boegehold (KA OH II).

62. CFK to Sloan, March 18, 1924 (RR).

63. CFK and Allen Orth, *The New Necessity* (Baltimore: Williams and Wilkins, 1932), p. 83.

64. CFK to Sloan, undated (RR).

65. C. E. Summers to CFK, July 20, 1923 (RR).

66. J. H. Hunt to Clements, November 30, 1923 (RR).

67. J. H. Hunt to CFK, January 16, 1924 (RR).

68. "Automotive Research," *SAE Journal* (May 1925), p. 499.

69. CFK, "Minutes," Lubrication Committee, April 10, 1924 (RR).

70. CFK, "Minutes," Lubrication Committee, June 18, 1924 (RR).
71. Mougey to CFK, May 27, 1926 (RR).
72. A. R. Glancy to Sloan, December 30, 1926 (RR).
73. Sloan to CFK, January 3, 1927 (RR).
74. CFK to Sloan, March 25, 1925 (RR).
75. P. S. du Pont to R. Samuel McLaughlin, November 25, 1921 (Papers of P. S. du Pont, EMHL).
76. CFK, "Vibration," undated (RR).
77. J. Swinburne to CFK, May 5, 1925 (RR).
78. Boyd, Interview with Theron Chase (KA OH I).
79. CFK to J. McEvoy, March 26, 1926 (RR).
80. J. H. Hunt to CFK, October 6, 1923 (RR).
81. CFK to McEvoy, March 26, 1928 (RR).
82. CFK to G. Hannum, September 20, 1923 (RR).
83. O. E. Hunt to CFK, April 25, 1925 (RR).
84. T. Van DeGrift, "Design Book," April 7, 1925 (KA).
85. CFK to O. E. Hunt, April 29, 1925 (RR).
86. CFK, "Conference with C. R. Alling, J. H. Hunt," undated; O. T. Kreusser to W. O. Kennington, April 17, 1923 (RR).
87. CFK, "Report of Laboratories Activities for Month of December 1925" (RR).
88. CFK to Sloan, November 28, 1927 (RR).
89. Interview with Hooven (KF).
90. Pierre Schon to CFK, February 7, 1923 (RR).
91. Sloan to CFK, October 22, 1923 (RR).
92. Thomas A. Boyd, *More Tales of Boss Ket* (Detroit: privately published, 1974), pp. 37–39.
93. *New York Times*, August 19, 1923, VIII, 13:1.
94. Sloan to CFK, November (?), 1927 (RR).
95. CFK, "The Present Day View-Point of Science," copy of address to the American Association for the Advancement of Science, p. 31 (RR).

9/The Challenges of Management

1. Thomas A. Boyd, *Research—The Pathfinder of Science and Industry* (New York: Appleton-Century, 1935), p. 283.
2. Thomas Midgley, "Critical Examination of Some Concepts in Rubber Chemistry," *Industrial and Engineering Chemistry* (July 1942), 34:891.
3. Richard Weil, "Synthetic Rubber," *Industrial and Engineering Chemistry* (November 1926), p. 1176.
4. C. C. Burgdorf, "Artificial Rubber During the War in Germany," *Industrial and Engineering Chemistry* (November 1926), p. 1174.
5. William Geer, "Future Commercial Prospects for Synthetic Rubber," *Industrial and Engineering Chemistry* (November 1926), p. 1136.
6. Boyd to CFK, January 20, 1926 (RR).
7. CFK to Sloan, December 23, 1925 (RR).
8. Sloan to CFK, January 18, 1926 (TT).

9. CFK to Sloan, January 22, 1926 (RR).

10. *Ibid.*

11. James McEvoy to Sloan, March 11, 1926 (TT).

12. *Ibid.*

13. *Ibid.*

14. W. Lovett to McEvoy, March 6, 1926 (TT).

15. Sloan to McEvoy, March 15, 1926 (TT).

16. Midgley to Sloan, November 17, 1926 (RR).

17. *Ibid.*

18. CFK to Sloan, December 7, 1926; Sloan to CFK, November 20, 1926 (RR).

19. Sloan to Lammot du Pont, January 21, 1927 (TT).

20. Du Pont to Sloan, January 25, 1927 (TT).

21. Sloan to du Pont, February 3, 1927 (TT).

22. Sloan to du Pont, January 21, 1927 (TT).

23. Sloan to du Pont, February 3, 1927 (TT).

24. Sloan to du Pont, January 21, 1927 (TT).

25. Frank A. Howard, *Buna Rubber* (New York: Van Nostrand, 1947), pp. 1–2.

26. Thomas Midgley, "Natural and Synthetic Rubber I," *Journal of the American Chemical Society* (April 1929), 51:1215. See also Midgley, "Natural and Synthetic Rubber XIII," *Journal of the American Chemical Society* (June 1934), 56:1325.

27. Sloan to du Pont, February 3, 1927 (TT).

28. Sloan to J. Brooks Jackson, February 3, 1927 (TT).

29. Sloan to Midgley, March 8, 1927 (TT).

30. CFK to Sloan, March 10, 1927 (TT).

31. McEvoy to John Pratt, December 3, 1927 (TT).

32. CFK, "Trouble as an Approach to Research," in Malcom Ross and Maurice Holland, eds., *Profitable Practice in Industrial Research* (New York: Harper and Brothers, 1932), p. 53.

33. Sloan to CFK, November 17, 1928 (RR).

34. Matthew Josephson, *Edison: A Biography* (New York: McGraw-Hill, 1959).

35. Aaron Ihde, *The Development of Modern Chemistry* (New York: Harper and Row, 1963).

36. Midgley to Sloan, September 5, 1928 (TT).

37. Alfred Sloan, *My Years with General Motors* (New York: Doubleday, 1963), p. 355.

38. *Ibid.*, p. 356.

39. H. R. Colby to R. H. Grant, April 12, 1918 (RR).

40. John T. Flynn, "Big Changes Ahead: Interview with C. F. Kettering," *American Magazine* (January, 1930), p. 13.

41. CFK to E. G. Biechler, April 13, 1925 (RR).

42. Advice of Action, April 13, 1921 (RR); Sloan, *My Years with General Motors*, p. 355; Boyd, Interview with Edward B. Newill (KA OH II).

43. CFK to E. G. Biechler, April 13, 1925 (RR).

44. Boyd, Interview with Newill (KA OH II).

45. *Ibid.*

46. CFK to Biechler, October 14, 1925 (RR).

47. CFK to Biechler, April 13, 1925 (RR).

48. Boyd, Interview with Newill (KA OH II).

49. CFK to Biechler, March 2, 1926 (RR).

50. CFK to L. Keilholz, March 2, 1926 (RR).

51. Boyd to CFK, March 15, 1926 (RR).

52. CFK to Biechler, October 14, 1925 (RR).

53. Lovell to CFK, December 2, 1926 (RR); Lovell, "Report No. 10, Absorption Refrigeration," August 25, 1928 (RR).

54. Donaldson Brown, "Report on Operations of Kinetic Chemicals, Inc." (October 1944), p. 7 (TT).

55. CFK to Biechler, August 21, 1926 (RR); H. M. Williams to Biechler, May 13, 1927 (RR).

56. Biechler to CFK, June 30, 1928 (RR).

57. Midgley, "From Periodic Table to Production," *Industrial and Engineering Chemistry*, (1937), 29:244.

58. CFK, "Running Errands for Ideas" (KF).

59. Midgley, "From Periodic Table to Production."

60. Boyd to Williams, August 23, 1928 (RR).

61. Midgley and A. Henne, "Organic Fluorides as Refrigerants," *Industrial and Engineering Chemistry* (1930), 25:544.

62. *Ibid.*

63. Biechler to Pratt, July 31, 1929 (TT).

64. Biechler to Pratt, March 11, 1930 (RR).

65. Thomas A. Boyd, "Thomas Midgley," *Journal of the American Chemical Society* (June 1953), p. 2794.

66. Boyd to Williams, May 3, 1930 (RR).

67. Brown, "Report on Operations of Kinetic Chemicals, Inc."

68. CFK, "Direct Testimony," p. 3604 (TT).

69. CFK to E. B. Newill, June 22, 1931 (RR).

70. CFK, "General Motors Memorandum," June 28, 1930 (RR).

71. General Motors Patent Department, "Progress Report on Fluorides," June 26, 1930 (RR).

72. CFK, "Thomas Midgley, Jr." *National Academy of Sciences; Biographical Memoirs* (1948), 24:361–80.

10/The Diesel and the Depression

1. Interview with Fred Hooven (KF).

2. Alfred Sloan, *My Years with General Motors* (New York: Doubleday, 1963), p. 348.

3. Lynwood Bryant, "Diesel and His Rational Engine," *Scientific American* (August 1969).

4. Elmer A. Sperry to CFK, September 27, 1920 (RR).

5. Maschinenfabrik-Augsburg-Nurnberg A. G. to CFK, August 5, 1925 (RR).

6. Charles Short to CFK, November 25, 1925 (RR).

7. Arthur W. Gardiner to F. O. Clements, March 12, 1927 (RR).

8. Carl Fisher to O. D. Trieber, January 31, 1926 (RR).

9. Boyd, Interview with H. J. Defoe (KA OH I).

10. Interview with Hooven (KF).

11. CFK to Carl Fisher, July 5, 1928 (RR).

12. W. S. Jackson to CFK, June 16, 1928 (RR).

13. CFK to Jackson, July 5, 1928 (RR).

14. CFK to H. M. Waite, July 30, 1928 (RR).

15. CFK to Carl Fisher, August 25, 1928 (RR).

16. CFK to Carl Fisher, September 14, 1928 (RR).

17. George Codrington to CFK, August 27, 1928 (RR).

18. CFK to George Codrington, September 4, 1928 (RR).

19. Sloan, *My Years with General Motors*, p. 344.

20. J. L. Pratt to CFK, September 18, 1928 (RR).

21. CFK to J. L. Pratt, September 20, 1928 (RR).

22. CFK to J. J. Raskob, June 14, 1928 (Papers of J. J. Raskob, EMHL).

23. Sloan to CFK, June 8, 1925 (RR).

24. Henry B. Joy to CFK, October 11, 1929 (RR).

25. C. L. Cummins, *My Days with the Diesel* (Philadelphia: Chilton, 1967), p. 30.

26. Sloan, *My Years with General Motors*, p. 347.

27. W. E. Whitehouse to CFK, August 15, 1929; CFK to W. S. Knudsen, September 14, 1929 (RR).

28. H. J. Defoe to CFK, November 12, 1929 (RR).

29. "Memorandum for Mr. Hallett on Electrical Synchronizing Equipment on Mr. Kettering's Yacht," May 16, 1931 (RR).

30. CFK to H. W. Asire, April 15, 1931 (RR).

31. *New York Times*, November 8, 1929, 46:2.

32. Eugene Kettering to CFK, April 14, 1927 (KA).

33. CFK to Eugene Kettering, February 29, 1928 (KA).

34. Dayton *Journal*, April 6, 1930, 1:1.

35. Robert Lanphier, "Diary of the Voyage of the *Olive K* to the Galapagos Islands, 1930" (KA).

36. CFK to E. A. Deeds, March 29, 1930 (RR).

37. Thomas A. Boyd, *Professional Amateur: The Biography of Charles Franklin Kettering* (New York: E. P. Dutton, 1957), p. 168.

38. F. G. Shoemaker to G. E. Hallett, July 8, 1929 (RR).

39. U.S. Congress, Senate, Committee on the Judiciary, *Hearings Before the Subcommittee on Anti-Trust and Monopoly*, 84th Cong., 1st sess., part 6 (November 8–10, 1955), p. 2429.

40. CFK to Eugene Kettering, October 5, 1928 (RR).

41. F. G. Shoemaker, "Log Book," October 6, 1928 (KA).

42. Shoemaker, "Log Book," June 18, 1929 (KA).

43. Sloan, *My Years with General Motors*, p. 346; CFK, "Memorandum on Diesel History," March 1, 1944 (RR).

44. Boyd, Interview with George Codrington (KA OH I).

45. CFK, "Report of Research Laboratories for Jan. 1931" (RR).

46. Shoemaker, "Log Book," December 10, 1928 (KA).

47. CFK to G. Hallett, January 19, 1933 (RR).

48. CFK, "Report of Research Laboratories for Nov. 1931" (RR).

49. Dayton *Journal*, August 30, 1931 (clipping, Kettering File, DPL).

50. Boyd, Interview with Mrs. A. R. Maynard (KA OH II).

51. CFK to Roy McClure, January 20, 1932 (RR); *New York Times*, February 20, 1932, 20:2.

52. CFK to A. Schein, August 31, 1931 (RR).

53. Thomas A. Boyd, *More Tales of Boss Ket* (Detroit: privately published, 1974), p. 44.

54. George Smith, "Common Clay" (unpublished MS., 1939), pp. 202–3 (KF).

55. CFK to W. W. Constantine, November 12, 1931 (RR).

56. CFK, "Research as Related to Banking," *The Cleveland Trust Monthly* (December 1926).

57. J. J. Raskob to CFK, June 19, 1928, and CFK to Raskob, June 22, 1928 (Papers of John J. Raskob, EMHL).

58. CFK, "The Present Day View-Point of Science," copy of address to the American Association for the Advancement of Science, p. 31 (RR).

59. CFK, "Research and Industry," *Scientific American* (May 1937), p. 285.

60. CFK, "Unemployment and the Industrial System," *Saturday Evening Post* (September 26, 1931), p. 125).

61. CFK, "Industry at the Crossroads," *Saturday Evening Post* (September 26, 1931), p. 8.

62. *New York Times*, June 18, 1931, 25:1.

63. CFK, "The Present Day View-Point of Science."

64. *New York Times*, June 18, 1931, 25:1.

65. CFK, "The World Isn't Finished Yet," *Saturday Evening Post* (April 23, 1932), p. 84.

66. *Time* (January 9, 1933), p. 56.

67. H. C. Ray to Bruce Barton, January 10, 1933 (RR).

68. Bruce Barton to CFK, March 2, 1933 (RR).

69. R. O. Brundage to CFK, July 3, 1934 (RR).

70. Boyd, *More Tales of Boss Ket*, p. 98.

71. Secretary of the Franklin Institute to CFK, January 20, 1936 (RR).

72. Rexmond Cochrane, *The National Academy of Sciences: The First Hundred Years, 1863–1963* (Washington, D.C.: The Academy, 1978), p. 342.

73. *Centennial Celebration of the American Patent System* (Washington, D.C.: Government Printing Office, 1937), p. 53.

74. *Business Week* (December 10, 1938), p. 14.

75. U.S. Congress, Senate, Temporary National Economic Committee, *Technology and Concentration of Economic Power*, 77th Cong., 3d sess., 1939, pt. 30:342.

76. *Ibid.*, p. 360.

77. *New York Times*, December 11, 1938, IV, 7:2.

78. Paul de Kruif, "Boss Kettering," *Saturday Evening Post* (July 15, 29; August 12, 26; September 9, 23, 1933).

79. Emma Culler to CFK, August 2, 1933 (RR).

80. Reuben Schrank to CFK, April 23, 1933 (RR).

81. Clipping from San Antonio *Evening News* (RR).

82. Boyd, *More Tales of Boss Ket*, p. 79.

83. F. O. Clements to George Smith, June 13, 1932 (RR).

84. Emma Culler to CFK, May 21, 1933 (RR).

85. CFK to Charles F. Heyde, April 2, 1934 (RR).

86. Bernard Weisberger, *The Dream Maker: William C. Durant, Founder of General Motors* (Boston: Little, Brown, 1979), p. 354.

87. CFK, "America Comes Through A Crisis," *Saturday Evening Post* (May 13, 1933).

88. CFK, "Relation of Chemistry to the Individual," *Industrial and Engineering Chemistry* (May 1933), p. 484.

89. CFK to E. M. Clark, August 18, 1930 (RR).

90. F. G. Shoemaker to CFK, February 4, 1932 (RR).

91. CFK to V. Shaughnessy, December 21, 1932 (RR).

92. Harold F. Bowen, *Ships, Machinery, and Mossbacks* (Princeton, N.J.: Princeton University Press, 1954), p. 127.

93. *Ibid.*, p. 133.

94. CFK to V. Shaughnessy, December 28, 1933 (RR).

95. CFK to J. Crawford, March 18, 1936 (RR).

96. CFK to E. M. Clark, January 27, 1932 (RR).

97. CFK to Pierre S. du Pont, November 12, 1931 (Papers of P. S. du Pont, EMHL).

98. CFK to J. Muhlfield, November 21, 1933 (RR).

99. *New York Times*, May 28, 1933, 1:4.

100. CFK to Robert Lanphier, May 5, 1933 (RR).

101. CFK to V. Shaughnessy, May 19, 1933 (RR).

102. CFK to John E. Muhlfield, August 22, 1933 (RR); Richard Overton, *The Burlington Route* (New York: Knopf, 1965), p. 394 ff.

103. Overton, *The Burlington Route*, p. 395.

104. G. Hallett to CFK, April 26, 1934 (RR).

105. F. G. Horner to Ralph Budd, September 5, 1933; CFK to V. Shaughnessy, November 9, 1933; CFK, "Travel Expense Report," December 28, 1933 (RR).

106. Overton, *The Burlington Route*, pp. 391–95.

107. *New York Times*, May 27, 1934, 1:2.

108. *New York Times*, May 25, 1934, 11:2.

109. Sloan, *My Years with General Motors*, p. 350; Sloan to CFK, June 15, 1934 (RR).

110. Sloan to CFK, June 15, 1934 (RR).

111. CFK, "Industry Research," *Scientific American* (August 1934), p. 243.

112. CFK to Charles E. Wilson, August 9, 1934 (RR).

113. CFK, "Consultation with E. W. Kettering at Winton," May 13, 1935 (RR).

114. CFK to R. C. Lanphier, December 7, 1934 (RR).

115. E. V. Rippingille to CFK. February 6, 1935 (RR).

116. *Ibid.*

117. CFK to J. L. Pratt, July 15, 1935 (RR).

118. J. C. Fetters to F. G. Shoemaker, September 19, 1935 (RR).

119. Boyd, *More Tales of Boss Ket*, p. 68.

120. *Railway Age* (November 23, 1935), p. 344.

121. *Railway Age* (November 23, 1935), p. 684.

122. Robert Binkerd, "What About the Steam Locomotive," *Railway Age* (May 25, 1935), p. 800.

123. Sloan, *My Years With General Motors*, p. 351.

124. CFK to H. Hamilton, May 11, 1934 (RR).

125. Sloan to Pierre S. du Pont, October 18, 1937 (Papers of P. S. du Pont, EMHL).

126. *New York Times*, September 16, 1937, 21:2.

127. CFK to Sloan, October 21, 1937 (RR).

128. *New York Times*, December 7, 1938, 1:1.

129. CFK to Daniel Cox, August 24, 1939; CFK to Mark C. Honeywell, October 25, 1938 (RR).

11/Some Biological Diversions

1. Paul de Kruif, *The Sweeping Wind* (New York: Harcourt, Brace, and World, 1962), p. 180.

2. Thomas A. Boyd, *Professional Amateur: The Biography of Charles Franklin Kettering* (New York: E. P. Dutton, 1957), p. 190.

3. CFK, "The Functions of Research," *Industrial and Engineering Chemistry,* (November 1927), 19:1215.

4. *New York Times*, November 11, 1936, 45:1.

5. See Martin Kaufman, *Homeopathy in America* (Baltimore: Johns Hopkins University Press, 1971).

6. CFK, "Minutes of Proceedings of the Board of Trustees, Ohio State University," April 4, November 11, 1916 (KA).

7. *Ibid.*, February 3, March 11, 1920.

8. CFK, "Address to American Institute of Homeopathy," July 1920 (KA).

9. CFK, "Minutes of Proceedings of the Board of Trustees, Ohio State University," June 14, 1920 (KA).

10. *New York Times*, June 16, 1920, 5:4.

11. CFK to B. F. McCann, March 10, 1922 (RR).

12. B. F. McCann to W. O. Thompson, June 22, 1922 (KA).

13. CFK to W. O. Thompson, June 22, 1922 (KA).

14. B. F. McCann to W. O. Thompson, April 9, 1923 (KA).

15. CFK to C. W. Lieb, January 27, 1923 (RR).

16. *Ibid.*

17. George B. Smith, "Common Clay" (unpublished autobiography) p. 191 (KF).

18. Boyd, Interview with H. Worley Kendall (KA OH I).

19. De Kruif, *The Sweeping Wind*, p. 180.

20. CFK to W. R. Whitney, May 26, 1931 (RR).

21. CFK to W. R. Whitney, June 8, 1931, and November 11, 1931 (RR).

22. CFK to W. R. Whitney, November 11, 1931 (RR).

23. De Kruif, *The Sweeping Wind*, p. 194.

24. W. Simpson, "The Fever Therapy Research Project at Miami Valley Hospital," January 1, 1937 (KA).

25. *Ibid.*, p. 9.

26. W. Simpson to CFK, March 31, 1932 (RR).

27. W. Simpson, "The Fever Therapy Research Project at Miami Valley Hospital" p. 10.

28. W. Simpson to C. F. Tenny, October 31, 1933 (RR).

29. W. Simpson, "Artificial Fever Treatment of Syphilis," *Journal of the American Medical Association* (December 28, 1934), 26:2132.

30. Ellice McDonald to CFK, February 1, 1933; CFK to McDonald, March 2, 1933 (RR).

31. W. C. Teagle to CFK, February 15, 1934; CFK to W. C. Teagle, February 20, 1934 (RR).

32. CFK to W. C. Teagle, February 20, 1934, (RR).

33. *New York Times*, March 21, 1937, 14:2.

34. CFK to W. C. Teagle, February 20, 1934 (RR).

35. Boyd, Interview with Frank W. Hartman (KA OH II).

36. Boyd, Interview with Roy D. McClure (KA OH II).

37. R. McClure to CFK, February 17, 1940 (RR).

38. W. Simpson to CFK, January 8, 1935 (RR).

39. Algo Henderson and Dorothy Hall, *Antioch College: Its Design for Liberal Education* (New York: Harper and Brothers, 1946).

40. C. W. Adams to K. G. Matheson, June 19, 1924 (RR).

41. Thomas A. Boyd, ed., *Prophet of Progress: The Speeches of Charles F. Kettering* (New York: E. P. Dutton, 1961), p. 31.

42. Boyd, Interview with Clyde S. Adams (KA OH I).

43. *New York Times*, December 25, 1927, 3:6.

44. CFK, "Address to American Homeopathic Institute," July 1920 (KA).

45. Boyd, *Professional Amateur*, p. 192.

46. CFK to L. W. James, January 10, 1938 (RR).

47. B. L. Williams to CFK, September 9, 1926 (RR).

48. CFK to B. L. Williams, September 14, 1926 (RR).

49. Boyd, *Professional Amateur*, p. 190.

50. C. L. Cummins, *My Days with the Diesel* (Philadelphia: Chilton, 1967), p. 29.

51. CFK to F. O. Clements, June 26, 1929 (RR).

52. *Ibid.*

53. W. G. Lovell to CFK, July 1, 1929 (RR).

54. *New York Times*, June 16, 1930, 11:4.

55. CFK, "Memorandum on Organization of Photosynthesis Investigations," undated (RR).

56. *Ibid.*

57. CFK to O. L. Inman, September 22, 1932 (RR); Boyd, Interview with Harry V. Knorr (KA OH I).

58. O. L. Inman to CFK, March 3, 1931 (RR).

59. Boyd, Interview with Paul Rothemund (KA OH I).

60. CFK, L. W. Shutts, and D. H. Andrews, "A Representation of the Dynamic Properties of Molecules by Mechanical Models," *Physical Review* (August 1, 1930), vol. 36.

61. O. L. Inman to CFK, March 7, 1931 (RR).

62. Inman to CFK, March 3, 1931 (RR).

63. Inman to CFK, March 7, 1931 (RR).

64. Inman to CFK, undated (RR).

65. Inman to CFK, August 25, 1933 (RR).

66. CFK to F. H. McDonald, November 10, 1938 (RR).

67. CFK to Inman, November 8, 1938 (RR).

68. "Minutes of Annual Meeting of Board of Trustees, Antioch College," May 9, 1932 (AA).

69. CFK to George Smith, December 26, 1933 (RR).

70. Ernest Morgan to CFK, March 31, 1932 (AA).

71. CFK to Algo Henderson, December 20, 1938 (AA).

72. CFK to Algo Henderson, July 11, 1940 (RR).

73. O. L. Inman to CFK, August 9, 1934; Inman to CFK, August 3, 1937 (RR).

74. *New York Times*, January 12, 1935, 23:1; *ibid.*, July 14, 1937, 1:5.

75. *Ibid.*, September 19, 1937, IV, 2:1.

76. *Ibid.*, July 25, 1937, XIII, 6:1.

77. *Ibid.*, May 7, 1940, 1:5.

78. *Ibid.*, May 21, 1935, 15:1.

12/World War II

1. *New York Times*, December 13, 1940, 15:1.

2. Henry H. Arnold, *Global Mission* (New York: Harper, 1949), pp. 260–61.

3. CFK to H. H. Arnold, September 7, 1939 (RR).

4. Arnold to CFK, November 3, 1939 (RR).

5. CFK to Arnold, November 3, 1939 (RR).

6. Boyd, Interview with Gerald M. Rassweiler (KA OH II).

7. *Ibid.*

8. CFK to W. S. Knudsen, September 3, 1940; CFK, "Record of Telephone Conversation," September 6, 1940 (RR).

9. Arnold to CFK, March 3, 1941 (RR).

10. CFK to George V. Holloman, March 23, 1942 (RR).

11. Arnold, *Global Mission*, p. 261.

12. CFK to Sloan, September 19, 1941 (RR).

13. Arnold to CFK, December 30, 1944 (RR).

14. Boyd, "The Story of Triptane," p. 3 (RR).

15. T. O. Richards to CFK, October 3, 1942 (RR).

16. Sloan to CFK, October 10, 1942 (RR); S. D. Heron, *Development of Aviation Fuels* (Cambridge, Mass.: Division of Research, Graduate School of Business Administration, Harvard University, 1950), p. 657.

17. CFK, "Notes on First Meeting of Triptane Exploratory Committee, Mr. Kettering's Office," October 15, 1943 (RR).

18. J. M. Campbell to CFK, October 12, 1942 (RR).

19. B. A. D'Alleva to CFK, March 30, 1944 (RR).

20. CFK to M. R. Mandelbaum, February 22, 1944 (RR).

21. J. M. Campbell to CFK, December 11, 1944 (RR).

22. CFK to Boyd, February 19, 1945 (RR).

23. Gerald M. Rassweiler, *Retrospect* (Detroit: privately published, 1974), pp. 140–50.

24. CFK to E. V. Rippingille, February 12, 1941 (RR).

25. CFK to Rippingille, February 27, 1941 (RR).

26. *New York Times*, June 9, 1941, 1:4.

27. H. G. Bowen to CFK, June 11, 1941 (RR).

28. CFK to Bowen, June 18, 1941 (RR).

29. Clipping from Washington *Evening Star*, June 29, 1941 (RR).

30. CFK to Bowen, July 30, 1941 (RR).

31. CFK to Bowen, October 23, 1941 (RR).

32. CFK to Rippingille, October 23, 1941 (RR).

33. Joseph Lash to CFK, March 20, 1943 (RR).

34. Rassweiler, *Retrospect*, p. 150.

35. CFK to Rippingille, March 6, 1945 (RR).

36. CFK, "Horsepower Is War Power," *Scientific American* (July 1942), p. 4.

37. J. C. Fetters, "Development of a Light Weight Diesel Engine for the Navy," *Automotive and Aviation Industries* (June 15, 1943), p. 25.

38. CFK to Julius F. Stone, October 25, 1945 (RR).

39. John B. Rae, *The American Automobile* (Chicago: University of Chicago Press, 1965), p. 153.

40. CFK to Sloan, May 20, 1942 (RR).

41. Bascom N. Timmons, *Jesse H. Jones* (New York: Holt, 1956), p. 307; Frank A. Howard, *Buna Rubber* (New York: Van Nostrand, 1947), p. 207.

42. Sloan to Lammot du Pont, May 29, 1943 (TT).

43. *Ibid.*

44. CFK to Sloan, April 28, 1941 (RR).

45. H. M. Welch to CFK, May 28, 1940 (RR).

46. CFK to Harry Hopkins, July 17, 1940 (RR).

47. U.S. Congress, Senate, Committee on Military Affairs, Subcommittee of the Committee on Military Affairs, *Technological Mobilization: Hearings*, 77th Cong., 2d sess., 1943, pp. 783–98.

48. *New York Times*, June 9, 1941, 1:4.

49. B. H. Mossinghoff to CFK, January 4, 1941; CFK to Mossinghoff, January 8, 1941 (RR).

50. *New York Times*, August 20, 1942; *ibid.*, June 9, 1941, 1:4.

51. CFK, "Minutes of Meeting Held at D.A.C.," May 21, 1941 (RR).

52. *New York Times*, September 23, 1942, 12:2.

53. *Ibid.*, May 22, 1944, 21:3.

54. *Ibid.*, May 23, 1945, 15:1.
55. Boyd, Interview with Conway P. Coe (KA OH I).
56. *New York Times*, September 22, 1945, 9:6.
57. Boyd, Interview with Allen Orth (KA OH I).
58. CFK, "George Washington—Patriot, Statesman, and Scientist," NBC Symphony of the Air (July 9, 1944) (KA).
59. CFK, "Frontiers Unlimited," NBC Symphony of the Air (July 21, 1946) (KA).
60. *New York Times*, December 2, 1943, 15:1.
61. *New York Times*, December 20, 1944, 16:1.
62. CFK, "Comment," *SAE Journal* (July 1943), p. 57.

13/The Last Hero

1. CFK, "The Future of Science," *Science* (December 27, 1946), p. 613.
2. CFK, "Fuels and Engines for Higher Power and Greater Efficiency," *SAE Journal* (June 1945), 53:357.
3. R. V. Hutchinson, "The 'Whys' of the Kettering Triptane Engine of 1946/47," pp. 3–4 (KA).
4. Boyd, Interview with Carl F. Caris (KA OH II).
5. CFK to Sloan, January 2, 1947 (RR).
6. *New York Times*, May 20, 1947, 50:3.
7. Boyd, Interview with Jack Wolfram (KA OH II).
8. Thomas A. Boyd, ed., *Prophet of Progress: The Speeches of Charles F. Kettering* (New York: E. P. Dutton, 1961), p. 158.
9. Boyd, Interview with Caris (KA OH II).
10. *Newsweek* (June 16, 1947), p. 68.
11. Alfred Sloan, *My Years with General Motors* (New York: Doubleday, 1963), p. 260.
12. Boyd, Interview with C. Fred Huddle (KA OH II).
13. CFK to George A. Lundberg, July 17, 1946 (RR).
14. *New York Times*, May 17, 1956, 1:2.
15. Thomas A. Boyd, *Professional Amateur: The Biography of Charles Franklin Kettering* (New York: E. P. Dutton, 1957), p. 232.
16. CFK to E. V. Cowdry, September 4, 1942 (RR).
17. CFK to H. V. Knorr, December 5, 1942 (RR).
18. CFK to W. Simpson, May 14, 1943 (RR).
19. CFK to Adam Kettering, December 19, 1944 (KMHM).
20. C. P. Rhoads, "Cancer University," *Kettering Digest* (Dayton, Ohio: National Cash Register Co., 1950), p. 79.
21. CFK, "General Motors Press Release," August 8, 1945 (RR); *Time* (August 20, 1945), p. 64.
22. CFK to Mr. and Mrs. W. O. Kennington, January 16, 1947 (RR).
23. CFK to Calvin P. Bentley, February 25, 1946 (RR).
24. Thomas A. Boyd, *More Tales of Boss Ket* (Detroit: privately published, 1974), p. 92.

25. CFK to Carrie E. Hays, August 20, 1946 (RR).

26. Boyd, Interview with Milton Stoner (KA OH II).

27. Boyd, Interview with Virginia W. Kettering (KA OH II).

28. Susan Kettering to CFK, undated; CFK to Susan Kettering, October 31, 1946, (RR).

29. C. P. Rhoads to CFK, February 4, 1954 (RR).

30. CFK to Arthur Compton, June 2, 1948 (RR).

31. Sloan to CFK, November 15, 1945 (RR).

32. Rhoads to CFK, February 4, 1954 (RR).

33. *New York Times*, December 28, 1946, 1:6.

34. *New York Times*, May 4, 1950, 47:1.

35. CFK to Algo Henderson, January 2, 1947 (RR).

36. Boyd, Interview with Paul V. Rothemund (KA OH II).

37. CFK to Henderson, May 6, 1947, (RR).

38. Interview with William Treharne (KF).

39. Boyd, Interview with William E. Laesh (KA OH II).

40. *New York Times*, June 20, 1948, III, 1:2.

41. CFK to Adam Kettering, February 29, 1953 (KMHM).

42. Interview with Samuel B. Gould (KF).

43. Samuel Gould, "Speech for Kettering Memorial Program" (AA).

44. *New York Times*, October 6, 1955, 31:1.

45. "Minutes of Annual Meeting of Board of Trustees, Antioch College," May 11–12, 1956 (AA).

46. Interview with William Treharne (KF).

47. CFK, Handwritten note on newspaper clipping (Solar Laboratory, Antioch College).

48. Boyd, Interview with Howard Tanner (KA OH II).

49. Boyd, Interview with Glenn Elmore (KA OH II).

50. Interview with William Treharne (KF).

51. Boyd, Interview with Tanner (KA OH II).

52. Interview with Treharne (KF).

53. Marginalia in Louis De Broglie, *An Introduction to the Study of Wave Mechanics* (London: E. P. Dutton, 1930) (Solar Laboratory, Antioch College).

54. CFK to F. O. Clements, September 8, 1930 (Solar Laboratory, Antioch College).

55. Robert Lanphier, "Diary of Voyage of the *Olive K* to the Galapagos Islands, 1930," January 19, 1930 (KA).

56. CFK and G. G. Scott, "Inertia of the Carrier of Electricity in Copper and Aluminum," *Physical Review* (November 1944), 66:9–10.

57. Zay Jeffries, "Charles Franklin Kettering," *National Academy of Sciences, Biographical Memoirs* (1960), 34:111.

58. G. G. Scott, "Inertia of the Carrier of Electricity in Cadmium," *Physical Review* (August 1, 1951), 83: 656; G. G. Scott, "The Gyromagnetic Ratio of the Ferromagnetic Elements," *Physical Review* (September 1, 1952), 87:697–99.

59. S. R. Williams to CFK, September 28, 1949 (RR).

60. CFK to Julius F. Stone, October 25, 1945 (RR).

61. *New York Times*, September 4, 1954, 18:4, *ibid.*, June 5, 1955, IV, 11:6.
62. *New York Times*, June 18, 1947, 21:2.
63. Boyd, Interview with J. H. Hunt (KA OH II).
64. *New York Times*, July 1, 1950, 6:6.
65. *New York Times*, October 5, 1956, 27:3; *ibid.*, October 16, 1955, 80:1.
66. CFK, talk at University of Cincinnati, April 20, 1956 (AA).
67. *New York Times*, November 17, 1949, 35:5.
68. Mark C. Honeywell to CFK, April 19, 1951 (RR).
69. Arthur Morgan to CFK, November 8, 1947 (Morgan Papers, AA).
70. Boyd, *Prophet of Progress*, p. 222.
71. *New York Times*, June 3, 1952, 24:2.
72. Ashland *Times-Gazette*, August 30, 1946, p. 6.
73. *Business Week* (September 8, 1951), p. 25.
74. *New York Times*, September 11, 1951, 28:4.
75. CFK to Mark Honeywell, September 24, 1951 (RR); *New York Times*, February 1, 1952, 13:2.
76. CFK, "Testimony" (TT); *New York Times*, April 9, 1953, 45:2.
77. *New York Times*, March 25, 1953, 30:3.
78. CFK to Harvey Firestone, Jr., December 16, 1946 (RR).
79. CFK and H. G. Bowen, *A Short History of Technology* (West Orange, N.J.: Thomas Alva Edison Foundation, 1952).
80. Interview with Treharne (KF).
81. Interview with Frederick Hooven (KF).
82. CFK, "Running Errands for Ideas" (KF).
83. *New York Times*, April 23, 1947, 21:3.
84. *New York Times*, April 15, 1954, 43:1.
85. Interview with Gould (KF).
86. H. Eugene Kneiss to Dwight D. Eisenhower, July 24, 1956 (DDE, Personal Presidential File 1573).
87. D. D. Eisenhower to CFK, August 29, 1956 (DDE).
88. *New York Times*, December 19, 1957, 33:6.
89. *New York Times*, November 27, 1957, 15:1.
90. Dayton *Journal Herald*, October 9, 1958 (clipping in Kettering File, DPL).
91. Interview with Gould (KF).
92. Dayton *Journal Herald*, October 9, 1958 (clipping in Kettering File, DPL).
93. *Newsweek* (July 21, 1958), p. 50.
94. Interview with Gould (KF).
95. *New York Times*, November 25, 1958, 6:4.
96. Interview with Gould (KF).
97. Dayton *Journal Herald*, November 28, 1958 (clipping in Kettering File, DPL).
98. *New York Times*, November 26, 1958, 1:2.
99. Dayton *Journal Herald*, December 5, 1955 (clipping in Kettering File, DPL).
100. *New York Times*, November 27, 1958, 28:1.
101. Harold Vagtborg, *Research and American Industrial Development* (New York: Pergamon Press, 1973), p. 422.
102. Paul de Kruif, *Life Among the Doctors* (New York: Harcourt, Brace, 1949), p. 445.

INDEX